8

ENVIRONMENTAL ISSUES IN CHEMICAL PERSPECTIVE

Environmental Issues in Chemical Perspective

by THOMAS G. SPIRO

Professor, Department of Chemistry,
Princeton University

and WILLIAM M. STIGLIANI

Research Associate,
Atmospheric Sciences Research Center,
State University of New York at Albany

State University of New York Press | *Albany*

Grateful acknowledgement is made to the American Chemical Society for permission to reprint illustrative material in this volume.

Published by
State University of New York Press, Albany

For information, address State University of New York
Press, State University Plaza, Albany, N.Y., 12246

Library of Congress Cataloging in Publication Data

Spiro, Thomas G   1935–
  Environmental issues in chemical perspective

  Includes bibliographies and index.
  1. Environmental chemistry. I.   Stigliani,
William M., joint author. II. Title.
QD31.2.S66   540   79-23756
ISBN 0-87395-427-0

To our families—

Helen, Michael, and Peter Spiro
Sarah, Anthony, and Nicholas Stigliani

CONTENTS

PREFACE

Several years have elapsed since a wave of concern for environmental causes swept across the United States, culminating in the celebration of Earth Day in 1970. The enthusiasm of the moment has ebbed, but environmental issues have not gone away and there is no prospect that they will disappear in the foreseeable future. The debates over what to do about these issues have steadily grown, in volume and in complexity, as hard choices are faced. This is also true in other countries where the initial wave of environmental concern was less pronounced or absent. The environment is now ineradicably lodged in our consciousness, even if our perceptions of it change with time, as indeed they must.

The aim of this book is to make sense of the environmental debates by examining the natural cycles that human activities may be upsetting. The issues involved are very difficult. Should the plutonium breeder reactor be developed? Do fluorocarbon aerosol cans pose a serious threat to the atmosphere's ozone layer? Are streams fouled with detergent phosphates? Is saccharin a dangerous food additive? None of these questions has an easy answer, but in following the arguments pro and con, it helps to understand the natural balances that are threatened.

At a deeper level, it is highly satisfying to understand the world we inhabit in terms that are relevant to our age. To an important extent these terms are chemical in nature. Plutonium, fluorocarbons, phosphates, and saccharin are all chemical substances. We live in a chemical age, not only in the narrow sense that industrial society produces new chemicals in abundance, but also in the broader sense that we have come to a general understanding of the molecular relationships that underlie and determine natural phenomena. There are still innumerable gaps in our knowledge, but the chemical context of the natural world is reasonably coherent and provides the unifying principle of this book.

Chemistry is not, of course, the only perspective on environmental issues. Ecological, social, political, and economic questions are all vitally bound up in them, and some of these necessarily enter into any description of environmental issues. No attempt has been made to keep them out of the present discussion, even though the primary emphasis is on chemistry.

This book is structured in four sections: energy, atmosphere, hydrosphere, and biosphere. These divisions are for our convenience; environmental problems do not fall into neat categories, and we can expect them to pop up in more than one place in the book, as in real life.

PART I | ENERGY

1 | Introduction

The question of energy use underlies virtually all environmental issues. We are coming to realize that supplies of energy that we have taken for granted will be exhausted before long. At the same time there is a heightened awareness of adverse impacts on the environment that stem from increased energy consumption, such as air and water pollution, the spread of toxic materials, and the scarring of land by strip mining. Increasingly, there seems to be a clash between those who place greatest emphasis on maintaining an expanding supply of cheap energy, and those who are more concerned with the environmental costs of such expansion. In this part of the book, we will explore the background of energy production and energy consumption. We will see that protecting the environment and meeting the energy needs of society are not necessarily incompatible, and that there are avenues for resolving the apparent conflict.

2 | Natural Energy Flows

It is instructive to view our energy problems against a backdrop of the continual and massive daily flow of energy that occurs at the surface of the earth. This flow is diagrammed in Figure 1.1. In the figure, the magnitudes of the energy fluxes are given in calories per year. A calorie is the amount of energy needed to raise the temperature of 1 g of water by 1° C (see the Appendix for a comprehensive listing of the common forms and units of energy). The sun radiates a nearly unimaginable number of calories every year—28×10^{32}.

A very small fraction of the total, 13×10^{23} calories per year, is intercepted by the earth, which is 93 million miles from the sun. Of this quantity, about 34% is reflected or scattered back into space. This fraction is called the *albedo*, and it determines the total energy balance of the earth. The figure of 34% is an average value; it is difficult to estimate accurately because the reflectivity of the earth varies a great deal from place to place. The ocean reflects very little of the light, about

1

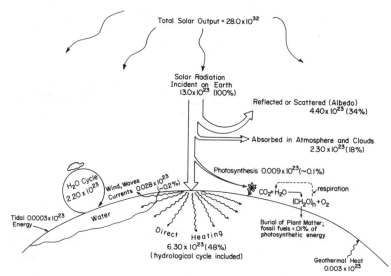

Figure 1.1   Yearly Energy Fluxes on Earth (in calories)

6%, whereas areas covered with snow reflect a large fraction, 80–90%; land areas an amount somewhere in between, depending on their covering, such as vegetation or sand. The extent of cloudiness is also an important determinant of the albedo.

The rest of the light is absorbed by the earth or its atmosphere, and its energy is used to drive a number of natural processes. About 48% is converted directly into heat. More than one-third of this is used to drive the hydrologic cycle—the massive evaporation and precipitation of water, upon which we depend for our freshwater supplies. While it takes 1 calorie to heat a gram of water 1° C, 540 calories is required to convert that same gram of water to vapor. This is called the *latent heat* of water. The same 540 calories of heat is released when a gram of water vapor condenses into rain; this is the reason that rainfall is associated with storms. A huge amount of energy is released by even a modest rainfall. The estimate of the total amount of energy involved in the hydrologic cycle is based on the heat released by the known amount of rainfall plus the energy required to raise the water up into the atmosphere. We use the energy available from falling water through dams and hydroelectric projects, which constitute an indirect tapping of the daily solar energy flow.

A small fraction, about 0.2%, of the incident sunlight is converted into the energy of wind and water currents and waves. An even smaller fraction, 0.1%, is used by green plants and algae in photosynthesis, which is vital for our food supply. A tiny part of the earth's energy comes from nonsolar sources: tidal energy, which arises from the gravitational attraction between the moon and the earth, and geothermal heat, which emanates from the earth's molten core.

3 | Carbon Cycle

The fraction of the sunlight that is used by plants in photosynthesis is converted to chemical energy. It is stored in the form of carbohydrates such as glucose, surose, and starch. They contain two atoms of hydrogen and one of oxygen for every atom of carbon. The carbohydrates are formed by the reduction of carbon dioxide, and at the same time, water is oxidized to form molecular oxygen. The reduced carbon is reoxidized to carbon dioxide in the process of respiration, which provides the energy needs of biological organisms. Plants themselves use up about 20% of their carbohydrates for their own energy needs. The remainder, which represents stored photochemical energy, is called *net primary productivity*.

The processes of photosynthesis and respiration are balanced closely, and the cycling of carbon between the carbon dioxide of the atmosphere and the reduced organic compounds of biological organisms is essentially a closed loop. A very small fraction of plant and animal matter, however, estimated at less than 1 part in 10,000, is buried in the earth and removed from contact with atmospheric oxygen. Over the millennia this small fraction adds up to a large amount of reduced carbon compounds, and it is generally felt that essentially all the oxygen in the atmosphere has been produced by this process. The original atmosphere of the earth is thought to have been devoid of oxygen. It was the evolution of green plants, some 600 million years ago, that led to the accumulation of oxygen through photosynthesis and the burial of organic matter.

Some of the buried carbon compounds accumulated in deposits and were subjected to high temperatures and pressures in the earth's crust. They became coal, oil, and gas, which we now use to fuel our industrial civilization. We are, therefore, living off the store of solar energy of past ages.

Since the burial of organic compounds is thought to have been responsible for the evolution of atmospheric oxygen, you might wonder whether we are in danger of using up our oxygen supply if these same compounds are now being mined and burned as fuel. Evidently only a small fraction of the buried carbon is available in recoverable deposits of fuel; the rest is presumably widely dispersed in the earth's crust. The total energy that is estimated to be available in recoverable fossil fuels is about 0.7×10^{23} calories. This is about 100 times the annual net primary productivity. Burning all this fuel would consume about 1.6% of the oxygen in the atmosphere. While the percentage decrease in oxygen would be small enough to be scarcely noticeable, the increase in carbon dioxide would be very significant. The concentration of carbon dioxide in the atmosphere is very much lower than that of oxygen. Converting 1.6% of the oxygen to carbon dioxide would increase its concentration by a factor of nearly ten. This has serious implications for warming up the earth's surface through the greenhouse effect, as we will see in the next part of the book.

Origins of Fossil Fuels

Petroleum and natural gas

Petroleum and natural gas deposits are of marine origin. Photosynthesis in the oceans is estimated to produce 25 billion tons of reduced carbon annually.[1] Most of this is recycled to the atmosphere as carbon dioxide, but a minute fraction settles to the bottom, where oxidation is negligible. This biological debris is covered by clay and sand particles and forms a compacted organic layer in a matrix of porous clay or sandstone. Anaerobic bacteria digest the biological matter, releasing most of the oxygen and nitrogen. As the sediment becomes more deeply buried, the temperature and pressure rise. Bacterial action decreases, and organic disproportionation reactions are thought to occur, with the release and accumulation of large quantities of methane and light hydrocarbons. The heavy organic compounds remaining are thought to be carried along, as an emulsion, with the water that is squeezed out of the compacted sediment. The oil could be trapped in the overlying porous layers.

Gas and petroleum deposits are thought to have developed in this manner over a period of about a million years. The biological origin of oil is evidenced in the similarities of its major constituents to abundant biological molecules. The saturated hydrocarbons found in oil have structural and carbon number distributions similar to those found in the lipids of living organisms. The accompanying structural formulas show the similarities between the common petroleum constituents 2,6-dimethyl octane and 2-methyl-3-ethyl heptane, and the plant terpenes geraniol and limonene.

2,6-Dimethyl octane   Geraniol   2-Methyl-3-ethyl heptane   Limonene

Coal

Coal composed of the remains of plant matter from the huge, thickly wooded swamps that flourished 250 million years ago during a period of mild, and moist climate. Woody plants are made up of lignin as well as cellulose and protein. Lignin is a complex, three-dimensional polymer that contains aromatic groups.

OH
/OCH₃

CH
‖
CH
|
CH₂OH
Coniferyl alcohol

OH
CH₃O—⟋⟍—OCH₃

CH
‖
CH
|
CH₂OH
Sinapyl alcohol

The building units are coniferyl and sinapyl alcohol for lignins from coniferous and deciduous plants, respectively. While aerobic bacteria rapidly oxidize cellulose to carbon dioxide and water when the plant dies, lignin is much more resistant to bacterial action. In swamps, the lignin accumulates under water, compacting into a substance called peat.

Over the geological ages, the peat layers of the primeval swamps metamorphosed into coal. Depression and thrusting of the earth's crust buried the deposits and subjected them to high pressures and temperatures for long periods of time. Under those conditions the lignin gradually lost its oxygenated groups via the expulsion of water and carbon dioxide gas, and the aromatic groups were bound together. The ultimate product is graphite, which contains layers of fused

Graphite   layer

benzene rings. During this process, somewhat more open structures were also formed, such as bituminous coal. As the metamorphosis continues, the moisture content drops and the coal becomes harder and richer in carbon.

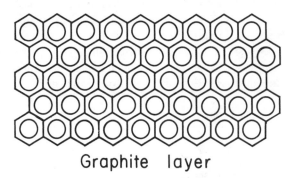

Bituminous coal

4 | Human Energy Consumption

Table 1.1 shows some of the quantities that have been discussed. It also shows that the total energy consumed by the burning of fossil fuels amounted to 6.0 × 10^{19} calories in 1975. This is about one-twelfth of the net primary productivity. The energy content of the food consumed by human beings in the same year was only 3.2 × 10^{18} calories. This is 2.2 million calories per person per day, which is close to the minimum estimated to be required for the daily energy needs of humans. Some people consume much more than this, while a large fraction of the world's population has an inadequate diet. (It should be noted that measurements of nutritionists are usually in Calories with a capital C, which are 1,000 ordinary calories. The average human diet is usually given as 2,200 Calories. This notation can be a source of confusion.)

Table 1.1 also shows that the total external energy consumed in the United States was about 30% of the worldwide energy consumption in 1975, although the United States had only 5% of the total population. The growth curves for both U.S. and world energy consumptions are given in Figure 1.2. World energy consumption has been increasing at a faster rate than that of the United States, but so has the population in the rest of the world. Both curves in the figure show nearly exponential growth, which means that consumption is increasing at a rate that is proportional to the amount already present; there is a constant percentage increase from year to year. The curves in Figure 1.2 show that this type of growth is not reasonable for the long term. Something that increases at a rate of 4% a year takes only 18 years to double, and then another 18 years to double again. Nothing in the natural world can grow through too many doubling periods before it runs into some constraint. Eventually all exponential growth curves have to

Table 1.1   Global Energy Fluxes

Energy Transfer	Rate (calories/year)
Energy radiated by the sun into space	2.8 × 10^{33}
Solar energy incident on earth	1.3 × 10^{24}
Solar energy affecting earth's climate and biosphere	8.6 × 10^{23}
Energy used to evaporate water	2.2 × 10^{23}
Solar energy used in photosynthesis	9.4 × 10^{20}
Energy used in net primary productivity	7.2 × 10^{20}
Energy conducted from earth's interior to its surface	3.0 × 10^{20}
Total energy consumed externally by humans, 1975	6.0 × 10^{19}
Energy content of food consumed by humans, 1975	3.2 × 10^{18}
Total energy consumed in the United States, 1975	1.8 × 10^{19}
Electrical energy produced in the United States, 1975	1.7 × 10^{18}

Source: Adapted from J. Harte and R. H. Socolow, *Patient Earth* (New York: Holt, Rinehart and Winston, Inc., 1971), p. 277; 1975 values from "World Energy Supplies, 1971–1975," U.N. Statistical Papers, Series J, No. 20 (New York: United Nations, 1977).

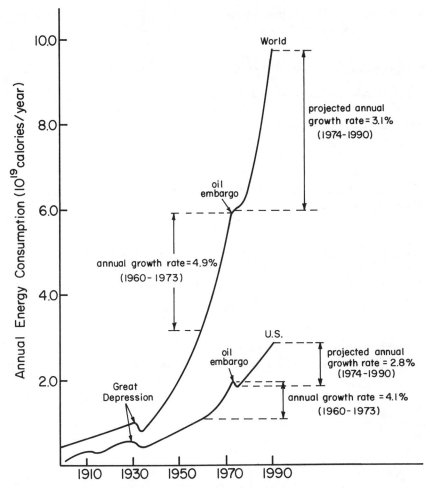

Figure 1.2 Trends in U.S. and World Energy Consumption

Source: Data up to 1970 taken from J. Harte and R. H. Socolow, *Patient Earth* (New York: Holt, Rinehart and Winston, Inc., 1971), p. 285. Data from 1971 to 1975 from "World Energy Supplies, 1971–1975," U.N. Statistical Papers, Series J, No. 20 (New York: United Nations, 1977). Projected U.S. values from "National Energy Outlook, Executive Summary, 1976," Federal Energy Administration (Washington, D.C.: U.S. Government Printing Office, 1976). Projected world values estimated from "Energy Facts II," Subcommittee on Energy Research, Development and Demonstration, U. S. House of Representatives, 94th Congress, Library of Congress, Serial H, August 1975, p. 44.

level off, and the growth of energy consumption is no exception. In the long run, energy inputs and outputs for human society must be in a steady state, just as they are for the earth as a whole. The present era of rapid energy use represents a transition to a new level of energy consumption. There remains considerable debate, however, about what that level will be and at what rate it is to be attained.

Already the immediate projections for the next decade or so are for lower annual growth rates for both U.S. and world energy consumption.

Exponential Growth and Decay; Resource Exhaustion

If a substance disappears at a rate that is proportional to the amount of it Q, present at any time, it is said to undergo *exponential decay*. The rate of disappearance is expressed by

$$-\frac{dQ}{dt} = kQ$$

where t is time and k is the proportionality constant (rate constant). Integration of this expression gives an equation for the exponential dependence of Q on time:

$$Q = Q_0 e^{-kt}$$

where Q_0 is the amount present initially. This dependence is shown in Figure 1.3. It is characterized by a constant half-life, $t_{1/2}$, i.e., the time it takes for Q to decrease to half its initial value ($Q/Q_0 = \frac{1}{2}$):

$$t_{\frac{1}{2}} = \frac{-\ln(\frac{1}{2})}{k} = \frac{0.693}{k}$$

Radioactivity is a process that follows exponential decay, since it involves spontaneous (random) disintegration of unstable atomic nuclei. This is shown in

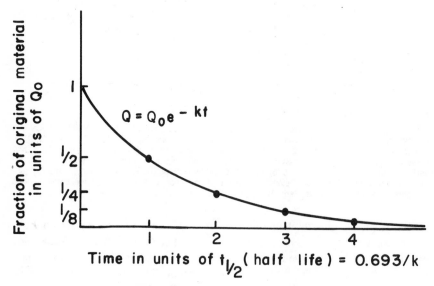

Figure 1.3   Plot of Exponential Decay

Figure 1.16 for plutonium decay. The number of disintegrations per second depends only on the number of nuclei present (Q) and on the probability of disintegration (k), which is characteristic of the particular composition of the nucleus. Each type of unstable nucleus (isotope) has a characteristic half-life.

Similarly, if Q increases at a rate proportional to the amount present, then

$$\frac{dQ}{dt} = kQ \tag{1}$$

and it undergoes *exponential growth:*

$$Q = Q_0 e^{kt} \tag{2}$$

The form of this dependence is shown in Figure 1.4. There is a constant doubling time, in which Q increases to twice its initial value ($Q/Q_0 = 2$):

$$t_2 = \frac{\ln (2)}{k} = \frac{0.693}{k} \tag{3}$$

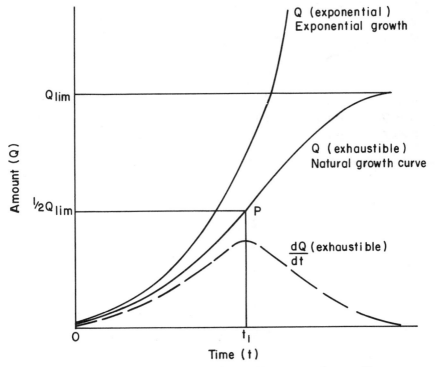

P is an inflection point where the rate of growth shifts from increase to decrease

Figure 1.4 Exponential and Natural Growth Curves

Often the rate of growth, R, is expressed as a percentage per unit of time, e.g., an annual percentage growth. If this percentage is not large,* it can be approximated as

$$R \approx \frac{dQ}{Qdt}$$

which, as we can see from equation (1) is equal to k. Therefore

$$t_2 \approx \frac{0.693}{R}$$

that is, a 7% annual growth rate corresponds to a doubling time of just about ten years.

   Growth curves in nature often look like the S-shaped curve in Figure 1.4. In the early part of the curve, growth is rapid, resembling the exponential curve, but after a time it slows down as the limit (e.g., resource exhaustion) is approached. The dotted curve represents the rate of production of Q, dQ/dt, as a function of time. This rate also increases rapidly at first, but then reaches a peak and afterwards declines as the total production of Q reaches its limit. This is the shape of the projected curves for petroleum production, shown in Figure 1.7. The equation for the bell-shaped curve is

$$\frac{dQ}{dT} = \frac{Q_{\lim}}{\sqrt{2\pi}} e^{-(t-t_1)^2/2} \tag{4}$$

where $Q_{\lim}$ is the limiting quantity of Q and t_1 is the time at which dQ/dt reaches its maximum value. The S-shaped curve is represented by the integral of equation (4).

---

*If the percentage is large, then the differential is a poor approximation. The exact relation is

$$R = \frac{Q - Q_0}{Q_0} = \frac{Q}{Q_0} - 1, \quad \text{since } t = 1$$

or

$$\frac{Q}{Q_0} = R + 1$$

Using equation (2), with $t = 1$, we have

$$\ln \frac{Q}{Q_0} = \ln(R + 1) = k$$

and, from equation (3),

$$t_2 = \frac{0.693}{\ln(R + 1)}$$

5 | Petroleum

The most immediate constraint on energy growth is the availability of petroleum and natural gas. The Industrial Revolution was initially fueled by coal, but we have increasingly switched to oil and gas, which are cleaner fuels and are transported more easily. Figure 1.5 illustrates that coal displaced fuel wood as an energy source in the late 1800s, but since the early part of this century it has been losing ground to gas and oil, which now account for nearly 80% of total energy consumption in the United States.

Oil is a complex mixture of hydrocarbons, which are molecules that contain only carbon and hydrogen. Figure 1.6 shows a diagram of an oil refinery, in which the various fractions of petroleum are separated by distillation. The table at the bottom of the figure gives the range of molecular sizes for the different fractions. The lightest liquid fraction is used for gasoline, the heaviest for lubricating oil.

We have become very dependent on petroleum and gas, but the rate of increase

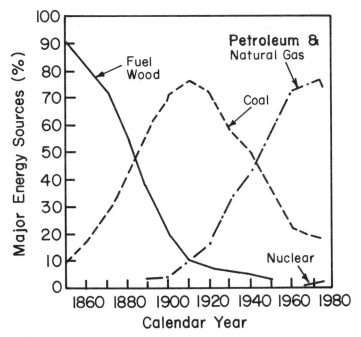

Figure 1.5 U.S. Energy Consumption Patterns

Source: "Historical Statistics of the United States Bureau of the Census," U.S. Bureau of Mines (Washington, D.C., 1974).

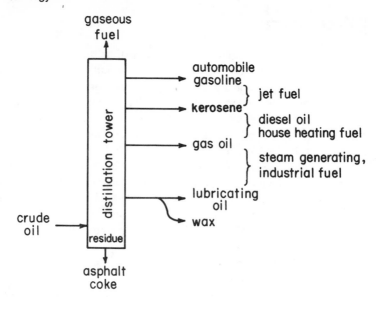

Chemical Composition

fraction	carbon atoms	molecular weight	boiling range, °C
gaseous	1 – 4	16 – 58	-126 – 0
gasoline	5 – 12	72 – 170	0 – 204
kerosene	10 – 16	156 – 226	180 – 274
gas oil	15 – 22	212 – 294	260 – 371
lube oil	19 – 35	268 – 492	338 – 468
residue	36 – 90	492 – 1262	468+

Figure 1.6 Crude Oil Refining

in production has begun to fall off, at least for U.S. reserves. Figure 1.7 shows past consumption and production curves, and projects two different estimates for future domestic production. There is some controversy about the total size of the reserves, which are represented by the area under the production curves in Figure 1.7. The lower curve is projected from a continuation of present trends, which

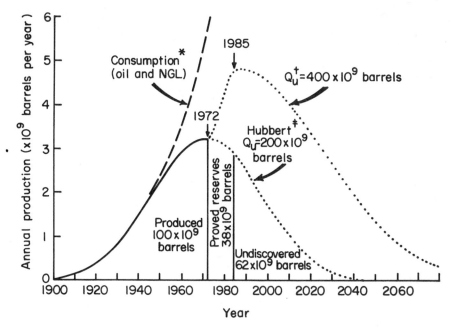

Figure 1.7   History and Trends for U.S. Oil Production

*Consumption curve includes crude oil and natural gas liquids (NGL), the latter accounting for about 15 percent of consumption.

†Q_u refers to the total quantity of produced oil—proved reserves plus potentially undiscovered reserves.

‡Hubbert estimate of Q_u from M. K. Hubbert, *Am. Assoc. Petrol. Geol. Bull.* 51 (1967):2207.

Source: R. R. Berg, J. C. Calhoun, and R. L. Whiting, *Science* 184 (1974):332. Copyright 1974 by the American Association for the Advancement of Science.

show a decrease in the rate of productive drilling in the United States. It is possible that drilling rates are influenced to some extent by the availability of less expensive foreign oil, however, and the upper curve represents a more optimistic assessment of total U.S. reserves based on a different set of assumptions. In any case, the amount of oil available is clearly inadequate to meet the ever-increasing demand.

The prognosis for worldwide petroleum reserves is similar. As shown in Figure 1.8 world production has increased more than fivefold from 1950 to 1976, when it amounted to 22×10^9 barrels. Table 1.2 lists the petroleum reserves for various areas of the world, as well as the production and consumption patterns. The total estimate of easily recoverable petroleum, perhaps 800×10^9 barrels, is only 36 times the amount produced in 1976. Among the four largest consumers, the United States, Western Europe, the communist countries, and Japan, only the communist countries produce enough petroleum to supply their present needs. The United States, Western Europe, and especially Japan must continue to de-

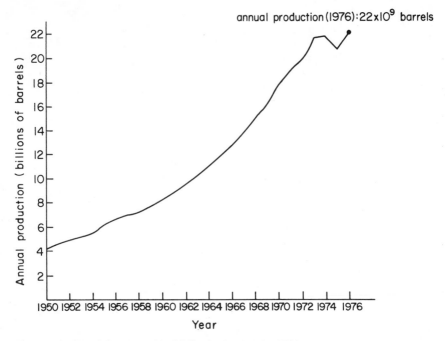

annual production (1976): 22×10^9 barrels

Figure 1.8 Trends in Worldwide Oil Production, 1950–1976*

*Includes crude petroleum and natural gas liquids.
Source: From data compiled in "World Energy Supplies, 1971–1975," U.N. Statistical Papers, Series J, No. 20 (New York: United Nations, 1977), Table I.

pend on the surplus oil of other areas, the Middle East in particular, to supplement their internal supplies. A large oil deposit has recently been found in Mexico, and similar discoveries may occur in China and other unexplored regions, and these will extend the world's oil supplies somewhat. Nevertheless, the surpluses are dwindling and will certainly be depleted sometime in the next century.

The energy crisis, then, really boils down to the question of how to respond to this fairly imminent exhaustion of our most versatile and convenient fuel. While there are many conceivable alternatives, as we shall see, the choices to be made are difficult and complex because of the massiveness of the energy supply system, which undergirds so many of our activities, and the long lead times needed to produce any significant change in this system.

Oil Refining

The gasoline fraction of crude oil, which is typically 20% by volume, is increased to 40–45% by reactions in the refinery. One of these reactions is the

Table 1.2   Worldwide Petroleum Resources

Distribution of Easily Extractable Reserves

Area	Reserve (barrels)
Middle East	326.3×10^9
Communist countries*	101.1×10^9
Africa	60.6×10^9
Mexico†	$50-200 \times 10^9$
United States	31.3×10^9
Other countries in Western Hemisphere	35.8×10^9
Western Europe	24.5×10^9
Far East and Oceania	19.4×10^9
Japan	Negligible
Estimated total	$649-799 \times 10^9$

Distribution of Consumption and Production, 1975

Area	Consumption (barrels)	Production (barrels)
United States	5.3×10^9	3.6×10^9
Western Europe	4.1×10^9	0.3×10^9 (1976)
Communist countries	3.7×10^9	4.5×10^9
Japan	1.5×10^9	Negligible
All other areas	3.5×10^9	12.6×10^9

*China may have significant untapped reserves.

†A new large reserve has recently been discovered; its size is presently uncertain. [See *Science* 202 (1978): 1261.]

Source: Top table: U.S. Department of the Interior, press release, *New York Times,* July 31, 1977. Bottom table: "World Energy Supplies, 1971–1975," U.N. Statistical Papers, Series J, No. 20 (New York: United Nations, 1977), Tables I and II.

"cracking" process for breaking down large alkanes:

$$C_{(m+n)}H_{2(m+n)+2} \longrightarrow C_mH_{2m}+ C_nH_{2n+2}$$

Kerosene or   alkene   alkane
gas-oil size   (gasoline size)

which occurs at about 800° C, or with the aid of a catalyst (K on SiO_2 and Al_2O_3) at 400–600° C. There are also alkylation reactions to build up small hydrocarbons:

$$RH + \underset{\substack{H}}{\overset{\substack{H}}{C}}=\underset{\substack{R''}}{\overset{\substack{R'}}{C}} \xrightarrow[20°C]{acid} \underset{\substack{R \quad H}}{\overset{\substack{H \quad R'}}{H-C-C-R''}}$$

light hydrocarbons   gasoline
(3,4, or 5 carbon atoms)

Reaction conditions are arranged to produce hydrocarbons that have a high degree of branching; these have higher octane ratings (less tendency to preignite, or "knock," during piston compression) than straight-chain hydrocarbons. Aromatic hydrocarbons (benzene derivatives) have even higher octane ratings, and an additional process carried out in the refinery is catalytic reforming, whereby straight-chain alkanes are converted to aromatics:

$$CH_3CH_2CH_2CH_2CH_2CH_3 \xrightarrow{-H_2} \text{(cyclohexane)} \xrightarrow{-H_2} \text{(benzene)}$$

Cyclohexane   Benzene
(C_6H_{12})   (C_6H_6)

These reactions are run at high pressure (15–20 atm) and temperature (500–600° C) with a Re-Pt-Al$_2$O$_3$ catalyst.

Estimation of Petroleum Reserves

Considerations of production curves led M. K. Hubbert to his estimate of the total U.S. oil reserves in the lower curve of Figure 1.7.[3] The solid curve is the actual production record up to 1972. Hubbert noticed that this curve is very similar to the time-averaged curve of the oil discovery rate, but with a time lag of 10 to 15 years. Since the latter reached a maximum in 1956 and has since declined, Hubbert inferred that the production rate would reach a maximum in the early 1970s and would thereafter decline, following the bell-shaped curve of Figure 1.4. Since the peak of this curve corresponds to the point at which half the ultimate production has been achieved, Hubbert concluded that the total oil reserve was twice the cumulative production to 1972, or 200×10^9 barrels. This is also close to the estimate advanced by the oil industry.

This reasoning has been challenged, however, on the grounds that both production and discovery rates are subject to economic factors.[4] In particular the availability of cheap foreign oil from the 1950s onward reduced the incentive for domestic exploration and production. The upper curve of Figure 1.7 is based on a higher estimate of the total reserve. This was arrived at by multiplying the total volume of sedimentary rock available for exploration on land and offshore by the fraction of petroleum it is expected to contain on the basis of past production experience. It is likely, of course, that even if the higher estimate is correct, the remaining oil is more difficult and expensive to produce.

While the difference of a factor of two in the reserve estimates is obviously important to energy economics and politics, the overall message of the production curves is the same: In a relatively short time, historically speaking, we will have used up the petroleum deposits that have accumulated over the millennia.

6 | Survey of Alternative Energy Sources

Table 1.3 is a survey of the energy sources potentially or actually available to the United States. There are two kinds of sources: depletable and renewable. The former, tabulated in the first part, includes all the fossil fuel deposits, including coal, petroleum, and natural gas, as well as oil shales, which are rocky deposits impregnated with oil. Depletable resources also include nuclear fuel, uranium, and possibly deuterium for the fusion reaction. Renewable sources, shown in the second part of Table 1.3, include sunlight and various indirect forms of solar energy such as hydropower, wind power, the energy stored in photosynthesis, and tidal energy. The estimates of the amounts of energy available are expressed in units of the national energy consumption in 1975. Thus the numbers in the columns are equivalent to the number of years the resource would last if all our energy came from that source alone, and if consumption remained at the 1975 level. In the first part, the numbers in the middle column show the relative amounts of depletable resources that are available at current energy prices in the United States. Coal is much more abundant than petroleum and natural gas, and could last for many decades even at present energy prices. The amount of energy available in uranium deposits is relatively small, comparable to that stored in the oil and gas reserves, unless the breeder reactor comes into use; this question will be examined shortly. Geothermal energy is listed as a depletable energy source because, although energy flows continuously from the interior of the earth, it can

Table 1.3   Estimates of Sources of Energy in the United States*

Depletable Sources†

Resource	Known and Economically Recoverable Reserves	Potential Reserves under Certain Economic and Technological Conditions
Petroleum	11.2	21–37‡
Natural gas	10.9	20–36‡
Coal	169	~440‡
Oil shale	16.9	82
Nuclear fission		
Conventional reactors	25.3	
Breeder technology		~1,800
Nuclear fusion		
Deuterium-deuterium		~10^9§
Deuterium-tritium		~275ǁ
Geothermal heat		
Steam, hot water, and		
geopressured fluids	0.2§	~11#
Hot rock		>100#

Renewable Resources§

Resource	Amount of Energy Continuously Supplied Per Year
Solar radiation	650
Wind power	4
Ocean thermal gradients	>5
Hydropower	0.12
Photosynthesis	0.20
Organic wastes	0.1
Tidal energy	0.1

*Numbers in both tables are in units of total U.S. energy consumption in 1975, or 1.79 × 10^{19} calories. They are equivalent to the number of years the resource would last if all energy came from that source alone.

†Except as noted, data are from "A National Plan for Energy Research, Development and Demonstration: Creating Energy Choices for the Future," Vol. I, ERDA (Washington, D.C.: U.S. Government Printing Office, 1975), chap. II.

‡"Energy Facts, II" Subcommittee on Energy Research, Development, and Demonstration, U.S. House of Representatives, 94th Congress, Library of Congress, Serial H, August 1975, p. 44.

§Adapted from A. Hammond, Science 177 (1972): 875, using 1975 energy consumption value.

ǁAssumes tritium is obtained from lithium-6, the U.S. supply of which is ~74 × 10^9 g; from A. Hammond, Science 191 (1976): 1037.

#D. E. White and D. L. Williams, eds., "Assessment of Geothermal Resources of the U.S.—1975," Geological Survey, Circular 726 (Washington, D.C., 1975).

be extracted practically only from concentrated deposits where it has been stored in hot rocks and water. At present prices, this appears to be a fairly small resource.

The right-hand column lists the resources that are potentially available at greater expense. These figures are much less certain than those in the middle column. Fuel deposits come in a wide range of concentrations, and the amount that is economically recoverable obviously depends on what price it makes sense to pay. The eventual limit is a concentration so low that it takes more energy to obtain the fuel than is recovered from it. This depends, however, on the efficiency of the extraction technology, which can change with time. Oil shale is a good example of this uncertainty. Very large amounts of hydrocarbons are trapped in oil shale, but at the moment extracting them requires that the shale be crushed and heated to quite high temperatures, thus limiting the attractiveness of the process from both an economic and an energy utilization point of view. This situation is changing as more effective means are found to extract the hydrocarbons from the rock. The amounts of energy that are potentially available from the fusion reaction dwarfs any of the other figures, if this technology can be made to work.

The numbers for the renewable sources in the second part of Table 1.3 represent the amounts of energy available per year. The annual solar flux is much larger than the total energy consumption. The main problem in harnessing the sun's rays is that they are widely dispersed over the surface of the land and are easily obstructed by clouds. Also, the sun shines during only 12 hours a day on the average, and much less than this in the winter at high latitudes.

Wind power represents a smaller, but still significant, resource. The technology for extracting the energy from wind is available now and may soon be practical. Again, the main problem is the intermittent nature of wind. A comparable resource is the ocean thermal gradients. The sun heats the surface of the ocean, producing a thermal gradient with respect to the underlying waters. In the tropical oceans the temperature difference is 20° C between the surface and the waters 1,000 m below. A large amount of energy is stored in this gradient, which is available on a continuous basis. The temperature difference is rather small, however, and the efficiency with which the energy can be extracted is very low. Also, the energy would have to be transported over large distances.

The amount of energy potentially available in hydropower is limited, and most of the suitable dam sites have already been developed. Photosynthesis taking place on the surface of the United States represents a relatively small fraction of the total energy consumption, but there are possibilities for increasing the photosynthetic yield and putting it to better use. Organic wastes represent that part of the current yield that is discarded. Converting these wastes to fuel would solve an environmental problem as well as contribute to the energy supply. Tidal energy is difficult to harness and represents a relatively unimportant resource.

7 | Coal

Having looked at the overall picture with respect to the magnitude of energy resources that are potential alternatives to oil and gas, let us now examine these forms of energy in greater detail. The first one to look at is coal, which is, of course, a resource that is already in use.

The size of the U.S. coal reserve is substantially larger than that of oil and gas. There are potential coal deposits to meet the total 1975 U.S. domestic energy consumption at current prices for 169 years and considerably more than that which would be more expensive to extract. Coal is also substantially more abundant than oil or gas on a worldwide basis.

As shown in Figure 1.9, worldwide recoverable reserves of coal are estimated to be about 7.4×10^{12} metric tons, with the Soviet Union and the United States owning about 75% of the supply. Countries in Latin America and other parts of the world would have to depend heavily on foreign imports if coal were to become the chief energy currency. The total coal reserve is equivalent to about 4.7×10^{22} calories. This is almost 800 times the value of world energy consumption from all fuel sources in 1975.

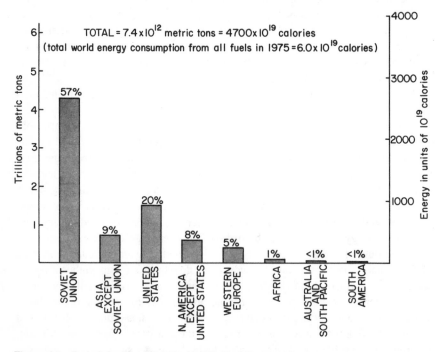

Figure 1.9 Remaining Identified Worldwide Coal Reserves*

*Total reserve includes sources that could be made available under certain economic and technological conditions.

Gasification:
  Individual steps
    Methane production

$$C + 2H_2 \quad \rightarrow \quad CH_4 \qquad\qquad\qquad \text{hydrogasification (1)}$$

    Hydrogen production

$$C + H_2O \quad \rightarrow \quad CO + H_2 \qquad\qquad \text{water-gas reaction (2)}$$

$$CO + H_2O \quad \rightarrow \quad CO_2 + H_2 \qquad\qquad \text{water-gas shift (3)}$$

  Overall reaction: (1) + (2) + (3)

$$2C + 2H_2O \quad \xrightarrow{900°\,C} \quad CH_4 + CO_2 \qquad\qquad (4)$$

Desulfurization:

$$S + H_2 \quad \rightarrow \quad H_2S \qquad\qquad (5)$$

$$CaCO_3 + H_2S \quad \rightleftharpoons \quad CaS + CO_2 + H_2O \qquad\qquad (6)$$

Liquefaction:
  Hydrocarbon liquids by Fischer-Tropsch synthesis

$$nCO + (2n + 1)H_2 \quad \xrightarrow[\substack{200°\,C \\ \sim 15\ \text{atm}}]{\text{catalyst}} \quad C_nH_{2n+2} + nH_2O \qquad\qquad (7)$$

  Methanol synthesis

$$CO + 2H_2 \quad \xrightarrow[\substack{>300°\,C \\ >200\ \text{atm}}]{\text{catalyst}} \quad CH_3OH \qquad\qquad (8)$$

  Direct catalytic hydrogenation

$$nC + (n + 1)H_2 \quad \xrightarrow[\substack{450°\,C \\ >100\ \text{atm}}]{\text{catalyst}} \quad C_nH_{2n+2} \qquad\qquad (9)$$

Figure 1.10 Conversion of Coal to Natural Gas and Liquid Fuels

One major problem with coal is that it is a dirty fuel to burn. Of particular concern is the sulfur dioxide emitted, which is a serious health hazard in urban areas. Also, being a solid, coal is much less convenient to use than petroleum or natural gas. One can imagine the inconvenience of running automobiles with steam engines into which the coal has to be shoveled. Even for railroad locomotives, the advantages of liquid fuel long ago led to the replacement of the steam engine by the diesel engine.

It is possible to convert coal to liquid or gaseous fuels by appropriate chemistry. The reduced carbon in coal, in which most of its energy content resides, can be transformed into hydrocarbon molecules which are either liquid or gaseous, depending on their molecular weights and structures. The simplest hydrocarbon molecule, and the one for which the most practical current coal conversion technology has been developed, is methane, CH_4. Figure 1.10 shows the chemical reactions, in simplified form, that are associated with coal gasification technology. Equation (1) shows the hydrogasification reaction, the conversion of carbon to methane by the addition of molecular hydrogen. To run this reaction, a supply of hydrogen is needed. The most abundant source of hydrogen and the only one that is practical to use on a wide scale is water. In order to produce hydrogen, water must be reduced. Equations (2) and (3) show that the same carbon found in coal can serve as a reducing agent, producing successively carbon monoxide and then carbon dioxide, with the release of two molecules of hydrogen. The overall reaction, reaction (4), involves a combination of two atoms of carbon with two molecules of water to produce one molecule of methane and one of carbon dioxide. It appears that we are throwing half the carbon away to produce methane, but the energy value of the methane is about twice that of carbon, and if the reaction could be carried out with 100% efficiency, no energy would be lost. In practice, of course, this efficiency cannot be achieved and some fraction of the energy content in coal must be used in its conversion to gas.

An additional advantage of coal gasification is that it makes the removal of sulfur quite straightforward, as shown in reactions (5) and (6) in Figure 1.10. In the presence of the hydrogen that is needed to convert carbon to methane, sulfur is converted to hydrogen sulfide, which is easily trapped in a calcium carbonate bed, with the release of carbon dioxide and water, as in reaction (6). This reaction is reversible on heating, and the hydrogen sulfide can be regenerated in another location and used in a variety of industrial processes such as the production of sulfuric acid. Since the sulfur in coal would otherwise be converted to sulfur dioxide on combustion, coal gasification has the attractive feature of converting a source of pollution into a resource.

Natural gas, which contains mostly methane, is the most convenient energy source for heating and for generating electricity. It is also transported quite easily. Coal gasification would augment the dwindling supplies of this desirable fuel. Once carbon monoxide is generated via reaction (2), it is possible to convert it to higher molecular weight hydrocarbons, in the gasoline range, using what is known as Fischer-Tropsch chemistry, shown in reaction (7). This technology is not so advanced as coal gasification, and it is somewhat less efficient in its energy requirements. Another alternative is to convert carbon monoxide to methanol, CH_3OH, via reaction (8). Methanol is nearly as useful as gasoline in internal combustion engines. Finally, recent technology has been developed for the direct catalytic hydrogenation of coal to produce liquid hydrocarbons, under the conditions shown in reaction (9).

It is possible in principle to switch from an oil economy to a coal economy with the assurance of a much larger resource base. Coal can be burned directly in stationary furnaces and can be gasified or liquefied for use as a fuel in transportation. This scenario, however, has formidable problems. In the first place, coal is

Table 1.4   Composition and Heat Content of Common Coals Found in the United States

Rank	Location by State	Chemical Analysis				Heating Value (calories/g)
		Moisture	Volatile Matter	Fixed Carbon	Ash	
Anthracite	Pa.	4.4%	4.8%	81.8%	9.0%	7,288
Bituminous						
Low volatile	Md.	2.3	19.6	65.8	12.3	7,338
High volatile	Ky.	3.2	36.8	56.4	3.6	7,821
Subbituminous	Wyo.	22.2	32.2	40.3	4.3	5,334
Lignite	N. Dak.	36.8	27.8	30.2	5.2	3,863

Source: U.S. Bureau of Mines, Information Circular, No. 769, 1954.

quite variable in its composition and also in its geographic distribution. Table 1.4 lists various kinds of coal in order of their carbon content. The heating value of the coal depends on the amount of reduced carbon and hydrogen in relation to the amount of nonfuel constituents, such as water, listed in the moisture column, and inorganic materials, listed under the heading of ash. Volatile matter refers to the hydrocarbons, mostly methane, that are released upon heating, while fixed carbon is the combustible fuel that is left behind after the volatile matter is removed. There are basically four types of coal distributed throughout the United States as shown in Figure 1.11. The hard coal, anthracite, is found in only a few deposits in the East and constitutes a small fraction of the total resource. The extensive coal deposits in Appalachia and the Midwest are bituminous or soft coal, which has a relatively high fraction of volatile matter. Western coal reserves amount to more than half the total and consist of subbituminous coal and lignite. These have a high water content, and therefore their heating value per gram is much less than that of eastern and midwestern coal. This factor magnifies the expense involved in transporting western coal to major urban centers.

The sulfur content is highest in the bituminous coals of the East and lowest in the subbituminous and lignite coals of the West. The table in Figure 1.11 shows that 70% of the bituminous but only 0.4% of the subbituminous and 9% of the lignite have more than 1% sulfur by weight. U.S. air quality standards set an upper limit for the amount of sulfur dioxide that can be emitted per calorie of coal energy consumed in power plants. Currently it stands at 1.2 mg of sulfur dioxide emitted per kilocalorie of coal burned. At first glance it may appear that western coals are safer for the environment because of their lower sulfur content per unit weight. Actually, there is no marked advantage to western coals, since their low percentage of sulfur is offset by their low heating value. Consequently, more western coal has to be burned to obtain a given amount of energy. Moreover, much of the sulfur in bituminous coal is present as iron sulfide, the mineral pyrites, which can be removed fairly readily by grinding and screening the coal,

	Anthracite
	Bituminous
	Subbituminous
	Lignite

Average Sulfur Content of Coal by Rank

Rank	% of total coal reserves	% with sulfur content >1%
Anthracite	0.9	2.9
Bituminous	46.0	70.2
Subbituminous	24.7	0.4
Lignite	28.4	9.3
Total, all ranks	100	35.0

Figure 1.11   Coal Distribution in the United States and Average Sulfur Content of Coal
Source: P. Averitt, U.S. Geological Survey, Bulletin 1136, January 1960.

whereas the sulfur of western coal is almost all organically bound and cannot be removed in this fashion.

A major cost of coal consumption, in both economic and human terms, is the mining operation. Deep mines are expensive to dig and maintain and notoriously dangerous for miners. Accident rates have historically been high, and black lung disease is a serious occupational hazard. Compensatory payments to U.S. miners who suffer from black lung disease is expected to reach $8 billion by 1980. The recent operating experience of some mines shows, however, that the institution of proper safety procedures can cut the accident rate to those of other industries, and that exposure to coal dust can be significantly reduced. In recent years strip mining, in which the surface soils are removed to expose the seams of coal, has increased steadily in importance and now accounts for almost half the total coal produced. Strip mining is safer and costs much less than deep mining, but takes its toll on the ecology of the land. In Appalachia, strip mining on steep hillsides has led to serious erosion and fouling of local waterways. Equally serious problems are encountered in the western states, where the topsoil is thin and the climate is semiarid. With considerable effort and expense, it is possible to restore strip-mined land to productive use, although restoration to the original condition is problematic.

Probably the most difficult environmental questions concern the exploitation of the extensive western U.S. coal deposits. As we have seen, these deposits are relatively low grade and are expensive to transport over long distances. The energy companies are thinking of building coal conversion plants on site and shipping the upgraded fuel, gas or liquid, instead. The difficulty here is the lack of water in the region. As shown in Figure 1.10, coal gasification requires the generation of hydrogen, which only water can supply in sufficient quantities. Two molecules of water are required for each molecule of methane that is produced. Large quantities of water are required for the reactions and for cooling. Additional water would be required for the mining activities themselves and for reclamation of the strip-mined land. Water resources, however, have historically been in short supply in the western part of the United States. A study by the National Academy of Sciences concluded that there might be adequate water for mining but not for the coal conversion industries that are envisioned.[5] This is disputed, however, by the energy companies. The mining activities also present difficult problems. Many of the seams of coal in the West are also natural aquifers, and their stripping might disrupt water tables and water circulation patterns. Also, the social and economic disruption of small communities in the West as large energy enterprises get under way has recently caused much concern.

Coal Conversion

The basic problem in converting coal to liquid or gaseous fuel is to find an efficient way to combine hydrogen with solid carbon. The H/C atomic ratio is 4 for methane and about 2 for gasoline, but in coal it ranges from 0.8 (bituminous coal) to 0.3 (anthracite). The only abundant source of hydrogen is water, and energy is required to release the hydrogen. In the future this energy might be provided by nuclear or solar sources, but for the present the only practical source is coal itself via the reactions given in Figure 1.10. Shown below are the amounts of heat given off or absorbed in the reactions, along with the temperatures required for acceptable reaction rates consistent with the position of equilibrium:

$$C + H_2O \rightleftarrows CO + H_2 - 31.4 \text{ kcal/mol} \tag{1}$$
$$(900° \text{ C, water-gas reaction)}$$

$$CO + H_2O \rightleftarrows CO_2 + H_2 + 9.9 \text{ kcal/mol} \tag{2}$$
$$(450° \text{ C, water-gas shift reaction)}$$

Since reaction (1) requires heat (endothermic), the equilibrium shifts toward the products when the temperature is raised, whereas for reaction (2), which gives off heat (exothermic), the products are favored by lowering the temperature.

The hydrogen produced is now available for addition to carbon. The direct reaction

$$C + 2H_2 \rightleftarrows CH_4 + 17.9 \text{ kcal/mol} \tag{3}$$
$$(800° \text{ C, Hydrogasification)}$$

produces methane but is quite slow. A high temperature is needed for reasonable rates, but because the reaction is exothermic, the equilibrium is then unfavorable. Reaction with carbon monoxide,

$$CO + 3H_2 \rightleftarrows CH_4 + H_2O + 49.3 \text{ kcal/mol} \tag{4}$$
$$(400° \text{ C, methanation)}$$

is even more exothermic, but it can be accelerated with a nickel catalyst and therefore run at lower temperatures where the equilibrium is favorable.

Practical gasification of coal therefore relies mainly on reactions (1), (2), and (4), as shown in the first flow diagram of Figure 1.12. Coal and steam are heated to about 900° C. Some methane is given off directly from the volatile fraction of the coal, and some carbon is hydrogenated directly; but the main products of this stage are carbon monoxide and hydrogen from the water-gas reaction. At the lower temperature (450° C) of the next stage, some of the carbon monoxide is converted to carbon dioxide with the production of more hydrogen via the water-gas shift reaction. Carbon dioxide, water, and sulfur compounds are removed from the gas streams before they are passed over the catalyst, which induces the methanation reaction.

The overall reaction, obtained by multiplying reaction (1) by 2 and adding reactions (2) and (4), is:

$$2C + 2H_2O \rightleftarrows CH_4 + CO_2 - 3.6 \text{ kcal/mol} \tag{5}$$

In principle, only 3.6 kcal/mol of energy need be expended, and all the heating value of the coal is transferred to methane. In practice, however, the energy costs are much higher. The basic problem is that the overall process must be carried out in stages that are not thermodynamically matched. Since endothermic reac-

Production of Methane from Coal

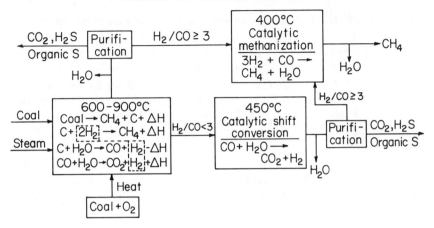

Production of Liquid Fuel from Coal by Fischer-Tropsch Synthesis

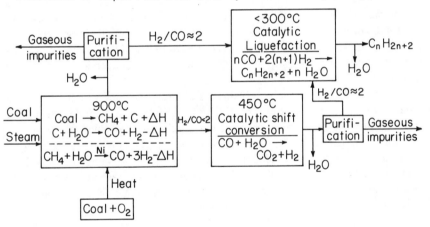

Production of Liquid Fuel from Coal by Direct Catalytic Hydrogenation

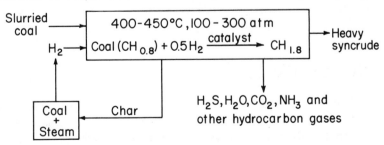

Figure 1.12 Coal Conversion Technology

tions run at high temperatures and exothermic ones at low temperatures, the heat produced in exothermic reactions cannot be fed back to run the endothermic ones. A high-temperature step is required to start the process, via reaction (1). Essentially the entire heat input for this reaction must be provided from an external source, e.g., the burning of some of the coal. Since 2 moles of carbon are needed for the production of 1 mole of methane, the external heat requirement is 62.8 kcal/mol, which is 30% of the heating value of the methane, 210.8 kcal/mol. Therefore the energy conversion efficiency of the process is no better than about 70%.

The production of liquid hydrocarbons from coal proceeds in a similar manner, as shown in the second diagram in Figure 1.12, except that the hydrogen and carbon monoxide are combined under different conditions to produce alkanes instead of methane,

$$n\text{CO} + (2n+1)\text{H}_2 \xrightarrow{\text{Catalyst}} \text{C}_n\text{H}_{2n+2} + n\text{H}_2\text{O} \quad (\text{Fischer-Tropsch reaction})$$

The operating temperature ($\sim 250°$ C) is lower and the gas pressure (25 atm) is higher than in the methanation reaction; a variety of catalysts can be used to control the product composition: iron, cobalt, nickel, ruthenium, zinc oxide, and thorium dioxide. The overall process is even less efficient than methane production; about half the energy value of the coal is lost in conversion to the liquid hydrocarbons.

Higher efficiencies could be obtained if a way was found to react hydrogen directly with coal, rather than with carbon monoxide. For example, the overall methane production process, reaction (5), could also be obtained by adding reactions (1), (2), and (3). Since only 1 mole of carbon would have to be converted to carbon monoxide, the external energy cost would be only 31.4 kcal/mol, instead of 62.8 kcal/mol. Unfortunately no way has yet been found to catalyze reaction (3). However, direct catalytic hydrogenation of coal, as in the third diagram in Figure 1.12, can be accomplished with the production of a heavy liquid with the consistency of crude oil, which is suitable as a heating fuel. A residue of char is left behind, which can be used to make the needed hydrogen by reaction with steam. The overall energy efficiency is higher than that with the other liquefaction or gasification processes.

8 | Nuclear Fission

Nuclear power is presently the most highly developed alternative to energy supplied by coal. The one significant form of energy on earth that is not related to the sun either directly or indirectly is energy that resides in the nuclei of atoms. Nuclei are made up of collections of protons and neutrons called *nucleons,* which

Table 1.5   Simple Nuclear Particles

Type	Schematic Representation	Charge	Mass*	Chemical Symbol†
Neutron	●	0	1.0087	$_{0}^{1}n$
Proton	⊕	+1	1.0078	$_{1}^{1}p$
Helium-4 (alpha particle)		+2	4.0026	$_{2}^{4}He$
Helium-3		+2	3.0160	$_{2}^{3}He$

*In atomic mass units (amu), where 1 amu = 1.6606×10^{-24} g.
†The superscript is the *mass number,* equivalent to the number of protons and neutrons in the nucleus; the subscript is the *atomic number,* equivalent to the number of protons. $_{2}^{4}He$ and $_{2}^{3}He$ are isotopes.

are held together by strong nuclear forces. As indicated in Table 1.5, protons are positively charged, while neutrons are neutral. The number of protons determines the number of negatively charged electrons that surround the nucleus, which determines the chemical properties of the element. The mass of the atoms is determined by the total number of nucleons. Isotopes of the elements, such as He-3 and He-4, have the same number of protons but different numbers of neutrons. The nuclear forces increase as the number of nucleons increases, but so does the electrostatic repulsion among the positively charged protons. Figure 1.13 is a graph of the total binding energy per nucleon with increasing mass of the nuclei. The highest nuclear stability is associated with atoms of intermediate atomic weight, in the vicinity of the element iron. For heavier elements, the repulsive forces gradually become more important, and elements heavier than bismuth, with 83 protons, are unstable. As illustrated in Figure 1.14, these heavier elements split off alpha particles, which are nuclei of the element helium that contain two protons and two neutrons. Some of these heavy elements can also undergo spontaneous fission, in which they split into two daughter atoms of intermediate atomic weights, with the release of a great deal of energy.

Isotopes of the elements can also be unstable with respect to the number of neutrons they contain. The ratio of neutrons to protons needed for stability increases slowly with increasing atomic number, as shown in Figure 1.15. Isotopes with too many neutrons can convert a neutron to a proton with the emission of a high-energy electron, called a beta ray. This corresponds to moving diagonally across the graph of Figure 1.15 toward the stability curve. Both alpha particle emission and nuclear fission produce isotopes with too many neutrons,

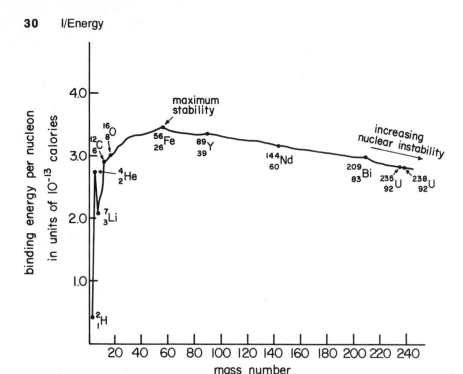

Figure 1.13 Nuclear Binding Energy Curve

and the products therefore are beta emitters. Unstable isotopes can also release some of their energy in the form of high-energy electromagnetic radiation, called gamma rays. The rate of nuclear decay, whether by alpha, beta, or gamma emission, varies from one isotope to another. It is generally expressed as the half-life, which is the time required for half of the nuclei to decay, as illustrated in Figure 1.16 for plutonium. Plutonium no longer exists naturally in the earth's crust but is produced in nuclear reactors. Half the plutonium that was initially formed on earth decayed after 24,360 years. After 100,000 years, i.e., approximately four half-lives, the original quantity of plutonium was reduced to one-sixteenth of its initial value. Thus, plutonium and other unstable elements have long since disappeared over the course of the earth's history. However, a few of them decay so slowly that they are still present in significant abundance. Among these, uranium is the only element that can undergo fission.

Spontaneous fission is an extremely rare event, but one of the isotopes of uranium, the one containing 235 nucleons and called U-235, can be induced to undergo fission with high probability if it encounters a neutron. In addition to the two fission fragments, two or three neutrons are produced in this process, as shown in the top part of Figure 1.17. If these neutrons, in turn, strike other atoms

Alpha Decay

example:

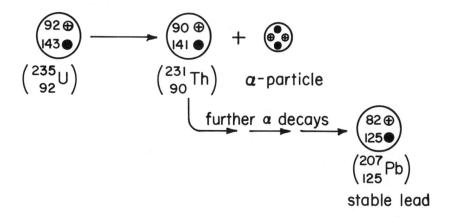

Spontaneous Fission

example[*]:

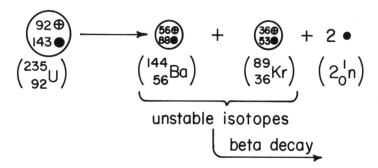

Figure 1.14   Reactions of Heavy Nuclei

*Example shows just one of more than 30 possible pairs of primary fission products that can occur when $^{235}_{92}$U splits up.

of uranium-235, they can produce further fission. Since the ratio of neutrons released to neutrons absorbed in each fission event is greater than one, a chain reaction can be built up in which all the atoms in a piece of uranium-235 undergo fission in a short period of time with a large release of energy. This is the basis of the first atom bomb, which was tested in New Mexico and exploded over Hiroshima in 1945.

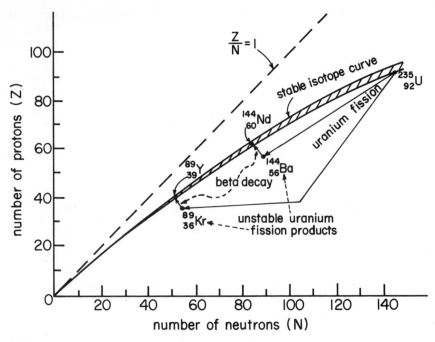

Figure 1.15 Proton-Neutron Ratio for Stable Isotopes: Beta Emission*

*Beta emission: neutron (^1_0n) → proton (^1_1p) + β^- (high-energy electron)

example: $^{239}_{94}$Pu (plutonium) decay

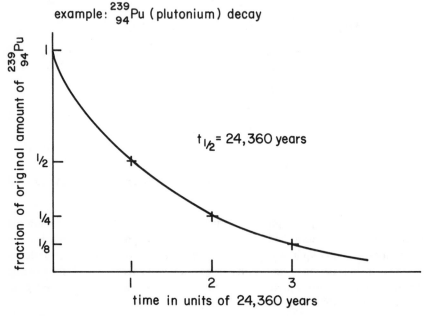

Figure 1.16 Half-Life $(t_{1/2})$ of Radioactive Isotopes

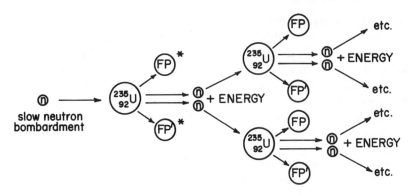

Pressurized Light Water Reactor

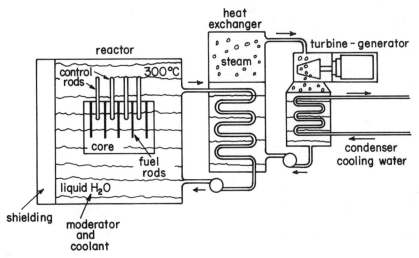

Figure 1.17 Chain Reaction by Induced with Slow (Thermal) Neutrons; Pressurized Light Water Reactor

*FP and FP' represent various fission products.

Naturally Occurring Radioisotopes

The most important radioisotopes found in the earth's crust, along with their half-lives, are:

	$t_{1/2}$ (years)		$t_{1/2}$ (years)
^{232}Th*	1.4×10^{10}	^{235}U	7×10^8
^{238}U	4.5×10^9	^{40}K	1.27×10^9

*The left superscript gives the mass number of the isotope, the number of neutrons plus protons. Sometimes the atomic number (number of protons) is also given as a left subscript, e.g., $^{235}_{92}$U. Since the element with atomic number 92 is uranium, the atomic number is implicit in the symbol U.

The first three are α emitters, while ^{40}K is a β emitter. ^{232}Th and ^{238}U are both quite abundant in the earth's crust. ^{235}U has become scarce, since 6.4 of its half-lives have elapsed since the formation of the earth. It is, however, the only naturally occurring isotope that can undergo fission. ^{40}K is a form of potassium in low abundance (0.001%), but since potassium is an important constituent of biological tissues, ^{40}K provides a significant fraction of the background radiation to which we are normally subject (see Table 1.8 on page 45).

Alpha emission often leaves a product isotope that is itself unstable with respect to β or further α emission, and decay of the heavy elements generally proceeds in a sequential cascade, as shown for ^{235}U in Figure 1.18. Consequently small quantities of daughter isotopes such as ^{231}Pa ($t_{1/2} = 3.25 \times 10^4$ years) exist in a steady state with the parent isotope.

Unstable isotopes can also be created by the interaction of stable nuclei with neutrons or with high-energy particles. Cosmic rays are charged particles from outer space that enter the earth's atmosphere at high velocity. Their collisions with N_2, the major constituent of the atmosphere, produce ^{14}C ($t_{1/2} = 5,730$ years), which reacts with the O_2 to form $^{14}CO_2$. This isotopic CO_2 enters the biological carbon cycle. All living things therefore contain the same fraction of ^{14}C as that produced in the atmosphere by the steady rain of cosmic rays. When

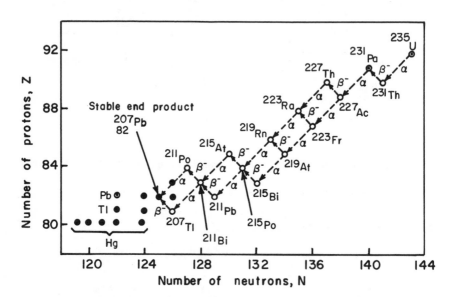

● Stable
◉ Stable but radioactive
○ Transient, radioactive

Figure 1.18 Natural Radioactive Decay of U-235

life stops, so does the exchange of carbon in the atmosphere, and the ^{14}C content of preserved organic matter gradually decreases. This is the basis of the radiocarbon dating method.

Neutrons are readily absorbed by many isotopes, since, being neutral, they do not have to overcome the coulombic forces experienced by charged particles. The product isotopes are often unstable and radioactive. The probability of a given nuclear reaction occurring is expressed as a *cross section* (σ), which can be thought of as an area around the target nucleus within which an incoming particle will produce the reaction. Nuclear cross sections are given in units of barns, one barn being 10^{-24} cm^2 (i.e., a square measuring 10^{-4} Å on a side; nuclei are on the order of 10^{-5} Å in radius). The neutron absorption cross section varies a good deal from one isotope to another, e.g.,

$$n + {}^1H \rightarrow {}^2H + \gamma \qquad \sigma = 0.33 \text{ barns} \tag{1}$$

$$n + {}^2H \rightarrow {}^3H + \gamma \qquad \sigma = 0.51 \times 10^{-3} \text{ barns} \tag{2}$$

These cross sections are an important consideration in choosing materials for the construction and operation of nuclear reactors.

9 | Nuclear Power

Pressurized light water reactor

Since the grim dawn of the nuclear age, scientists have dreamed of harnessing the power of the nucleus for peaceful purposes, and from this impetus the nuclear power reactor program arose. The lower part of Figure 1.17 shows the operating principles of one common nuclear reactor design—the pressurized light water reactor. The fuel rods of this reactor contain pellets of uranium or uranium oxide. Naturally occurring uranium is made up mostly of the isotope that contains 238 nucleons, U-238, which does not fission. U-235 constitutes only 1 out of 140 uranium atoms. In order to build up a chain reaction in the light water reactor, the uranium is concentrated in the U-235 isotope to a level of 2–3%. Control rods containing cadmium or boron, which absorb neutrons effectively, are lowered automatically among the fuel rods to a level that adjusts the neutron flux so that the chain reaction is maintained but does not run out of control. Surrounding the fuel and control rods is a bath of water, which acts both as a coolant to carry away the energy generated in the fission reaction and as a moderator, that is, a substance that slows down the neutrons to increase the fission probability. Neutrons released by the fission travel at such high velocities that, in the absence of a moderator, they would escape before inducing further fission. The water circulates through a heat exchanger that generates steam from a secondary water coolant, and this steam is then used to drive a turbine to generate electricity. Basically the reactor is a conventional steam generator in which the heat source is fissioning uranium instead of burning coal. The amount of energy concentrated in uranium, however, is vastly greater than that in coal. Whereas the highest heating value found for coal is about 7,000 calories/g, a gram of U-235 can release 20 billion calories. One gram of uranium-235 is equivalent to about 3 metric tons of high-grade coal. The U-235 cannot be completely used up in the reactor, however, because of the buildup of fission products, which themselves absorb the neutrons and eventually slow the chain reaction down. After about a year, the fuel rods must be replaced with new ones. The spent fuel can be reprocessed by chemical extraction of the fission products and reconcentration of the U-235.

Breeder reactor

Although U-235 represents an extremely concentrated form of energy, there is not a great deal of it present in the world. As we saw in Table 1.3, at present uranium prices, the total U-235 resource in the United States amounts to 25.3 units of the annual energy consumption in 1975. Nuclear fission would therefore represent a short-lived energy resource if it were not for the potential of breeder reactions, one of which is diagrammed in the upper part of Figure 1.19. While U-235 is the only naturally occurring fissionable isotope, isotopes of other heavy elements, which are no longer present on earth naturally, can also undergo induced fission. Of particular interest is plutonium-239, which can be made by neutron bombardment of uranium-238, the abundant form of uranium. The scheme, shown in the figure, offers the promise of converting inactive uranium-238 to fissionable plutonium-239, thereby converting all the uranium to nuclear fuel. As diagrammed, uranium-238 absorbs a fast-moving neutron to produce a very unstable isotope, uranium-239. This isotope forms a new element, neptunium-239, by beta emission. Neptunium undergoes a similar transformation to plutonium-239.

The reactions for the formation of plutonium can be carried out in a breeder reactor, which is shown in the lower part of Figure 1.19. This reactor is designed to extract power from the fission of either U-235 or Pu-239, but at the same time to produce plutonium from U-238 at a fast rate so that more fuel is produced than is consumed. Again, the reactor core contains uranium fuel rods and cadmium or boron control rods but in this case there is also a blanket of U-238 from which the plutonium is to be bred. A moderator is not wanted because the conversion of uranium-238 to plutonium-239 is most efficient with fast neutrons. With the faster neutrons, however, the induced fission reaction is less efficient, so the fuel must be enriched to the extent of 15–20% with a fissionable isotope, either uranium-235 or plutonium-239. The chosen coolant is liquid sodium, which does not slow down the neutrons, has good heat transfer properties, and is a liquid

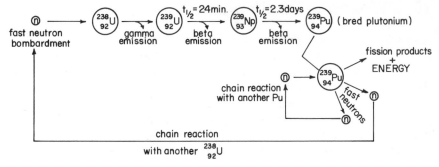

Liquid Sodium Breeder Reactor

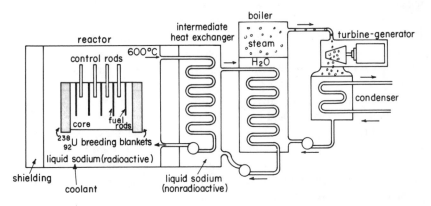

Figure 1.19   Breeder Reaction with Fast Neutrons; Liquid Sodium Breeder Reactor

over a wide temperature range, 98–808° C. The primary sodium coolant transfers its heat to a secondary liquid sodium coolant, which in turn transfers heat to a steam generator that runs the turbine for producing electricity. The purpose of the secondary sodium coolant is to prevent any accidental contact of the primary sodium coolant with water, since some of the sodium atoms do absorb neutrons and become radioactive.

There are inevitable losses in the system, but use of the breeder reactor would still stretch the supply of uranium fuel by at least a factor of 50 and would transform nuclear fission into an energy resource much larger than coal. The technology of the breeder reactor is far more complex than that of the ordinary fission reactor, however, and it is still being developed. The most formidable problem seems to be associated with the plumbing of the heat exchanger, since leaks between the liquid sodium and the water would be disastrous. A practical breeder reactor is not yet in operation, although the British and French programs are quite far advanced.

10 | Weapons Proliferation

Despite its promise for providing cheap and abundant energy, nuclear power presents unique problems that have placed it at the center of the growing controversy about the whole direction of energy policy. One concern has to do with the relative ease with which fission fuel could be diverted to the production of nuclear weapons. Table 1.6 lists the sources, processes, and levels of technology required to construct nuclear weapons from nuclear fuels. The uranium fuel of ordinary fission reactors is only slightly enriched in the fissionable U-235 and is not itself of weapons grade. In order to produce a nuclear explosion, U-235 must be concentrated to at least 90%. Isotope separation is a difficult process and currently is done only at large industrial facilities. In the United States isotope separation plants are of the gaseous diffusion variety, in which the volatile compound, uranium hexafluoride, is passed through many diffusion barriers. The lighter molecules containing U-235 move slightly ahead of their counterparts containing U-238 and are gradually enriched. Other feasible methods involve gas centrifugation or gas nozzle technologies. All these require large and expensive plants.

One of the more acute controversies surrounding nuclear power is the question of whether such plants would be built in countries that import nuclear fission reactors. From the point of view of the importing countries, such plants are highly desirable in that they eliminate dependence on foreign supplies of enriched uranium fuel. The same plants can, however, be used to enrich U-235 to weapons-grade material and could directly contribute to the spread of nuclear armaments. Moreover, it is likely that a new and less costly isotope separation process, based on the use of lasers, will become available before long.

Plutonium presents an even more immediate concern. Since it is a different element than uranium, plutonium is easily extractable from nuclear fuel by conventional chemical methods. Indeed, India has recently demonstrated that it

Table 1.6   Weapons from Nuclear Fuels

Source	Process of Attainment of Weapons-Grade Material	Level of Technology Required
Uranium-235	Enrichment of natural uranium (0.7% U-235) to 90% U-235 by gaseous diffusion, gas centrifuge, or laser techniques	Extremely sophisticated
,Plutonium-239	Chemical separation of plutonium from other elements (there are no other plutonium isotopes)	Simple

is possible to extract sufficient plutonium from spent reactor fuel to build and explode an atom bomb.

Fuel reprocessing plants routinely separate plutonium during the regeneration of the spent uranium. If this plutonium is then itself used to fashion new fuel rods, substantial quantities of plutonium could be transported from reprocessing plants to fuel fabrication plants and then to the reactors themselves. There is much concern that the plutonium fuel could be stolen, perhaps by criminal or terrorist groups, to manufacture clandestine nuclear weapons. It has been claimed that 5 kg of plutonium could be assembled into a crude but usable weapon by a small group, or even a single individual, working from unclassified published government documents.

These problems of nuclear proliferation and diversion will be greatly magnified when large quantities of plutonium are in circulation, which will happen when plutonium breeder reactors come into widespread use. The issues are sufficiently serious and difficult that, as of the summer of 1979, the entire U.S. breeder program was under reevaluation and its future was in doubt. In the meantime nuclear alternatives to the plutonium breeding cycle have been discussed increasingly. One of these is based on the conversion of the element thorium to a fissionable isotope. As shown in Figure 1.20, the reaction of thorium-232 with a neutron leads to the production of fissionable uranium-233, which can be used as nuclear fuel. A breeder reactor to convert thorium to uranium-233 would be similar to a plutonium breeder reactor, except that the thorium reaction works best with slow neutrons, so a moderator is needed. Thorium-232 is almost as plentiful as uranium-238, the abundant isotope of uranium; consequently, a thorium breeding cycle would extend the nuclear fuel supply by about the same amount as would the plutonium breeder. The security advantage is that the fissionable uranium-233 could be denatured by the addition of uranium-238, making it unsuitable for the manufacture of bombs. Similar denaturing is not possible with plutonium-239, for which no naturally occurring

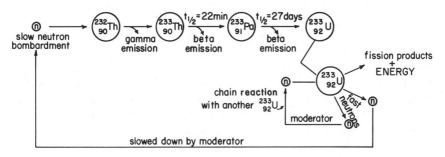

Figure 1.20 Thorium-232–Uranium-233 Cycle

isotope is available. The technical feasibility of the thorium cycle, as well as other alternatives to the plutonium breeder, have only begun to be seriously evaluated.

Fission Chain Reaction

When ^{235}U absorbs a neutron and undergoes fission, it releases two or three additional neutrons, depending on the exact composition of the fission products (see Figure 1.17). The average number of neutrons produced per neutron absorbed is 2.47. If each of these product neutrons induces an additional fission event, then a chain reaction can quickly build up. There are other possibilities for the neutrons, however. Some of them are absorbed by ^{235}U without inducing fission:

$$n + {}^{235}U \rightarrow {}^{236}U + \gamma$$

In a sample of natural uranium, many neutrons are absorbed by the nonfissionable isotope ^{238}U:

$$n + {}^{238}U \rightarrow {}^{239}U + \gamma$$

These neutron-capture reactions compete with fission, but the cross section of the fission reaction is high enough so that a chain reaction is still possible, even in unenriched uranium. Whether it will occur depends mainly on the amount of uranium present, since some neutrons escape from the system before they are absorbed by the uranium nuclei. This tendency decreases as the surface-to-volume ratio of the total sample decreases, i.e., the mass of the uranium increases. A *critical mass* is that amount of uranium for which the probability, k, that a neutron produced in a fission reaction induces another fission reaction is equal to unity. This is the break-even point for a self-sustaining chain reaction. A fission explosion is set off by assembling a *supercritical mass ($k > 1$)* of ^{235}U (or ^{239}Pu, a man-made fissionable isotope) very rapidly, using a chemical explosive for the trigger. For pure ^{235}U, the critical mass is 15 kg, while for pure ^{239}Pu, it is 4.4 kg.

The fission cross section is sensitive to the neutron energy and reaches a maximum at around 0.025 ev, near the average energy of the surrounding molecules, called the *thermal energy*. The fission neutrons are released with high energy (velocity), so in a reactor, they must be slowed down to propagate the chain reaction effectively. This is the role of the moderator, a substance whose constituent atoms slow down the colliding neutrons. The lighter the atom, the greater the amount of energy is removed per collision. This makes water, with its two hydrogen atoms per molecule, an attractive moderator. Heavy water, D_2O, is less effective as a moderator because of the larger deuterium mass, but it has the advantage that it absorbs neutrons much less than hydrogen, as seen from the cross section for the absorption of neutrons by protons and deuterium [see reactions (1) and (2) on page 35]. As a result, it is possible to maintain a chain reaction even with unenriched uranium (0.7% ^{235}U) if D_2O is used as a moderator. This is the operating mode of the CANDU reactor designed in Canada. American commercial reactors use ordinary water and require uranium enriched to 2-3% in ^{235}U to maintain the chain reaction. The relative merits of the two designs depend in large measure on the relative costs of separating D_2O from H_2O versus separating ^{235}U from ^{238}U. The costs of the latter have been somewhat hidden by the preexistence of large ^{235}U separation plants constructed for nuclear weapons production, which have been used to supply the fuel for the American commercial reactor program. As this capacity becomes increasingly strained, the large and uncertain costs of new separation plants make the heavy water–natural uranium design more attractive, since D_2O separation is much less demanding. On the other hand, the development of cheaper isotope separation methods could again increase the attractiveness of enriched uranium.

Isotope Separation

Because isotopes of a given element have the same chemistry, their separation must be based on the slight differences in their properties resulting from their differences in mass. The greater the isotope to mass ratio, the easier it is to exploit these differences. The rates of chemical reactions involving hydrogen, for example, are appreciably faster than those involving deuterium, and electrolysis of water to H_2 and O_2 leaves a liquid that is increasingly rich in D_2O.

The mass ratio of ^{235}U and ^{238}U is too close to unity to utilize reaction rate differences, but physical separations that are sensitive to this ratio can be operated in many successive stages to produce gradual enrichment. The method used at present is gaseous diffusion, using the gaseous compound UF_6, which is passed through a succession of porous diffusion barriers. At each of these, the lighter $^{235}UF_6$ is enriched by a factor equal to the square root of the $^{238}UF_6/^{235}UF_6$ mass ratio, i.e., $\sqrt{352/349} = 1.004$. The enrichment factor after n diffusion barriers is $(1.004)^n$. To enrich ^{235}U by a factor of three, from its natural abundance of 0.7% to the 2% minimal requirement for light water reactors, requires 263 diffusion stages, i.e., $3 = (1.004)^{263}$. The plants required for this process are very large and expensive, and a large amount of energy is required to force UF_6 through so many barriers.

The application of centrifugal force offers a somewhat more efficient route to isotope separation, since for a given centrifugal velocity and radius, the force is directly proportional to the mass, rather than to its square root. Gas centrifuge and gas nozzle techniques are both based on this principle and are being developed actively.

The most promising new approach, however, is laser isotope enrichment.

Lasers are devices that produce light of very well-defined (monochromatic) energy. When a photon of appropriate energy is absorbed by a molecule, it undergoes a transtion to an excited state, in which it may be considerably more reactive than it is in its ground state. The excited-state energy levels depend

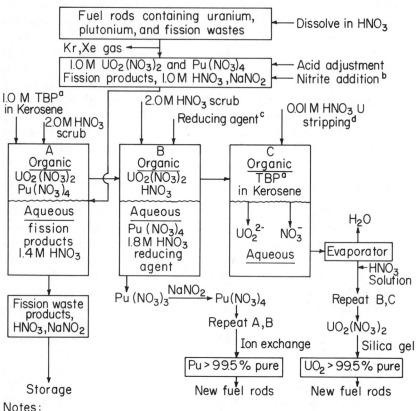

Figure 1.21 Purex Process for the Extraction of Plutonium and Uranium from Fission Wastes

slightly on the isotopic composition, and with a sufficiently well-tuned laser it is sometimes possible to excite molecules that contain one isotope, while exciting only a small fraction of the molecules that contain the other isotope. If the excited-state reactivity can be properly exploited, then large enrichments are possible with a single pass. Successful enrichment has already been reported for several lighter elements with this approach, and intensive research on uranium compounds is under way. Laser enrichment has the potential of substantially lowering the complexity and cost of ^{235}U separation.

Low-cost isotope separation would improve the economics, although the effect is limited by the fuel cost, which is a minor component of the cost of nuclear power (capital costs are the major component). It would also place nuclear technology within the means of many currently nonnuclear nations and complicate the problems of nuclear weapons proliferation.

Nuclear Fuel Reprocessing

The reprocessing of spent reactor fuel involves cutting up the old fuel rods, chemically extracting the uranium and plutonium from the fission products, and preparing the latter for radioactive waste disposal. A flow chart for the most widely accepted process is shown in Figure 1.21. While the chemical steps are all straightforward, involving acid dissolution, solvent extraction, and ion exchange, the technology is complicated by the need for remote handling of the intensely radioactive material. Maintenance and safety problems are much more severe than those in the operation of a nuclear reactor, and the possibilities for accidental release of radioactivity are much greater.

11 | Radioactivity

Another major nuclear safety concern is with radioactivity and radioactive isotopes. Table 1.7 indicates some of the hazards. We have seen that elements that are too heavy to be stable decay by the loss of alpha particles. These particles are ejected with high energy. Since they are helium nuclei, with a doubly positive charge, they efficiently ionize atoms in their path, losing energy with each ionization. They do not travel far but produce intense ionization within a short path. In water or biological tissue, their range is only 0.005 cm, so alpha emitters are not harmful to us if they remain external to our bodies. The danger lies in their being inhaled as small particles. Once lodged in the lungs, an alpha particle can produce intense damage in a localized region. One of the known consequences is the eventual induction of cancer.

The absorption of neutrons by uranium produces very unstable heavy isotopes

Table 1.7   Radioactivity

Paths of Energetic Particles in Biological Tissue		
Type of Radiation	Range in Biological Tissue	Relative Biological Effectiveness*
alpha	0.005 cm	10–20
beta	3 cm	1
gamma	~20 cm	1

Some Hazardous Radioactive Isotopes			
Element	Type of Radiation	Half-Life	Site of Concentration
$^{239}_{94}$Pu	alpha	24,360 years	Bone, lung
$^{90}_{38}$Sr	beta	28.8 years	Bone, teeth
$^{131}_{53}$I	beta, gamma	8 days	Thyroid
$^{137}_{55}$Cs	beta, gamma	30 years	Whole body

*Accounts for the fact that cell damage increases as the density of the damage sites increases.

including plutonium-239, which not only is fissionable but also emits alpha particles. As we noted earlier, the half-life of plutonium-239 is about 24,000 years. Once created, plutonium-239 will be around for much longer than all of recorded history. Because of its cancer-inducing potential, plutonium is one of the most dangerous substances to humans. Its oxide is a finely divided powder and susceptible to inhalation. The maximum permissible dose is a matter of considerable controversy, however. At the moment, it is set at $6 \mu g$ for the total body burden. By the end of the century there may be as much as 80,000 kg of plutonium produced per year if plutonium breeder technology is fully developed. Keeping these quantities of plutonium from contaminating the environment will be a formidable problem.

The products of uranium or plutonium fission are also radioactive, decaying by beta and gamma emission, as we have seen. Both forms of radiation travel greater distances than do alpha rays, although they produce a lower intensity of damage. Most fission products decay very rapidly, but some are relatively long-lived, with half-lives on the order of 30 years. Some of these radioisotopes are particularly hazardous because they are specifically concentrated in biological tissue. For example, strontium-90, which has a half-life of 29 years, can replace calcium in bones. During the period of atmospheric testing of nuclear weapons, there was much concern that strontium-90 from the radioactive fallout was being concentrated in the milk of cows that grazed on contaminated grass. Children were particularly at risk since their bone development, and consequently the deposition of strontium-90 from the affected milk, is rapid. Another isotope of particular concern is iodine-131. Although it has a half-life of only eight days, it selectively concentrates in the thyroid where it can produce thyroid cancer. Cesium-137 has a half-life of 30 years. It can replace potassium, an essential biological element, and is distributed throughout the body.

The problem of radioactivity should be viewed against the background of natural and anthropogenic sources of radiation to which we are all exposed even in the absence of the nuclear industry. The major sources of radiation are tabulated in Table 1.8 in which the units are millirads, a convenient measure of radiation dose. We receive a total of about 115 millirads per year in radiation from cosmic rays and from radioisotopes in the earth around us as well as internal to our own bodies. In addition, we receive about 100 millirads per year of radiation due to human activity, chiefly from diagnostic x-rays. Current guidelines for the operation of nuclear reactors call for the release of radiation that produces no more than 20 millirads per year for any individual. This is less than one-fifth of the background dose, and most nuclear plants currently operate well within this limit. (See the Appendix for definitions of the common units of radiation.)

While the radiation released from nuclear reactors in normal operation is quite low, the reactors themselves contain a huge quantity of intense radioactivity, roughly equivalent to that in a Hiroshima-sized atomic bomb. This radioactivity

Table 1.8   Sources of Radiation Dose to Persons in the United States

Source	Average dose per year (millirads*)
Human activity (1978)	
Diagnostic x-ray	75
Therapeutic x-ray	15
Radioactive fallout	5
Nuclear industry, including mining and fuel processing	5
Subtotal	100
Natural background	
Terrestrial radiation, external to body	60
Cosmic rays	30
Radioisotopes, internal to body	25
Subtotal	115
Total	215

*1 millirad = absorption of 0.1 erg of energy per gram of tissue.
Sources: J. Harte and R. H. Socolow, *Patient Earth* (New York: Holt, Rinehart and Winston, Inc., 1971), p. 309.; J. L. Marx, *Science* 204 (1979): 162.

could be released in the event of a disastrous accident, which might be caused by a violent earthquake or a crash from a large aircraft. There is also concern about the possibility of massive rupture of the primary plumbing system with rapid loss of the coolant. Although control rods would come down immediately to stop the chain reaction, intense heat generated by radioactivity would accumulate in the reactor. This heat could be sufficient to melt the core and the concrete floor beneath the reactor. Under these circumstances it is feared that the containment vessel itself would be breached and the radioactive fuel spread around the countryside. To avoid such a loss of coolant, each reactor is provided with a backup emergency cooling system designed to flood the reactor core with water. However, there is some concern that this system might fail in an actual crisis situation.

This concern was raised considerably after an accident at the Three Mile Island nuclear plant hear Harrisburg, Pennsylvania, in March, 1979. The sequence of events in the accident scenario demonstrated the inherent probability, however small it might be, of mechanical and human failure leading to a core meltdown.

The problem began when a pump in the primary cooling system shut down. Auxiliary feedwater pumps were not operational, although they should have been, as prescribed by governmental regulations. The temperature of the water in the reactor soared and pressure within the reactor vessel caused a relief valve in the primary coolant loop to open, as it should have, to let out the overheated water. Then the valve failed to close. This caused the pressure to drop low enough for thousands of gallons of water to vaporize and escape out of the reactor core. Thus the fuel rods were left partially exposed above the cooling water level, and they became so hot that some melting of the fuel rod cladding occurred.

At least one water level indicator appears to have given a faulty reading, causing a technician to think the system was full of water when it was not. This made him think wrongly that the situation was under control. The high temperatures caused water molecules to break up into hydrogen and oxygen gas with the formation of a 1000 cubic foot gas bubble in the upper part of the core. Within minutes the emergency cooling system had gone into operation, but the gas bubble kept the coolant from reaching the top of the fuel rods, causing them to remain overheated and dangerously close to complete melting. To exasperate the problem, a technician confusedly turned off the emergency cooling system for a short time at the peak of the crisis.

The bubble formation was a new and unexpected event and for some time left the experts, who arrived on the scene after the accident, perplexed as to how to cope with it. A catastrophe was averted when the bubble was gradually reduced and the core was cooled off.

The consequences of a major accident, in terms of the potential for dispersal of long-lived radioactive materials, are so disastrous that it is difficult to establish a rational notion of the risk involved. This is reflected in the inability of the nuclear industry to obtain accident insurance through normal commercial channels. Under the long-standing Price-Anderson Act, the U.S. Congress has limited the liability for an accident to $560 million and has underwritten the bulk of the insurance for this sum. Critics of the nuclear industry have long called for repeal of this act on the grounds that actual damage might well be considerably greater than the $560 million limit, and that whatever risks are involved with nuclear reactors should be assessed against their operation through appropriate insurance premiums. Such premium payments are a standard market device for encouraging the development of more effective safety procedures, from which the nuclear industry is currently exempt. Proponents of the industry argue that calling for a repeal of the Price-Anderson Act is tantamount to destroying the industry, which needs government backing in this form if it is to provide energy for U.S. needs.

Aside from the question of nuclear reactor operations, there are several points in the entire nuclear fuel cycle, diagrammed in Figure 1.22, where the dispersal of radioactive materials is an actual or potential problem. In the first place, uranium mining itself is a hazardous occupation. Miners have a high risk of developing lung cancer because they inhale dust that contains radioactive radium, which is present in uranium deposits, as well as daughter products of radium decay including the radioactive gas, radon. Moreover, uranium mining produces large hills of waste tailings, fine particles that are left over after the uranium ore is extracted from the rocks. The tailings also contain radium and are dispersed by winds over the surrounding area, posing a threat to people in nearby

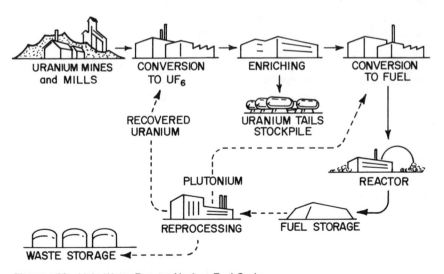

Figure 1.22 Light Water Reactor Nuclear Fuel Cycle

Source: "Energy Facts II," Subcommittee on Energy Research, Development and Demonstration, U.S. House of Representatives, 94th Congress, Library of Congress, Serial H, August 1975, p. 262.

communities. Another place where the release of radiation is potentially serious is the fuel reprocessing plant, where the spent fuel rods are dissolved in acid and the fission products and the heavy element contaminants are separated before the uranium or plutonium is sent back to the fuel fabrication plants. The operation of a reprocessing plant is much more difficult than that of a reactor because of the need to handle intensely radioactive materials, and the release of radiation from such plants is more difficult to prevent. Because of safety and other technical difficulties, no reprocessing plant is currently operating in the United States and spent fuel rods are simply piling up in storage tanks filled with water. A new plant has been built in South Carolina, but current uncertainties about the reprocessing of plutonium leave its opening in doubt.

Another area of uncertainty concerns the eventual disposal of the radioisotopes that are extracted at the reprocessing plant. They must be isolated from the human environment for exceedingly long periods of time. A rule of thumb is that radiation sinks to negligible levels after ten half-lives. For the fission products this is a few hundred years, but for plutonium and the other heavy elements ten half-lives is on the order of a quarter of a million years. Various waste disposal schemes have been suggested, including melting the hot wastes into the Antarctic snow cap or firing them with rockets into space or into the sun. The scheme currently favored, however, involves burying the wastes in underground salt domes, which are extremely dry and geologically stable. There is concern, however, that in due course water could intrude into the salt formation and dissolve the radioisotopes along with the salt. A site chosen near Lyons, Kansas, had to be abandoned when it was subsequently discovered that the area had been infiltrated with water from a salt-mining operation. At present, new sites are being sought in New Mexico.

Finally, the elaborate transportation network required in the nuclear fuel cycle presents many opportunities for accidents or sabotage.

In summary, the energy stored in uranium or in thorium atoms can provide us with a significant energy resource if breeder technology can be mastered. On the other hand, the price of fission energy includes unprecedented possibilities of long-term harm resulting from the unique hazards of nuclear weapons and radioactive isotopes.

Biological Effects of Ionizing Radiation

When unstable nuclei decay, α, β, or γ rays are released with very high energy, in the range of millions of electron volts (Mev). On encountering molecules in their path, they knock electrons out of the atomic shells. Enough energy is deposited in the ionized molecules to break chemical bonds and induce reactions. In biological tissues the result is generalized damage and the production of reactive chemical fragments (e.g., free radicals).

Some biological molecules are more susceptible than others to the effects of ionizing radiation. The nucleic acids, which make up each cell's genetic apparatus, are particularly vulnerable. A single ionization in the cell's nucleus can produce an error in the genetic instructions for assembling the protein constituents of the cell. Certain kinds or combinations of such errors are believed to transform normal cells into cancerous ones, and there are well-established correlations between radiation exposure and the incidence of cancer. If the nuclei of reproductive cells are damaged, the result may be genetic mutations and, thus, the transmission of hereditary disorders to succeeding generations.

An α ray, being a doubly charged helium nucleus, produces intense damage over a short distance. It ionizes half the atoms in its path, losing about 30 ev per collision. A 6-Mev α ray would therefore produce about 200,000 ionizations among the first 400,000 atoms it encounters. In a substance with the density of water or biological tissue, the distance traveled, or range, is about 0.05 mm. This is less than the thickness of the skin's protective outer layer of dead cells. If, however, an α emitter is ingested into the body, it produces a high density of localized damage, with an appreciable potential for cancer induction. The likeliest route of ingestion is inhalation of dust particles that carry radioisotopes. Uranium miners are at high risk of developing lung cancer. The uranium itself is relatively harmless because of its very slow decay ($t_{1/2} = 7 \times 10^8$ years for ^{235}U and 4.5×10^9 years for ^{238}U). Some of the daughter isotopes, which accumulate in the mines, are much more radioactive and therefore more hazardous. Radon ($t_{1/2} = 3.82$ days), which is a gas, and radium ($t_{1/2} = 1,620$ years), which can circulate on particles, are thought to be primary causes of lung cancer.

Both radium and plutonium seek out bone after they are absorbed into the body following inhalation, so that bone cancer, as well as lung cancer, is a major concern. It is uncertain how to estimate the biological exposure due to small radioactive particles lodged in the lung. There is considerable debate over whether the probability of cancer production from a "hot" particle is greater or less than that associated with the same amount of radioactivity spread evenly through the body.

A β ray, being an energetic electron, is much lighter than an α ray and is only singly charged. It also loses about 30 ev per collision, but it ionizes only about 1 in 1,200 atoms in its path. The damage density is therefore lower, but the range of a β ray is larger; a 6-Mev β ray travels 3 cm in water or biological tissue. External β radiation is therefore hazardous, and β-emitting isotopes must be shielded.

A γ ray is a high-energy photon and has a different mode of interaction with matter than do charged particles. The probability of a γ ray hitting an atom in its path is quite low, but when it does so, it transfers a large amount of energy, and the ionized electron carries away enough energy to ionize many other electrons (secondary ionizations). Because of this, γ rays do not have a well-defined range but rather a distribution of path lengths. For 6-Mev γ rays, the median path length, at which half the γ rays have stopped, is 20 cm in water or biological tissue. Energetic γ emitters require heavy shielding.

Finally, neutrons interact with matter by penetrating the electron shells and reacting directly with the nuclei of matter, displacing them and causing ionization or producing radioisotopes, which in turn release ionizing radiation. Neutrons decay spontaneously ($t_{1/2}$ = 12 minutes) into protons and electrons and are therefore of concern only in the immediate vicinity of nuclear reactions.

Radioactive Waste Disposal

The radioactive isotopes of fission reactors are of two main varieties: the fission products, which have too many neutrons and emit β rays, and very heavy elements (actinides) produced by neutron absorption reactions of ^{235}U and ^{238}U or ^{232}Th, which are subject to α as well as β decay. Some radioisotopes are also generated via neutron absorption by the reactor materials: moderator, control rods, and housing.

The problem of disposing of these radioisotopes is difficult since there is no way to render them unradioactive. They must be kept isolated from the biosphere for a time sufficient for them to decay to the background level, which requires about ten half-lives. Most fission products are very unstable and decay quickly, but some half-lives measure in tens of years. Two fission products of major concern are strontium-90 ($t_{1/2}$ = 28.1 years) and cesium-137 ($t_{1/2}$ = 30.2 years). These require isolation for hundreds of years.

Some of the actinides produced in a reactor have much longer half-lives. Plutonium-239 has a 24,000-year half-life. Some other actinides produced in a fast neutron reaction include neptunium-237 ($t_{1/2}$ = 2.14 $\times$ 10^6 years), americium-243 (7.37 $\times$ 10^3 years), curium-245 (9.3 $\times$ 10^3 years), and californium-251 ($\sim$800 years). The rate of production of these heavy nuclides increases rapidly with the neutron flux of the reactor. It is possible to produce microgram amounts of californium isotopes from 1 g of ^{239}Pu in about three years.[6] Although ^{239}Pu is intended to be reprocessed into new fuel, some of it inevitably is lost to the waste stream, as are the other actinides. They require isolation for hundreds of thousands of years. It has been suggested that reprocessing be modified to carefully extract essentially all the actinides and send them back to reactors to be burned via neutron-induced transformation.[7] This would leave only fission products for waste disposal. No plans exist for doing this, however, so the radioisotope waste disposal problem has a time span much longer than all of recorded human history.

The accepted disposal plan is to bury nuclear wastes in geologically secure strata of the earth. The prime geological formations are salt domes—deep deposits of sodium chloride that have been undisturbed for millions of years. Salt is plastic when heated, and the heat produced by the nuclear wastes could seal them into the salt. The main concern over this disposal method is the extent to which one can be certain that the salt beds will remain undisturbed by water over time. Another proposal is to inject the wastes, in a self-hardening cement slurry, into stable granite layers.

12 | Fusion Power

Much greater energy is available from nuclear sources via the fusion reaction. As we saw in Figure 1.13, the most stable nuclei are those of elements with intermediate masses. Consequently the lighter elements are potentially unstable with respect to fusion to heavier ones, and very large amounts of energy could be released in the process. Extreme reaction conditions are necessary, however, because in order for two nuclei to fuse, they must overcome a huge energy barrier caused by the repulsion between their positive charges before the strong nuclear forces take over when the nucleons actually intermingle. Such conditions are achieved in the centers of stars, including our sun, whose energy outputs are due to fusion reactions. They can also be observed in hydrogen bombs, which use the explosive force of a fission bomb as a trigger. The easiest fusion reactions to carry out are those of the heavy isotopes of hydrogen. These are deuterium, with one neutron and one proton, and tritium, with two neutrons and one proton. Fusion reactions of these particles are shown schematically in the first part of Figure 1.23. Reaction 1 shows that two deuterium nuclei can fuse to produce a helium-3 nucleus, with one neutron and two protons, plus a free neutron; or, as in reaction 2, they can produce a tritium nucleus with the release of a proton. Reaction 3 shows that a deuterium nucleus can fuse with a tritium nucleus to produce helium plus a neutron. Tritium, with a half-life of 12.3 days, does not exist in nature and must be synthesized from lithium as shown in reactions 4 and 5. Since reaction 3 has the lowest activation barrier, it is the one that scientists are concentrating on for the production of useful energy. Even so, the tempera- ture required for this reaction, the so-called ignition temperature is 40,000,000° C. Needless to say, at this high temperature, which is characteristic of the interior of the sun, all earthly materials would be vaporized. The overriding obstacle to harnessing the fusion reaction is that there is no conceivable container capable of withstanding such high temperatures.

One answer to this dilemma is to suspend the fusion fuels in free space with the use of powerful magnetic fields. At the high temperatures under consideration, the atoms are completely ionized and can therefore be controlled with magnetic fields. The upper part of Figure 1.24 shows a diagram of a proposed magnetic containment fusion reactor. The plasma would be in a doughnut-shaped elec-

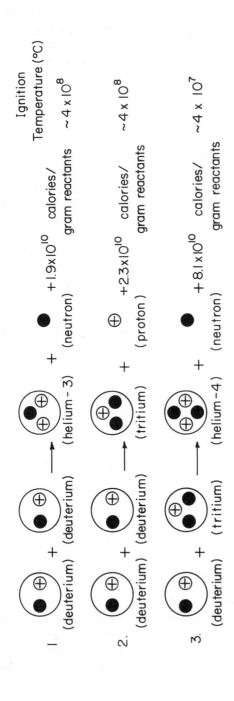

Figure 1.23 Some Energy-Producing Fusion Reactions

(i)
Magnetic Containment

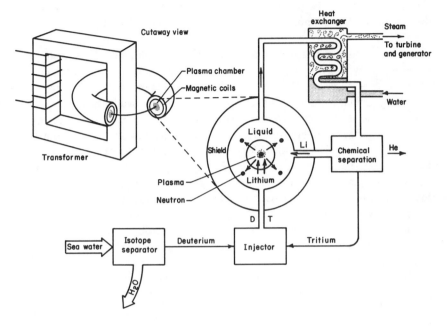

(ii)
Laser Induced

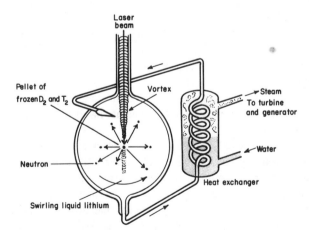

Figure 1.24   Deuterium-Tritium Fusion Reactors

Source: G. Gordon and W. Zoller, *Chemistry in Modern Perspective* (Reading, Mass.: Addison-Wesley Publishing Company Inc., 1975), figs. 6-3 and 6-4. Copyright © 1975. Reprinted with permission.

tromagnetic field and would be heated to the desired temperature by the induction of an electric current. The tritium would be supplied by a blanket of liquid lithium surrounding the plasma. This blanket absorbs the neutrons given off in the fusion reaction and produces tritium as a by-product, via reactions 4 and 5 in Figure 1.23.

Lithium itself is a relatively scarce element, and high-grade deposits are not plentiful. They probably correspond to an energy resource comparable to the fossil fuels themselves. On the other hand, with appropriate technology for extracting lithium from lower grade sources, the energy available may be much larger. If the deuterium-deuterium reactions can be made to work, then the supply of energy available from fusion is essentially limitless. Deuterium is a naturally occurring isotope of hydrogen and is readily separated in the form of heavy water. There is enough of it in the ocean to provide a resource 50 million times larger than the fossil fuel deposits. However, the deuterium-deuterium fusion process has a higher activation energy and the temperature would have to be ten times higher than that for the deuterium-tritium reaction.

At the present time, fusion technology is far from practical. The high-temperature plasmas are subject to various instabilities, and they escape from their confining magnetic fields in short order. These instabilities are gradually being eliminated in experimental plasma machines, but there is still a long way to go before hot plasma can be contained long enough to produce more energy than the machine consumes. Even after this point is reached, the problems of constructing a practical power source are formidable. Among these is the neutron flux produced by the reactor, which is so intense that most ordinary construction materials would have a very short lifetime.

A different design for a fusion reactor has recently been proposed and is shown schematically in the lower part of Figure 1.24. In this method, a small pellet of frozen deuterium and tritium is dropped into a laser beam that has sufficient intensity to compress the pellet suddenly and produce a tiny fusion explosion. Again, a blanket of lithium would absorb the neutrons and the energy produced. Repeated firings of the laser at successive pellets would then produce a steady energy source. This design has the advantage of eliminating the need for very large magnets, but it is presently uncertain whether lasers of sufficient power and stability can be produced.

In terms of environmental hazards, fusion reactors would avoid the problems associated with fission products. Nevertheless, the radioactivity involved is not negligible because large quantities of radioactive tritium would be used. Tritium is a fairly dangerous material because it is readily incorporated into water and biological tissues. Tritium gas, like hydrogen gas, can diffuse through metals and is difficult to contain. Moreover, the material in the reactor structure itself becomes radioactive from the constant neutron bombardment. The reactors will have a finite lifetime, perhaps 20 years, due to the gradual breakdown of materials, and dismantling the structures will present a problem in radioactive waste disposal.

Current research on fusion is being pursued vigorously in several countries. The scientists involved in the work are optimistic that all outstanding problems will be overcome, but no one can be sure whether the concept will work. If it can, it will still take many years to produce useful power.

Fusion Reactors; Unresolved Problems

The primary requirement for the generation of power from the fusion of nuclei in a plasma is that the energy input needed to sustain the plasma conditions be less than the energy output gained from fusion.* The break-even point where the energy input is exactly balanced by the output has yet to be achieved in experimental fusion reactors. The realization of this goal depends on the simultaneous attainment of two physical conditions within the reactor. One is that the plasma be maintained at a temperature high enough to "ignite" the fuel. The other condition is that the plasma be contained at sufficiently high densities for some period of time (called the *confinement time*) in order that an abundance of nuclear collisions can occur. The confinement time depends on the density of the plasma. The criterion for plasma containment at the break-even point has been expressed succinctly by Lawson,[8] and is given in the equation:

$$\text{density} \times \text{confinement time} = 10^{14} \text{ particles sec/cm}^3 \qquad (1)$$

Particle densities in magnetic confinement reactors range from about 10^{14} to 10^{16} particles per cubic centimeter, so that the required confinement times are in the range of 1 to 0.01 second.

Confining the plasma at such high temperatures even for short periods of time is a formidable engineering task. The plasma must be contained by nonmaterial means. This is true not only because solid containers cannot hold a gas at 40,000,000°C, but also because if the plasma comes in contact with cold reactor walls, its high temperature will be quenched. Although great progress has been made in magnetic containment technology through the development of the Tokamak reactor and other promising designs, serious problems still exist. Confinement times are limited by "plasma instability." Plasma leaks out of the field and into the reactor walls at rates that are considerably higher than would be predicted from classical electromagnetic theory. Plasma leakage has been reduced considerably in the Tokamak design by introducing a strong electrical current within the plasma, thereby inducing a secondary magnetic field to augment the larger field of the superconducting toroidal magnets.

---

*At required temperatures for fusion reactions, all reactants exist as completely ionized gases (plasma) consisting of free electrons and bare atomic nuclei.

Another problem is the highly charged impurities that come off the reactor walls from bombardment by escaping plasma particles. Impurities can interact strongly with the plasma to emit high-energy radiation (bremsstrahlung), thus causing a rapid cooling to below the ignition temperature. Additional correction fields called *divertors* must be incorporated near the reactor walls to trap the impurities. Divertors add considerably to the complexity of the reactor, and their long-term effectiveness is unproved.

Apart from technological problems stemming from plasma physics, there is a practical economic problem regarding the anticipated size of a magnetic containment reactor. At fusion temperatures the fuel density must be maintained at a tiny fraction of normal atmospheric density. Otherwise, the magnets would have to contain plasmas that exert hundreds of thousands of atmospheres of pressure. The generated power density varies with the square of the fuel density, and power densities on the order of 1 Mw/m^3 are produced in the plasma chamber. This number may be compared with the value of 100 Mw/m^3 or more in the core of a light water or fast breeder reactor. Because of the necessary scale-up in size (and especially in the size of the toroidal magnets), it is generally estimated that the cost of a fusion reactor will be three to four times that of a fast breeder reactor. Furthermore, it is expected that maintenance costs will be high because of chronic material damage to the inner chamber walls due to high-energy neutron bombardment. Improved, more resistant materials may reduce such costs in the future.

Laser implosion offers a completely different approach to harnessing fusion power. This method takes advantage of inertial rather than magnetic confinement by using lasers to heat plasmas. A cryogenic pellet of liquid or solid deuterium-tritium is uniformly irradiated by a high-power pulsed laser which deposits energy in the pellet surface. The pellet implodes, compressing the material at the center and heating it to thermonuclear temperatures. The Lawson criterion, expressed in equation (1), is also applicable to laser fusion. Whereas in magnetic containment the plasma is typically confined for about a second at a density of about 10^{14} particles per cubic centimeter, in inertial containment the objective is to implode fuels to densities as high as 10^{26} particles per cubic centimeter for times as short as 10^{-12} seconds. The confinement time is thus determined by the inertia of the plasma, i.e., by the finite time required to accelerate and move the material a significant distance.

Enormously powerful lasers are needed to compress the fuel, which must be imploded to 10,000 times the normal liquid density, corresponding to pressures as high as 10^{12} atm.* At present the lasers that are available for experimental study of pellet compression cannot meet the power and efficiency requirements

---

*These densities are comparable to those found in the core of stars, where they are maintained gravitationally by the overlying mass.

needed for economic fusion power production. It has been estimated that such a laser system must deliver 300,000 joules in a nanosecond (3×10^{14} w) at a pulse rate of more than one per second while operating at an overall efficiency of 10%.[9] Each of these operational parameters is at least an order of magnitude more than those of current laser systems. Laser technology is improving rapidly, however, and construction of such systems may be realized in the not too distant future.

Even if the required laser system is built, the success of laser fusion is still not guaranteed. Feasibility depends on computer predictions of compression and subsequent ignition, which have not been proved experimentally. One major concern is whether high enough densities can in fact be achieved in light of the possibility of asymmetric implosion. Although theory suggests that symmetric implosion is attainable, it is experimentally unproved in the appropriate parameter range.

13 | Solar Energy

The alternative to fossil and nuclear fuels is to harness renewable energy sources that are derived directly or indirectly from sunlight. We have already seen in Table 1.3 that the annual energy deposited by sunlight on the continental United States is 650 times the total annual external energy consumption. Enough sunlight falls yearly on each square meter to equal the energy content of 420 pounds of high-grade bituminous coal. The sun already provides us, in fact, with our most basic energy needs including heat, freshwater, and plant life. There is plenty left over for our other cultural energy needs if we develop the technology to harness it. The difficulty is that sunlight is diffuse and intermittent. The technology required to harness and store solar energy is currently expensive; until now it has been much cheaper to pump oil from the ground and burn it. With fuel prices rising and the end of petroleum deposits in sight, however, the economic balance is shifting. There is now considerable interest in developing solar technology, with a reasonable prospect of substantial cost reductions from engineering improvements and mass production.

The most convenient and straightforward application of solar energy is in heating buildings and providing hot water, which currently consumes 20–25% of our fuel supply. This is an ideal application for a uniformly dispersed energy source. Figure 1.25 shows a detailed design for a solar-heated house. The sunlight is collected on plates in the roof and the heat is transferred to a circulating water system. It has been estimated that the average house in the central United States could obtain its energy needs for heating and hot water in December with a collection area of 1,300 ft², well within the average roof area.

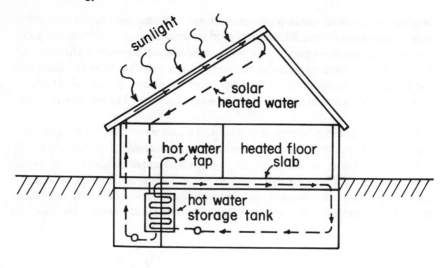

Details of Heating System

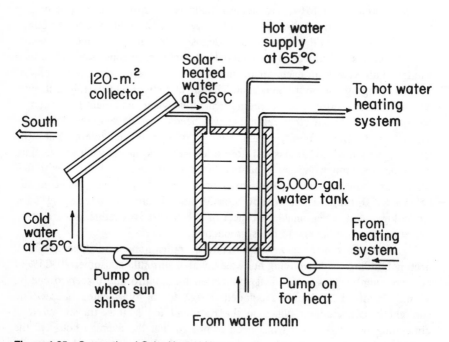

Figure 1.25 Conventional Solar-Heated House

Source: W. E. Morrow, *Technol. Rev.*, December 1973, p. 34.

Various solar-heating designs are currently being tested, and there is little doubt that they will come into widespread use in the coming years. The main problem is that it is relatively expensive to refit older houses with solar units.

A more difficult application is the generation of electricity from sunlight. It would take an area of 1,600 mi² to supply the total electrical energy needs of the United States if sunlight were converted to electricity with 30% efficiency. While this area is only slightly larger than Rhode Island, it still represents a very large collection surface. One approach to this is to use collected heat to run a boiler in a steam generator. To achieve high enough temperatures for efficient operation, the sunlight must be focused from many collecting units. One possible design is diagrammed in Figure 1.26. To achieve efficient operation throughout the day, the mirrors must track the path of the sun. The cost of reliable collectors and tracking machinery is one uncertainty surrounding the design of solar thermal plants. Keeping the mirrors clean and scratch-free, especially in deserts, is another major problem.

Another approach is direct transformation of sunlight into electricity via the photovoltaic effect. Light is absorbed in a material with the generation of positive and negative charges that are collected at electrodes at either side. The most successful current design is the silicon solar cell diagrammed in Figure 1.27,

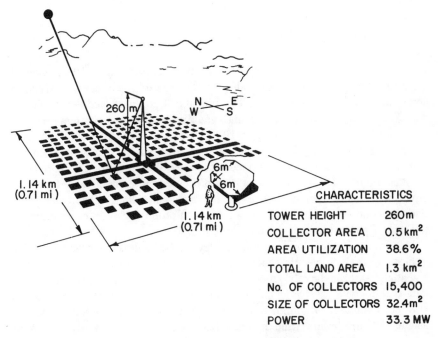

CHARACTERISTICS	
TOWER HEIGHT	260m
COLLECTOR AREA	0.5 km²
AREA UTILIZATION	38.6%
TOTAL LAND AREA	1.3 km²
No. OF COLLECTORS	15,400
SIZE OF COLLECTORS	32.4m²
POWER	33.3 MW

Figure 1.26 Electricity from Sunlight: Central Receiver Design

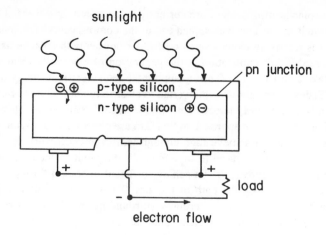

sunlight

pn junction

p-type silicon

n-type silicon

load

electron flow

p - type silicon conducts positive charges
n - type silicon conducts negative charges

Figure 1.27 Diagram of Solar Cell for Generation of Electricity

which was developed for the space program. This consists of a sandwich of
n-type and *p*-type silicon semiconductors; the charge separation is developed
across the junction between them. The silicon cell produces electricity reliably,
but it is quite expensive, since very high-grade crystalline silicon is required. The
efficiency of conversion of light is 10–15%, and an array of such cells sufficiently large to produce a substantial amount of electricity would be prohibitively
expensive at current prices. It is hoped, however, that the price can be reduced
substantially through new manufacturing processes and more advanced technology. The recent development of cells that contain amorphous rather than crystalline semiconductor materials is one of the most promising avenues for reducing
the cost of photovoltaic devices in the future.

Meanwhile, indirect forms of solar energy can be harnessed for the production
of electricity. Hydroelectric generation has been with us for a long time, and its
potential has been largely tapped. Another source is wind power which, as
indicated in Table 1.3, has an energy potential each year of four times the current
U.S. consumption. Windmills have a long history of use throughout the world,
and in the midwestern United States there were 50,000 backyard windmills
generating electricity until 1950, after which they were phased out by the Rural

Electricity Administration. The strongest and steadiest winds are those on the Great Plains and on the Atlantic seaboard. As shown in Figure 1.28, there have been many technical advances in the design of windmills and wind turbines, and it seems quite likely that wind power will be an economical source of electricity in the near future.

Much solar energy is also stored in the ocean as thermal gradients between the warm surface layer and the colder waters beneath. Extracting this energy requires new and difficult technology. Figure 1.29 illustrates a design for a large-scale low-temperature heat engine for producing electric power from the thermal gradients.

Emission and Absorption of Radiation

Photons act like oscillating dipoles traveling through space; their energy is proportional to the frequency of oscillation, $E = h\nu$, where h is Planck's

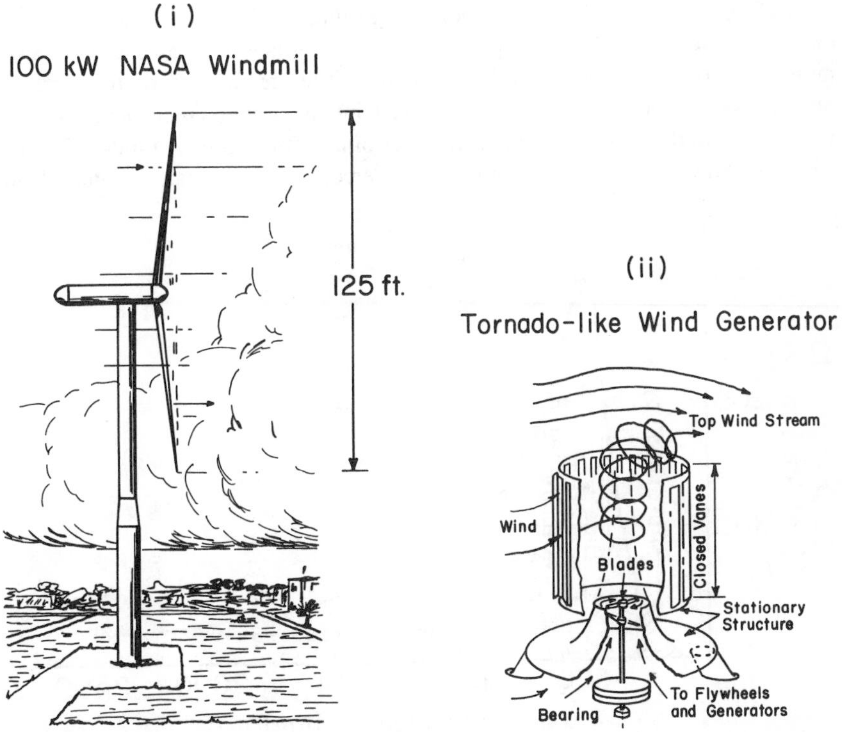

Figure 1.28 Wind Power

Source: Upper diagram: N. Wade, *Science* 184 (1974):1056. Lower diagram: A. Hammond, *Science* 190 (1975):257. Copyright 1975 by the American Association for the Advancement of Science.

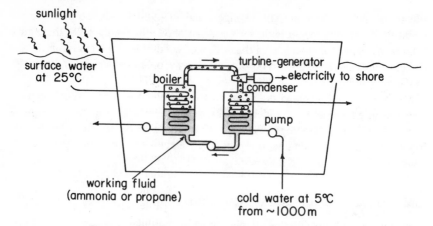

sunlight

surface water at 25°C

boiler

turbine-generator

electricity to shore

condenser

pump

working fluid (ammonia or propane)

cold water at 5°C from ~1000m

Figure 1.29 Electricity from Ocean Thermal Gradients

constant. Photons are emitted from hot surfaces. The higher the temperature of the surface, the greater is the radiation energy flux leaving it, and the higher are the frequencies of the departing photons. The sun radiates with an energy flux of more than 100,000 calories/cm² per minute. The frequencies of the emitted photons vary over a wide range. The most intense rays contain photons with frequencies in the visible region of the electromagnetic spectrum (400–700 nm). About 0.002% of the solar photons are intercepted by the earth. Figure 1.30

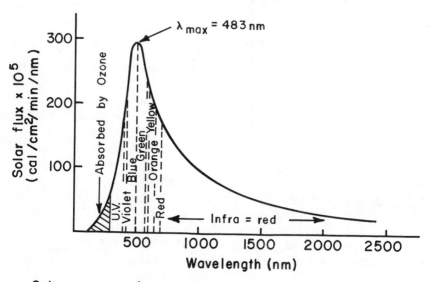

Solar constant (area under curve) = 1.95 cal/cm²/min

Figure 1.30 Spectrum of Solar Radiation Incident on Earth's Atmosphere

shows the flux of solar energy impinging perpendicularly on the earth's outer atmosphere as a function of photon wavelength. The dotted lines mark the visible portion of the spectrum to which the human eye has been adapted. The total energy flux is the area under the curve and equals 1.95 calories/cm^2 per minute.

The solar photons that encounter the earth's atmosphere or surface are either scattered back into space or absorbed. When a molecule absorbs a photon, its own energy is increased by the amount of the photon energy. An oscillating dipole is created in the molecule, with a frequency characteristic of the photon. The probability of this happening depends on the match between the frequency of the photon and the fundamental frequencies at which the electrons and nuclei of the molecule move. Quantum mechanics tells us that there are discrete energy levels corresponding to these motions, and that the photon energies must match these exactly if the photons are to be absorbed. Molecules usually have many energy levels that are too closely spaced to be distinguished. Their absorption spectra, plots of the intensity of absorption against wavelength, contain relatively broad bands. Figure 1.31 shows the absorption spectrum of chlorophyll, one of the molecules the solar photon is likely to encounter. Chlorophyll is a complicated molecule, as the structural formula in the figure shows, with an extended system of conjugated double bonds. These are responsible for the intense absorption peaks in the red (~663 nm) and blue (~433 nm) regions. Between these peaks the absorption intensity is lower but tapers off slowly. Chlorophyll is an efficient collector of solar photons. (The red peak is mainly responsible for the green color of chlorophyll. Reflected light is the incident light minus the absorbed light, so the colors of absorbed and reflected light are complementary.)

Once a molecule has been excited by the absorption of a photon, it can lose its excess energy in several ways. It can reemit a photon, a process called *luminescence* (which may be subdivided into fluorescence and phosphorescence, corresponding to fast and slow reemission); or it can dissipate the energy through collision with other molecules, heating them up in the process. Eventually all absorbed photons are converted to heat. This is the basis of all solar heat collection systems, whether for space heating or thermal electricity generation. The amount of heat collected per unit area is equal to the solar emission spectrum multiplied by the collector absorption spectrum. The collector surfaces are usually black, corresponding to a very broad absorption band (from many overlapping molecular transitions), to match the solar spectrum. The effective area of the collector can be increased by concentrating the light with mirrors.

Another possibility is that after absorbing a photon, the excited molecule is transformed chemically. The products of photochemistry may be higher or lower in energy than the starting material. If their energy is higher, they represent a chemical form of stored photoenergy. Whether they release this energy in subsequent reactions depends on their chemical surroundings. It is possible to envision the harnessing of solar energy by the photochemical generation of high-

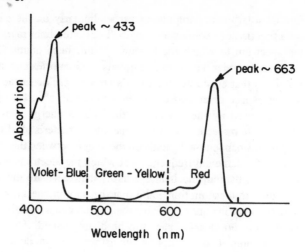

Structural Formula of Chlorophyll a

Figure 1.31 Absorption Spectrum of Chlorophyll a

energy molecules—synthetic fuels that could be induced to release their energy under controlled conditions for conversion to useful work. Many photochemical reactions have been proposed for this purpose. The main difficulty is preventing rapid energy loss (back-reactions) from the photochemical products. There must be a kinetic barrier to prevent this, which can later be overcome in a controlled way (with catalysts, for instance) to harness the energy.

The prototype of photochemical energy storage is, of course, photosynthesis, nature's method of harnessing the sun's rays, which permitted the evolution of life on this planet. The photosynthetic solar collector is chlorophyll. The manner in which the photons are then used to generate biochemical fuel is exceedingly intricate and has been the subject of intense and continuing research. As shown in Figure 1.32 the basic picture that emerges from these studies is that light is harvested by numerous "antenna" chlorophyll molecules packed together in the chloroplasts of green plants, and then fed into a special pair of chlorophyll molecules in the photoreaction center. Here the photon induces a separation of charge in the chlorophyll pair. The electron generated in this fashion is then captured by an acceptor molecule, which feeds it along a chain of electron transfer molecules until it is used to reduce NAD (nicotinamide adenine dinucleotide) to its hydride form, NADH, which is subsequently used in the reduction of carbon dioxide.

Meanwhile, the hole generated in the chlorophyll pair is filled by an electron extracted from water via another specialized set of transfer molecules, with the production of oxygen. The kinetic barriers that keep electrons flowing in one

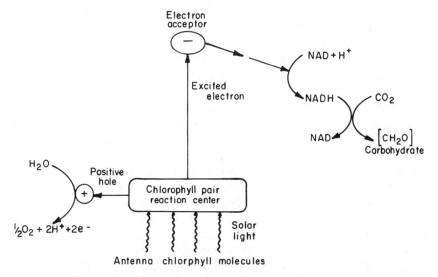

Figure 1.32 Photochemical Energy Storage by Photosynthesis

direction only are maintained by the spatial arrangement of the molecular components of the chloroplast. It is likely that any manufactured photochemical energy storage system will also have to make use of spatial segregation of the products, e.g., using surface chemistry at the interface between two phases.

The Photovoltaic Cell

One device that successfully makes use of an interfacial kinetic barrier in solar energy conversion is the photovoltaic cell. In this case the solar collector is a semiconductor, such as crystalline silicon. In the solid state, the energy levels of the individual atoms merge with one another and spread out, forming energy bands. An energy level diagram for silicon is shown below:

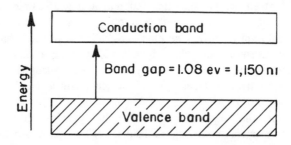

The lower valence band is filled with electrons; in an isolated silicon atom, it would be the ground-state energy level. The conduction band corresponds to the first excited state of isolated silicon atoms; the energy spreads into a band by the interactions among the silicon atoms in the crystal. This band has no electrons and is separated from the valence band by the band gap, which is the excitation energy. In silicon it is 1.08 ev, corresponding to a photon with a wavelength of 1,150 nm. A photon of this wavelength or shorter would excite the silicon, leaving an electron in the conduction band and a hole in the valence band. Both of these are free to move from one silicon atom in the crystal to another, freely carrying charge. In a short time, however, they would find one another and recombine, producing light and/or heat.

It is possible to alter the electrical balance in crystalline silicon by introducing a few impurity atoms (called "doping") with a different number of valence electrons. Boron, for example, has three valence electrons, compared with silicon's four. When it sits at a silicon site in the crystal, boron attracts electrons from the surrounding silicon atoms. At thermal energies it is easy for a silicon electron to transfer to the boron atom, producing a fixed (on boron) negative charge and a hole that is free to wander among the silicon atoms. This produces a p (positive) type semiconductor, which can be diagrammed as follows:

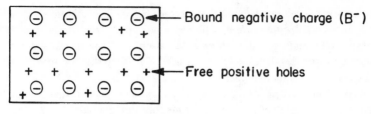

p-type semiconductor

An *n* (negative) type semiconductor is produced by doping arsenic, which has five valence electrons and a strong tendency to lose one electron when it is at a silicon lattice site. This leaves a fixed (on arsenic) positive charge and an electron that is free to move in the silicon conduction band.

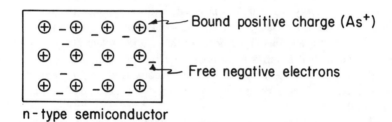

n-type semiconductor

When a *p*-type semiconductor is joined with an *n*-type (*p-n* junction), the free charges move away from the interface because of repulsion by the fixed charges.

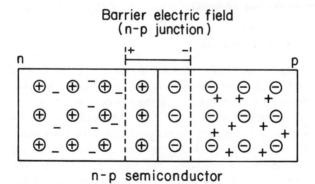

n-p semiconductor

This leaves a separation of charge and a potential difference across the interface. If a photoelectron is now created in the *p*-type semiconductor, it will have a chance of being accelerated across the interface before it recombines with a hole. This produces an electric current, which can be carried from the n-type back to the p-type semiconductor through an external circuit. The spatial separation of fixed charges provides the kinetic barrier needed to keep the electrons flowing in one direction. The actual geometry used in a solar cell is shown in Figure 1.27. The p-type semiconductor is the outer layer that faces the sun. It should be thick enough to capture most of the solar photons, but thin enough to give the photoelectrons a chance to reach the junction before recombining with a hole. In practice a compromise has to be made between these competing requirements because recombination inevitably reduces the available photoenergy. An actual silicon solar cell has a maximum operating voltage of 0.5–0.6 v, about half the potential available at the band gap, 1.08 v.

Even in the absence of recombination, solar energy could not be used at 100% efficiency because of its spectral distribution. About a third of the photons have energies below the band gap and cannot be utilized. For the remainder, 1.08 ev is the maximum energy that can be extracted, and energy increments above the band gap are wasted as heat. Consequently only half the solar energy can be converted to photoelectrons. Together with the efficiency loss due to recombination, this means that the maximum possible efficiency of silicon cells is about 25%. Because of imperfect junctions and surface reflectivity, together with adverse temperature effects, commercially produced cells currently operate at about 10–16% efficiency.

While many other semiconductors are available, silicon offers the best and most reliable performance so far, and silicon cells have been used extensively in the space program. They are costly to produce because of the difficulty of making sufficiently pure crystalline silicon. Hopes for reducing costs sufficiently to make solar cells attractive for general use rest on new continuous processes for fabricating silicon and the search for less costly but effective semiconductors.

Photoassisted Electrolysis

Another possible application of semiconductors is to use them for the photogeneration of hydrogen and oxygen from water in an electrolysis cell like the one shown in Figure 1.35. In this case a strontium titanate semiconductor is placed in an electrolyte and connected electrically to a platinum electrode. When strontium titanate is excited at its band gap, the generated hole has enough potential to oxidize water to oxygen (analogous to the hole generated in the chlorophyll pair of photosynthetic reaction centers). The free electron is carried through the current to the platinum electrode, where it reduces water to hydrogen. The main difficulty is that the strontium titanate absorbs in the near ultraviolet range at 400 nm. While there are many semiconductors with band gaps in the visible region, the ones examined to date are unstable upon photoexcitation. They tend to dissolve in the solution, rather than produce oxygen.

14 | Energy Storage

The main drawback to the production of direct solar or wind electricity is the intermittent nature of the energy source. Electricity is produced only when the sun shines or the wind blows. What is needed is a means of storing energy to provide an even and continuous supply. This would be desirable even with current power plants, since there are large fluctuations in the daily demand for electricity. Extra generating capacity is required to meet the peak demands during daylight hours, particularly during the summer when air-conditioners draw a heavy load, and the extra capacity is left idle much of the time. A few electric companies have developed water pump storage, in which excess electricity is used to pump water uphill to reservoirs and the water running back downhill can then be used to run turbines to meet peak demands. Other energy storage schemes under consideration include storage of compressed air in caverns, mechanical energy storage in flywheels, and direct electrical storage in large superconducting magnets. We are all familiar with the lead storage battery, which represents chemical storage of electrical energy in portable form. While it is very efficient in converting electrical to chemical energy and back, the chemical battery is a heavy and expensive storage medium. Much research is now being directed to finding lighter and cheaper versions.

Probably the most attractive general storage scheme is chemical storage in the form of molecular hydrogen. This can be generated directly by electrolysis of water as shown in the upper diagram of Figure 1.33. Electric current is passed between electrodes immersed in a conducting water solution. Hydrogen is generated at the negative electrode and oxygen at the positive one. The energy stored in the hydrogen can then be reconverted into electricity using the reverse of the electrolytic cell, called the *fuel cell*, diagrammed in the lower diagram of Figure 1.33. Here hydrogen is oxidized at the negative electrode, where electrons are produced and passed through the circuit to the positive electrode, where oxygen is reduced. The overall efficiency of this conversion and reconversion is fairly low because of various energy barriers connected with the electrode processes. Lowering these barriers is an important target of current electrochemical research.

The ability to store energy in the form of hydrogen would help also to solve the problem of energy transport. The cost of electrical transmission over large distances is high, and there are serious losses. The areas with the greatest amount of sunlight, where solar plants would be most efficient, are far from northern centers of population. Transmission problems for ocean-generating plants are even more severe. Hydrogen transport by pipeline is much more efficient and less expensive. Instead of electricity, remote plants could generate hydrogen, which could be piped to urban centers. These considerations have led to the concept of the hydrogen economy shown graphically in Figure 1.34 in which hydrogen gas would become the main energy currency. It would be consumed

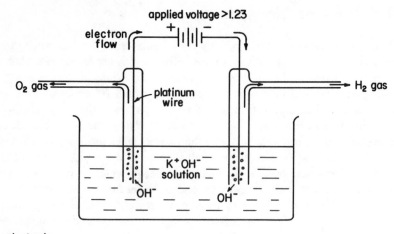

electrode
reactions: $2\,OH^- \rightarrow H_2O + \frac{1}{2}O_2 + 2e^-$ $2H_2O + 2e^- \rightarrow H_2 + 2OH^-$

overall
reaction: $H_2O \rightarrow H_2 + \frac{1}{2}O_2$

Electricity Production from Hydrogen – Oxygen Fuel Cell

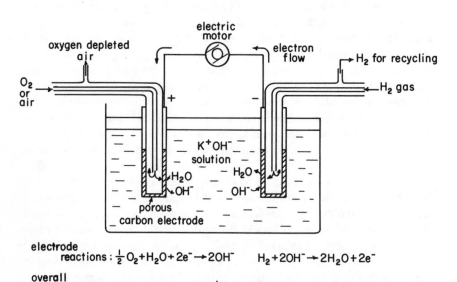

electrode
reactions : $\frac{1}{2}O_2 + H_2O + 2e^- \rightarrow 2OH^-$ $H_2 + 2OH^- \rightarrow 2H_2O + 2e^-$

overall
reaction: $H_2 + \frac{1}{2}O_2 \rightarrow H_2O$

Figure 1.33 Storage and Production of Electricity with Hydrogen

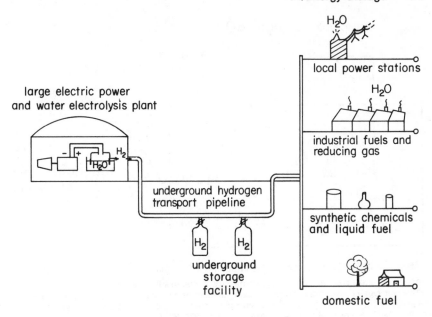

Figure 1.34   The Hydrogen Economy

directly for electrical generation and heating and could be used to synthesize liquid fuels by chemistry similar to that described in connection with coal gasification.

Another possibility is to generate hydrogen directly from sunlight by photochemistry. The energy of visible light is sufficient to split water molecules into hydrogen and oxygen atoms. Water is transparent to sunlight, however, and therefore some other agent must be used such as a catalyst that absorbs light and transfers the energy to the water-splitting reaction. Figure 1.35 shows one scheme for doing this. It consists of an electrochemical cell with platinum and strontium titanate electrodes dipped into a sodium hydroxide solution. When light strikes the strontium titanate electrode, oxygen is produced and electrons flow through the circuit to the platinum electrode, where they generate hydrogen. The main problem is that light in the ultraviolet region is required to activate the strontium titanate. A satisfactory electrode that works with visible light has not yet been found; however, there is considerable interest in the possibility of developing chemicals that can absorb light and transfer the energy directly to the splitting of water molecules.

Of course, green plants have been carrying out photochemical synthesis for millions of years and we use their products for our food supply as well as for fiber and wood. The entire biomass of plants represents an energy resource, some of which could practically be tapped for our energy needs. Figure 1.36 shows one

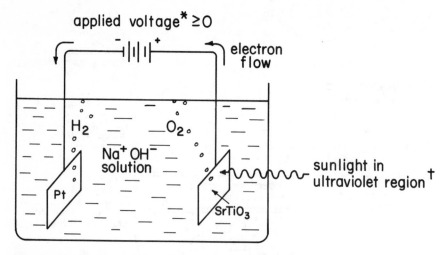

Figure 1.35 Direct Production of Hydrogen from Sunlight by Photoassisted Electrolysis

*0.5 ma of current flows at 0 applied volt; 2 ma (50% of maximum) flows at 0.25 applied volt.
†This prototype photoelectrode system is not an efficient device for converting solar energy into stored chemical energy, since only ~3% of solar energy comes from light in the ultraviolet range.
Source: M. S. Wrighton, et al., *J. Am. Chem. Soc.* 98 (1976):2774.

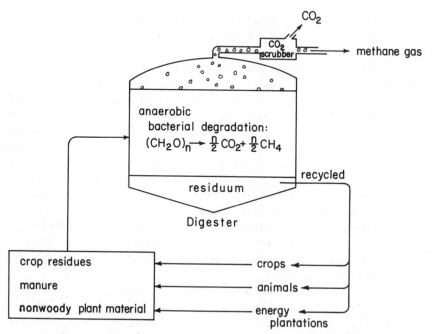

Figure 1.36 Flower Power: Energy from Decay Products of Photosynthesis

simple scheme for doing this. Bacteria that live in the absence of oxygen can effectively convert plant tissue into methane gas, which we have already seen is a high-grade fuel. Simple methane digesters of well-established design can produce methane from crop residues and manure—materials that are often wasted and in fact may cause pollution problems, as in the case of wastes from massive cattle feedlots. The methane digesters work on any nonwoody plant materials and it would be possible to harvest energy plantations, for example, swamp land that is photosynthetically productive but unsuited for agriculture. In wet areas of the world, this could be a simple and effective way of increasing the energy supply, particularly for poor countries with tropical climates. In addition to methane, the digester leaves a solid residue that is rich in nutrients and could be used as a soil conditioner or converted into animal feed.

Woody tissue is not appropriate for the methane digesters and neither is urban solid refuse, which is contaminated with metals and other substantially toxic materials. The energy content of urban waste as well as logging and pulp waste is significant, however, amounting to about 3% of our annual energy consumption. Some of this could be recovered through a pyrolysis technique shown in Figure 1.37 from which the product is methanol—a useful fuel. The same process could

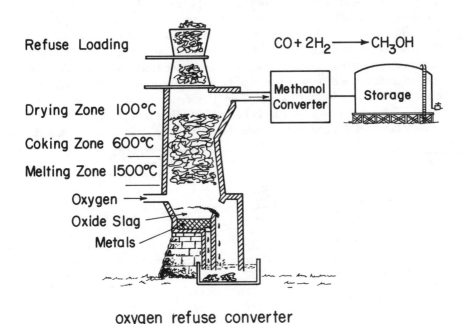

oxygen refuse converter

Figure 1.37 Fuel from Refuse

Source: T. B. Reed and R. M. Lerner, *Science* 182 (1973):1303. Copyright by the American Association for the Advancement of Science.

be used on trees harvested from forest plantations that are designed for energy production.

Overall, then, we can see many ways in which the energy of the sun can be tapped for human purposes. Because of the abundance of sunlight, the long-term prospects for renewable energy supplies are quite good. Some of the technologies, such as solar heating, conversion of plant matter to methane and methanol, and wind power generation of electricity, are already well developed and require only appropriate economic conditions for their implementation. Other techniques such as thermal or photovoltaic solar electricity production are well understood but require engineering development to reduce their costs before they will be attractive. Still other technologies such as direct photochemical production of hydrogen and ocean power generation are somewhat further off, but they have a long-term potential for the provision of abundant energy supplies.

15 | Thermal Pollution

Even if we could be supplied with unlimited amounts of energy, there are still difficulties associated with the ever-increasing use of energy. One general problem, which comes under the heading of thermal pollution, is how to get rid of all the heat that accompanies energy utilization. A station that generates electricity uses heat, whether it is supplied by the burning of fossil or nuclear fuels, to produce steam, which in turn runs a turbine. Only a fraction of the heat can be converted to useful work, however, even if everything works with perfect efficiency. The situation is illustrated in Figure 1.38. Heat is delivered to a boiler at a temperature of T_2, and after driving the turbine, the steam is condensed at a

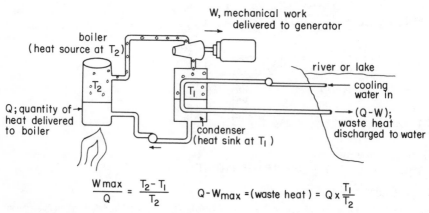

$$\frac{W_{max}}{Q} = \frac{T_2 - T_1}{T_2} \qquad Q - W_{max} = (\text{waste heat}) = Q \times \frac{T_1}{T_2}$$

Figure 1.38 Maximum Work and Waste Heat from Steam Electric Power Plant

temperature of T_1. The maximum ratio of work output to heat input is given by the temperature difference, $T_2 - T_1$, divided by the input temperature, T_2. This ratio is a consequence of the second law of thermodynamics and is a fundamental property of nature. No matter what the design of the power plant, the ratio can never be exceeded.

The temperatures in the formula are absolute temperatures. On the centigrade scale, absolute zero is $-273°$. To obtain the absolute temperature, we add 273 to the centigrade temperature. This is called the *Kelvin scale*. Since the temperature at the surface of the earth is, on the average, not far from 27° C, we know that T_1 in the formula will always be roughly 300° K. This means that if the boiler is run at 327° C, or 600° K, the maximum theoretical efficiency would be 50%. Actual efficiencies of generating plants are always lower than the theoretical maximum because of inevitable losses in transferring heat in real systems. The efficiency of coal-fired plants has been improved from initial values of about 10% to about 40% in the most modern one. A plant operating at 40% efficiency produces 4 calories of electrical energy and 6 calories of waste heat for every 10 calories of fuel burned. This means that for every calorie of electricity produced, 1½ calories of waste heat have to be carried away. The operating efficiency of current pressurized water nuclear reactors is about 30%, because of the relatively low temperature, 300° C, of the primary water coolant. This means that 3 calories of electricity and 7 calories of waste heat are produced for each 10 calories of nuclear energy input. For every calorie of electricity produced, 2.3 calories of waste heat must be removed, which is about 50% more than with modern coal-fired plants. Moreover, in nuclear plants all the waste heat must be removed at the steam condenser, whereas in a coal plant, some of the waste heat exits from the boiler chimney with the exhaust gases.

The condenser coils are cooled with water, which in most designs flows straight through from some nearby source and is discharged back to the environment, with its temperature increased by about 10° C. Already more than 10% of the total water streamflow in the United States is used for this purpose. Immense amounts of flowing water are needed for the very large power plants of current design, and it is becoming increasingly difficult to find sites where this much water is available. Moreover, there are ecological consequences of the cooling water streamflow. For one thing, fish and other marine life can be sucked into the intake and killed in large numbers. There is also concern that the increase in the temperature of the discharge water may be deleterious to aquatic life, although few effects have actually been observed so far. In the case of nuclear reactors on lakes with slow outflows, there is a possibility that traces of radioactivity released in the discharge water might eventually build up to a dangerous level.

It is possible to transfer the waste heat to the atmosphere rather than to the surrounding waters through cooling towers. As shown in Figure 1.39, these can be of the wet or dry variety. In the case of wet cooling towers, the waste heat is

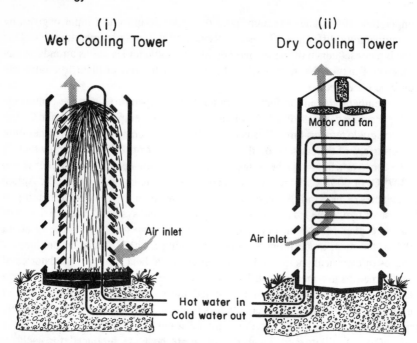

(i)
Wet Cooling Tower

(ii)
Dry Cooling Tower

Motor and fan

Air inlet

Air inlet

Hot water in
Cold water out

Figure 1.39 Transfer of Waste Heat from Electric Power Generation to the Atmosphere from Cooling Towers

Source: W. L. Masterton and E. J. Slowinski, *Chemical Principles,* 3rd ed. (Philadelphia: W. B. Saunders Company, 1973). Copyright © 1973. Figure 11.11 reprinted with permission.

removed through the evaporation of water. We recall that it takes 540 calories to evaporate a gram of water but only 10 calories to heat it by 10° C, so that the amount of water needed for wet cooling towers is a factor of 50 less than that used for direct flow cooling. However, this water is now transferred to the atmosphere and may disturb the local climate. Wet cooling towers often produce fog in the local area. Dry cooling towers operate by direct heat exchange from the closed loop condenser coolant to the atmosphere. Large fans are needed to force sufficient air past the heat exchange surfaces, and this produces a high noise level in the vicinity and drains power from the plant. Because heat transfer to the air is appreciably less efficient than transfer to water, dry cooling towers lower the overall efficiency of electricity generation.

In addition to the acute problem of cooling power plants, there is concern about the more general effects of increasing thermal pollution. As we use more and more energy, we disturb the natural energy balances. Cities such as Manhattan already produce more heat than they absorb from the sun, and the effects on the local climate are noticeable. In the long run, it is conceivable that we could upset the overall energy balance of the earth if energy production continues to grow exponentially. We saw in Table 1.1 that the total energy consumed is currently only abut 0.007% of the total energy absorbed from the sun. However, the annual energy consumption growth rate is 3.1%, as shown in Figure 1.2, which corresponds to a doubling time of 23 years. At that rate, heat from fuel energy consumption would equal the energy absorbed from the sun in another 320 years. This would certainly produce a marked increase in the earth's surface temperature, as we will see in the next part. Long before this, serious effects on the climate would be observed, including melting of the polar ice caps and flooding of coastal cities as a result of the rising levels of seawater. This sort of problem would be caused by any energy source that adds to the total heat budget, whether it is fossil or nuclear fuel. The only significant exception is solar energy, since the sun's rays are being converted to heat in any event. If we divert some of this solar energy flow to useful purposes, there is no net increase in the earth's energy budget. It is conceivable, of course, that if we begin to absorb a significantly larger fraction of the solar radiation than the earth does already, by blanketing the deserts with solar collectors, for example, then the total heat flow could increase. The increase would be much smaller, however, than that from the direct burning of fossil or nuclear fuels.

Power Plants; Thermal Efficiencies

As shown in Figure 1.38, a power plant generates electricity by boiling water and forcing the steam through a turbine. The steam is then condensed and returned to the boiler. In this way, heat from the burning of fuel, whether fossil or nuclear fuel, is converted to electricity. Some heat has to be transferred to the environment (cooling water) to condense the steam, however. The first law of thermodynamics tells us that energy is conserved, so that

$$Q_h = W + Q_c$$

where Q_h is the quantity of heat used to boil the water, Q_c is the quantity of heat transferred to the environment, and W is the quantity of work produced, in the form of electricity. A diagram of the energy flow is:

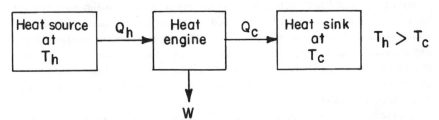

where T_h is the absolute temperature of the heat source (boiler) and T_c is the absolute temperature of the heat sink (cooling water).

The second law of thermodynamics puts a limit on the fraction of heat that can be converted to work:

$$\frac{W_{max}}{Q_h} = \frac{T_h - T_c}{T_h} \tag{1}$$

The physical basis for equation (1) is that the entropy of a system and its surroundings cannot decrease; the universe always tends toward greater disorder. Entropy, S, which is a measure of disorder, is defined as Q/T. The entropy change for the power plant and its surroundings is:

$$\Delta S_{total} = \Delta S_{source} + \Delta S_{sink}$$

$$S_{total} = \frac{-Q_h}{T_h} + \frac{Q_c}{T_c}$$

where the plus and minus signs indicate a gain and loss in entropy, respectively. The overall change must be positive. Therefore

$$\frac{-Q_h}{T_h} + \frac{Q_c}{T_c} > 0$$

Substituting

$$Q_c = Q_h - W$$

into this expression and rearranging it leads to

$$\frac{W}{Q_h} < \frac{T_h - T_c}{T_h}$$

which is another form of equation (1).

16 | Energy Consumption and Conservation

We have learned that there are limits to energy growth. Although there are large energy resources that can be tapped to replace our dwindling supplies of petroleum and natural gas, we cannot continue to increase the energy supply exponentially without upsetting the earth's energy flows. There are also other environmental costs of energy production such as air and water pollution and the exhaustion of mineral resources, which become increasingly important as energy consumption increases.

It is useful at this point to look at the other side of the ledger and ask how much energy we actually need. It is generally assumed that the standard of living increases with increasing energy consumption. This assumption is supported by

Figure 1.40, which is a plot of per capita energy consumption against per capita gross national product for many countries. There seems to be a roughly linear correlation between the two, with poor countries clustered near the bottom and the United States at the top. It is arguable, however, whether gross national product, which is the aggregate value of all economic activities, is an accurate measure of the standard of living. Most people who have lived in both countries would agree that the average standard of living is as high in Sweden as it is in the United States, despite a substantially lower per capita gross national product in Sweden. Yet the per capita energy consumption in Sweden is less than half that of the United States. Even within the terms of the overall correlation in Figure 1.40, one can draw a box around the countries of Western Europe and see that in this limited range there is no correlation, with wide variations in per capita energy consumption for comparable per capita gross national product.

These differences may reflect peculiarities of the economies of the individual

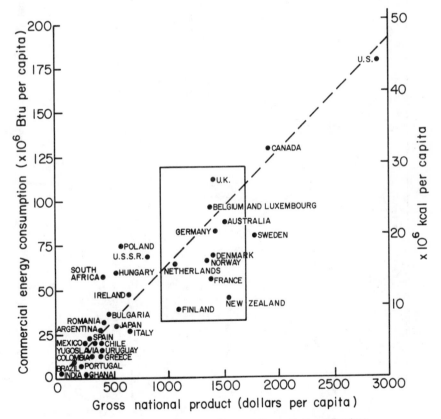

Figure 1.40 Energy Consumption and Gross National Product

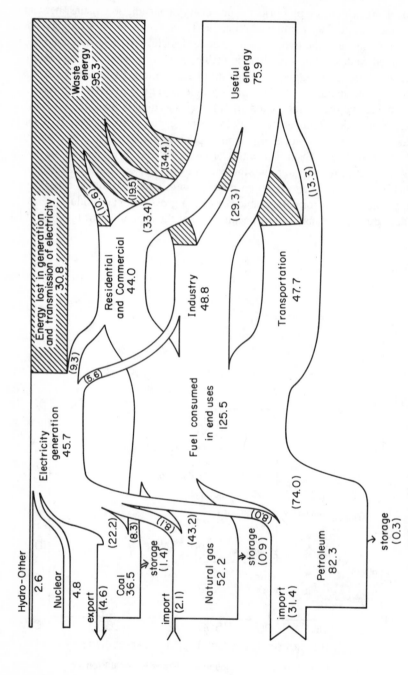

Figure 1.41 Production and Consumption of Energy in the United States, 1975 (in 10^{17} calories)

countries, but they may also reflect the effectiveness with which energy is actually used. It is reasonable that the amount of energy we need depends on how efficiently we use it. Figure 1.41 is a diagram of how energy actually flows through the U.S. economy. On the left side are the inputs from coal, petroleum, natural gas, water, and nuclear power in units of 10^{17} calories. The total consumption is 171.2 units. Of this, 45.7 goes to electricity production and the rest for other uses—household and commercial heating, transportation, and industry all taking comparable shares. Finally, on the right we have a division into useful energy versus waste heat. Fully 95.3 units, or 56% of the total, is wasted. Electricity production results in 30.8 units of waste, representing the inevitable waste heat mentioned earlier, as well as transmission losses.

Transportation produces 34.4 units of waste out of 47.7 total units, an efficiency of only 28%. Some of this waste has to do with inevitable losses in converting heat into motion, but much of it is due to inefficient modes of transportation. Table 1.9 compares the energy efficiency as well as the current economic cost of various modes of transportation for both freight and passengers. We see that pipelines and railroads are far more energy-efficient than trucks in

Table 1.9   Efficiencies of Freight and Passenger Transport

Energy and Price Data for Intercity Freight Transport		
Mode	Energy (kcal/ton-mile)	Price (cents/ton-mile)
Pipeline	110	0.27
Railroad	170	1.4
Waterway	170	0.30
Truck	710	7.5
Airplane	11,000	21.9

Energy and Price Data for Passenger Transport		
Mode	Energy (kcal/ton-mile)	Price (cents/passenger-mile)
Intercity		
Bus	400	3.6
Railroad	730	4.0
Automobile	860	4.0
Airplane	2,100	6.0
Urban		
Mass transit	960	8.3
Automobile	2,000	9.6

Source: E. Hirst and J. C. Moyers, *Science* 179 (1973): 1299.

freight transport and that airplanes are extremely inefficient. For passenger transport the differences are less extreme, but airplanes are still more than twice as wasteful as railroads and automobiles, whereas mass transit is twice as efficient as the automobile for urban transportation. These efficiency factors have to be balanced against convenience in making transportation choices, but it is clear that there is much room for energy savings when planning a transportation system. For example, rapid intercity trains would be both more efficient and more convenient up to a distance of about 500 miles, considering the time spent in traveling to and from airports.

In assessing the potential for energy conservation, a flow diagram such as that in Figure 1.41 is only a starting point. Some of the numbers in the waste column actually underestimate the potential. For example, household and commercial heating seems to be fairly efficient, wasting only 10.6 units or 24% of the input energy. However, the figure for waste includes only calories that are expelled directly to the environment rather than used for heating. If electrical resistance heating is used, for example, the conversion from electricity to heat is nearly 100% efficient, but this ignores the approximately 65% heat loss of the electrical generating plant. A more effective way to use the electricity would be to run a heat pump, which is diagrammed in Figure 1.42. This is just an air-conditioner run in reverse, with heat transferred from the colder outdoors to the warmer

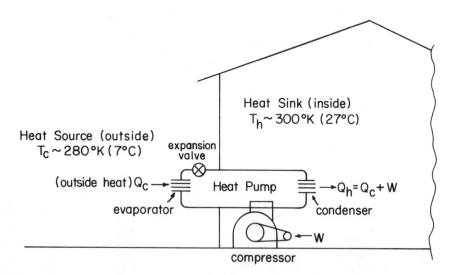

$$\text{Theoretical Efficiency: } \frac{Q_h \text{ (heat delivered)}}{W \text{ (work)}} = \frac{T_h}{T_h - T_c} = \frac{300}{20} = 15$$

Figure 1.42 The Heat Pump: An Efficient Means of Residential Space Heating

indoors. The theoretical amount of heat that can be produced from a unit of work is the inverse of the amount of work that can be extracted from heat in a heat engine; that is, the theoretical heat output of the heat pump is given by the ratio of the interior temperature to the difference in temperature between the outside and the inside. If the interior temperature is about 300° on the absolute scale, and the outside temperature is 20° colder, the heat pump could theoretically deliver 15 calories of heat for every calorie of electricity needed to run it. Because of resistances to heat transfer, actual pumps are much less efficient than this, but they nevertheless can be expected to deliver at least 2 calories of heat for every calorie of electricity. This is twice as good as electrical resistance heating and recovers some of the energy wasted at the electrical generating plant.

There are ways to use the waste heat from electrical generation purposefully. As diagrammed in Figure 1.43, one way is simply to use the hot water outflow to heat residential or commercial buildings. This is already being done in urban areas such as New York, but it requires close proximity of the power plant and the units to be heated.

Another possibility is to combine electrical generation with the production of industrial process heat. At the moment much of the fuel consumed by industry goes to generate heat for various chemical and manufacturing processes. These industrial heating plants could be combined with electricity generators to extract

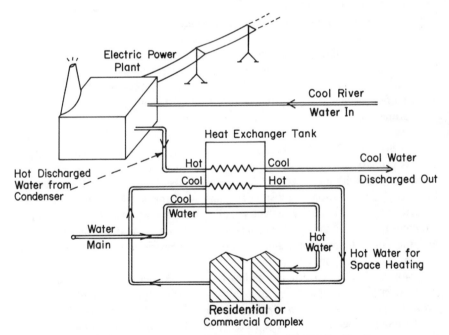

Figure 1.43 Integrated Electric Power Plant—Residential Heating Source

$$CaBr_2 + 2H_2O \rightarrow Ca(OH)_2 + 2HBr \qquad \text{at } 730° \text{ C (1)}$$
$$Hg + 2HBr \rightarrow HgBr_2 + H_2 \qquad \text{at } 250° \text{ C (2)}$$
$$HgBr_2 + Ca(OH)_2 \rightarrow CaBr_2 + HgO + H_2O \qquad \text{at } 100° \text{ C (3)}$$
$$HgO \rightarrow Hg + \tfrac{1}{2}O_2 \qquad \text{at } 500° \text{ C (4)}$$

$$\text{Net: } H_2O \rightarrow H_2 + \tfrac{1}{2}O_2$$

Figure 1.44 Thermochemical Cycle
Source: G. DeBeni and C. Marchetti, *Eur. Spectra* (1970): 46.

greater energy value from the fuel. The main obstacle to this is that all electricity production is currently centralized in a single electrical utility in a given area. Another possibility that depends on further technical development is the use of some of the wasted heat to generate hydrogen through a thermochemical cycle of reactions. For example, Figure 1.44 shows a set of simple chemical reactions that sum up to give the water-splitting reaction. Although the direct thermal dissociation of water requires temperatures of about 2,500° C, all the individual reactions in the cycle shown occur at temperatures below 730° C. In essence, calcium bromide and mercury serve as catalysts for the dissociation of water by the four reaction steps shown. The overall reaction still requires energy and represents an energy-storing mechanism, but lower grade heat can be used for that purpose. The hydrogen produced in this fashion would be an input into the overall hydrogen economy discussed previously.

There are many opportunities to save substantial amounts of energy in manufacturing processes as well. The production of steel, aluminum, and paper consumes more than 20% of the total industrial energy expenditure in the United States. A substantial savings would arise from more systematic recycling of these and other industrial commodities. The bar graph in Figure 1.45 shows the amount of energy required to produce a metric ton of steel, paper, and aluminum from primary materials compared with the energy required for production from recycled materials. We see that aluminum production from ore is particularly energy-intensive. Recycled aluminum requires only 5% as much energy to process as primary aluminum ore. The savings from using steel scrap and paper waste are not so high—52% and 70%, respectively. Nevertheless, the potential for energy conservation is substantial when we consider the volume of these materials produced annually. Effective solid waste management could transform the environmental liability of millions of tons of waste products into new raw material assets. It would also help to eliminate the problem of finding more land for landfill disposal operations.

Historically, U.S. government policy has been skewed in favor of using primary materials rather than recycled materials. Most companies that mine primary ores are given about a 15% depletion allowance—a favorable tax incentive. Furthermore, federally regulated freight rates for transporting scrap iron and steel, nonferrous metals, paper, rubber, and textile wastes have been considera-

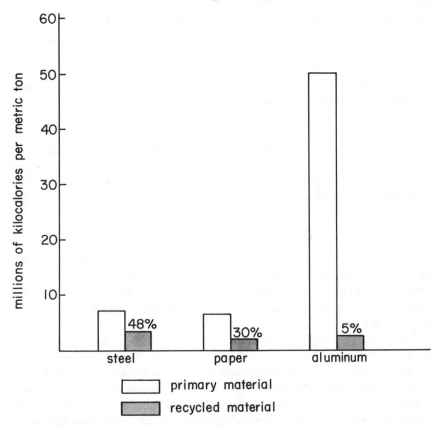

Figure 1.45 Comparison of Energy Requirements for Production of Steel, Paper, and Aluminum from Primary and Recycled Materials

Source: Ford Foundation, *A Time to Choose America's Energy Future* (Cambridge, Mass.: Ballinger Publishing Company, 1975), pp. 458, 464. E. T. Hays, "Energy Implications of Materials Processing," in *Materials: Renewable and Nonrenewable Resources*, ed. P. H. Abelson and A. L. Hammond (Washington, D.C.: American Association for the Advancement of Science, 1976), p. 33.

bly higher than the freight rates paid by producers of competitive primary materials. These policies have made it more profitable to continue to rely on production from primary materials despite the major energy savings that recycling would provide.

The trend is changing, however, and recycled wastes will come to play a more important role in materials production. As part of the 1978 United States National Energy Act, equipment purchased for recycling wastes was given a 10% investment tax credit in addition to the 10% credit that already exists. Furthermore, the energy legislation contains a recycling targets provision, which authorizes the Department of Energy to set industrial goals maximizing the use of recycled materials. Specific targets are to be set for each industry for the next ten years. Also, the Interstate Commerce Commission has been mandated to review the freight rate structure for primary and scrap material.

The trend toward recycling is one example of how energy can be saved by examining the energy flow patterns in our society in depth, from both technological and social perspectives. Energy analysis is a new and rapidly developing area of study that is very important for energy policy. It is becoming clear that answers to the questions of what energy supplies are available to us and over what period of years they must be developed depend critically on having an accurate assessment of how much energy we really need. We cannot rely on extrapolations from past consumption patterns since they are based on the assumption of plentiful, cheap energy.

Heat Pumps; Heat Quality

Because of the importance of temperature in limiting the energy conversion efficiency, the quality of heat, i.e., the temperature of the heat reservoir, is as important as its quantity. One calorie of heat is worth much more at 400° K than at 350° K. High-grade heat can actually be converted into a much larger quantity of low-grade heat.

The simplest device for doing this is the heat pump, illustrated in Figure 1.42. This is a small version of a power plant run in reverse. Mechanical work is used to condense a working fluid, usually freon, CF_2Cl_2, at the temperature of the heat sink. The fluid is then allowed to evaporate, thereby absorbing heat from the heat source. In this way heat can be pumped from lower to higher temperatures by the expenditure of work. This is how refrigerators and air-conditioners operate. A house can be heated in cold weather by reversing the direction of the air-conditioner.

The conversion of work to heat is governed by the same entropy considerations as the reverse process. The maximum degree of conversion is simply given by the inverse of equation (1) on page 78:

$$\frac{Q_{max}}{W} = \frac{T_h}{T_h - T_c}$$

but T_h and T_c are reversed, since the heat source (T_c) is now colder than the heat sink (T_h).

It has been suggested that, when considering energy use for heating, it is more sensible to measure conversion efficiency by the standard of the second law of thermodynamics than by that of the first law.[10,11] Rather than simply counting calories, which gives electrical resistance heating a "first-law" efficiency rating of nearly 100%, one should divide the heat production by that available from a perfect heat pump. For the house illustrated in Figure 1.42, the "second-law" efficiency would be 1/15 or 6.7% if heat were provided by electrical resistance heating. However, if the house were fitted with an actual heat pump to produce 2 calories of heat per calorie of electricity, the efficiency would be 2/15 or 13.4%.

17 | Summary

Our survey of sources has shown that energy is supplied to us in abundance by the sun, and this steady energy flow is sufficient to maintain the human population at a steady state, which we must, in any event, achieve over a period of time. Capturing the sun's energy and putting it to useful work are challenges to science and technology. At the moment it is much more expensive to do this than to tap the solar energy that has been stored over the millennia in fossil fuels, which we have used to develop our industrial civilization. We are currently completely dependent on fossil fuels and particularly on petroleum and natural gas. These fuel stocks are being drawn down and will inevitably run out, in a matter of decades for oil and gas and perhaps in a few centuries for coal. In the meantime, the development of atomic science has begun to release the very large amounts of energy stored in the nuclei of uranium atoms, and potentially in hydrogen atoms as well, both for destructive and for constructive purposes. The development of nuclear power on a large scale, however, poses unprecedented problems for humanity in terms of the dangers of nuclear weapons proliferation and the long-term hazards associated with massive amounts of radioisotopes.

On the supply side of the energy equation, the key questions are to what extent coal and nuclear fuels can be used safely with acceptable environmental costs, and how long it will take to introduce alternative technologies involving solar power and possibly the fusion reaction. Equally important questions exist on the demand side of the energy equation; these are just beginning to be recognized. It is obvious that energy consumption cannot continue to grow exponentially forever. A close examination of how energy is actually used shows that significant savings are possible in situations where the use of energy has been historically predicated on the availability of a cheap and plentiful supply. Energy savings have a greater impact on the equation than energy supplies because of the low efficiency with which fuels are used. Each calorie of electricity that is not used represents a saving of 3 calories of oil, coal, or nuclear fuels. Savings on the demand side of the energy equation are desirable because they increase the range of human choices with respect to the energy supply. The lower the projected energy requirements, the greater is the flexibility for providing energy from a variety of sources, and the more time there is to develop the safest, most efficient, and least environmentally harmful technologies.

Problem Set

1. Calculate the amount of energy produced by the sun and the amount of solar energy intercepted by the earth each year. The solar constant at the earth is 2 calories/min/cm², the radius of the earth is 6,400 km, and its distance from the sun is 1.48×10^8 km.

2. How much energy is released in a 2-cm rainfall over an area 10 by 10 km? (It takes 540 calories to evaporate 1 ml of water.) This is equivalent to how many tons of TNT at 10^9 calories/ton?

The following table refers to problems 3 and 4. It lists the heating requirements for a typical well insulated one family house in the central United States, along with the sunlight per day (24 hour average) falling on a fixed 45° flat plate collector facing south.

	Monthly heating requirements	Daily sunlight (calories/cm²) 45° tilt
January	4.2×10^9 cal	283
February	4.0×10^9 cal	411
March	3.2×10^9 cal	383
April	1.7×10^9 cal	396
May	0.7×10^9 cal	391
June	0.2×10^9 cal	399
July	0	478
August	0	438
September	0.3×10^9 cal	428
October	1.3×10^9 cal	405
November	3.0×10^9 cal	243
December	4.1×10^9 cal	211

3. Plot energy need versus time over the course of a year. On the same graph draw a plot of available daily sunlight versus time. Comment on why most solar energy systems are not designed to provide 100% of the heating needs (typically, they may provide 50%).

4. Consider a house fitted with 50 m² of solar collectors capable of converting 40% of the available sunlight to warm the house. Calculate the amount of heat that can be extracted from the system to meet the heating needs of the house for one year. If the solar collectors are installed at a cost of $375 per m² what is the total cost of the system? Assume that the cost of home heating oil will be an average of $3 per gallon over the next 20 years and that the heat value of the oil is 2.50×10^7 calories/gal. Assume further that the oil is burned at 90% efficiency. What would be the return on the investment over the 20 year period?

5. The photosynthetic reaction

$$6CO_2 + 12H_2O \xrightarrow{h\nu} C_6H_{12}O_6 + 6O_2 + 6H_2O$$

absorbs 6.7×10^5 calories of solar energy per mole of glucose. The annual net primary productivity is 320 g (dry weight) of plant matter per square meter of the earth's surface, of which 50% is carbon. If plants respire 25% of the energy they absorb, estimate the total amount of solar energy used in photosynthesis per year. The earth's radius is 6.4×10^6 m.

6. The estimated amount of energy available in recoverable fossil fuels is 5.6×10^{22} calories. If all the oxygen in the atmosphere results from accumulation of photo-synthetic oxygen accompanying the burial of unrespired organic matter, estimate what fraction of the total *stored* photosynthetic energy is recoverable as fossil fuel. The atmosphere (dry) weighs 1,000 g/cm^2 and is 20% oxygen and 80% nitrogen by volume. (For other needed information see problem 5.) If all this fuel were burned, by how much would the carbon dioxide content of the atmosphere increase, if all of it stayed in the air? The present carbon dioxide content is 330 ppm by volume.

7. A subbituminous coal that contains 45% fixed carbon, 30% volatile gas (as methane), 20% water and 5% ash by weight is converted to methane. The heating value of the coal is 5.7×10^6 calories/kg. The coal is first heated to 800° C in the reaction:

$$\text{coal} + \text{heat} \rightarrow C_{\text{fixed}} + CH_4$$

and the methane is collected. The fixed-carbon residue is then completely converted to methane by the overall reaction:

$$2C + 2H_2O \rightarrow CH_4 + CO_2$$

How many grams of methane are produced per kilogram of coal? What is the heat value of this methane if a gram molecular weight of methane supplies 210.8 kcal of heat? How does this value compare with that of the original coal? How many grams of water are needed to produce the methane in the second reaction?

8. Describe three major environmental and security problems associated with nuclear power.

9. Explain how nuclear power based on the thorium breeding cycle has a security advantage in terms of nuclear proliferation over the plutonium breeding cycle.

10. How great an increase in the present genetically significant radiation background, 0.2 rad/year, would be expected to increase the estimated mutation rate, 10 per 10^6 genes per generation, by 10%? Assume that radiation induces 0.06 mutations per 10^6 genes per rad. One generation equals 30 years.

11. Complete the following nuclear reactions:
    a) Beta decay: $^{60}_{27}Co \rightarrow \beta^- +$
    b) Positron emission: $^{22}_{11}Na \rightarrow \beta^+ +$
    c) Electron capture: $^{41}_{20}Ca \rightarrow$
    d) Alpha decay: $^{239}_{94}Pu \rightarrow {}^4_2He +$
    e) Nuclear fission: $^{236}_{94}U \rightarrow {}^{99}_{42}Mo +$

12. Plutonium is very damaging when inhaled as small particles because of the ionization of tissue by its emitted alpha particles. One microgram of plutonium is known to produce cancer in experimental animals. From its atomic weight (239) and half-life (24,000 years), calculate how many alpha particles are emitted by a microgram of plutonium over the course of a year. About how many ionizations do the particles produce?

13. A neutron generated by fission typically possesses a kinetic energy of 2 Mev. When such a neutron collides with a hydrogen atom 18 times, its energy is reduced to its thermal energy of 0.025 ev, i.e., the kinetic energy it would possess by virtue of the

temperature of its surroundings. The same neutron would have to collide with a sodium atom more than 200 times to reduce its energy by the same amount. Explain how these characteristics make water a suitable coolant in the pressurized light water reactor that utilizes U-235 as the fuel, whereas sodium is the suitable coolant in the breeder reactor.

14. If world energy consumption continues to increase at the present annual rate of 3.6%, how long will it take to double? At this rate of increase, how long would it be before human energy consumption equals 1% of the solar energy absorbed by the earth, 2.1 $\times 10^{23}$ calories/year? The present world energy consumption is 4.8×10^{19} calories/ year.

15. a) Compare the costs per unit of the energy of electricity and gasoline. Current prices are $0.05 per kwh for the former and $1.50 per gallon for the latter. Gasoline weighs 5.51 lb/gal, and its energy release on combustion is 19,000 Btu (British thermal units) per pound. Energy units: 1 calorie = 4.18 joules = 1.16×10^{-6} kwh = 3.97×10^{-3} Btu.

b) Is this comparison fair?

16. An electric hot-water heater has a standard efficiency rating of 90% (i.e., for every 10 calories of electricity consumed, 9 go into heating the water). If the heater normally heats water from the ambient temperature, 68° F, to 176° F, what is its "second law" efficiency (i.e., what is the ratio of the amount of energy that an ideal heat pump would use to do the same job, to the amount of energy actually consumed)?

17. Calculate the theoretical efficiency of a heat pump when the room temperature is 65° F (18.3° C) and the outside temperature is −10° F (−23.3° C). If the heat pump were drawing heat from a water tank at 40° F (4.4° C) what would be the theoretical efficiency? Describe how solar energy in conjunction with a heat pump can provide an efficient means of heating a house.

18. 23% of total national energy consumption is used for space heating of residential and commercial buildings. Total national energy consumption is currently about 2.0 × 10^{19} calories/year. It is estimated that on the average space heating can be reduced by 50% by adding more efficient insulation, caulking, and weatherstripping. Using the heat value of oil given in problem 19 calculate the barrels of oil saved if all houses in the U.S. were efficiently insulated. In the peak year of 1977, 8.8×10^6 barrels per day were imported. By what percentage could our foreign oil imports be reduced if 50% better insulation were adopted?

19. a) The energy equivalent of how many barrels of crude oil are saved by recycling one ton of scrap aluminum rather than producing the ton from the ore. Use the following information:

1 barrel of oil = 1.46×10^9 calories
1 ton of finished aluminum requires 4.79×10^{10} calories from ore and
2.39×10^9 calories from recycled aluminum.

b) In 1979 about 8.0 million tons of aluminum were produced in the U.S. Of this about 2.0 million tons were produced from scrap metal. The equivalent of how many barrels of oil could have been saved if half of the total aluminum were produced from scrap metal? At $25 a barrel, how much money can be saved?

20. A large power plant is being constructed that will produce 1.6×10^{10} kcal/day of electrical energy. For every kcalorie of energy produced, 2 kcal of waste heat is

discharged. If the plant draws 2×10^9 l/day of river water at 20° C into its cooling condensers, calculate the rise in temperature of the cooling water. If the river has a flow rate of 10^{10} l/day, estimate the rise in temperature of the water downstream from the plant.

21. Assume you are asked by an electric utility in Chicago to assess the feasibility of using low sulfur subbituminous coal from Wyoming rather than locally available bituminous coal in order to meet EPA SO_2 emission standards (1.2 mg SO_2/kcalorie coal burned). Environmental impact and energy conservation should be considered in your assessment. You are given the following information:

	% S (by weight)	heat value (calorie/gram)
Bituminous (Chicago)	1.00	8,000
Subbituminous (Wyoming)	0.34	5,500

50% of the sulfur in the bituminous coal is in the mineral form of pyrite which is easily removed by mechanical means. The remainder of the sulfur is organically bound within the coal structure. All the sulfur in the subbituminuos coal is organically bound. The energy cost of transporting the coal by train is 170 kcalories/ton-mile. The distance from Wyoming to Chicago is 1,000 miles.

Notes

1. G. M. Woodwell, *Biol. Sci.* 24 (1974):81.
2. The structure depicted for bituminous coal is from: M. E. Bailey, *J. Chem. Educ.* 51 (1974):446.
3. M. K. Hubbert, *Am. Assoc. Petrol. Geol. Bull.* 51 (1967):2207.
4. B. Commoner, *The Poverty of Power* (New York: Alfred A. Knopf, Inc., 1976), pp. 43–65.
5. "Study Committee on the Potential for Rehabilitating Lands Surface Mined for Coal in the Western United States" (Washington, D.C.: National Academy of Sciences, 1973).
6. B. G. Harvey, *Introduction to Nuclear Physics and Chemistry,* 2nd ed. (Englewood Cliffs, N.J.: Prentice-Hall, Inc., 1969), p. 391.
7. A. A. Kubo and D. J. Rose, *Science* 182 (1973):1205.
8. J. D. Lawson, *Proc. Phys. Soc.* B70 (1957):6.
9. J. L. Emmett, J. Nuckolls, and L. Wood, *Sci. Am.* 230 (June 1974):28.
10. K. W. Ford, et al., eds., "Efficient Use of Energy: A Physics Perspective, American Physics Society Studies on the Technical Aspects of the More Efficient Use of Energy" (New York: American Institute of Physics, 1975).
11. R. H. Socolow, *Phys. Today* 28 (August 1975):23.

Suggestions for Further Reading

Energy

"Energy and Power" issue of *Scientific American* 225 (September 1971).
a) Energy issue of *Science* 184 (April 19, 1974).

b) This issue was also published along with other relevant *Science* articles in: Abelson, P. H., ed. *Energy—Use, Conservation and Supply*. Washington, D.C.: American Association for the Advancement of Science, 1974.

Science 199 (February 10, 1978), devoted largely to articles on energy.

Abelson, P. H., and Hammond, A. L., eds. *Energy II: Use, Conservation and Supply*. Washington, D.C.: American Association for the Advancement of Science, 1978.

"Energy Review." *Nature* 249 (June 21, 1974):697–737.

Ford Foundation. *A Time to Choose America's Energy Future*, final report by the Energy Policy Project of the Ford Foundation. Cambridge, Mass.: Ballinger Publishing Company, 1974.

Makhijani, A., and Poole, A. *Energy and Agriculture in the Third World*. Cambridge, Mass.: Ballinger Publishing Company, 1975.

Commoner, B. *The Poverty of Power. Energy and the Economic Crisis*. New York: Alfred A. Knopf, Inc., 1976.

Fossil fuels

Levorsen, A. *Geology of Petroleum*. San Francisco: W. H. Freeman and Co. Publishers, 1967, pp. 499–537.

Murchison, D. *Coal and Coal-Bearing Strata*, edited by T. S. Westoll. London: Oliver and Boyd, Ltd., 1968, pp. 197–268.

Griffith, E. D., and Clarke, A. W. "World Coal Production." *Sci. Am.* 240 (January 1979):38.

Flower, A. R. "World Oil Production." *Sci. Am.* 238 (March 1978):42.

Myerhoff, A. A. "Economic Impact and Geopolitical Implications of Giant Petroleum Fields." *Am. Sci.* 64 (September–October 1976):536.

Klass, D. L. "Synthetic Crude Oil from Shale and Coal." *Chem. Technol.* August 1975, p. 499.

Hammond, O. H., and Baron, R. E. "Synthetic Fuels: Prices, Prospects and Prior Art." *Am. Sci.* 64 (July–August 1976):407.

Worthy, W. "Synfuels: Uncertain and Costly Fuel Option." *Chem. Eng. News,* August 27, 1979, p. 20.

Maugh, T. "Tar Sands: A New Fuels Industry Takes Shape." *Science* 199 (1978):756.

Gillette, R. "Western Coal: Does the Debate Follow Irreversible Commitment?" *Science* 182 (1973):456.

Koppenaal, D., and Manahan, S. "Hazardous Chemicals from Coal Conversion Processes." *Environ. Sci. Technol.* 12 (1976):1104.

Fission

Harvey, B. G. *Introduction to Nuclear Physics and Chemistry*, 2nd ed. Englewood Cliffs, N.J.: Prentice-Hall, Inc., 1969.

Vendryes, G. A. "Superphénix: A Full-Scale Breeder Reactor." *Sci. Am.* 236 (March 1977):26.

Metz, W. D. "European Breeders (II): The Nuclear Parts Are Not the Problem." *Science* 191 (1976):368.

Zare, R. N. "Laser Separation of Isotopes." *Sci. Am.* 236 (February 1977):86.

Kubo, A. S., and Rose, D. J. "Disposal of Nuclear Wastes." *Science* 182 (1973): 1205.

Rochlin, G. I. "Nuclear Waste Disposal: Two Social Criteria." *Science* 195 (1977):23.

deMarsily, G., Ledoux, E., Barbreau, A., and Margat, J. "Nuclear Waste Disposal: Can the Geologist Guarantee Isolation?" *Science* 197 (1977):519.

Cohen, B. L. "The Disposal of Radioactive Wastes from Fission Reactors." *Sci. Am.* 236 (June 1977):21.

Sagan, L. A. "Human Costs of Nuclear Power." *Science* 177 (1972):487.

Lovins, A. B., and Patterson, W. C. "Plutonium Particles: Some Like Them Hot." *Nature* 254 (1975):278.

Lichtenstein, G. "Ill Wind Blows No Good in Uranium County." *New York Times,* May 22, 1976, p. 27.

Cohen, B. L. "Impacts of the Nuclear Energy Industry on Human Health and Safety." *Am. Sci.* 64 (September–October 1976):550.

Morgan, K. "Cancer and Low-Level Ionizing Radiation." *Bull. Atom. Sci.* 34 (September 1978):30.

Roblat, J. "The Risks for Radiation Workers." *Bull. Atom. Sci.* 34 (September 1978):41.

Edsall, J. T. "Toxicity of Plutonium and Some Other Actinides." *Bull. Atom. Sci.* 32 (September 1976):27.

Kerr, R. "Geologic Disposal of Nuclear Wastes: Salt's Lead Is Challenged." *Science* 204 (1979):603.

Marx, J. "Low-Level Radiation: Just How Bad Is It?" *Science* 204 (1979):160.

Carter, L. "Uranium Mill Tailings: Congress Addresses a Long-Neglected Problem." *Science* 202 (1978):191.

Angino, E. "High Level and Long-Lived Radioactive Waste Disposal." *Science* 198 (1977):885.

Hammond, R. P. "Nuclear Wastes and Public Acceptance." *Am. Sci.* 67 (March–April 1979):146.

Marshall, E., Carter, L., and Holden, C. "The Crisis at Three Mile Island: Nuclear Risks Are Reconsidered." *Science* 204 (1979):152.

Burwell, C. C., Ohanian, M. J., and Weinberg, A. M. "A Siting Policy for an Acceptable Nuclear Future." *Science* 204 (1979):1043.

Hammond, A. L. "Nuclear Proliferation (I): Warnings from the Arms Control Community." *Science* 193 (1976):126.

Feiveson, H. A., Taylor, T. B., von Hippel, F., and Williams, R. H. "The Plutonium Economy, Why We Should Wait and Why We Can Wait." *Bull. Atom. Sci.* 32 (December 1976):10.

Feiveson, H. A., and Taylor, T. B. "Security Implications of Alternative Fission Futures." *Bull. Atom. Sci.* 32 (December 1976):14.

von Hippel, F., and Williams, R. H. "Energy Waste and Nuclear Power Growth." *Bull. Atom. Sci.* 32 (December 1976):18.

Lovins, A. B. "Thorium Cycles and Proliferation." *Bull. Atom. Sci.* 35 (February 1979):16.

Kross, A. S. "Laser Enrichment of Uranium: The Proliferation Connection." *Science* 196 (1977):721.

Wilson, R. "How to Have Nuclear Power Without Weapons Proliferation." *Bull. Atom. Sci.* 33 (November 1977):39.

Roblat, J. "Controlling Weapons-Grade Fissile Material." *Bull. Atom. Sci.* 33 (June 1977):37.

Bebbington, W. P. "The Processing of Nuclear Fuels." *Sci. Am.* 235 (December 1976):30.

Walsh, J. "Fuel Reprocessing Still the Focus of U.S. Nonproliferation Policy." *Science* 201 (1978):692.

Lewis, K. N. "The Prompt and Delayed Effects of Nuclear War." *Sci. Am.* 241 (July 1979):35.

Rose, D., and Lester, R. "Nuclear Power, Nuclear Weapons and International Stability." *Sci. Am.* 238 (April 1978):45.

Rose, D. J., Walsh, P. W., and Leskovjan, L. L. "Nuclear Power Compared to What?" *Am. Sci.* 64 (May–June 1976):291.

Hohenemser, C., Kasperson, R., and Kates, R. "The Distrust of Nuclear Power." *Science* 196 (1977):25.

Flowers, B. "Nuclear Power." *Bull. Atom. Sci.* 34 (March 1978):21.

Weinberg, A. M. "Is Nuclear Energy Acceptable?" *Bull. Atom. Sci.* 33 (April 1977):54.

Rossin, A., and Rieck, T. "Economics of Nuclear Power." *Science* 201 (1978):582.

Kulcinski, G. L., et al. "Energy for the Long Run—Fission or Fusion?" *Am. Sci.* 67 (January–February 1979):78.

Fusion

Post, R. F., and Ribe, F. L. "Fusion Reactors As Future Energy Sources." *Science* 186 (1974):397.

Emmett, J. L., Nuckolls, J., and Wood, L. "Fusion Power by Laser Implosion." *Sci. Am.* 230 (June 1974):24.

Ashby, D. "Laser Fusion." *J. Br. Nucl. Energy Soc.* 14 (1975):311.

Holmes-Siedle, A. "Radiation Effects in the Fusion Power Programme." *Nature* 251 (September 20, 1974):191.

Metz, W. D. "Fusion Research (I): What Is the Program Buying the Country?" 192 (1976):1320.

Metz, W. D. "Fusion Research (II): Detailed Reactor Studies Identify More Problems." *Science* 193 (1976):38.

"Fusion Focus Shifts to Practical Aspects." *Chem. Eng. News,* October 11, 1976, p. 24.

Holdren, J. "Fusion Energy in Context: Its Fitness for the Long Term." *Science* 200 (1978):168.

Steiner, D., and Clarke, J. "The Tokamak: Model T Fusion Reactor." *Science* 194 (1978):1395.

Parkins, W. E. "Engineering Limitations of Fusion Power Plants." *Science* 199 (1978):1403.

Furth, H. P. "Progress Toward a Tokamak Fusion Reactor." *Sci. Am.* 241 (August 1979):50.

Yonas, G. "Fusion Power with Particle Beams." *Sci. Am.* 239 (November 1979):50.

Dingee, D. "Fusion Power." *Chem. Eng. News,* April 12, 1979, p. 32.

Solar Energy

Daniels, F. *Direct Use of the Sun's Energy,* (New York: Ballantine Books, Inc., 1974.

Wrighton, M. S. "Photochemistry: Power and Fuel from the Sun." *Chem. Eng. News,* September 3, 1979, p. 29.

Calvin, M. "Photosynthesis As a Resource for Energy and Materials." *Am. Sci.* 64 (May–June 1976):260.

Poole, A. D., and Williams, R. H. "Flower Power: Prospects for Photosynthetic Energy." *Bull. Atom. Sci.* 32 (May 1976):48.

Hammond, A. L. "Alcohol: A Brazilian Answer to the Energy Crisis." *Science* 195 (1977):564.

Burwell, C. "Solar Biomass Energy: An Overview of U.S. Potential." *Science* 199 (1978):1041.

Anderson, E. V. "Gasohol: Energy Mountain or Molehill?" *Chem. Eng. News,* July 31, 1978, p. 8.

Wade, N. "Windmills: The Resurrection of an Ancient Energy Technology." *Science* 184 (1974):1055.

Gustavson, M. R. "Limits to Wind Power." *Science* 204 (1979):13.

Pollard, W. G. "The Long-Range Prospects for Solar-Derived Fuels." *Am. Sci.* 64 (September–October 1976):509.

Bezdek, R., Hirshberg, A., and Babcock, W. "Economic Feasibility of Solar Water and Space Heating." *Science* 203 (1979):1214.

Hammond, A., and Metz, W. "Capturing Sunlight: A Revolution in Collector Design." *Science* 201 (1978):36.

Metz, W. "Energy Storage and Solar Power: An Exaggerated Problem." *Science* 200 (1978):1471.

Worthy, W. "Passive Solar Heating Systems Show Promise." *Chem. Eng. News,* September 11, 1978, p. 23.

Chalmers, B. "The Photovoltaic Generation of Electricity." *Sci. Am.* 235 (October 1976):34.

Hildebrandt, A. F., and Vant-Hull, L. L. "Power with Heliostats." *Science* 197 (1977):1139.

Duguay, M. A. "Solar Electricity: The Hybrid System Approach." *Am. Sci.* 65 (July–August 1977):422.

Hammond, A. L., and Metz, W. D. "Solar Energy Research: Making Solar After the Nuclear Model?" *Science* 197 (1977):241.

Caputo, R. S. "Solar Power Plants: Dark Horse in the Energy Stable." *Bull. Atom. Sci.* 33 (May 1977):46.

Johnston, W. D. "The Prospects for Photovoltaic Conversion." *Am. Sci.* 65 (November–December 1977):729.

Pollard, W. G. "The Long-Range Prospects for Solar Energy." *Am. Sci.* 64 (July–August 1976):424.

Rawls, R. "Prospects Improving for Wider Solar Energy Use." *Chem. Eng. News,* August 20, 1979, p. 22.

von Hippel, F., and Williams, R. H. "Toward a Solar Civilization." *Bull. Atom. Sci.* 33 (October 1977):12.

Lovins, A. "Energy Strategy: The Road Not Taken?" *Foreign Affairs,* October 1976.

Energy Conservation

Ford, K. W., et al., eds. "Efficient Use of Energy: A Physics Perspective, American Physics Society Studies on the Technical Aspects of the More Efficient Use of Energy." New York: American Institute of Physics, 1975.

Socolow, R. H. "Efficient Use of Energy."*Phys. Today* 28 (August 1975):23.

Schipper, L., and Lichtenberg, A. J. "Efficient Energy Use and Well-Being: The Swedish Example." *Science* 194 (1976):100.

Robinson, A. L. "Energy Storage (I): Using Electricity More Efficiently." *Science* 184 (1974):785.

Robinson, A. L. "Energy Storage (II): Developing Advanced Technologies." *Science* 184 (1974):884.

Fickett, A. P. "Fuel-Cell Power Plants." *Sci. Am.* 239 (December 1978):70.

Hirst, E. "Residential Energy Use Alternatives: 1976 to 2000." *Science* 194 (1976):1247.

Karkheck, J., Powell, J., and Beardsworth, E. "Prospects for District Heating in the United States." *Science* 195 (1977):948.

Hayes, E. T. "Energy Implications of Materials Processing." *Science* 191 (1976):661.

Hayes, E. "Energy Resources Available to the United States, 1985 to 2000." *Science* 203 (1979):233.

Reddy, A. K. "Energy Options for the Third World." *Bull. Atom. Sci.* 34 (May 1978):28.

PART II | ATMOSPHERE

1 | Earth's Radiation Balance

As we have seen, the sun provides us with a very large input of energy every day. Consequently, the earth must get rid of this energy at the same rate if it is to maintain a steady state. It does so by radiating light. Of course, the earth does not glow the way the sun does. The wavelengths of the earth's rays are too long to be detected by our eyes. A hot body gives off radiation with a range of wavelengths that decreases with increasing temperature. This is why a piece of iron when heated in a furnace glows red and then white as its temperature increases. Wavelengths are expressed in terms of billionths of meters, or nanometers (nm). The eye is sensitive to wavelengths between 400 and 700 nm, corresponding to the blue and red ends of the spectrum.

Figure 2.1 shows the spectral distribution of radiation from the sun as well as from the earth. The sun is a very hot body, and most of its rays fall in the region of visible wavelength. This is reasonable since our visual organs have evolved in response to sunlight. As shown by equation 1 in Figure 2.1, known at *Wein's law,* one can calculate the peak wavelength of the rays given off by a hot body by dividing its absolute temperature into a constant number, 2,900,000. The solar spectrum peaks at 483 nm, giving an estimate of the temperature at the surface of the sun of about 6,000° K. The earth, of course, is much cooler than this. If we take the average temperature to be about 290° K, we would expect from equation 1 a peak wavelength of about 10,000 nm, which is in good agreement with the earth's spectrum shown in Figure 2.1. In summary, while the earth absorbs radiation mainly in the visible region, characteristic of the high temperature at the surface of the sun, it gives off radiation at the same rate but at the much longer wavelengths characteristic of the earth's surface temperature.

The rate at which a hot body radiates energy is proportional to the fourth power of its absolute temperature, as shown by equation 2 in Figure 2.1, known as the *Stefan-Boltzmann law.* From the rate at which the earth absorbs energy from the sun, one can calculate the steady state temperature.

The solar flux incident on the earth is known to be 1.95 calories/cm²-minute. The fraction absorbed by the earth is one minus the average albedo, or 0.66.

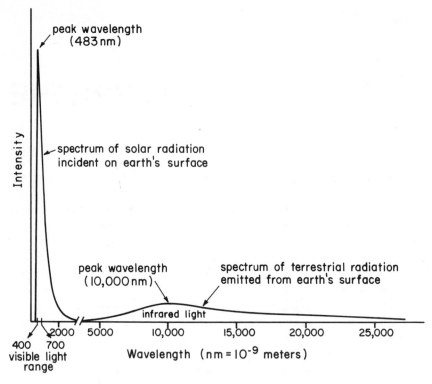

1. peak wavelength = $\dfrac{2.90 \times 10^6}{T}$ nm

2. total energy flux from
   surface of radiator = $82 \times 10^{-12}\, T^4$ calories/cm²- minute

(T = temperature in degrees Kelvin)

Figure 2.1 Spectral Distribution of Solar and Terrestrial Radiation

Averaging over the surface of the earth means dividing by four, because as seen from the sun the earth is a disk of area πr^2, where r is the earth's radius, whereas the total surface area of the earth is $4\pi r^2$. If the rate of radiation follows the Stefan-Boltzmann law, then energy balance requires that

$$82 \times 10^{-12} T^4 = \frac{1.95}{4} \times 0.7 \text{ calories/cm}^2\text{-minute}$$

This gives $T = 254°$ K, or $-30°$ C, which is actually the average temperature that prevails about 5 km above the surface of the earth. The earth-air system acts as if it radiates from somewhere in the middle of the atmosphere.

If the heat input to the earth is increased or decreased, the outflux will adjust accordingly, and the average temperature will move up or down. In the first part of this book, we mentioned that human consumption of energy in the form of fossil or nuclear fuels will equal the solar heat flux within another 14 doubling periods, which at current rates of increase corresponds to about 320 years. Using the fourth-power dependence of the total heat flux on the temperature, it is easy to calculate that the average temperature would then increase by 19%, or 46° C. Long before then severe effects, including the melting of the polar ice caps, would be felt.

Another way that human activities could upset the heat balance is by inadvertently changing the albedo. As mentioned earlier, the average value for the fraction of sunlight reflected and scattered back into space without being absorbed is about 34%. As illustrated in Figure 2.2, this represents an average over very large local variations, which could be affected by human activities. For example, the clearing of forest land for agriculture increases the albedo from about 15% to 20%. If erosion sets in, leading to dust bowl and eventually desert conditions, the albedo is further increased to about 28%. An area of particular

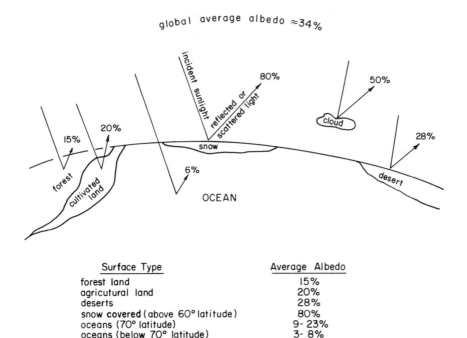

Surface Type	Average Albedo
forest land	15%
agricutural land	20%
deserts	28%
snow covered (above 60° latitude)	80%
oceans (70° latitude)	9- 23%
oceans (below 70° latitude)	3- 8%
clouds (average over all types)	50%
over entire surface	~ 34%

Figure 2.2 Variations in Albedo with Type of Surface on Earth

concern is the Arctic ice sheet—large masses of ice that melt and reform every year. This is a potentially unstable situation since the melting of ice leads to a decrease in the albedo from 80% to less than 25%. Therefore, a greater absorption of solar heat would cause an increased degree of melting with an accompanying decrease in the overall albedo. This would cause even more ice to melt in a positive feedback loop. There is a possibility that the instability might be increased if areas of the ice were covered with foreign matter that decreases the albedo, for example, oil that might spill and spread on the ice as a result of drilling and transporting petroleum in the Arctic region.

A related concern has to do with the dispersal of airborne particles in the atmosphere as a result of human activities. Both agriculture and industry release quantities of dust and fumes into the air, as do heating plants and automobiles. The increased particle loading of the atmosphere might affect the radiation balance. Figure 2.3 is a graphical estimate of the amounts of particles dispersed in the atmosphere over the past 100 years. The contribution from human activity, shown by the solid curve, is much less than the contribution from wind and other natural sources, but it is rising rapidly. Large temporary increases in particle concentrations have resulted from volcanic eruptions in the past. The effect of more particles in the atmosphere has generally been thought to be a cooling of the earth's surface as a result of increased scattering of the sun's rays. However, particles can absorb light as well as scatter it, as shown in Figure 2.4. Dark particles absorb light, whereas light particles reflect light. The absorbed light contributes to the heating of the earth's atmosphere, while the reflected light

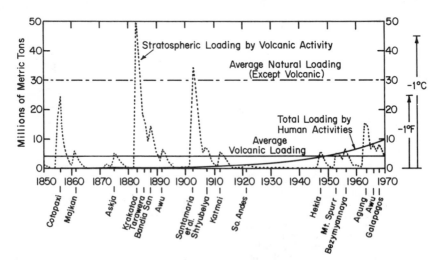

Figure 2.3 Natural and Man-made Particle Loading of Atmosphere

Source: "The Natural Stratosphere of 1974," Monograph 1, U.S. Department of Transportation, Climatic Impact Assessment Program (DOT-TST-75-51), September 1975, p. 8–24.

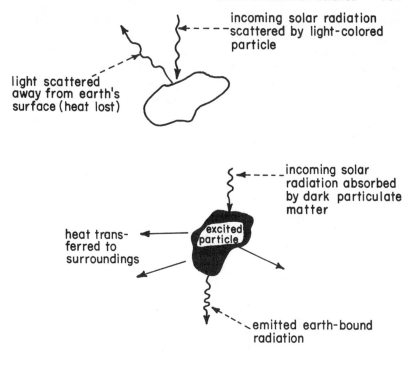

incoming solar radiation
scattered by light-colored
particle

light scattered
away from earth's
surface (heat lost)

incoming solar
radiation absorbed
by dark particulate
matter

heat trans-
ferred to
surroundings

excited
particle

emitted earth-bound
radiation

Earth's Surface

Figure 2.4   Scattering and Absorption of Radiation from Particulate Matter

takes heat away. Consequently, whether particles have a cooling or heating effect depends on their optical properties, which vary depending on their source. Coal dust absorbs more light than does sand. Understanding the effect of particles on climate therefore requires a detailed analysis of the sources as well as the overall loading.

Atmospheric Particles

Sources and sinks

Most airborne particles have natural sources: volcanic emissions, sea spray, dust carried from arid areas by wind, organic products of plant excretions. A small but increasing contribution arises from human activities: dust from plowing and overgrazing of arid land, mineral dust from mining and smelting, ash and smoke from industry, oxidation products of hydrocarbons and sulfur dioxide from burning petroleum and coal.

The particles in air have a wide size distribution, as shown in Figure 2.5, as a result of the dynamics of particle growth and removal. Small particles grow to larger ones via collisions and aggregation and gradually settle out. The settling velocity in wind-free air is given by the Stokes formula,

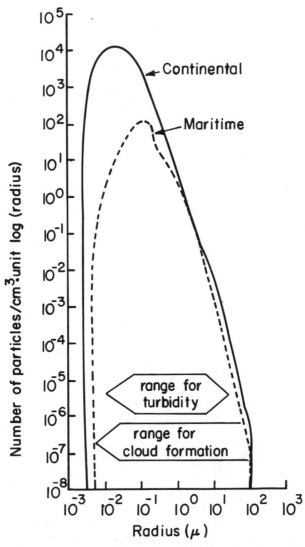

Figure 2.5 Size Distribution of Particulate Matter in the Lower Troposphere

$$v_s = \frac{2gr^2(\rho_p - \rho_a)}{9\eta} \tag{1}$$

where η is the viscosity of air (171×10^{-6} g/cm-sec), g is the gravitational force constant (978 cm/sec^2), r is the radius of the particle, and ρ_p and ρ_a are the densities of the particle and of the air, respectively. If the particle density is about that of water, 1 g/cm^3 (for which $\rho_a/\rho_p \ll 1$), equation (1) gives $v_s = 1$ cm/sec for $r = 10\ \mu$ (10^{-3} cm), and 10^{-4} cm/sec for $r = 0.1\ \mu$ (10^{-5} cm). From a height of 5 km, it would take the 10-μ particle 6 days and the 0.1-μ particle 159 years to settle to the earth.

The atmosphere is a turbulent region, however, and settling is a relatively minor mechanism (estimated at 10–20% of the total deposition rate) for particle removal.[1] Impaction by wind is a significant mechanism, but the major removal processes are "washout" and "rainout" associated with rainfall. Washout is the capture of particles by raindrops as they fall, while rainout is the removal of particles that actually serve as condensation points for the formation of raindrops.

Cloud formation

Particles are essential to the formation of raindrops and clouds. In principle, water condenses from the gas phase when its partial pressure, p, exceeds the equilibrium vapor pressure of liquid water, p_0. This is expressed in the free energy change, ΔG, for the phase change:

$$H_2O(g) \rightleftarrows H_2O(l)$$

$$\Delta G = -RT \ln \frac{p}{p_0}$$

where R is the gas constant (1.99 calories °K^{-1}) and T is the absolute temperature (°K). As the relative humidity, p/p_0, exceeds unity (100%), ΔG becomes negative, and liquid water forms spontaneously at equilibrium.

In pure air, however, the water molecules must first find a way to get together to form raindrops. Very small drops evaporate quickly, even at relative humidities higher than 100%, because of their large surface tension. In the condensation of a small number of molecules:

$$nH_2O \rightleftarrows (H_2O)_n$$

the surface free energy of the droplet is a significant part of the free energy change,

$$\Delta G = -nRT \ln \frac{p}{p_0} + 4\pi r^2 \gamma \tag{2}$$

where γ is the surface tension, r is the droplet radius, and n is the number of moles of water contained in the droplet, which can also be written as

$$n = \frac{4\pi}{3} r^3 \frac{\rho}{M} \tag{3}$$

where $\frac{4}{3}\pi r^3$ is the volume of the drop, ρ is its density (1 g/cm³), and M is the gram molecular weight (18 g). Thus ΔG is the result of two opposing terms that have a different dependence on r. Figure 2.6 is a plot of ΔG against r for a given value of p/p_0 (1.001, or 100.1% relative humidity). The curve goes through a maximum, which defines a critical radius, $r_c = 1$ μm. Droplets larger than this will accumulate more water molecules and become stable, but droplets smaller than 1 μm in radius will evaporate. A 1-μm drop contains 0.23×10^{-12} mole of water [see equation (3)] or 1.38×10^{11} molecules. (There are 6.02×10^{23} molecules in a mole.) It is very improbable that this many molecules can come together simultaneously to form a growing droplet; consequently water vapor in pure air at 100.1% humidity is stable indefinitely with respect to precipitation. The critical droplet radius depends on the extent to which p/p_0 exceeds unity, i.e., the extent to which the air is "supersaturated" with water. The dependence [obtained by differentiating equation (2) and setting $d(\Delta G)/dr$ equal to zero] is given by

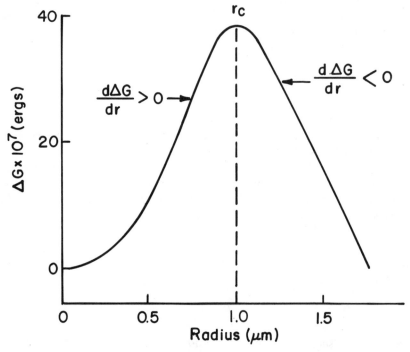

Figure 2.6   Variation of ΔG with Drop Size at $p/p_0 = (T = 20°C)$

$$r_c = \frac{2M\gamma}{\rho RT \ln (p/p_0)}$$

Thus r_c decreases slowly as p/p_0 increases. Pure air can be supersaturated to a high degree without precipitation.

In nature, however, condensation actually occurs in the range 100.1–101% relative humidity, corresponding to $r_c = 1$–0.1 μm. This is because there are many suspended particles in this size range, and they serve as condensation "nuclei." A film of water surrounding particles of this size or larger has sufficiently low surface tension to permit droplet growth rather than evaporation. The principle of rain-making by "cloud-seeding" is to inject into supersaturated vapor particles that are effective in nucleating rain drops.

There is a trade-off between droplet size and the number of condensation nuclei. A given amount of water vapor can form a small number of large drops or a large number of small ones. An excess of condensation nuclei can produce a cloud of droplets that are too small to fall as rain. The fogs that often hover over cities probably reflect the large number of condensation nuclei in polluted air. It is possible that a general increase in the number of atmospheric particles will lead to a corresponding increase in the cloud cover.

Light scattering and absorption

For very small particles and molecules, the amount of light scattering (Rayleigh scattering) is given by

$$s = \frac{128\pi^5 r^6}{3\lambda^4} \times \frac{m^2 - 1}{m^2 + 1}$$

where r and m are the radius and refractive index of the particle, respectively, and λ is the wavelength of light. Because of the $1/\lambda^4$ dependence, blue light is scattered more strongly than red. This is why the sky, which is seen in scattered light, is blue, while sunsets, which are seen in transmitted light, are red. The blue haze over the Smokey Mountains of the eastern United States is due to light scattering from small particles formed by the oxidation of volatile terpenes emitted by the sap of coniferous trees.

For particles that are large compared with the wavelength of light (0.4–0.7 μm in the visible region), the scattering is more complex, being the result of light waves that originate from different parts of the molecule. Their phases and intensities are related in a complex manner, described by the Mie scattering theory.[2,3] The wavelength dependence is less pronounced, and scattered light from large particles is white.

While the light scattering properties of particles can be taken into account, their effect on the radiation balance also depends on their absorptivities. Dark particles absorb more light than they scatter and, therefore, heat up the atmosphere. If the particles absorb more strongly than the earth's surface beneath them (e.g., snow and sand), then their net effect could actually be to heat up the earth rather than cool it off. This makes general quantitative estimates of the effect of particles very difficult.

The transmission of light upon passage through M absorbing molecules is given by

$$T = \frac{I}{I_0} = e^{-kM} \qquad (4)$$

where I_0 and I are the incident and transmitted light intensities, respectively, and k is the absorptivity, which depends on the wavelength and the nature of the molecular transitions. A plot of k against wavelength shows the absorption spectrum of the molecule. Equation (4) has the same exponential form as does the equation for radioactive decay (see page 8) and has a similar derivation. Each molecule in the light path has the same probability of absorbing a photon, and the fractional loss in intensity is proportional to the number of molecules:

$$\frac{dI}{I} = -k \, dM \qquad (5)$$

Equation (4) is the integrated form of equation (5).

Exactly the same equation applies for the loss of light due to scattering from a turbid sample,

$$\frac{I}{I_0} = e^{-k_s n} \qquad (6)$$

where n is the number of scattering particles and k_s is a scattering parameter, which is the reciprocal of the number of particles required to reduce the incident light intensity by a factor of e (2.718). Equation (6) can be rewritten as:

$$\frac{I}{I_0} = e^{-K\pi r^2 c_n l} \qquad (7)$$

where l is the light path length, c_n is the number of particles per unit volume, r is the radius of the particle, and K is the total scattering coefficient, which equals 2.0 for particles that are large compared with the wavelength of the light. The product $\pi r^2 c_n l$ is the number of particles times the fraction of the cross-sectional area they occupy.

The turbidity of clouds increases with the number of condensation nuclei. The liquid content, W, per unit volume in a cloud is

$$W = \frac{4}{3} \pi r^3 c_n$$

Solving for r and substituting in equation (7), we obtain

$$\frac{I}{I_0} = e^{-K(3/4\pi \frac{1}{3}W)^{2/3}c_n^{1/3}l}$$

For a given cloud size (i.e., constant W and l), the scattering increases as the particles decrease in size (r decreases) and increase in number (c_n increases). Particles increase the albedo indirectly by increasing the number of cloud droplets.

2 | Greenhouse Effect

What about the air molecules through which radiation passes to and from the earth? How do they affect the heat flow? Table 2.1 shows the gaseous composition of the atmosphere. It is 78% nitrogen, by volume, 21% oxygen, 0.9% inert gas argon, and 0.03% carbon dioxide. There are many other gases present in trace quantities. All of them together make up less than 0.01% of the total. The units usually used for measuring atmospheric gases present at low concentrations are parts per million, which can be obtained from the percentage by multiplying by 10,000.

The table gives no value for water vapor, whose contribution varies greatly from place to place. While all the other constituents are well mixed throughout the atmosphere, this is not true of water. The amount of water in the air depends

Table 2.1   The Gaseous Composition
of Unpolluted Air (dry basis)

	Volume (%)	Volume (ppm)
Nitrogen	78.09	780,900
Oxygen	20.94	209,400
Water	—	—
Argon	0.93	9,300
Carbon dioxide	0.03	325
Neon	Trace	18
Helium	Trace	5.2
Methane	Trace	1.0–1.2
Krypton	Trace	1.0
Nitrous oxide	Trace	0.5
Hydrogen	Trace	0.5
Xenon	Trace	0.08
Organic vapors	Trace	~0.02

Source: A. C. Stern, H. C. Wohlers, R. W. Boubel, and W. P. Lowry, *Fundamentals of Air Pollution* (New York: Academic Press, 1973), p. 21.

on the vapor pressure of liquid water, which depends strongly on the temperature. Moreover, water molecules are being constantly evaporated and reprecipi-
tated as rain. The total number of water molecules in the atmosphere at any time
is about 0.4% of the air molecules.

All the constituents listed in Table 2.1 are transparent to most of the sun's
rays. None of them absorbs light significantly in the visible region of the spectrum. The situation is different in the infrared region, however, where the earth
emits its radiation. Neither nitrogen nor oxygen absorbs infrared rays, but carbon
dioxide and water vapor do. Figure 2.7 shows the absorption spectra of these
molecules, that is, the intensity of light absorption as a function of wavelength.
These two spectra add up to effectively block a large fraction of the earth's
emitted radiation, as illustrated in the top graph of the figure. Some of the
terrestrial radiation does escape without absorption in a relatively small fre-

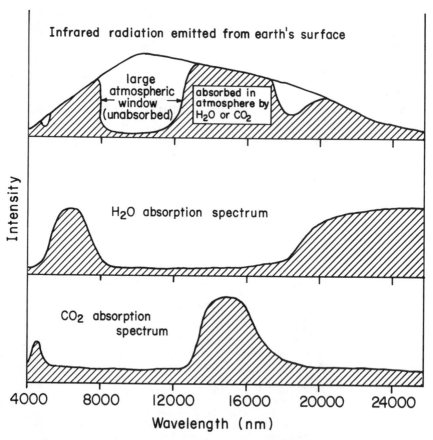

Figure 2.7   Absorption of Terrestrial Radiation by Water and Carbon Dioxide

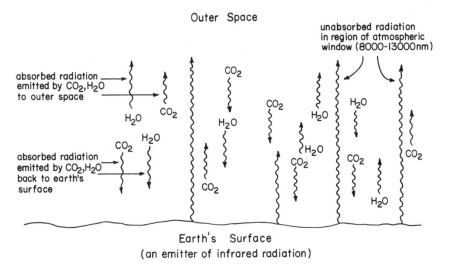

Figure 2.8   The Greenhouse Effect

quency range between 8,000 and 13,000 nm. This is called the *atmospheric window*.

The absorption of the earth's rays by carbon dioxide and water is of great importance to the climate on our planet. The overall effect is to heat up the earth's surface by a phenomenon commonly called the *greenhouse effect,* which is shown schematically in Figure 2.8. The light absorbed by carbon dioxide and water can be emitted again. The radiation can be reemitted in all directions, with equal probability upward and downward. The net result of this is that part of the earth's radiation returns to the surface and raises the surface temperature to warmer than what it would be in the absence of an atmosphere. This effect causes a change of about 35° C, the difference between the 254° K temperature calculated earlier for the earth as a radiating body and the actual average temperature at the surface. The overall radiation balance is not affected by this, of course, since the earth must still lose as much energy as it absorbs; what changes is the temperature distribution in the atmosphere. The surface of the earth is heated up at the expense of the upper layers of the air.

As far as we surface dwellers are concerned, however, it is the surface temperature that counts, and there has been concern that the greenhouse effect will be magnified by the increasing amounts of carbon dioxide produced by the rapid burning of the fossil fuel stores. We saw earlier that the burning of fossil fuels has a negligible effect on the oxygen content of the atmosphere, which is very large, but an appreciable effect on the carbon dioxide content which is currently only 325 ppm. The upper part of Figure 2.9 shows the increase in industrial carbon dioxide production during the last century. The curve is exponential,

(i)
Industrial CO_2 Production Since 1860

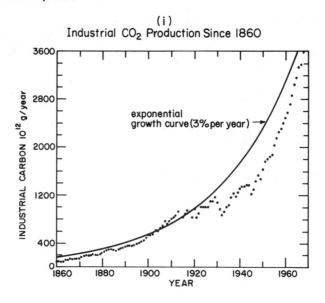

(ii)
Mean Monthly Values of CO_2 Concentration at Mauna Loa, Hawaii (1958 – 1971)

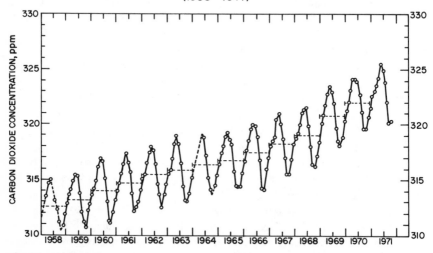

ANNUAL→ 0.60 0.80 0.62 0.82 0.35 0.60 0.37 0.67 0.77 0.77 1.79 1.20
CHANGE, ppm year⁻¹

Figure 2.9   Buildup of Carbon Dioxide in the Atmosphere

Source: G. M. Woodwell and E. V. Pecan, eds., *Carbon and the Biosphere* (Springfield, Va.: Technical Information Center, U.S. Atomic Energy Commission, August 1973), pp. 22, 90.

paralleling the curve of energy consumption. The second graph in the figure shows the mean monthly carbon dioxide concentrations in the atmosphere over a measuring station in Hawaii for the past two decades. There are large seasonal fluctuations associated with the yearly cycle of plant life. The plants grow in the spring and summer and decay in the fall and winter, giving their carbon dioxide back to the atmosphere. Underlying this seasonal variation is a steady upward trend in the average value. Since 1958, the value has increased from about 312 ppm to the present average value of 325 ppm.

However, the rate of increase is only about 50% of that expected if all the carbon dioxide emitted by human activity during those years were added to the total. Evidently 50% of the carbon dioxide produced does not stay in the atmosphere. Figure 2.10 diagrams the sources of atmospheric carbon dioxide and also the removal mechanisms, commonly known as the *sinks*. One sink is the ocean, which contains very large amounts of carbon dioxide in the form of the bicarbonate ion and accounts for most of the carbon dioxide removal, according to recent studies. Another possible sink is the biomass, that is, the living green plants themselves. It is known from laboratory experiments that green plants increase their rate of photosynthesis in response to an increase in the carbon dioxide concentration. This could be happening on a global scale. But the growth and shrinkage of the biomass depend on much more than the carbon dioxide concentration. They depend on other factors that affect plant growth and on human activities, particularly the widespread clearing of forested areas for agricultural purposes. It is very difficult to estimate the size of the total biomass, and we do not know whether it is presently growing or shrinking.

The temperature effects of carbon dioxide and water vapor are coupled. As the surface temperature rises, because of increased amounts of carbon dioxide, more water evaporates, and the water vapor increases the temperature further. The combined effect can be calculated to be a 3° C rise in the surface temperature for a doubling of the carbon dioxide concentration. Also general precipitation in-

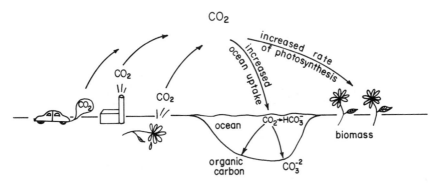

Figure 2.10   Sources and Sinks of Carbon Dioxide

creases by 7% because of the increased rate of water evaporation. Extrapolation of the present trend suggests that the carbon dioxide concentration will double by the year 2050.

New considerations in studying the greenhouse effect are the chlorofluoro-methane gases, called CFMs, which are used in refrigerators and as spray can propellants. There are two kinds of CFMs: $CFCL_3$ and CF_2CL_2. Both are very inert, which is one of their desirable properties from the point of view of the consumer, and they accumulate in the atmosphere. The major controversy about CFMs has to do with their impact on the ozone layer, which we will discuss shortly. It has been pointed out that these molecules also absorb infrared light

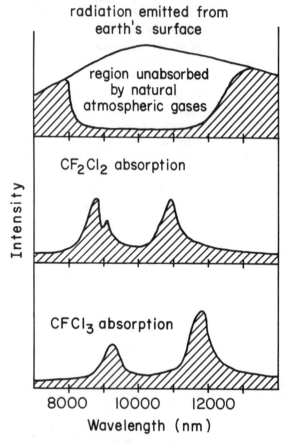

Figure 2.11 Absorption Spectra of Chlorofluoromethanes, CF_2Cl_2 and $CFCl_3$, Coincidence with Atmospheric Window Region*

*Region from 8,000 to 13,000 nm (see Figure 2.7)

strongly and that their absorption bands fall in the window region of carbon dioxide and water absorption, which, as we saw in Figure 2.7, is the region of maximum radiation from the earth. The CFM spectra and the window region are shown in Figure 2.11. The effect is strong enough so that an increase in the surface temperature of nearly a degree might result from CFM concentrations on the order of 2 parts per billion (ppb), which would be expected by the year 2000 if levels of injection of CFMs into the atmosphere were maintained at the 1975 level.

The mean global temperature has been increasing gradually throughout the first half of this century, as shown in the top graph of Figure 2.12, in which a smooth curve is drawn through the yearly temperature fluctuation. This rise correlates with the increase in carbon dioxide production associated with the Industrial Revolution. It has been suggested that the greenhouse effect is respon-

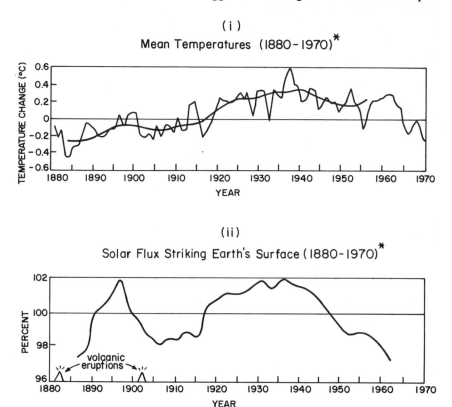

Figure 2.12   Recent Trends in Temperature and Solar Radiation Flux (Northern Hemisphere)

*Baselines have been arbitrarily set.
Source: Adapted from "The Natural Stratosphere of 1974," Monograph 1, U.S. Department of Transportation, Climatic Impact Assessment Program (DOT-TST-75-51), September 1975, p. 8–47.

sible. On the other hand, the temperature seems to have peaked in about 1940 and has been declining perceptibly since then. This downward trend might be associated with the increasing production of particles, according to our previous discussion. The second graph in Figure 2.12 shows the solar radiation flux at the surface of the earth. There is a suggestive similarity with the overall shape of the temperature record including the dip in the early 1900s. This dip and the earlier one before 1890 can be associated with atmospheric dust from large volcanic eruptions, as shown in Figure 2.3, and it is likely that the radiation curve reflects the amount of particles in the air.

The average temperature can be traced back over a longer period of time using a variety of geophysical techniques as well as fossil records. When this is done, much larger temperature fluctuations are observed, as illustrated in Figure 2.13. The graph on the left shows that over the past few hundred years, temperature fluctuations of more than 1° C were experienced. Temperatures were appreciably lower from about 1400 to 1850. This period is known as the Little Ice Age in Europe. As seen in the graph on the right, there were larger fluctuations over a

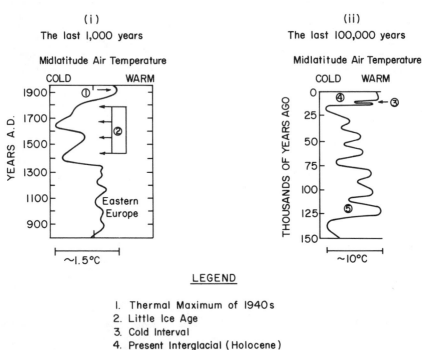

LEGEND

1. Thermal Maximum of 1940s
2. Little Ice Age
3. Cold Interval
4. Present Interglacial (Holocene)
5. Last Previous Interglacial (Eemian)

Figure 2.13   Natural Fluctuations in Earth's Temperature

Source: *Understanding Climatic Change, A Program for Action* (Washington, D.C.: National Academy of Sciences, 1975), p. 130.

span of hundreds of thousands of years. These reflect the Ice Ages, the last one of which reached its lowest temperature about 20,000 years ago.

We see that the assessment of human impacts on the climate must be superimposed on this large natural variation. Figure 2.14 shows an attempt to do this for the carbon dioxide greenhouse effect. The expected 0.3° C rise per 10% increase in carbon dioxide concentration is added to a projection of the natural temperature fluctuations obtained from an examination of the temperature record over the past several hundred years. If this approach is correct, then the current cooling trend should soon level off and be followed by a rather steep rise in temperature. This calculation does not consider contributions to the greenhouse effect by the chlorofluoromethanes, and conceivably by other organic molecules currently being emitted into the atmosphere, which would magnify the predicted temperature increase.

Relatively small average temperature changes could seriously disrupt world food production. A 1° C decline would decrease the growing period in the northern latitudes sufficiently to eliminate much of the wheat crop in Canada and large areas in the Soviet Union. On the other hand, an increase in average temperature would shift the wheat-growing zones toward the poles, away from fertile soils and onto poorer quality ground. Also, a warming of the surface layers of the ocean would reduce the vertical circulation that carries nutrients to the surface from the deeper layers. Biological productivity would therefore decrease.

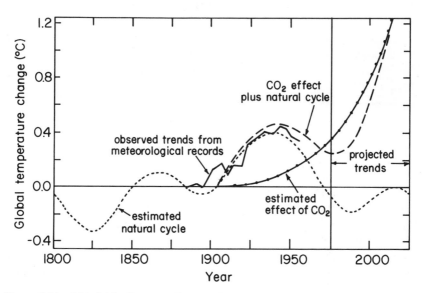

Figure 2.14 A Model for Projected Trend in Global Temperature Due to the Greenhouse Effect

Source: W. S. Broecker, *Science* 189 (1975):461.

At the moment we simply do not know enough about the determinants of long-term effects on climate to make any predictions with confidence. This is an active and important area of research.

Infrared Absorption
and the Greenhouse Effect

While absorption of visible and ultraviolet radiation is associated with electronic transitions in molecules, absorption in the infrared region is associated with vibrational transitions. The atoms in molecules behave much as if they were balls connected by springs, the springs being the chemical bonds. The resistance of the bonds to stretching and bending determines the stiffness of the springs. The stiffer the springs, the greater is the frequency of the vibrations.

Light may induce molecular vibrations when its frequency matches the vibrational frequency.* The absorption of light depends both on this frequency match and on the change in the dipole moment of the molecule during the vibration. Some vibrations do not change the dipole moment and are therefore "infrared-inactive." The major air constituents, nitrogen and oxygen, do not absorb infrared radiation, because their vibrations, which stretch the bond between two identical atoms, produce no charge separation. If the atoms are not the same, as in carbon monoxide and nitric oxide, then the vibrations absorb infrared light; these gases are insignificant constituents of the atmosphere on a global basis, however.

Polyatomic molecules have more numerous vibrations, at least some of which are "infrared-active." The main infrared absorbers in the atmosphere are water and carbon dioxide. At the long wavelengths of terrestrial radiation, the bending vibrations of these molecules

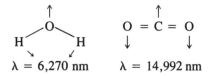

$$\lambda = 6{,}270 \text{ nm} \qquad \lambda = 14{,}992 \text{ nm}$$

are chiefly responsible for absorption.

The vibrationally excited molecules lose their energy either by colliding with other molecules and heating up their surroundings, or by reemitting the radiation. Either process occurs in all directions. At any level of the atmosphere half the absorbed energy flows up and the other half flows back down. The absorption of terrestrial radiation retards the flow of energy to space. The total flux is unal-

---

*The relationship between wavelength and frequency of light is given by: $\lambda = c/\nu$ where λ is the wavelength, c is the speed of light and ν is the frequency.

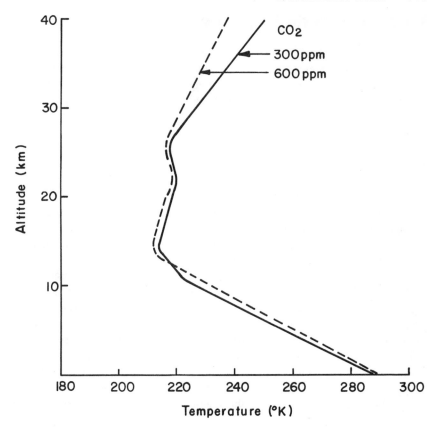

Figure 2.15   Effect of Doubling the Carbon Dioxide Concentration on the Temperature Profile of the Atmosphere

Source: S. Manabe and R. Wetherald, *J. Atmos. Sci.* **24** (1967):241.

tered, but the flux gradient and therefore the temperature gradient are altered. The earth's surface and the lower levels of the atmosphere are heated, while the upper layers are cooled. The negative lapse rate (slope of the temperature versus the altitude curve) of the troposphere, shown in Figure 2.16, is established in this way.

Raising the carbon dioxide concentration is expected to increase the lapse rate. The earth's surface would be warmed further and the upper atmosphere would be cooled further. The effect would be amplified by the increased evaporation of water at the higher surface temperature, thereby increasing the atmospheric infrared absorption by water. A plot of this coupling effect is shown in Figure 2.15.

3 | Atmospheric Structure

Our gaseous envelope extends many miles up from the surface of the earth. With respect to its major chemical constituents, which we examined in Table 2.1, the atmosphere is quite uniform throughout its extent, except for water vapor, which is concentrated in the lower region. In other respects, the air is far from uniform. It grows thinner with increasing altitude. The density falls off roughly logarithmically with increasing distance from the surface. About 70% of the mass of the atmosphere is contained in a blanket 10 km thick. Even less uniform than the density is the temperature, which depends on altitude as shown in Figure 2.16. The slope of the curve of temperature versus altitude is called the *lapse rate*. Figure 2.16 shows several reversals of the lapse rate. Up to about 10 km, temperature decreases uniformly with increasing altitude. This reflects the fact that the atmosphere in this lower region is heated from below by the earth's radiation. Above 10 km, however, the temperature increases again with increasing altitude, reaching a maximum near 50 km and decreasing once again beyond this. The maximum in the temperature profile reflects a heating process high in the atmosphere due to the absorption of solar radiation in the near ultraviolet region by a band of ozone, O_3. We will examine the ozone layer and its properties shortly. Beyond about 90 km, the temperature rises once more due to the absorption of solar rays in the far ultraviolet region by atmospheric gases, principally oxygen. These far ultraviolet rays are sufficiently energetic to ionize molecules and break them into their constituent atoms. Because of the thinness of the atmosphere at such high altitudes, fragments recombine only rarely, and an appreciable fraction of the gases in this region, called the *thermosphere,* exist as atoms or ions.

The structure of the temperature profile reflects a physical layering of the atmosphere as well. A negative lapse rate leads to convection of the air; warm air rises from below and cool air sinks. But a positive lapse rate reflects a region of stability with respect to convection, since warm air overlies cool air. The change from negative to positive lapse rate is called a *temperature inversion,* and the point at which this change occurs marks a stable boundary between two physically distinct layers of air. Local temperature inversions are quite common over many cities, particularly those nestled in surrounding mountains or, as in the case of Los Angeles, where prevailing winds from the ocean blow cool air into a region ringed on three sides by mountains. Warm air flowing over the mountain tops traps the cool air below, allowing pollutants to build up for considerable periods. Anyone flying into Los Angeles on a sunny day is likely to see the local temperature inversion and the quite distinct boundary between the clear air above and the brown smoggy air below.

The temperature inversion shown in Figure 2.16 at an altitude of about 10 km is called the *tropopause.* It marks a global layering of the atmosphere into the

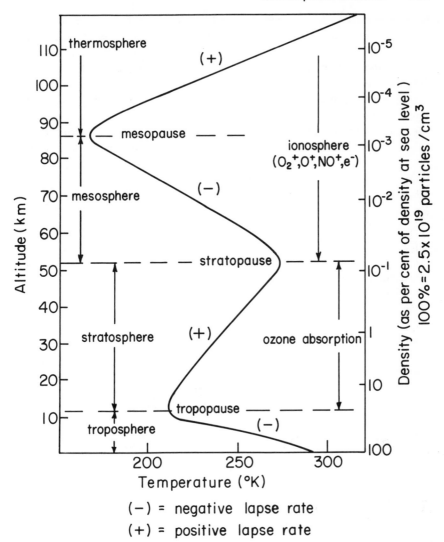

(−) = negative lapse rate
(+) = positive lapse rate

Figure 2.16   Layer Structure of the Atmosphere

troposphere below and the stratosphere above. The troposphere contains 70% of the mass of the atmosphere. Because of its negative lapse rate, the air it contains is mixed rapidly by convection. It is also a region of much turbulence due to the global energy flow that results from the imbalances of heating and cooling rates between the equator and the poles. The stratosphere, on the other hand, is a quiescent layer; because of its positive lapse rate, it mixes slowly. The tropopause itself is a stable boundary and the flux of air across it is low. Residence times of molecules or particles in the stratosphere are measured on a scale of years. The air in it is quite thin so that pollutants that reach, or are injected into, the stratosphere have a relatively greater global impact than they would in the much denser troposphere.

Concern about pollution of the stratosphere centers on possible threats to the layer of ozone it contains. This triatomic form of the element oxygen serves two essential functions in the stratosphere. It protects living matter on earth from the harmful effects of the sun's ultraviolet rays, and it provides the heat source

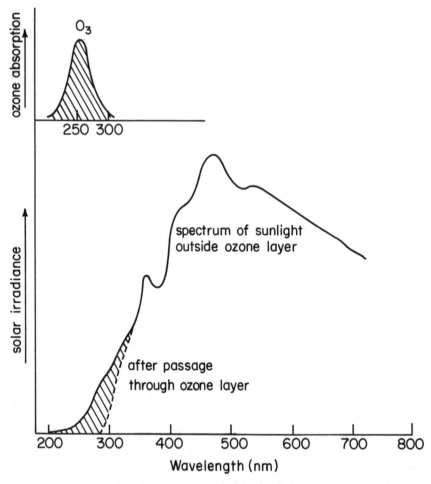

Figure 2.17 Absorption of Sun's Ultraviolet Light by Ozone

for layering the atmosphere into a quiescent stratosphere and a turbulent troposphere.

Figure 2.17 shows the spectrum of the sun's rays in the visible and ultraviolet regions. Also shown is part of the absorption spectrum of ozone. It has a peak at about 260 nm. Although the ozone layer extends over tens of kilometers in altitude, if compressed to 1 atm pressure its thickness would be only 3 mm on the average. Nevertheless, its ultraviolet absorption is strong enough to eliminate much of the ultraviolet tail of the solar radiation spectrum at the surface of the earth. These ultraviolet rays are harmful to life. They carry enough energy to break the bonds of organic molecules and produce reactive fragments. Ultraviolet radiation produces sunburn and also skin cancer, particularly in people who have light pigmentation. The damage done to living tissue as a function of solar wavelength is shown in Figure 2.18 and is commonly known as the *action spectrum*. The solid curve in the figure shows the spectrum of the skin's sunburn sensitivity at constant light intensity. Also shown is the spectrum of the solar rays at ground level. The product of these two curves gives the actual action spectrum for sunburn, that is, the response of the skin to solar radiation. The overlap of ground-level radiation with the sunburn sensitivity curve would be much greater if it were not for the filtering effects of the ozone layer.

Figure 2.19 shows data that support the connection between exposure to solar ultraviolet radiation and the incidence of skin cancer. Both the incidence of skin cancer and the solar ultraviolet flux decrease with increasing distance from the

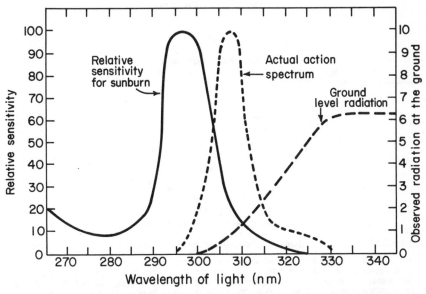

Figure 2.18 Action Spectrum of Ultraviolet Radiation Damage to Living Tissue

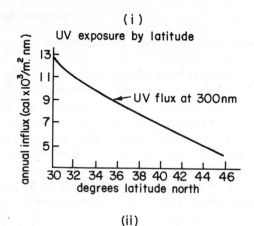

(i)
UV exposure by latitude

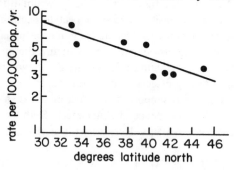

(ii)
Malignant melanoma skin cancer by latitude

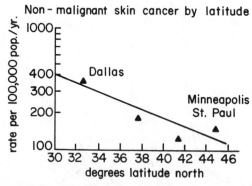

(iii)
Non-malignant skin cancer by latitude

Figure 2.19 Correlation Between Skin Cancer Incidence* and Ultraviolet Exposure

*Caucasian total age-adjusted incidence in the United States, 1970.
Source: Top graph: Adapted from data of F. S. Johnson, et al., *Photochem. Photobiol.* **23** (1976):179. Middle and bottom graphs: A. J. Grobecker, et al., "The Effects of Stratospheric Pollution by Aircraft" (DOT-TST-75-50) (Springfield, Va.: National Technical Information Service, U.S. Atomic Energy Commission, December 1974), p. 35.

equator. The sun's rays fall more directly at lower latitudes, and also the ozone layer is thinner over the equator than over the poles. As shown in the figure, between 30 and 46 degrees latitude north, the ultraviolet flux is reduced by a factor of three, the incidence of malignant skin cancer appears to decrease by a factor of nearly three, and nonmalignant cancer decreases by a factor of nearly four. Green plants are also susceptible to damage by ultraviolet rays. Their light-harvesting photosynthetic apparatus is tuned to visible radiation and can be destroyed by sufficiently intense ultraviolet radiation. Also, the genetic material of both plants and animals, the DNA molecules, is known to be susceptible to ultraviolet radiation damage. It is likely that higher forms of life could not have evolved on earth until the protective ozone layer had developed.

Ultraviolet Absorption by Ozone

For an absorbing constituent of the atmosphere, the total number of molecules through which the light passes can be expressed as an equivalent thickness, l, of a global layer of the gas, brought to standard temperature ($0°$ C) and pressure (1 atm). Then equation (4) on page 106 can be written,

$$T = \frac{I}{I_0} = e^{-\epsilon l} \tag{1}$$

where ϵ is the absorptivity (sometimes called the *extinction coefficient*) expressed in units of inverse length. The transmittance depends strongly on ϵl. If this product is 1.0, then 37% of the incident light is transmitted, whereas if it is 10.0, only 0.005% is transmitted.

The equivalent thickness of ozone at $0°$ C and 1 atm is 0.34 cm on the average. Figure 2.20 shows a plot, on a log scale, of the ozone absorptivity versus wavelength. The product ϵl (value of the graph times 0.34) goes from 1 to 10 between 310 and 290 nm, the critical region for sunburn and perhaps skin cancer (see Figures 2.18 and 2.19).

The effect of a small decrease in the ozone thickness can be estimated by differentiating equation (1):

$$dT = -\epsilon e^{-\epsilon l}\, dl$$

Dividing through by equation (1) gives the relative response:

$$\frac{dT}{T} = -\epsilon\, dl = -\epsilon\, l\, \frac{dl}{l}$$

Thus a given fractional decrease in l produces a fractional increase in T which is amplified by the product ϵl. A 1% decrease in the ozone layer gives a 1% increase in ultraviolet transmittance at 310 nm, a 3% increase at 300 nm, and 10% at 290 nm.

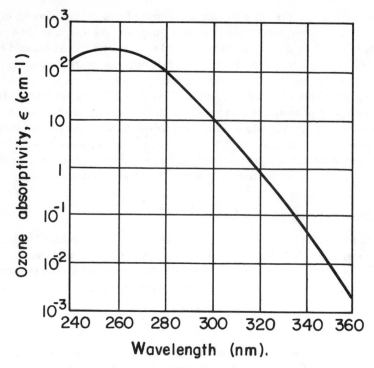

Figure 2.20 Ozone Absorptivity As a Function of Wavelength

4 | Ozone Chemistry

Figure 2.21 shows the reactions that are responsible for the buildup of ozone in the stratosphere. As we mentioned earlier, the ultraviolet photons of the sun have enough energy to split oxygen molecules into oxygen atoms high in the atmosphere. This is shown in reaction 1. Reaction 2 shows an oxygen atom combining with another oxygen molecule to form the triatomic molecule, ozone. Because the oxygen atom is very energetic, a third molecule labeled M must be present at the encounter in order to carry away some of the excess energy, otherwise the ozone molecule would fly apart as fast as it was formed. M can be any molecule that happens to be present. In the atmosphere it is most likely to be nitrogen or another molecule of oxygen. Reactions 3 and 4 are ozone destruction reactions. As we have seen, ozone can absorb solar rays in the ultraviolet region. When this happens, there is a high probability that the excited ozone molecule will dissociate into an oxygen molecule and an oxygen atom, as shown in reaction 3. Also, an oxygen atom can combine with an ozone molecule to form two oxygen molecules, as in reaction 4.

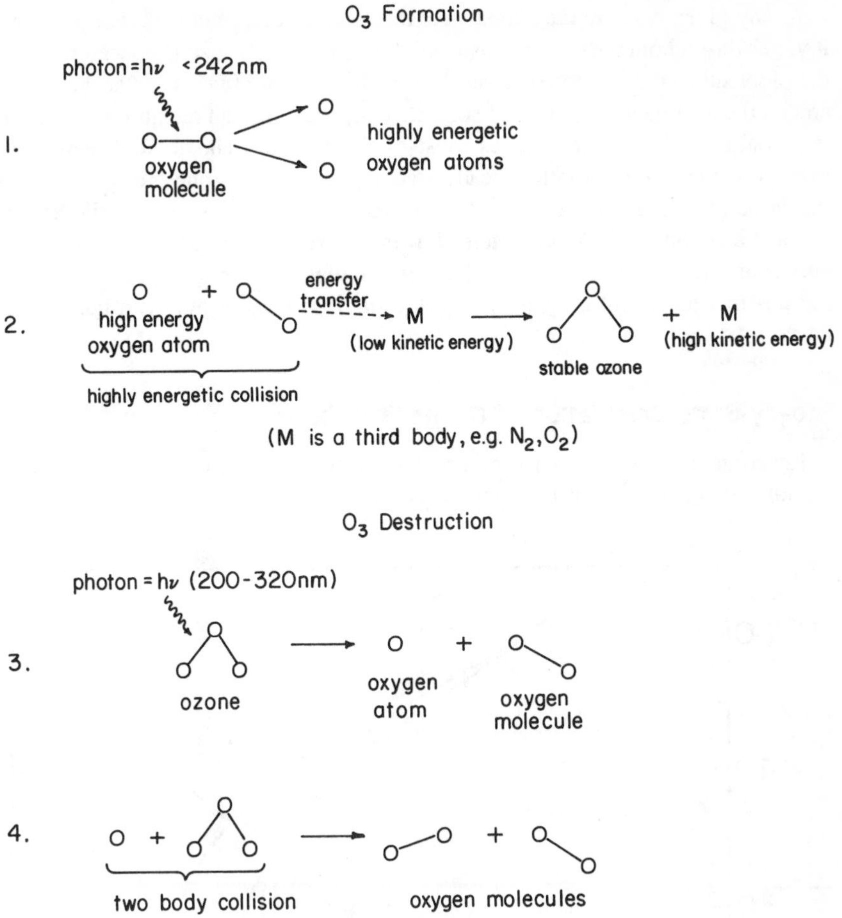

O₃ Formation

(M is a third body, e.g. N_2, O_2)

O₃ Destruction

Figure 2.21   Reactions of Ozone

Ozone is highly unstable compared with the normal form of oxygen, O_2. At equilibrium, less than 1 part in 10^{25} of the oxygen in the atmosphere is present as ozone. The actual ratio of ozone to oxygen reaches values as high as about 1 part in 30,000 at an altitude of 30 km. Evidently the ozone layer is very far from being at equilibrium because the ozone-destroying reactions are not instantaneous. The actual ozone concentration depends on the rate of the destruction reactions compared with the rate of the formation reactions. The rate of formation depends on the flux of ultraviolet solar radiation in the stratosphere. If this flux were constant, we would have a steady-state condition in which the rate of formation is equal to the rate of destruction. We could then write down the rate equations and solve them for the steady-state concentration of ozone.

At any given place in the atmosphere the solar flux is, of course, not constant. It varies throughout the day and also with the seasons. The ozone concentration is therefore subject to large variations. These variations are fairly regular, however, and on the average the ultraviolet solar flux depends only on the altitude, becoming smaller at lower altitudes as most of the rays are absorbed. When these average values are used in the steady-state equation, the ozone profile shown as the dashed line in Figure 2.22 can be calculated. Also shown, as the solid line, is the actual ozone profile as obtained from averaged measurements. The two curves are quite similar in shape, but the calculated curve gives ozone concentrations that are about a factor of two too high, at least at the maximum in the curve.

Steady-State Calculation of Ozone Distribution

Reaction rates are given by the products of the reactant concentrations times the rate constants, k. For the four reactions in Figure 2.21:

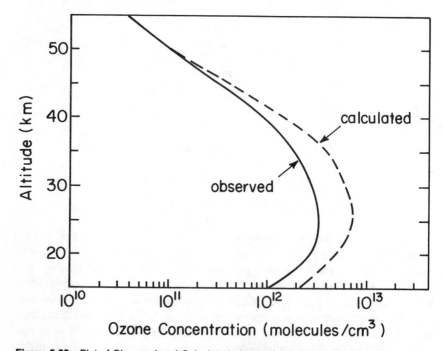

Figure 2.22 Plot of Observed and Calculated* Atmospheric Ozone Concentrations

*Calculation does not include reactions with NO_x and Cl (see Figures 2.23 and 2.24).
Source: *Report of the Study of Man's Impact on Climate (SMIC)* (Cambridge, Mass.: MIT Press, 1971), p. 268.

rate 1 $= k_1(O_2)$
rate 2 $= k_2(O)(O_2)(M)$
rate 3 $= k_3(O_3)$
rate 4 $= k_4(O)(O_3)$

The rate of ozone production is rate 2, while the loss rate is rate 3 + rate 4. The ozone steady-state condition is

$$\text{rate 2} = \text{rate 3} + \text{rate 4}$$

or

$$k_2(O)(O_2)(M) = k_3(O_3) + k_4(O)(O_3) \tag{1}$$

In this expression (O_2) and (M) (the concentration of air molecules) are known, and the rate constants are known from experiments. There are two unknowns, (O_3) and (O). In order to eliminate one of them, an additional equation is needed. This can be provided by the steady-state condition for oxygen atoms, whose production and loss rates must also balance. Their rate of production is twice the rate of reaction 1 (two oxygen atoms produced per O_2 molecule split) plus the rate of reaction 3, while the loss rate is rate 2 + rate 4:

$$2(\text{rate 1}) + \text{rate3} = \text{rate2} + \text{rate4}$$

or

$$2k_1(O_2) + k_3(O_3) = k_2(O)(O_2)(M) + k_4(O)(O_3) \tag{2}$$

Equations (1) and (2) can now be solved for the steady-state concentrations of O and O_3. For example, subtraction of equation (2) from equation (1) gives:

$$2k_2(O)(O_2)(M) = 2k_1(O_2) + 2k_3(O_3) \tag{3}$$

which can be solved for (O). The expression is simplified if we assume that $k_1(O_2) \ll k_3(O_3)$, i.e., that photolysis of O_2, reaction 1, produces far fewer O atoms than does photolysis of O_3, reaction 3. This assumption turns out to be valid for the lower reaches of the stratosphere, where O_3 is important because the flux of solar photons is much smaller in the far ultraviolet region (O_2 splitting) than in the near ultraviolet (O_3 splitting). Dropping $2k_1(O_2)$ from equation (3), we obtain

$$(O) = \frac{k_3}{k_2(M)} \frac{(O_3)}{(O_2)} \tag{4}$$

Addition of equations (1) and (2) gives

$$2k_1(O_2) = 2k_4(O)(O_3) \tag{5}$$

After substituting equation (4), we can solve for the $(O_3)/(O_2)$ ratio:

$$\frac{(O_3)}{(O_2)} = \left(\frac{k_1 k_2 (M)}{k_3 k_4} \right)^{\frac{1}{2}} \tag{6}$$

The value of this quantity depends strongly on the altitude. The concentration of air molecules, (M), decreases strongly with increasing altitude, both k_1 and k_3 increase because the photon flux increases, while k_2 and k_4 increase slightly because the temperature increases with increasing altitude in the stratosphere. At an altitude of 30 km, the concentration of air molecules is $10^{17.7}$ molecules/cm^3, while the approximate values of the rate constants, expressed with this concentration unit (and averaged over the earth's surface), are $k_1 = 10^{-11}$, $k_2 = 10^{-32.7}$, $k_3 = 10^{-3}$, and $k_4 = 10^{-15}$. Inserting these numbers into equation (6) gives $(O_3)/(O_2) = 10^{-4}$. This calculation can be repeated at other altitudes, with appropriate modification of the constants, and the result is the dotted curve in Figure 2.22. The $(O_3)/(O_2)$ ratio peaks at about 30 km. At higher altitudes, ozone photolysis (reaction 3 in Figure 2.21) is increasingly rapid, whereas at lower altitudes, net ozone formation is limited by the decreasing supply of O atoms from reaction 1.

The calculated ozone distribution has the same shape as the measured distribution (solid line in Figure 2.22), but the calculated values are about a factor of two too high. The likeliest explanation of the discrepancy is that there are other mechanisms for ozone destruction than those so far considered.

5 | Nitrogen Oxides

The likeliest reason for the discrepancy between the actual and the calculated ozone concentrations is that we have not considered reactions that can significantly speed up the destruction of ozone. Many such reactions have been considered. The most important ones appear to be reactions 5 and 6 in Figure 2.23. In reaction 5, a molecule of nitric oxide, NO, reacts with ozone to give molecular oxygen and a molecule of nitrogen dioxide, NO_2. In reaction 6, the nitrogen dioxide reacts with an oxygen atom to regenerate nitric oxide and produce another molecule of oxygen. The sum of reactions 5 and 6 is reaction 4 of Figure 2.21. In other words, reactions 5 and 6 act to speed up the combination of ozone and atomic oxygen to give molecular oxygen. The nitrogen oxides are not used up in this process; they are simply interconverted between nitric oxide and nitrogen dioxide. Therefore they act as a catalyst in the destruction of ozone.

Although present in relatively small amounts, nitrogen oxides are natural constituents of the atmosphere. The largest source of nitrogen oxides on a worldwide basis is microbial action, which produces nitrous oxide, N_2O. As shown in the lower part of Figure 2.23, nitrous oxide is quite inert in the lower atmosphere, but it can react with oxygen atoms that are available in the strato-

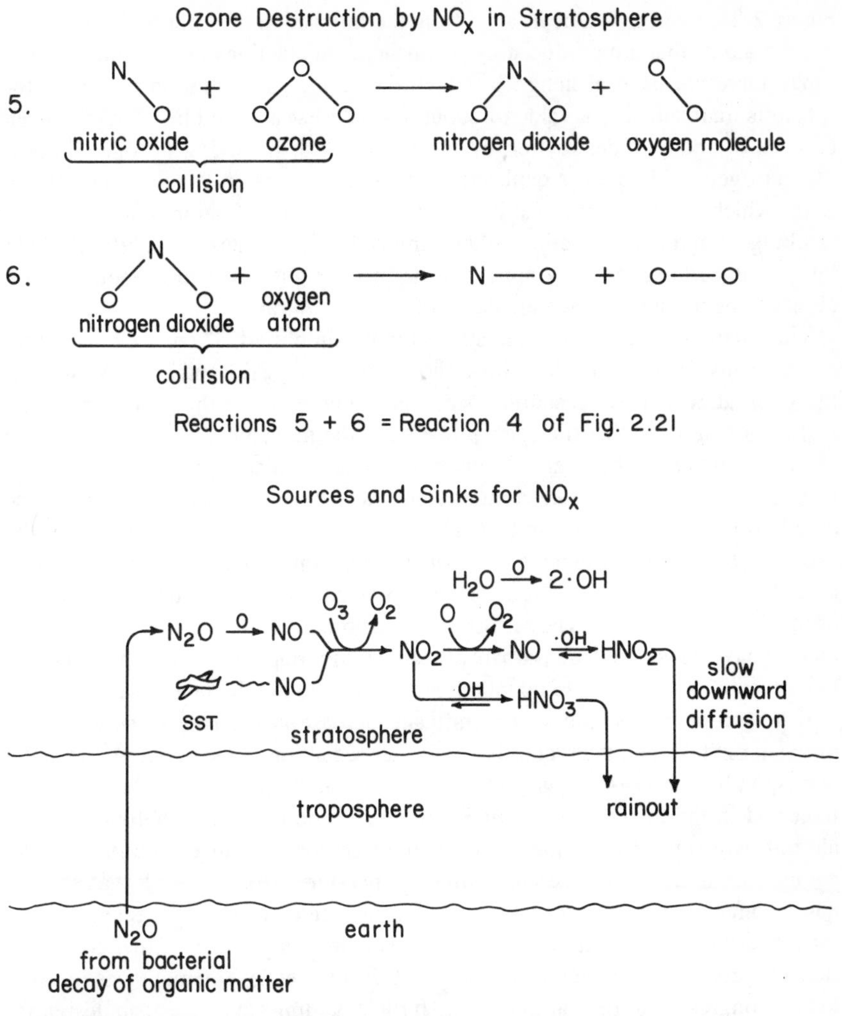

Ozone Destruction by NO_x in Stratosphere

5.   nitric oxide   ozone   →   nitrogen dioxide   oxygen molecule

collision

6.   nitrogen dioxide   oxygen atom   →   N—O + O—O

collision

Reactions 5 + 6 = Reaction 4 of Fig. 2.21

Sources and Sinks for NO_x

Figure 2.23 NO_x Reactions in the Stratosphere

Source: Lower diagram: From reactions given in "The Natural Stratosphere of 1974," Monograph 1, U.S. Department of Transportation, Climatic Impact Assessment Program (DOT-TST-75-51), September 1975, chaps. 1 and 5.

sphere to produce nitric oxide, and thereby enter the ozone destruction cycle. Eventually this cycle is broken when the nitrogen dioxide reacts with the hydroxyl radical, OH, to produce nitric acid, HNO_3, and nitric oxide reacts similarly to produce nitrous acid, HNO_2. These acids diffuse back out of the stratosphere and, being very soluble in water, are quickly rained out. As shown in

Figure 2.23, hydroxyl radicals arise from the interaction of water molecules with oxygen atoms that are produced by photochemical reactions in the atmosphere.

We therefore have a picture in which the ozone concentration in the stratosphere is maintained at a value of about half of what it would be in pure oxygen because of catalytic destruction by a reaction cycle involving nitrogen oxides. The nitrogen oxide pool is depleted by gradual conversion to nitric and nitrous acids, which are rained out, and it is replenished by the activation of nitrous oxide resulting from microbial action on the earth below. Estimates of the nitrous oxide flux are uncertain, but they appear to be in the right range to account for the observed depression in the calculated ozone concentration.

This picture of the ozone chemistry is highly simplified. There are many more reactions involving ozone than those shown in Figures 2.21 and 2.23. Moreover, the rates at which the reactions occur in many parts of the stratosphere are sufficiently slow so that transport processes—the movement of air masses from one location to the other—are as important as the chemistry. In order to deal with these complexities, elaborate computer programs have been devised to model the distribution of gases in the stratosphere. These calculations have highlighted the need for better measurements of stratospheric constituents than are currently available. As the new measurements are obtained, they permit better refinement of the computer models. The results obtained so far do indicate that the reactions that we have considered are probably the most important ones, even though many more reactions may have to be taken into account to obtain an accurate picture.

If human activities lead to a significant increase in the load of stratospheric nitrogen oxides, then there could be a further reduction in the ozone shield and a corresponding increase in ultraviolet radiation at the surface of the earth. As indicated in the lower diagram of Figure 2.23, one concern is with supersonic aircraft, which must fly in the stratosphere where air resistance is minimized. Jet engines are designed to operate at high temperature with the result that exhaust gases contain considerable quantities of nitric oxide, which is injected directly into the stratosphere. The supersonic speeds require high rates of fuel consumption and produce large quantities of exhaust. Before its development was forestalled by congressional refusal to provide further funding, the American design for the supersonic transport, the SST, was estimated to produce nitric oxide at a rate of one million grams per hour. An eventual fleet of 500 SSTs, as initially projected, flying 7 hours per day might have produced about as much nitric oxide per year as is presently found in the stratosphere. Since residence times of gases in the stratosphere are generally on the order of a year or so, this could have led to a doubling of the stratospheric concentration of nitrogen oxides with a resultant further decrease of the ozone concentration by a factor of about 40%, predicted by the steady-state approximation. The more complicated and realistic computer calculations project a more modest reduction. Moreover, newly measured rates of important reactions involving the hydroxyl radical have increased the estimated efficiency of nitrogen oxide removal from the stratosphere. At present the problem of SST emissions appears less serious than was thought, although considerable uncertainty persists and studies of the problem are being actively pursued.

A more serious increase in nitrogen oxide levels would be brought about by the explosion of many nuclear weapons, as would occur in a nuclear war. Nuclear explosions heat the surrounding air to very high temperatures, producing large quantities of nitrogen oxides. The force of the explosion causes these oxides to be injected directly into the stratosphere. While the matter is still controversial, it appears likely that the extensive nuclear tests conducted by the United States and the Soviet Union during 1961 and 1962 temporarily reduced the ozone concentration by as much as 4%. There is little doubt that an all-out nuclear war would significantly deplete the ozone layer. The Pentagon estimates the reduction as 50–75% if the nuclear arsenals of the Soviet Union and the United States were unleashed. A similar conclusion was reached by a National Academy of Sciences committee in a 1975 report.[4] Such a large reduction in the ozone shield might conceivably be disastrous to food production through ultraviolet radiation damage to plants. Thus, the production of nitric oxides by nuclear weapons might put humanity at even greater risk from nuclear war than it would be from the direct effects of the explosions and from radioactive fallout.

Nitrogen Oxide Effect on the Ozone Steady-State

The effect of a given quantity of nitrogen oxides on the ozone steady-state concentration depends on the rate constants for reactions 5 and 6 in Figure 2.23. At an altitude of 30 km, the values are $k_5 = 10^{-14.4}$ and $k_6 = 10^{-11}$. The rate of ozone depletion is augmented by the rate of reaction 5, while the rate of oxygen atom depletion is augmented by the rate of reaction 6. The O_3 and O steady-state conditions now read:

$$O_3: \quad \text{rate 2} = \text{rate 3} + \text{rate 4} + \text{rate 5}$$

or

$$k_2(O)(O_2)(M) = k_3(O_3) + k_4(O)(O_3) + k_5(NO)(O_3) \qquad (1)$$

$$O: \quad 2(\text{rate 1}) + \text{rate 3} = \text{rate 2} + \text{rate 4} + \text{rate 6}$$

or

$$2k_1(O_2) + k_3(O_3) = k_2(O)(O_2)(M) + k_4(O)(O_3) + k_6(NO_2)(O) \qquad (2)$$

A steady-state condition can also be written for NO_2 (or NO), on the assumption that the average concentration of nitrogen oxides does not change rapidly:

$$NO_2: \quad \text{rate 5} = \text{rate 6}$$

or

$$k_5(NO)(O_3) = k_6(NO_2)(O) \tag{3}$$

Once again, these steady-state equations can be solved for the variables (O) and (O_3). Subtracting equation (2) from the sum of equations (3) and (1) gives:

$$2k_2(O)(O_2)(M) = 2k_1(O_2) + 2k_3(O_3) \tag{4}$$

which is the same as equation (3) on page 127 and yields the same expression for (O) [after dropping $2k_1(O_2)$],

$$(O) = \frac{k_3}{k_2(M)} \frac{(O_3)}{(O_2)} \tag{5}$$

Adding equations (1), (2), and (3) gives

$$2k_1(O_2) = 2k_4(O)(O_3) + 2k_6(NO_2)(O) \tag{6}$$

and substitution of equation (5) gives

$$k_1(O_2) = \frac{k_4 k_3}{k_2(M)} \frac{(O_3)^2}{(O_2)} + \frac{k_6 k_3}{k_2(M)} \frac{(NO_2)(O_3)}{(O_2)} \tag{7}$$

This equation can be rearranged in the following form:

$$X^2 + bX - 1 = 0 \tag{8}$$

where

$$X = \frac{(O_3)/(O_2)}{R_0} \quad \text{and} \quad b = \frac{(NO_2)}{(O_2)} \frac{k_6/k_4}{R_0} \tag{9}$$

The quantity $R_0 = [k_1 k_2(M)/k_3 k_4]^{1/2}$ is the $(O_3)/(O_2)$ ratio in the absence of nitrogen oxides [see equation (6) on page 128]. Therefore, the variable X is the extent to which the ozone concentration is reduced by nitrogen oxides. Since the actual $(O_3)/(O_2)$ ratio measured in the stratosphere is a factor of two less than that calculated by equation (6) on page 128, X must be ½, if nitrogen oxides are the source of the discrepancy. The quantity b is a parameter that is directly proportional to the NO_2 concentration. We can solve equation (8) for b in terms of X:

$$b = X^{-1} - X \tag{10}$$

If $X = $ ½, then $b = 3/2 = 1.50$. The NO_2 concentration is readily found by substituting the constants in the expression for b in equation (9). At an altitude of 30 km, $R_0 = 10^{-4}$, $k_6/k_4 = 10^{-11}/10^{-15} = 10^4$, and $(O_2) = 10^{17}$ molecules/cm³. (The total concentration of air molecules is $10^{17.7}$ and O_2 is one-fifth of the total.) Therefore $(NO_2) = 1.50 \times 10^9$ molecules/cm³. To obtain the relative concentration of NO_2, we divide by the total concentration of air molecules and obtain:

$$\frac{(NO_2)}{(air)} = \frac{1.50 \times 10^9}{10^{17.7}} = 3.00 \times 10^{-9} \text{ or 3 ppb}$$

If we want to know the total level of nitrogen oxides needed to account for O_3 depletion, we also have to calculate the NO concentration. For this we can use equation (3), which rearranges to

$$\frac{(NO)}{(NO_2)} = \frac{k_6(O)}{k_5(O_3)} \tag{11}$$

The $(O)/(O_3)$ ratio is given by equation (5):

$$\frac{(O)}{(O_3)} = \frac{k_3}{k_2(O_2)(M)} \tag{12}$$

Substitution into equation (11) gives

$$\frac{(NO)}{(NO_2)} = \frac{k_6 k_3}{k_5 k_2(O_2)(M)} = 10^{-1.6} = 0.025 \tag{13}$$

using the values given above for 30 km. It appears, therefore, that essentially all the nitrogen oxides exist as NO_2 at steady state.

An additional reaction, reaction 6', has been neglected, however, which modifies this conclusion. NO_2 is itself subject to photolysis by visible and near ultraviolet radiation:

$$NO_2 + h\nu \text{ (260-400 nm)} \rightarrow NO + O \qquad 6'$$

$$\text{rate } 6' = k_{6'} (NO_2)$$

At 30 km, $k_{6'} = 10^{-2.3}$. This is the key reaction in initiating smog formation in polluted air. In the stratosphere, its main effect is to push the steady state back toward NO. [It also is a source of oxygen atoms, but its contribution to the O atom steady-state concentration, equation (2), is negligible, since $k_{6'} (NO_2)$ $<<k_3(O_3)$.] The NO_2 steady-state condition becomes

$$\text{rate } 5 = \text{rate } 6 + \text{rate } 6'$$

or

$$k_5(NO)(O_3) = k_6(NO_2)(O) + k_{6'}(NO_2)$$

and

$$\frac{(NO)}{(NO_2)} = \frac{k_6(O)}{k_5(O_3)} + \frac{k_{6'}}{k_5(O_3)}$$

The first term is 0.025, as before, but the second term is substantially larger: $10^{-2.3}/10^{-14.4} \times 10^{12.5} = 10^{-0.4} = 0.40$. Therefore $(NO) = 0.42(NO_2)$ and total concentration of nitrogen oxides is:

$$(NO_x) = (NO) + (NO_2) = 1.42(NO_2) = 2.1 \times 10^9 \text{ molecules/cm}^3$$

According to our steady-state calculation, the ozone concentration is reduced by a factor of two from its pure air value (10^{13} molecules/cm^3 at 30 km) by the presence of only 2×10^{-4} as many nitrogen oxide molecules. The actual concentration of nitrogen oxides in the stratosphere has been measured, and at an altitude of 30 km, the estimated value is between 3×10^9 and 5×10^9 molecules/cm^3.

This agrees rather well with our calculations. In fact the agreement is better than we have a right to expect, since there are many other reactions that have some (though not major) influence on the ozone balance, and since the steady-state approximation is not very realistic. A steady state can be achieved only if the contributing reactions are fast compared with the fluctuations in the concentrations. The stratosphere experiences major fluctuations due to the day-night and seasonal cycles. Above an altitude of 30 km, the chemical reactions are fast on this time scale, but below 30 km the photochemical processes are greatly slowed. Moreover, the ozone distribution is not uniform over the globe but exhibits marked latitudinal variations, being more concentrated at the poles than at the equator. In the lower stratosphere, ozone chemistry is slower than the rate of ozone transport from one part of the globe to another and even from the stratosphere into the troposphere. These factors all tend to make the steady-state calculation overestimate the effect of nitrogen oxides (or other catalysts) on the ozone balance.

Stratospheric Nitrogen Cycle

The main mechanism for the removal of nitrogen oxides from the stratosphere is believed to be the reaction of NO_2 with hydroxyl radicals:

$$HO\cdot + NO_2 + M \rightarrow HNO_3 + M \tag{1}$$

Hydroxyl radicals are formed from water molecules by reaction with energetic oxygen atoms, which are in their singlet D (^{1}D) electronic state, with all electrons paired. These are formed by ozone photolysis by reaction 3 in Figure 2.21. The electronic state of the O atoms resulting from reaction 3 depends on the wavelength of the photons. At wavelengths longer than 310 nm, the O atoms are produced in their low-energy triplet state (^{3}P). Below 310 nm, the photons have enough energy to produce ^{1}D O atoms. These can react with water molecules to produce hydroxyl radicals

$$O(^1D) + H_2O \rightarrow 2HO\cdot \tag{2}$$

Hydroxyl radicals can also destroy ozone, abstracting an oxygen atom to form the hydroperoxyl radical, HOO:

$$HO\cdot + O_3 \rightarrow HOO\cdot + O_2 \tag{3}$$

Reaction of HOO with oxygen atoms can then regenerate HO:

$$HOO\cdot + O \rightarrow HO + O_2 \tag{4}$$

Reactions (3) and (4) form another catalytic cycle, similar to reactions 5 and 6 in Figure 2.23, for ozone depletion. This cycle is quantitatively less important, however, and the main influence of hydroxyl radicals on the ozone balance is to limit the effect of NO_2 by converting it to HNO_3.

If this is the sink for stratospheric nitrogen oxides, there must be a source of the same magnitude. A small amount of NO is formed directly in the stratosphere by the action of cosmic rays. In the troposphere, NO and NO_2 are formed in large quantities by combustion and electrical discharge (lightning), but they are converted to HNO_3 and rained out before reaching the stratosphere. Nitrous oxide, N_2O, is quite inert, however, and eventually drifts into the stratosphere. There it can generate nitric oxide by reacting with $O(^1D)$:

$$N_2O + O(^1D) \rightarrow 2NO \tag{5}$$

However, most of the N_2O, about 96%, is removed by photodissociation to N_2:

$$N_2O + h\nu \rightarrow N_2 + O(^1D) \tag{6}$$

while an additional ~2% also yields N_2 by reacting with $O(^1D)$:

$$N_2O + O(^1D) \rightarrow N_2 + O_2 \tag{7}$$

Consequently only ~2% of the N_2O diffusing into the atmosphere reacts via reaction (5). Nevertheless this is considered to be the main source of NO_x in the stratosphere.

N_2O is a side product of biological denitrification, the process whereby microbes reduce nitrates and nitrites to N_2. A small fraction of the nitrogen is released as N_2O instead. There is some concern that N_2O production may be increasing in parallel with the increasing use of chemical fertilizers, which now account for a significant fraction of total worldwide nitrogen fixation. In 1974 this total was estimated to be 237 MT (megaton = 10^{12} g), with industrial fixation accounting for 57 MT, or 24%.[5] It is reasonable to expect that biological denitrification would increase in response to the increased fixed-nitrogen loading. If nitrogen fixation and denitrification are in balance, and if the fraction of the N_2O side product is constant, then it follows that chemical fertilizers already account for 24% of the stratospheric NO_x flux, and that further increases would increase stratospheric NO_x in proportion. If this were true, however, then a measurable reduction in ozone should already have occurred over the past few decades with the introduction of chemical fertilizers, but there is no evidence of this.

There is no direct relationship between nitrogen fixation and denitrification, and the ratio of N_2O to N_2 produced in denitrification is quite variable, according to a number of experiments, and seems to depend on soil conditions, especially the degree of aeration. Also, there is some evidence that there are large unidentified sources and sinks of N_2O in the troposphere. Measurements of ambient N_2O concentrations have suggested a large reservoir (about 1,300 MT) with yearly fluctuations indicating a residence time of about 10 years and therefore a production rate of 130 MT/year.[5] The stratospheric N_2O flux, however, is only about 35 MT/year, if 2% of it produces the stratospheric NO_x flux (0.7 MT/year) as discussed above. It has also been found that ocean waters are supersaturated with respect to N_2O, implying that the oceans release N_2O, and a global production rate of 100 MT/year has been estimated. These numbers are all highly tentative; they indicate that much more work needs to be done to understand the N_2O cycle.

6 | Chlorofluoromethanes

Another reaction cycle that could be effective in destroying ozone is shown in Figure 2.24. In reaction 7 a chlorine atom reacts with ozone to produce an oxygen molecule and chlorine oxide, which then combines with an oxygen atom in reaction 8 to produce another oxygen molecule and regenerate the chlorine atom. The sum of reactions 7 and 8 gives reaction 4 in Figure 2.21 and the high rate of these reactions makes this an effective catalytic cycle. In fact, they are six times more efficient than the nitrogen oxide cycle reactions 5 and 6 of Figure 2.23. If present in equal concentration, chlorine atoms would be six times more effective than nitric oxide in destroying ozone.

Concern about this reaction sequence has centered on the production and use of the chlorofluoromethanes (CFMs) as refrigerants and aerosol spray can propellants. In news articles they have often been referred to as fluorocarbons, but it is, in fact, the chlorine they contain that is of central concern to the ozone question. These chemicals undergo no known reactions in the lower atmosphere, and it had been accepted that this inertness precludes any harmful environmental impact. However, in 1974 two scientists, Dr. M. J. Molina and Professor F. S. Rowland, pointed out that a danger does exist in the stratosphere when the CFMs split off chlorine atoms.[6] As shown in the lower part of Figure 2.24, in this region CFMs are subjected to ultraviolet radiation at wavelengths of around 200 nm. At these short wavelengths the radiation flux is negligible in the troposphere due to the ozone shield, but it becomes significant in the stratosphere. The same ultraviolet

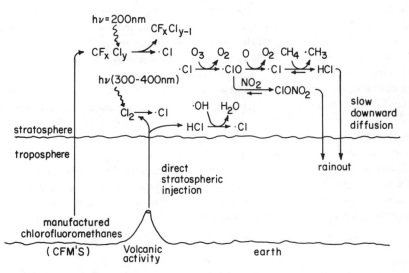

Figure 2.24 Chlorine Reactions in the Stratosphere

Source: From reactions given in "The Natural Stratosphere of 1974," Monograph 1, U.S. Department of Transportation, Climatic Impact Assessment Program (DOT-TST-75-51), September 1975, chap. 5; and "Halocarbons: Environmental Effects of Chlorofluoromethane Release" (Washington, D.C.: National Academy of Sciences, 1976).

radiation that is absorbed by the ozone can convert CFMs into a source of chlorine atoms that can efficiently destroy the ozone. Precisely because the CFMs undergo no known reactions in the troposphere, they eventually diffuse up into the stratosphere and are a continuing source of chlorine atoms. Eventually, by reaction with methane, CH_4, the chlorine atoms are trapped as hydrochloric acid, HCl, which, because of its solubility in water, is rained out of the atmosphere.

It takes a few years for the CFM molecules to diffuse up to the altitude of peak photoefficiency, about 25–35 km. Therefore, there is a considerable time lag between the production of CFM and the eventual effects on the ozone layer that may be observed. These effects may be substantial. However, there are many uncertainties in the calculations that could move the predicted effects upward or downward. For example, it has recently been discovered that chlorine oxide and nitrogen dioxide can react to give a fairly stable product, chlorine nitrate, as shown in reaction 9 of Figure 2.24. This has the effect of lowering the rate of both the chlorine and nitrogen oxide catalytic cycles for ozone destruction, leading to somewhat lower overall ozone depletion rates.

A U.S. government task force concluded that at the 1973 level of chlorofluoromethane production, the eventual ozone reduction would be about 7%, according to the best current estimates. After this study, the federal government decided to ban all CFM use in spray cans as of December 1978. This ban has decreased U.S. production of CFMs by about 50%, since other uses, mainly as refrigerants, accounted for the remaining 50%. Before the ban, the United States made half the CFMs in the world; hence, the ban has reduced the global CFM production by about 25%. With the exception of Sweden, CFM use has not been restricted in other parts of the world, although Canada and Norway are considering similar legislation and the Netherlands has required the labeling of spray cans using CFMs as potentially dangerous. Other countries are aware of the problem and at an international conference in Munich in December 1978, the general consensus among the world producers was that production would either hold at its present level or decrease in the near future.

Other aerosol spray propellants are readily available, but finding a suitable substitute in refrigeration units is a more difficult problem. It should be possible to design the units so that the CFM does not escape into the atmosphere but is recycled at the end of the refrigerator's lifetime.

7 | Oxide Chemistry

The reactivity of oxygen also dominates the chemistry of the lower atmosphere. In the presence of molecular oxygen, the stable forms of almost all the

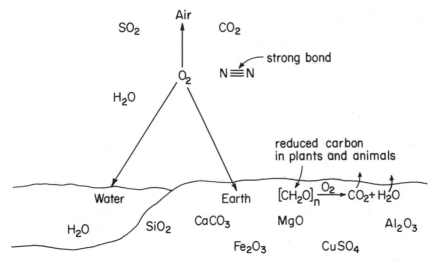

Figure 2.25 Most Elements, Except Nitrogen, Are Stable As Oxides

elements are oxides. This is shown graphically in Figure 2.25. The crust of the earth consists mainly of solid oxides of the various elements, iron, aluminum, magnesium, calcium, carbon, and silicon, while the oceans are filled with the oxide of the element hydrogen. The atmosphere also contains volatile oxides such as carbon dioxide and sulfur dioxide. Nitrogen, however, is stable in the presence of oxygen. The bond connecting the two nitrogen atoms is so strong that energy would be lost in converting N_2 to any of the nitrogen oxides.

Since carbon dioxide is the stable form of carbon in the presence of oxygen, we might wonder how reduced organic compounds, of which plants and animals are made, can exist in contact with the atmosphere. The answer to this is that the reactions of oxygen are quite slow under ordinary conditions. A substantial activation barrier must usually be overcome, as diagrammed in the top part of Figure 2.26. An activation barrier corresponds to the energy that the reactants must acquire before they can form the products, even if the overall reaction releases energy. In the combustion of reduced carbon, such as coal or oil, the activation barrier is manifested by the high ignition temperatures that are re-quired. The energy of the combustion products, carbon dioxide and water, is lower than that of the reduced organic compounds, but the reaction has to travel uphill in terms of energy before the products can be formed, with the liberation of heat.

One factor that determines the activation energy is the requirement that the bond between the oxygen atoms must be broken. Although not as strong as the bond between nitrogen atoms, this is quite a strong bond. The two carbon-oxygen bonds formed in the carbon dioxide product are worth more in energy,

(i)

Uncatalyzed Oxidation (combustion)

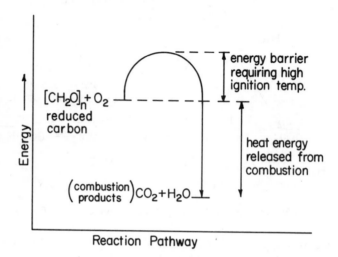

(ii)

Biologically Catalyzed Oxidation (respiration)

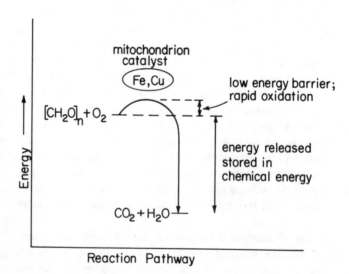

Figure 2.26 Oxidation Reactions, in the Absence of Catalysts, Are Quite Slow

but the oxygen-oxygen bond must still be broken first or at least appreciably weakened, and this requires energy. Another factor is that the oxygen molecule has two of its electrons unpaired, whereas most stable molecules have all their electrons paired. It costs energy to pair up electrons, and this is another contribution to the barrier to oxygen reactivity.

For these reasons we exist fairly comfortably with our oxygen atmosphere, except in certain circumstances such as in the intense heat of fire, which can provide the needed activation energy to cause oxygen to react. Indeed, biological organisms have developed a specialized biochemical apparatus inside their cells, called the *mitochondrion,* in order to be able to use oxygen to provide rapid energy through respiration, as illustrated in the lower part of Figure 2.26. The mitochondrion contains atoms of the elements iron and copper, which themselves have unpaired electrons and can lower the activation barrier to oxygen reactivity. The mitochondrion is designed not only to lower the barrier but also to channel the resulting energy into biochemical pathways useful to the organisms. Thus organisms require both the reactivity of oxygen and its control by the biochemical machinery that has evolved for the purpose. Both the energy source and the energy barrier, which can be selectively reduced for productive ends, are essential.

Turning our attention to the top part of Figure 2.27, we see that although molecular nitrogen is stable in the presence of oxygen, nitrogen oxides can be formed at sufficiently high temperature. Since the nitrogen-oxygen bonds that form are not so strong as the nitrogen-nitrogen and oxygen-oxygen bonds that are broken, heat must be supplied to the system to make the reaction go. This is shown for nitric oxide, represented by reaction 1 on the left side of the illustration. The energy diagram is the reverse of the one in Figure 2.26, with the products at a higher energy than the reactants. We know that reactions that absorb heat can be made to go forward if enough heat is supplied. This is the reason high-temperature processes such as combustion or the explosion of bombs are associated with the formation of nitrogen oxides in the atmosphere. Once the heat is taken away, nitric oxide is unstable with respect to nitrogen and oxygen. However, the reverse of reaction 1 is also slow at low temperature because a high activation barrier must still be overcome, as shown in the diagram. Again, a fairly strong bond between nitrogen and oxygen must be broken or considerably weakened before the stronger nitrogen-nitrogen and oxygen-oxygen bonds can form. Consequently, if the temperature is lowered quickly, as is the case in exhaust gases from a fire or an explosion, the nitric oxide does not have a chance to dissociate and the reaction is so slow that the molecule can last for a long time even though it is potentially unstable. Indeed, another reaction is more probable, namely, the oxidation of nitric oxide to nitrogen dioxide, represented by reaction 2 on the right side of the figure. This reaction is also downhill in energy, and it has a lower activation barrier because, while the oxygen-oxygen bond must still

(i)
Pathways of Nitrogen-Oxygen Reactions

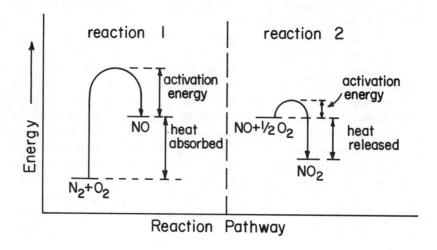

Reaction Pathway

(ii)
Oxidation Reactions of Nitrogen, Carbon, and Sulfur*

	stable at low temp.		stable at high temp.
1.	heat + N_2 + O_2	$\rightleftharpoons$	$2 NO$

	stable at high temp.		stable at low temp.
2.	$NO + \frac{1}{2} O_2$	$\rightleftharpoons$	NO_2 + heat
3.	$CO + \frac{1}{2} O_2$	$\rightleftharpoons$	CO_2 + heat
4.	$SO_2 + \frac{1}{2} O_2$	$\rightleftharpoons$	SO_3 + heat

Figure 2.27 Thermochemical Stability of Oxides

*Reactions are governed by Le Chatelier's principle; i.e., if temperature is lowered, the reaction system compensates by shifting the equilibrium toward the side where heat is given off, and vice versa.

be broken, the nitrogen-oxygen bond remains intact. The reaction is still slow but not so slow as the reformation of nitrogen and oxygen. Since heat is given off in reaction 2, it can be reversed at sufficiently high temperature. Consequently as indicated in reaction 1 in the lower part of Figure 2.27, nitric oxide is the main product of nitrogen oxidation associated with combustion and it is slowly oxidized to nitrogen dioxide as it cools in the atmosphere, as shown in reaction 2. This pattern also holds for other volatile oxides.

The oxidation of carbon monoxide to carbon dioxide, reaction 3 in Figure 2.27, is likewise accompanied by the liberation of heat and can be reversed at high temperature. The internal combustion engine in particular gives off substantial quantities of carbon monoxide, which slowly oxidizes to carbon dioxide in the atmosphere. Similarly, as shown in reaction 4 of Figure 2.27, the oxidation of sulfur dioxide to sulfur trioxide gives off heat and is reversed at high temperature. Sulfur dioxide is emitted by coal-burning power plants and it is slowly oxidized in the atmosphere.

Oxygen Reactivity

Electronic structure

The main factor in oxygen's slow reaction rates is its unusual electronic structure, which is readily understood by reference to its molecular orbital diagram:[7]

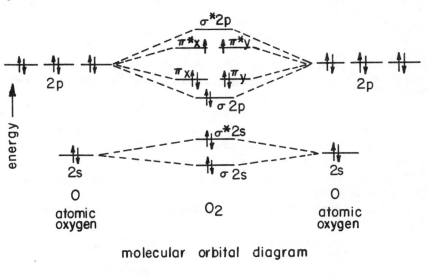

molecular orbital diagram

The $2s$ and $2p$ valence atomic orbitals on the oxygen atoms overlap to from bonding and antibonding combinations as shown. The valence electrons fill up these orbitals two at a time, in accordance with the Pauli principle. If there are ten valence electrons, as in N_2, four bonding and one antibonding orbitals are filled, and the net bond order (electron pairs in bonding minus those in antibonding orbitals) is three. If there are 14 valence electrons, as in F_2, two more antibonding orbitals are filled, and the bond order is one. O_2 has 12 electrons, and the net bond order is two. The last pair of electrons, however, has two orbitals available with equal energy (degenerate orbitals). The most stable arrangement is for the electrons to be placed in different orbitals (to reduce their mutual repulsion) with their spins aligned, since it takes energy to pair up electron spins (as it takes energy to oppose two magnets).[8] Thus oxygen has two unpaired electrons (triplet state) in its lowest energy (ground) state.

Free radicals; combustion

Oxygen is a highly electronegative element, and the production of oxides involves partial electron transfer to oxygen with the formation of polar $D^{\delta+}-O^{\delta-}$ bonds, where D is the element being oxidized. Reactions that proceed with partial electron transfer require an empty low-lying orbital on the acceptor molecule to receive the electrons from the donor molecule, i.e.,

In the case of O_2, however, the potential acceptor orbitals are each half filled and cannot accept an electron pair directly (see the lower part of Figure 2.28). One of the O_2 orbitals could be emptied by pairing electrons in the other, but pairing costs energy. An oxygen molecule with its electrons paired (singlet oxygen), as shown in the lower part of Figure 2.28, is in an excited state, which is 23.4 kcal/mol above the ground state. Moreover, spin pairing is a slow (improbable) process. The unavailability of empty acceptor orbitals is the main factor in slowing oxygen reaction rates, since most oxidizable molecules have fully paired electrons.

The situation is altered when the donor molecule has only one electron in its highest orbital:

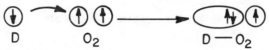

rapid reaction of O_2 with donor
containing one unpaired electron(free radical)

(i)

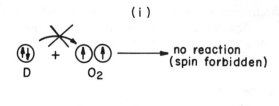

(ii)

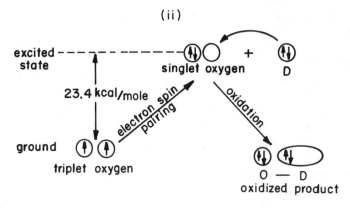

Figure 2.28   Slow Reaction of Oxygen with Donor Containing Two Unpaired Electrons

In this case there is a rapid transfer of the single electron to one of the half-filled O_2 orbitals. Molecules with one unpaired electron are called *free radicals*. They are generally very reactive, attacking other molecules to form electron-pair bonds. (There are some exceptions, such as ·NO and ·NO$_2$, in which the odd electron is in a relatively low energy orbital.) If the target molecule has fully paired electrons, as is usually the case, then one of the products must have an unpaired electron and is itself a reactive free radical. Consequently the high reactivity of free radicals is amplified by their tendency to participate in chain reactions, each reaction producing a reactive free-radical product. Such chains terminate when two free radicals find each other and react to form a fully paired product.

The most common chain reaction is combustion, in which the high temperature of a flame or spark in the presence of organic matter produces free radicals, usually by breaking $C-C$ bonds. The organic free radicals react rapidly with O_2:

$$R\cdot + O_2 \rightarrow RO_2\cdot$$

The product is itself a free radical (peroxyl radical) and its $O-O$ bond is considerably weakened since an electron has been added to an antibonding orbital of

O_2. It is an effective oxygen atom donor, producing oxidized organic products and another free radical, which in turn reacts with oxygen, and the cycle repeats. Thus free radicals serve to catalyze the reactions of O_2.

Transition metals; respiration

Oxygen molecules are also activated by binding to transition metal atoms. These often have unpaired electrons in their d orbitals, which can interact with the unpaired electrons of oxygen. The resulting complex, e.g., $Fe-O_2$, again has a weakened $O-O$ bond. In contrast to organic compounds, iron oxidizes rapidly in air (particularly moist air; the water provides protons that increase the reactivity of bound O_2).

Nature uses iron complexes to control biological O_2 reactions. Hemoglobin picks up O_2 from the lungs and transfers it to myoglobin in the body's tissues. Both proteins contain iron-porphyrin complexes, to which O_2 is bound. Next the O_2 is delivered to the mitochondrion, the subcellular apparatus for carrying out respiration. Here the electrons from reduced carbon compounds are fed to O_2 through several stages, and at each stage energy is extracted and stored via the synthesis of adenosine triphosphate (ATP), nature's energy currency. At the final stage, an enzyme called *cytochrome oxidase* reduces O_2 to water by the addition of four electrons at a time. This is accomplished by a protein that contains two iron-porphyrin complexes and two copper ions. In this way the reactivity of oxygen toward organic compounds is accelerated along specific pathways to maintain the essential flow of biological energy.

Thermodynamics and Equilibrium

Free energy

The relative stabilities of molecules can be expressed in terms of the energies involved when they interconvert. The energy change between the products and the reactants of a chemical reaction is called the *Gibbs free energy change, ΔG*. If the reaction is

$$a\text{A} + b\text{B} \rightleftarrows c\text{C} + d\text{D}$$

then:

$$\Delta G = \Delta G^\circ + RT \ln \frac{[\text{C}]^c [\text{D}]^d}{[\text{A}]^a [\text{B}]^b} \tag{1}$$

where [A] is A's *activity* (similarly for B, C, and D), which is a measure of its concentration. In aqueous solution, the customary unit of concentration is moles per liter; in the gas phase, concentration is usually expressed as the partial pressure in atmospheres, although molecules per cubic centimeter is also used commonly in atmospheric chemistry.* ΔG^0 is the *standard free energy* change for the reaction in which the reactants in their standard states at 298° K and 1 atm pressure go to products in their standard states.

If the system is at equilibrium, $\Delta G = 0$ and

$$\Delta G^0 = -RT \ln K \qquad (2)$$

where K, the equilibrium constant, is the quotient defined in equation (1) for the special case when the activities of the reactants and products are the *equilibrium activities*.

If ΔG^0 is negative, K has a value greater than unity and the equilibrium lies toward the products. If ΔG^0 is positive, K is less than unity and the equilibrium lies toward the reactants. It is possible to assign each compound a free energy value, G^0, from which ΔG^0 can be obtained by addition and subtraction (products minus reactants). The standard free energies of the elements (which cannot be chemically interconverted) are set equal to zero in their stable forms, i.e., O_2 for oxygen, N_2 for nitrogen, graphite for carbon, etc. Extensive tables of standard free energies are available. The standard free energies of several important atmospheric gases show them to be far out of equilibrium, as illustrated by the following examples.

Ozone

The standard free energy of ozone is 39.1 kcal/mol. If we write the chemical reaction for the formation of O_3 and O_2:

$$\frac{3}{2}O_2 \rightleftarrows O_3 \qquad (3)$$

its standard free energy change is 39.1 kcal, since the standard free energy of O_2 is zero by definition. This is a large positive value and indicates that the equilibrium lies far to the left. The equilibrium constant is given by equation (2), which can also be written as

$$\Delta G^0 = -RT(2.303)\log K$$

in which the factor 2.303 converts natural to base-ten logarithms. At 25° C, the factor $RT(2.303)$ is 1,366 calories/mol, or 1.37 kcal/mol. With ΔG^0 expressed in kilocalories per mole, it can be converted to log K at 25° C by dividing by

*The free energy change is not entirely independent of the individual concentrations, because of intermolecular interactions that are not connected with the reaction itself. It is, therefore, referenced to an idealized state of the molecules in which such intermolecular interactions are negligible, i.e., an infinitely dilute solution or a gas of infinitesimal pressure. Deviations from this value under actual conditions are taken into account by tabulating activity coefficients, $\gamma_A = [A]/(A)$, which are ratios of the activity defined for the idealized conditions, [A], and the actual concentration, (A). At the pressures and temperatures of the earth's atmosphere, these deviations are very small and can be neglected.

-1.37. For ozone formation, reaction (3), log K $= 28.5$ and K $= 10^{-28.5}$. The equilibrium expression is

$$K = 10^{-28.5} = \frac{[O_3]}{[O_2]^{3/2}} \tag{4}$$

with the activities expressed in atmospheres of partial pressure.*

The equilibrium ratio of O_3 to O_2 is:

$$\frac{[O_3]}{[O_2]} = [O_2]^{\frac{1}{2}} \times 10^{-28.5}$$

Since O_2 constitutes 20% of the atmosphere at sea level, $[O_2] = 0.20 = 10^{-0.7}$. Consequently,

$$\frac{[O_3]}{[O_2]} = 10^{-28.8}$$

The conversion of O_2 to O_3 at sea level is predicted to be exceedingly slight at equilibrium. The O_3/O_2 equilibrium is predicted to be even less in the stratosphere, where the air is much thinner and $[O_2]$ is much lower. But the actual ratio at an altitude of 30 km is more than 10^{-5} on the average, as we have seen. Evidently, the ozone is far from being at equilibrium with oxygen in the stratosphere.

Nitric oxide and nitrogen dioxide

The standard free energy of NO, 20.7 kcal/mol, is also ΔG^0 for the reaction

$$\tfrac{1}{2}O_2 + \tfrac{1}{2}N_2 \rightarrow NO$$

and log K $= -15.1$. The equilibrium expression is:

$$K = \frac{[NO]}{[O_2]^{\frac{1}{2}}[N_2]^{\frac{1}{2}}}$$

At sea level in the atmosphere,

$$[NO] = [O_2]^{1/2}[N_2]^{1/2}K = (0.2)^{1/2}(0.8)^{1/2}10^{-15.1} = 10^{-15.5} \text{ atm.}$$

*Reaction (3) might have been written with different coefficients, e.g.,

$$3O_2 = 2O_3$$

in which case the equilibrium expression would be

$$K' = \frac{[O_3]^2}{[O_2]^3} \tag{5}$$

The free energy change would be twice that of reaction (3) since 2 moles of O_3 are produced, and K' would be K^2. Equation (5) is equation (4) with both sides squared. The equilibrium concentrations are unaffected by how the reaction is written, but care must be taken to use the correct value of the free energy change.

The equilibrium conversion of O_2 and N_2 to NO is very slight. Once formed, however, NO does not decompose to N_2 and O_2 at a measurable rate, but instead is oxidized to nitrogen dioxide, NO_2, whose standard free energy is 12.4 kcal/mol, substantially less than the 20.7 kcal/mol free energy of NO. The free energy change for the reaction

$$NO + \tfrac{1}{2}O_2 \rightarrow NO_2 \qquad\qquad (6)$$

is the difference between these two numbers, -8.3 kcal/mol, and K is $10^{6.1}$. The equilibrium expression is:

$$K = \frac{[NO_2]}{[NO][O_2]^{\frac{1}{2}}}$$

and

$$\frac{[NO_2]}{[NO]} = K[O_2]^{\frac{1}{2}} = 10^{5.8}$$

at sea level. Reaction (6) is slow, however, as are all reactions of O_2 in the absence of free radical or transition metal catalysts.

Carbon monoxide and carbon dioxide

The standard free energy of CO_2, -94.3 kcal/mol, is also the free energy change of the reaction

$$C_{solid} + O_2 \rightarrow CO_2$$

This very large negative value ensures that at equilibrium carbon is oxidized until essentially all the available O_2 is used up. The equilibrium ratio of CO_2 to O_2 in the presence of carbon is given by the equilibrium constant:

$$\frac{[CO_2]}{[O_2]} = K = 10^{68.8}$$

Since the concentration of CO_2 in the atmosphere is currently 320 ppm, or 320×10^{-6} atm partial pressure, the actual value of $[CO_2]/[O_2]$ is $320 \times 10^{-6}/0.2$ or $10^{-2.8}$. In the presence of carbon, the atmospheric $[CO_2]/[O_2]$ ratio is out of equilibrium by a factor of $10^{71.6}$.

The effect of temperature; enthalpy

The free energy change of a reaction is not the same as the heat gain or loss. Some spontaneous reactions actually absorb heat from the surroundings. (When KNO_3 is dissolved in water, for example, the resulting solution is quite cold.) This is because the free energy depends on the degree of disorder of a system, the entropy, as well as its heat content, the enthalpy. It takes energy to increase order (decrease entropy). For example, it takes energy to compress a gas, even when the molecules are maintained at a constant temperature.

The relationship among changes in free energy, G, enthalpy, H, and entropy, S, is given by:

$$\Delta G = \Delta H - T \, \Delta S \tag{7}$$

Just as for free energy, data on enthalpy and entropy are available for many compounds, and changes in these quantities can be calculated for chemical reactions. Using equation (7), we can express the dependence of the equilibrium constant of a reaction on its enthalpy and entropy changes:

$$\ln K = - \frac{\Delta H}{RT} + \frac{\Delta S}{R} \tag{8}$$

The main effect of temperature on the position of equilibrium is due to the enthalpy. For a reaction that releases heat (exothermic), the equilibrium is expected to shift toward the reactants as the temperature increases, whereas for a reaction that absorbs heat (endothermic), the equilibrium is expected to shift toward the products. These expectations are confirmed by equation (8) (assuming ΔH and ΔS are independent of temperature). For negative ΔH (exothermic), K becomes smaller with increasing temperature, whereas for positive ΔH (endothermic), K becomes larger.

If the equilibrium constant is known at a given temperature (K_0 at T_0), it can be calculated at any other temperature if the enthalpy is known and the enthalpy and ΔS are assumed to be independent of temperature (not a bad assumption for gas-phase reactions). From equation (8), we obtain

$$\ln \frac{K}{K_0} = \frac{\Delta H}{R} \left(\frac{1}{T_0} - \frac{1}{T} \right) \tag{9}$$

At very high temperatures ($T \gg T_0$), equation (9) takes the limiting form:

$$\ln \frac{K}{K_0} \rightarrow \frac{\Delta H}{RT_0}$$

It is of interest to compare the low- and high-temperature equilibrium constants for the formation of the oxides of nitrogen, carbon, and sulfur. This is done in Table 2.2 in which the standard free energies and enthalpies are also listed. We can see that increasing temperature has a generally leveling effect and that the high-temperature equilibrium constants are much closer to unity than the low-temperature ones. Among the nitrogen oxides, the equilibrium constant for NO formation exceeds unity at high temperature. Consequently NO is always a side product of high-temperature combustion in air. Another feature revealed by the high-temperature equilibrium constants is that the relative stabilities of the lower and higher oxides are reversed. Thus, NO is less stable than NO_2 at low tempera-

Table 2.2   Thermodynamics of Nitrogen, Carbon, and Sulfur Oxides

			Low and high-temperature equilibrium constants of formation	
		At $T_0 = 298°$ K		At $T \gg T_0 = 298°$ K
	(kcal/mol)		log K_0	log K
Molecule	ΔH_f°	ΔG_f°	(log $K_0 = -\dfrac{\Delta G_f^\circ}{2.3RT_0}$)	(log K $= \dfrac{\Delta H_f^\circ}{2.3RT_0}$ + log K_0)
NO	21.6	20.7	−15.2	0.6
NO_2	8.1	12.4	−9.1	−3.2
N_2O	19.5	24.8	−18.1	−3.9
CO	−26.4	−32.8	24.0	4.7
CO_2	−94.0	−94.3	69.1	0.5
SO_2	−71.0	−71.8	52.6	0.8
SO_3	−94.4	−88.5	64.9	−4.0

| | Low and high-temperature interconversions | |
Reaction	log K (298° K)	log K (high temp.)
$NO + \frac{1}{2}O_2 \rightarrow NO_2$	+6.1	−3.8
$N_2O + \frac{1}{2}O_2 \rightarrow 2NO$	−12.3	+5.1
$CO + \frac{1}{2}O_2 \rightarrow CO_2$	+45.1	−4.2
$SO_2 + \frac{1}{2}O_2 \rightarrow SO_3$	+12.3	−4.8

ture but more stable at high temperature. Similarly CO and SO_2 gain stability relative to CO_2 and SO_3 at high temperature. This effect is illustrated by the equilibrium constants for oxidation of the lower to the higher oxides, which are also given in Table 2.2. These values of log K are obtained by adding and subtracting the appropriate formation reactions. The free energies, and therefore the values of log K, add and subtract in parallel. Because of the high-temperature stabilities of the lower oxides, CO and SO_2, as well as NO, are major pollutants from combustion processes.

Gas-phase oxidation reactions are rapid at high temperatures but become very slow at low temperatures. Since exhaust gases are rapidly cooled, the emitted NO, CO, and SO_2 persist for some time in the atmosphere, despite their instability. Their oxidation rates depend on the ambient concentrations of free radicals or other catalysts.

8 | Air Pollution

As shown in Table 2.3, the major air pollutants are sulfur dioxide, which is produced mostly from coal-burning power plants; carbon monoxide, mostly from

Table 2.3   Annual Emissions of Pollutants in the United States by Source*
(millions of metric tons per year)

	SO$_2$	CO	Hydrocarbons	NO/NO$_2$	Particles† ≤20 μ	≤3 μ
Transportation	0.8	69.7	10.8	10.1	1.2	1.0
Stationary fuel combustion	21.9	1.2	1.4	11.8	4.6	1.3
Industrial processes	4.1	7.8	9.4	0.7	6.3	2.7
Miscellaneous	0.1	8.5	6.3	0.4	1.3	—
Total	26.9	87.2	27.9	23.0	13.4	5.0

*Except as noted, data are from *National Air Quality and Emissions Trends Report, 1976*, U.S. EPA, Research Triangle Park, EPA-450/1-77-002, December 1977.
†Data for particles smaller than 3 μ are from L. J. Shannon, P. G. Gorman, and W. Park, *Feasibility of Emissions Standards Based on Particle Size*, prepared for the Office of Research and Development, U.S. EPA, EPA-600/5-74-007, March 1974.

automobiles; unburned hydrocarbons, from automobiles and industrial processes; and nitrogen oxide, which is contributed both by stationary power sources and by the internal combustion engine.

In addition to these gaseous pollutants, Table 2.3 lists pollution from the direct emission of particles to the atmosphere. These are primary particles, as distinct from secondary particles that are formed from chemical reactions in the atmosphere. Particle size is given in units of microns—a micron being one-millionth of a meter and denoted by μ. As we will see later, health effects are strongly related to particle size. The total quantity of each of the pollutants in the table does not reflect its relative impact on our environment since the effect of each pollutant depends on many different factors.

Carbon monoxide

The association of carbon monoxide with automobile traffic is graphically illustrated in Figure 2.29, in which both traffic density and carbon monoxide concentration at street level are shown to rise and fall in a regular daily pattern in Manhattan. A similar graph could be drawn for all other urban areas. Shown in the lower part of Figure 2.29 are carbon monoxide concentrations, averaged over an eight-hour period, for locations with increasing distance from traffic. The eight-hour average is chosen to reflect the fact that carbon monoxide is an asphyxiating poison that competes with oxygen for hemoglobin molecules, which are responsible for transporting oxygen from the lung to the tissues. It takes some time to establish this competition while the gases are breathed in and out and the blood circulates to the tissues. Thus, the eight-hour average represents the best measure of actual exposure. The reactions involved are shown in the upper part of Figure 2.30. Both oxygen and carbon monoxide are bound to the iron atoms in the hemoglobin molecules, but the binding of carbon monoxide

(i)

CO Build-up in Manhattan Air from Heavy Traffic

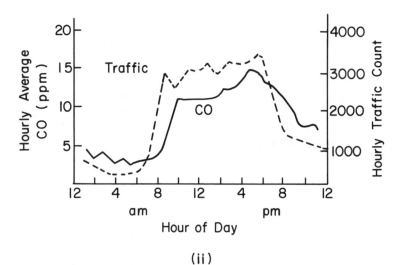

(ii)

8-Hour Average CO Concentration (ppm)

	exceeded at 5% of sites	exceeded at 50% of sites
Inside vehicles in downtown traffic	115	70
Inside vehicles on expressways	75	50
Commercial areas	40	17
Residential areas	23	16
Background	0.025– 1.0	

Figure 2.29   Carbon Monoxide Concentrations in Urban Atmospheres

Source: Upper graph: K. L. Johnson, L. H. Dworetzky, and A. N. Heller, *Science* 160 (1968):67. Copyright 1968 by the American Association for the Advancement of Science. Lower table :"Air Quality Criteria for Carbon Monoxide," U.S. Department of Health, Education and Welfare, Washington, D. C., March 1970, p. 6-22.

(i)

Replacement of Oxygen in Hemoglobin

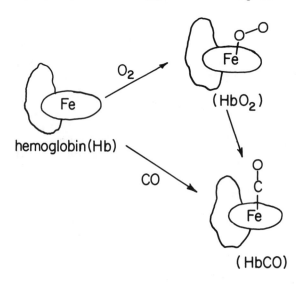

(ii)

Dose-Response Curves of HbCO Uptake in Blood

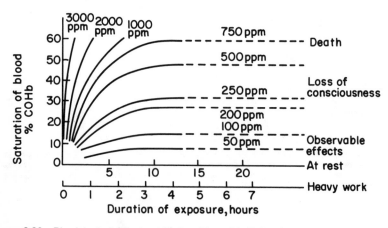

Figure 2.30 Physiological Effects of Carbon Monoxide Poisoning

Source: Lower diagram: P. C. Wolfe, *Environ. Sci. Technol.* 5 (1971):213.

is 320 times more effective than that of oxygen. This means that oxygen and carbon monoxide would be on an equal footing in competing for hemoglobin if the carbon monoxide concentration were as high as 1/320 of the oxygen concentration, or about 625 ppm. At this concentration, half the hemoglobin would bind to oxygen and half to carbon monoxide. At 100 ppm, about 16% of the hemoglobin would be tied up in the carbon monoxide complex. As the lower part of Figure 2.29 shows, 100 ppm is a concentration to which people can be exposed in heavy traffic. Bridge and tunnel workers and traffic police officers are especially at risk. As seen in the lower diagram in Figure 2.30, acute effects of carbon monoxide poisoning begin to occur at about 20% saturation of the hemoglobin, while 60% saturation can cause death. Some effects on heart and lung function can be seen down to about 5% binding of carbon monoxide. All of us have a background level of about 0.5% carbonmonoxyhemoglobin in our blood, and in smokers this level rises to 2%.

Acute exposure to carbon monoxide is reversible. Once the carbon monoxide is removed, the physiological functions return to normal. It is uncertain whether there are any long-term effects of chronic exposure to the carbon monoxide levels typical of urban areas. No such effects have yet been determined conclusively, although there is some statistical correlation between carbon monoxide levels and mortality rates in urban areas. Certainly individuals with heart problems are particularly at risk when the concentration of carbon monoxide increases.

Nitrogen oxides and hydrocarbons

Nitrogen oxides and unburned hydrocarbons are key ingredients in the formation of smog, a condition that afflicts an increasing number of cities. Smog can form whenever large quantities of automobile exhausts are trapped by an inversion layer over a locality that is, at the same time, exposed to sunshine. Los Angeles, with its dependence on the automobile, abundant sunshine, and frequent inversion layers, is the classic location for smog, but automobile traffic has introduced the problem to other cities as well. Smog is characterized by an accumulation of brown, hazy fumes, which irritate the eye and lung and lead to the cracking of rubber and to extensive damage of plant life.

Figure 2.31 shows the time course of the key atmospheric ingredients for a classic, smoggy day in Los Angeles. The peak in the concentration of hydrocarbons is during the early morning rush hour. The concentration of nitric oxide reaches a peak at the same time, and then begins to decrease as the nitrogen dioxide concentration increases. Subsequently there is a rise in the concentration of oxidants—materials that are active oxidizing agents and contain the irritating ingredients of smog. This coincides with the gradual reduction in the hydrocarbon concentration. Figure 2.32 shows that a somewhat similar time course can be observed in experiments with a smog chamber, a device into which controlled amounts of gases can be introduced and subjected to solar or artificial radiation.

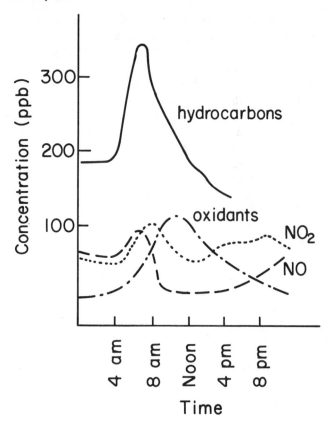

Figure 2.31 Concentration Profiles of Smog-Forming Chemicals in Los Angeles Air
Source: J. A. Kerr, J. G. Calvert, and K. L. Demerjian, *Chem. Br.* 8 (1972):253.

The experiment in the figure involves the irradiation of a mixture of pure air, nitric oxide, and the hydrocarbon, *trans*-butene. All these ingredients are needed for the reaction to work. As in the urban air, the concentrations of hydrocarbon and nitric oxide decrease in parallel while the nitrogen dioxide concentration increases and falls again. Replacing the hydrocarbon is an oxidized product, in this case acetaldehyde. Increasing at the same time is one of the most potent eye irritants found in smog—peroxyacetylnitrate (PAN). The computer simulation in Figure 2.32 was achieved by postulating a set of reactions with known rates, suggesting that the chemistry, at least in the smog chamber, is reasonably well understood.

A flow chart for the chemistry of smog formation is given in Figure 2.33. Basically it involves catalysis of the oxidation of hydrocarbons in air to form products that are themselves reactive and irritating to biological tissue. The

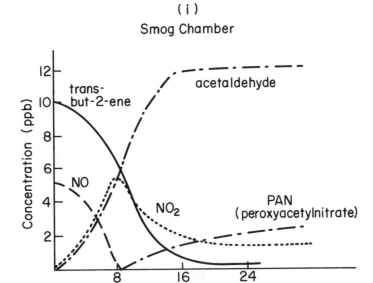

Figure 2.32 Simulated Smog Formation from *trans*-but-1-ene, Nitric Oxide, Nitrogen Dioxide, and Air

Source: J. A. Kerr, J. G. Calvert, and K. L. Demerjian, *Chem. Br.* 8 (1972):253.

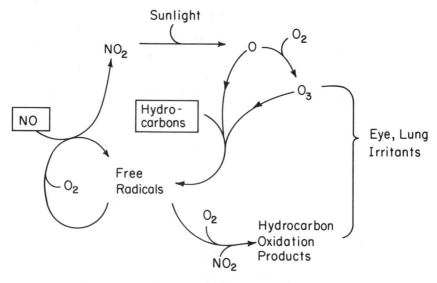

Figure 2.33 Flow Chart for Smog Formation

catalysis requires sunlight, and the key chemical ingredient is nitrogen dioxide, which is the only molecule present in significant quantities that is capable of absorbing solar light. Its absorption spectrum is shown in Figure 2.34 along with the spectrum of solar radiation. The absorption band of nitrogen dioxide is quite broad and has a peak at about 400 nm, not far from the peak in the solar spectrum. At the beginning of the smog formation reaction, however, there is only nitric oxide, which is transparent to sunlight, and we have to explain how nitric oxide is converted to nitrogen dioxide. As shown by the reaction in Figure 2.34, when nitrogen dioxide absorbs light, there is a high probability that it will split into nitric oxide and an oxygen atom. Referring back to Figure 2.33, we see that the oxygen atom is picked up by an oxygen molecule to form ozone in the same reaction that is responsible for forming ozone in the stratosphere. The ozone can transfer the oxygen atom back to nitric oxide, thus reforming nitrogen dioxide; but if this happens, we are back where we started. Indeed studies have shown that nitric oxide is not converted to nitrogen dioxide at a significant rate if the hydrocarbon is left out of the cycle. It is the hydrocarbon that accelerates the reaction of oxygen molecules with nitric oxide to form nitrogen dioxide. It does this by first reacting with the ozone to produce hydrocarbon free radicals, highly reactive molecules with an unpaired electron. Because of the unpaired electron, the free radicals combine readily with molecular oxygen, forming reactive oxygen species that can easily transfer an oxygen atom to nitric oxide, forming more nitrogen dioxide. This process regenerates the free radicals, which can continue to react with oxygen and nitric oxide many times in a chain reaction. This is how

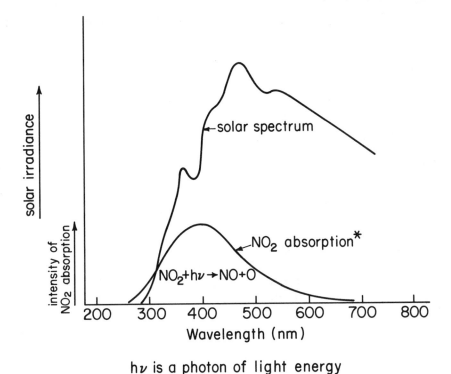

hν is a photon of light energy

Figure 2.34   Absorption of Solar Light by Nitrogen Dioxide to Form Oxygen Atoms

*The reaction shown under the absorption curve occurs when nitrogen dioxide absorbs light at wavelengths of less than 400 nm. For wavelengths greater than 400 nm, nitrogen dioxide is excited but does not decompose.

the absorption of sunlight by nitrogen dioxide, which is initially present in very low concentration, can lead to a rapid buildup of the nitrogen dioxide itself. It amounts to catalysis of the nitric oxide oxidation by the agency of free radicals formed from the hydrocarbons and the ozone, which are themselves generated photochemically from the nitrogen dioxide. The free radicals eventually combine with oxygen and nitrogen dioxide to form the oxidation products, which are eye and lung irritants, and gradually the hydrocarbon supply is depleted.

The upper part of Figure 2.35 shows in more detail some of the free-radical reactions that can take place and lead to the buildup of the concentration of nitrogen dioxide and oxidants. There are many other reactions possible, but the cycle shown here serves to illustrate the main features of smog formation. The initial event is the production of a hydrocarbon free radical symbolized by $RCH_2\cdot$, that is, a hydrocarbon with an unpaired electron in place of the bond to a hydrogen atom. This can be produced by the interaction of ozone with hydrocar-

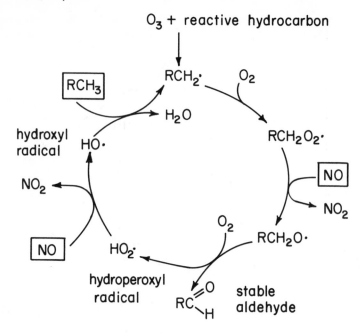

PAN Formation

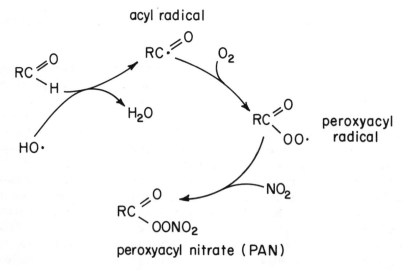

peroxyacyl nitrate (PAN)

Figure 2.35   Smog-Forming Reactions

bons from auto exhaust that have a reactive group, such as a carbon-carbon double bond. Once formed, the hydrocarbon free radical rapidly reacts with oxygen to form a new free radical with the two oxygen atoms incorporated. One of these oxygen atoms is readily donated to nitric oxide, producing nitrogen dioxide and leaving another free radical with only one oxygen atom. This radical can transfer a hydrogen atom to oxygen, thus producing a stable aldehyde molecule, which is an oxidation product of the original hydrocarbon. This reaction produces the hydroperoxyl radical, $HO_2\cdot$, which can donate an oxygen atom to another nitric oxide molecule, leaving the hydroxyl radical, $HO\cdot$. The hydroxyl radical is extremely reactive and can pull a hydrogen atom away from a stable hydrocarbon to produce water and regenerate the hydrocarbon free radical. We thereby close the loop. One circuit around it produces two molecules of nitrogen dioxide and one molecule of oxidized hydrocarbon, and regenerates the free radical to start all over again. It is this sort of chain reaction that leads to the rapid buildup of smog products. The lower part of Figure 2.35 shows another pathway leading to the peroxyacylnitrates, the most potent eye and lung irritants in smog. The hydroxyl radical pulls a hydrogen atom off the aldehyde, leaving an acyl radical, which combines with an oxygen molecule to form a peroxyacyl radical and then with nitrogen dioxide to give the final product, peroxyacylnitrate.

Tropospheric Chemistry

The chemistry of the lower atmosphere consists mainly of the oxidation of reduced molecules released by human and nonhuman activities at the earth's surface. Apart from CO_2, N_2, and N_2O, which are unreactive, the major emissions are of SO_2, H_2S, CO, NO and NO_2, NH_3, and hydrocarbons. As indicated in Table 2.4 hundreds of millions of tons of these are released each year, and their background concentrations are in the parts per million or parts per billion range. These figures can be combined for each gas to calculate a residence time, which ranges from a few days to a few years.

H_2S, NH_3, and CH_4 are all products of anaerobic biological decay, which takes place on a large scale in swampy areas. H_2S (100 MT) is rapidly oxidized to SO_2, in which form it joins a larger amount of anthropogenic SO_2 (146 MT), which is derived mostly from coal burning. The SO_2 is oxidized fairly rapidly to H_2SO_4 and rained out. NH_3 is produced naturally in much larger quantities (1,160 MT) and is oxidizable to NO and NO_2, of which large amounts (1,100 MT) are produced naturally and a relatively small amount (53 MT) from combustion. The nitrogen oxides are further oxidized to HNO_3 and rained out. Some of the NH_3, which is the only gas in this group with basic properties, reacts directly with acidic aerosols that contain H_2SO_4 or HNO_3, and is rained out as $(NH_4)_2SO_4$ or $(NH_4)NO_3$.

Table 2.4 Summary of Sources and Concentrations of Atmospheric Trace Gases

Molecule	Major Pollution Sources	Natural Sources	Estimated Annual Emissions		Atmospheric Background Concentration	Calculated Residence Time in Air
			Pollution (tons)	Natural (tons)		
SO_2	Combustion of coal and oil	Volcanoes	1.46×10^8	1.5×10^6	0.2 ppb	4 days
H_2S	Chemical processes, sewage treatment	Volcanoes, biological action in swamp areas	3×10^6	1.00×10^8	0.2 ppb	2 days
CO	Auto exhaust and other combustion	Forest fires	2.75×10^8	7.5×10^7	0.1 ppm	<3 years*
NO/NO_2	Combustion	Lightning, bacterial action in soil	5.3×10^7	NO: 4.30×10^8 NO_2: 6.58×10^8	NO: 0.2–2 ppb NO_2: 0.5–4 ppb	5 days
NH_3	Sewage treatment	Biological decay	4×10^6	1.16×10^9	6–20 ppb	7 days
N_2O	None	Biological action in soil	None	5.90×10^8	0.25 ppm	4 years
Hydrocarbons	Combustion exhaust, chemical processes	Biological processes	8.8×10^7	4.80×10^8	CH_4: 1.5 ppm non-CH_4: <1 ppb	16 years (CH_4)
CO_2	Combustion	Biological decay, release from oceans	1.4×10^{10}	10^{12}	320 ppm	2–4 years

*See T. H. Maugh, "Carbon Monoxide: Natural Sources Dwarf Man's Output," *Science* 177 (1972): 338. This suggests that 7.5×10^7 may be too low by a factor of 40, and a three-year residence time too high by a factor of 10. Source: A. C. Stern, H. C. Wohlers, R. W. Boubel, and W. P. Lowry, *Fundamentals of Air Pollution* (New York: Academic Press, 1973), pp. 30–31.

CH_4 makes up most of the 480 MT of natural hydrocarbon emission. It is a rather unreactive molecule and oxidizes only slowly in the atmosphere, with an estimated residence time of 16 years. Enough of it diffuses into the stratosphere to provide a significant source of H atoms, which serve in the removal of Cl atoms by conversion to HCl. A smaller contribution to the hydrocarbon total is provided by terpenes—green plant metabolites that contain double bonds and are therefore much more reactive than CH_4. Their oxidation produces complex products that form aerosols, which account for the blue haze that often hangs over forests. The anthropogenic hydrocarbons are mainly from automotive exhausts. They are a complex mixture of molecules whose partial oxidation can lead to smog formation. The principal oxidation product of CH_4 is CO, which is subsequently oxidized to CO_2. As indicated in the footnote to Table 2.4, the emission of CO from natural sources, principally from the degradation of chlorophyll in fallen leaves, is much greater than previously thought, and its residence time is measured in months rather than years.

In all cases except SO_2, the natural emissions of these gases greatly exceed the contribution from human activities, and in all cases the removal rates are fast enough so that the background concentrations are far less than the levels that might affect human health. These rates are not fast enough, however, to cope with the high local concentrations that result from urban congestion and lead to serious air pollution.

Because of the low reactivity of molecular oxygen, the rate of oxidation of the reduced gases depends on the concentration of catalysts in the air. For SO_2, which is water soluble, a significant pathway is oxidation to H_2SO_4 in water droplets that often contain particles of transition metal oxides (especially iron oxide) that can catalyze the oxidation. In other cases (and also for SO_2 in dry air), the major catalysts appear to be oxygen atoms and hydroxyl radicals. These are so highly reactive that even though they are present in the lower atmosphere in minute quantities, they provide the fastest routes to oxidation. The hydroxyl radical is especially important, since it is the only agent capable of reacting rapidly with CH_4:

$$HO\cdot + CH_4 \rightarrow H_2O + \cdot CH_3 \tag{1}$$

and CO:

$$HO\cdot + CO \rightarrow CO_2 + H\cdot \tag{2}$$

The free-radical products of these reactions readily react with the surrounding oxygen molecules:

$$\cdot CH_3 + O_2 \rightarrow CH_3O_2\cdot \tag{3}$$

$$\cdot H + O_2 + M \rightarrow HO_2\cdot + M \tag{4}$$

The resulting *peroxyl* radicals have a much weakened O–O bond (because the bond to H or C adds an electron to the already half-filled pair of O–O antibonding orbitals—see pages 143–144) and are good oxygen atom donors. In particular, they can convert NO to NO_2:

$$HO_2 \cdot + NO \rightarrow NO_2 + HO \cdot \qquad (5)$$

$$CH_3O_2 \cdot + NO \rightarrow NO_2 + CH_3O \cdot \qquad (6)$$

Reaction (5) regenerates HO·, which can again attack CH_4 or CO via reactions (1) and (2). Meanwhile, the *methoxy* radical from reaction (6) can donate a H atom to O_2, leaving CH_2O, which is the stable molecule formaldehyde:

$$CH_3O \cdot + O_2 \rightarrow CH_2O + HO_2 \cdot \qquad (7)$$

The resulting $HO_2 \cdot$ can oxidize NO [reaction (5)] and generate more HO·. Reactions (1) through (7) constitute a chain reaction for the catalysis of CH_4, CO, and NO oxidation. NO (or some other oxygen atom acceptor such as SO_2) is an essential ingredient since it accepts oxygen from the peroxyl radicals, permitting the regeneration of hydroxyl radical, which alone can attack CH_4 and CO. The chain reaction is terminated by reactions that convert the free radicals to stable molecules, e.g.,

$$HO \cdot + HO_2 \cdot \rightarrow H_2O + O_2 \qquad (8)$$

or

$$HO \cdot + NO_2 + M \rightarrow HNO_3 + M \qquad (9)$$

We still need an input of free radicals in order to initiate the chain reaction and to sustain it against the chain termination steps. Free radicals are high-energy species and their generation requires an energy source. In the atmosphere, this energy is provided by solar photons. Since the ultraviolet photons are mostly screened out by the ozone layer, photochemistry in the troposphere depends on molecules that absorb visible or near ultraviolet radiation.

A significant contribution to tropospheric photochemistry is likely to be the photolysis of formaldehyde, the product of reaction (7):

$$CH_2O + h\nu \rightarrow H \cdot + \cdot CHO \qquad (10)$$

which is known to proceed efficiently with photons in the near ultraviolet range. The hydrogen atoms can enter the radical chain at reaction (4), while the ·CHO radical can also give up its H atom to O_2, producing stable CO (and thereby completing the oxidation of CH_4 to CO). Other aldehydes, which are significant components of automotive exhausts, can similarly photolyze.

The splitting of NO_2:

$$NO_2 + h\nu \rightarrow NO + O \qquad (11)$$

is more important, however, since NO_2 is more abundant and more effective in absorbing solar photons (see Figure 2.34). At wavelengths shorter than 400 nm, reaction (11) proceeds efficiently. In the stratosphere, as we saw earlier, this reaction is a minor contributor to the oxygen atom balance, but in the troposphere it is the only source of oxygen atoms, and therefore of ozone, via

$$O + O_2 + M \rightarrow O_3 + M \tag{12}$$

Both O and O_3 are powerful oxidants. Neither is reactive enough to attack CH_4 or CO at a significant rate, but they readily react with unsaturated hydrocarbons, which contain $C=C$ double bonds. The mechanisms are complex, but the result is the breaking of the double bond with generation of hydrocarbon free radicals, as diagrammed in Figure 2.35. These radicals can themselves catalyze the symbiotic oxidation of hydrocarbons and NO, and also produce $HO_2\cdot$ and $HO\cdot$.

9 | Automotive Emissions

Since smog production depends on nitrogen oxides as well as hydrocarbons, clean air regulations require that both of these pollutants be controlled in automobile emissions. Figure 2.36 shows, however, that this is a difficult task. It shows the concentrations of carbon monoxide, hydrocarbons, and nitrogen oxides in auto exhaust as a function of the ratio of air to fuel, which is controlled by the carburetor. The dashed line shows the stoichiometric ratio, that is, the ratio at which there is just enough oxygen in the fuel to convert all the carbon and hydrogen to carbon dioxide and water, if the combustion were complete. In fact, combustion is not complete under the rapidly varying conditions of an internal combustion engine, and there is a residual amount of carbon monoxide and unburned hydrocarbons well beyond the stoichiometric ratio. At less than this ratio the amounts of both hydrocarbons and carbon monoxide increase rapidly. The formation of nitrogen oxide results, as we have discussed, from the high-temperature combination of nitrogen and oxygen that are present in the air. Combustion is hottest close to the stoichiometric air/fuel ratio and cools off on either side. This explains the bell-shaped curve shown for nitrogen oxide emission. Automobile carburetors are adjusted to the fuel-rich side of the stoichiometric ratio, because if more air is admitted, the engine tends to stall. The exact ratio can be varied somewhat without undue detriment to automobile performance.

When the smog problem in Los Angeles was first recognized to be associated with automobile exhaust, standards were imposed on the hydrocarbon and carbon monoxide levels in automobile emissions. At that time, the involvement of nitrogen oxides in smog production was not clearly appreciated. Automobile manufacturers found that the easiest way to meet the new emission standards was to adjust the carburetor to increase the air/fuel ratio. As we can understand from Figure 2.36, the result was to decrease the concentrations of hydrocarbons and

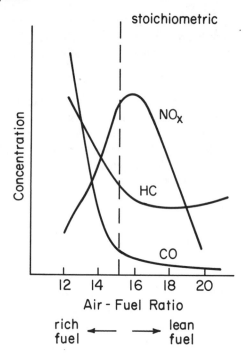

Figure 2.36 Auto Exhaust Composition

carbon monoxide but simultaneously to increase the nitrogen oxide level. It was found that the smog problem grew significantly worse after the initial standards were imposed.

Under the U.S. Federal Clean Air Act, nationwide standards have been set for the concentrations of nitrogen oxides as well as hydrocarbon and carbon monoxide. Imposition of the standards has been postponed repeatedly, however, pending resolution of the technical issues of how the standards can be met. Because of the conflicting requirements for getting rid of the different pollutants, that is, more complete combustion to lower the concentrations of hydrocarbons and carbon monoxide but lower temperatures to decrease the concentration of nitrogen oxides, the emission control problem turned out to be a difficult one.

The solution favored by the Detroit automobile manufacturers is the catalytic converter, which is diagrammed in Figure 2.37. The idea is to eliminate the

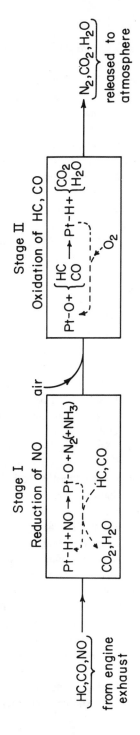

Figure 2.37 Catalytic Converter for Treating Auto Emissions

167

pollutants from the exhaust gases before they are vented to the atmosphere. Again, the different pollutants require different chemistries. Hydrocarbons and carbon monoxide can be oxidized to carbon dioxide and water, but oxidation of nitric oxide would produce nitrogen dioxide, which is itself a pollutant. Rather, the nitric oxide must be reduced to molecular nitrogen, which, as we have seen, is stable. The solution is to have two catalytic converters, one for reduction and the other for oxidation. Both use the same catalyst, finely divided platinum, but the conditions in each converter are different. In the first stage, reduction is induced by the presence of the hydrocarbons and carbon monoxide, which serve as the reducing agents. The nitric oxide gives up its oxygen to the surface of the catalyst, where it is picked up by the hydrocarbons or carbon monoxide. Following this stage, air is introduced to provide an oxidizing atmosphere for the second stage. Here the oxidation of carbon monoxide and hydrocarbon to carbon dioxide and water is completed. The overall chemistry of catalytic conversion is rather complicated and requires careful control of temperature and gas composition. One problem is that the reduction product of the first stage can be either molecular nitrogen or ammonia, NH_3. Ammonia, however, is rapidly reoxidized to nitrogen oxides in the second-stage unit. Careful control of the reduction stage is essential to minimize the production of ammonia. Another difficulty is that the catalyst itself is subject to poisoning by heavy elements. These combine with the reactive sites of the catalyst surface and inhibit the desired reaction.

Of particular concern is lead, which is normally added to gasoline to improve its combustion performance. Without lead the air/fuel mixture tends to ignite spontaneously as it is heated during the compression stroke in the cylinder. This sets off a small explosion that precedes the desired one, which is induced by the spark when the fuel is maximally compressed. This preignition, or knocking, decreases the efficiency of the engine and also sets up harmful stresses that increase engine wear. Preignition is caused by free radicals like the ones we have encountered in smog chemistry, which form in the engine due to the high temperature produced by the compression. As illustrated in Figure 2.38, tetraethyl lead is a good scavenger of free radicals. It reacts with them before they can build up the chain reaction that leads to combustion. Introduction of the catalytic converter, however, requires that lead be removed from gasoline, which may also be desirable from the point of view of curbing lead pollution. We will consider this subject later in the book.

Removal of lead from gasoline, however, poses difficulties with respect to engine performance. One solution is to change the composition of gasoline so that it is less likely to generate the free radicals that lead to knocking. Aromatic hydrocarbons, those that contain benzene rings, do not easily break down into radicals, and the quality of gasoline can be upgraded by increasing the content of aromatics. This can be done by changing the operating characteristics of refineries, although the process is costly. Another solution that has been introduced

piston of internal combustion engine

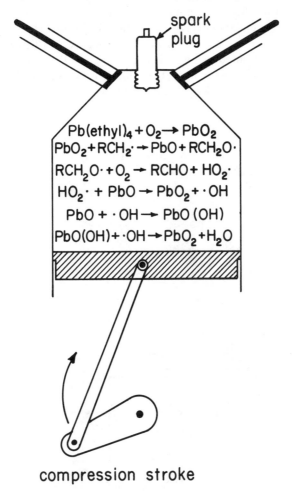

compression stroke

Figure 2.38   Radical Scavenging Reactions of Tetraethyl Lead

Source: Adapted from J. N. Bradley, *Flame and Combustion Phenomena* (London: Chapman and Hall, Ltd., 1972), p. 180.

is to lower the compression ratios of automobile engines, that is, the degree to which the air/fuel mixture is compressed in the cylinder before ignition. The lower the compression, the less tendency there is to produce free radicals. Consequently, ordinary gasoline with little or no lead becomes acceptable. Unfortunately, the engine efficiency also decreases with decreasing compression ratio, and the number of miles per gallon is reduced.

An alternative to the catalytic conversion of pollutants in the exhaust is to try to prevent their formation in the combustion process itself. Figure 2.39 shows one design that has been successfully tested, namely, the stratified charge engine. This is very similar to the normal internal combustion engine, but the head is modified to introduce an extra combustion chamber. In this prechamber, a fuel-rich mixture is introduced and ignited with a spark. Combustion therefore begins at a relatively low temperature which, as we saw in Figure 2.36, is associated with little formation of nitrogen oxides. The burning mixture is then

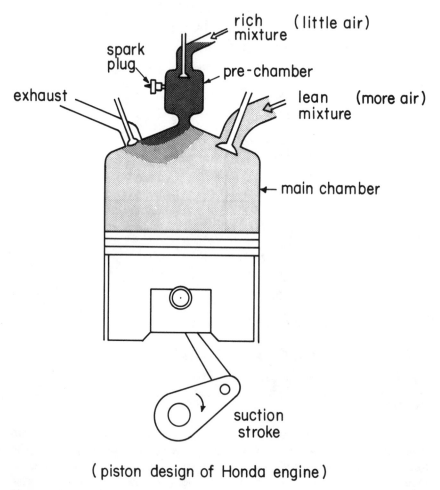

(piston design of Honda engine)

Figure 2.39 Stratified Charge Engine
Source: *Chem. Eng.* April 30, 1973, p. 39.

introduced into the larger main chamber, where it is mixed with a lean fuel mixture—one that has excess air in it. The combustion has already begun and goes to completion without stalling the engine. The excess air ensures complete combustion of the hydrocarbon and carbon monoxide, but the temperature remains low enough that the buildup of nitrogen oxides is limited. The stratified charge engine introduced by the Honda Corporation has been shown to meet the federal air pollution standards. There seem to be some questions about the extension of this design to large engines. If these can be satisfactorily answered, the stratified charge engine does offer the advantage over catalytic conversion of operating simplicity and more efficient performance.

10 | Sulfur Dioxide

Sulfur dioxide is largely associated with the burning of coal and some crude oils for electric power and heating. The sulfur content of refined petroleum is generally much lower. At the high temperatures of combustion, the sulfur is converted to sulfur dioxide. Sulfur dioxide itself is a lung irritant and is known to be harmful to people who suffer from respiratory disease. However, it is the sulfuric acid aerosol formed from the oxidation of sulfur dioxide that causes the most damaging health effects in urban atmospheres. The conversion process is shown graphically in Figure 2.40. As noted previously, sulfur dioxide is oxidized in the atmosphere to sulfur trioxide, the stable form at ambient temperatures, but the conversion is slow in the absence of a catalyst. Figure 2.40 shows two known pathways by which sulfur dioxide oxidation can be greatly accelerated in the atmosphere. In reaction a, ozone donates an oxygen atom to form sulfur trioxide, which in turn combines rapidly with water to form sulfuric acid. The sulfuric acid can condense to form aerosol droplets. In addition to ozone, other reactive gas-phase oxidants can cause a similar conversion. Alternatively, as shown in reaction b, the normally slow oxidation by oxygen can be catalyzed at the surface of particles such as soot, dust, or heavy metal oxides.

Sulfate aerosols in urban air are generally smaller than 2μ. Figure 2.41 shows that in the range smaller than 2μ, particles can quite effectively penetrate the innermost passages of the lung, called the pulmonary region. This is the region where oxygen is exchanged with carbon dioxide in the blood. Sulfuric acid aerosol irritates the fine vessels of the pulmonary region, causing them to swell and block the vessel passages. Severe breathing impairment may occur. The effect appears to be cumulative and older people suffer the most severe respiratory problems.

In order to reduce the level of sulfuric acid aerosols in urban air, power plants are often built with tall smokestacks to disperse the plume over a wide area. This

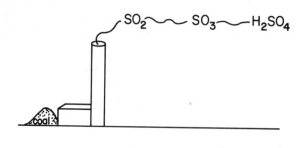

chemical pathways

a)

$$SO_2 + O_3 \longrightarrow SO_3 + O_2 \xrightarrow{+H_2O} \underset{\substack{\text{sulfuric} \\ \text{acid}}}{H_2SO_4} \longrightarrow \underset{\substack{\text{aerosol} \\ \text{droplet}}}{(H_2SO_4)_n}$$

b)

$$SO_2 + \tfrac{1}{2}O_2 \xrightarrow{\substack{\text{soot} \\ \text{dust} \\ \text{or} \\ \text{metal oxide}}} SO_3 \xrightarrow{+H_2O} H_2SO_4 \longrightarrow (H_2SO_4)_n$$

Figure 2.40 Formation of Sulfuric Acid Aerosol from Sulfur Dioxide

reduces the local problem but may increase the problem for areas that are far removed from the source of pollution. The sulfuric acid is washed out in rain or snowfall, resulting in an increase in the acidity of the local waters downwind from power plants and producing a condition that has come to be known as *acid rain*. Prevailing wind patterns bring acid rain to Scandinavia from the industrial areas of Europe and to New England and upstate New York from the industrial cities of the Northeast and Midwest of the United States. We will examine this problem in more detail in the next section.

Another approach to sulfur oxide abatement is to limit the sulfur content of fuels. This is one reason that coal has largely been displaced by petroleum and natural gas as a fuel in urban areas. With the tightening supply and higher prices of gas and petroleum, however, there is a strong incentive to return to coal. Unfortunately the supplies of low-sulfur coal are also quite limited, as mentioned earlier. There is consequently pressure to relax the sulfur emission standards currently in force. An alternative is to remove sulfur dioxide from the stack gases of the power plant by using chemical scrubbers of the type shown in Figure 2.42. In this design the stack gas is passed through a slurry of limestone, calcium carbonate, which removes sulfur dioxide quite efficiently according to the reaction shown to produce mostly calcium sulfite. Limestone is a cheap and abundant

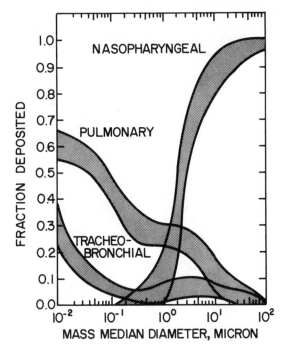

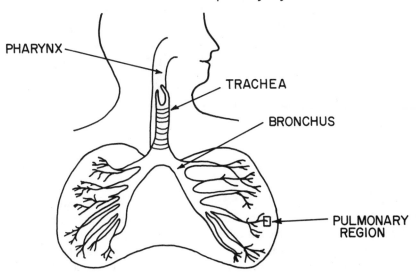

Schematic of Respiratory System

Figure 2.41 Penetration of Particles in the Human Respiratory System As a Function of Particle Size

Source: Upper graph: U.S. Department of Health, Education and Welfare, National Air Pollution Control Boards, "Air Quality Criteria for Particulate Matter," Publication No. AP-49, Washington, D.C., January 1969.

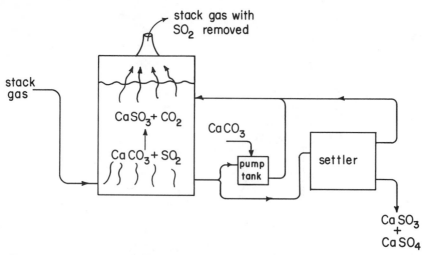

Figure 2.42 Scrubber Addition of Limestone for Removal of Sulfur Dioxide from Waste Gas

absorbent relative to other chemicals that are also under investigation. Power plant officials claim that the technology is expensive and not very reliable, and that the large quantities of calcium sulfite produced are a major waste disposal problem. The U.S. Environmental Protection Agency, on the other hand, asserts that the method is practical and is applying pressure for its widespread introduction. Another possibility is to remove the sulfur from the coal before it is burned. The inorganic sulfur can be removed fairly easily by screening powdered coal. Coal is already pulverized for large furnaces to improve its combustion characteristics. Organically bound sulfur is somewhat more difficult to remove, but several chemical processes are under investigation.

11 | Primary Particles

Sulfuric acid aerosol is a secondary particle since it is formed from a gas-to-particle conversion process in the atmosphere. In contrast, primary particles are emitted directly into the atmosphere with no intermediate conversion steps. They vary widely in their chemical composition, and hence it is difficult to assess their effects quantitatively. Soot, which arises from the residue of fuel combustion from power plants and automobiles, comprises about 50% of the particulate load in urban areas. But other particles from various industrial sources such as the cement and metallurgy industries also contribute.

As we saw in Table 2.3, 13.4 MT of primary particles is emitted annually in the United States, and of this, about 5.0 MT is smaller than 3 μ. These fine particles scatter light effectively and thereby reduce visibility. They are also the worst causes of lung damage because of their ability to penetrate into the deep air passages, as discussed in connection with sulfuric acid and shown in Figure 2.41. The larger particles are trapped in the nose and throat, from which they are easily eliminated. But the finer particles can remain lodged for years in the innermost regions of the lungs, which have no effective mechanism for particle removal.

Lodged particles can cause severe breathing impairment simply by the physical blockage and irritation of the delicate lung capillaries. Coal miners' black-lung disease, asbestos workers' pulmonary fibrosis, and the city dwellers' emphysema are all associated with the accumulation of such small particles.

Some particles are especially dangerous because they may carry toxic chemicals that can interact directly with lung tissue. A key example is soot, which is illustrated in Figure 2.43. Soot is mostly finely divided carbon with a loose structure that possesses a large surface area. It is often associated with toxic trace

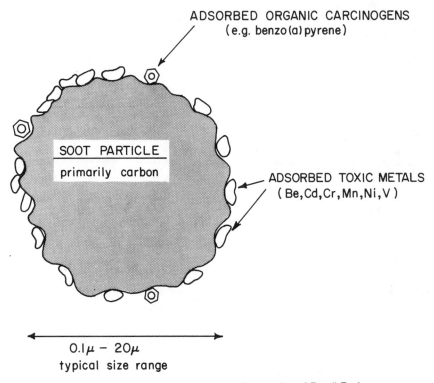

Figure 2.43   Soot Particle from the Combustion of Fossil Fuels

metals such as beryllium, cadmium, chromium, manganese, nickel, and vanadium adsorbed on its surface. Moreover, soot serves as a carrier for toxic organic molecules such as benzo(a)pyrene, which has been implicated as a cancer-causing agent. Asbestos is another insidious particulate that can lodge in the lung and cause cancer.

Control of particle emissions from stationary sources can be achieved by filtering the stack gas, by scrubbing it with a liquid spray, or by electrostatic precipitators, which charge the particles with an electric field and collect them on a grounded surface. These devices are effective for large particles but less so for the more dangerous fine particles. Nevertheless, when well designed, they are capable of achieving more than 90% collection of fine particles.

The amount of fine particles from automobile exhaust has been reduced by the use of nonleaded fuel in combination with the catalytic converter. However, the expanding use of diesel fuels in the 1980s will be an area of increasing concern in terms of particulate pollution. It has been estimated that light-duty diesel engines in passenger vehicles may produce 50 to 80 times as many particles as conventional engines with catalytic converters. Compounding this is the fact that 90% of the particulate matter is smaller than 2.5 μ, and that these particles contain relatively high concentrations of organic carcinogens. Control of diesel emissions will require an intensive research effort.

12 | Summary

Looking back on our survey of atmospheric issues, we see that atmospheric balances can be upset both on a global scale through the greenhouse effect and stratospheric ozone destruction and on a local and regional scale through the buildup of fossil fuel exhaust gases and their oxidation products. These problems are interrelated in complex and sometimes paradoxical ways. For example, nitrogen oxides catalyze ozone destruction in the stratosphere but are partly responsible for ozone formation in polluted urban air. The chlorofluoromethane gases are harmless locally but have potential global contributions to both the greenhouse effect and ozone destruction. Carbon monoxide and hydrocarbons are local pollutants, whose noxious qualities can be eliminated by oxidizing them to carbon dioxide, but an increase in the global carbon dioxide concentration will heat up the earth's surface. We do not know whether this in itself would be good or bad since the long-term trends in the climate are quite unpredictable. While scientists have learned a great deal about the atmosphere, partly in response to recent environmental concerns, there is an urgent need to learn much more in order to assess the human impact on it.

Problem Set

1. a) What is the energy in ergs of a photon of blue light that has a wavelength of 450 nm? What is the energy in kilocalories of a mole (6×10^{23}) of these photons? Calculate the same information for infrared light at 1,000 nm and for ultraviolet light at 250 nm.

   b) The energy required to break an oxygen-hydrogen bond in water is 110 kcal/mol. Since biological tissue consists of 80% water, when can radiation cause damage to such tissue? Photosynthesis requires the breaking of bonds in water. Briefly, describe how this can be accomplished using visible light. How does infrared light interact with water? The following information may be useful: Planck's constant (h) = 6.6256×10^{-27} erg-sec; speed of light (c) = 2.9979×10^{10} cm/sec; 1 kcal = 4.184×10^{10} ergs.

2. The polar ice caps have an albedo of about 0.80, while the polar seas have a maximum albedo of about 0.25. How could this difference in albedo cause the spontaneous melting of much of the ice cap if a small rise in ambient temperature occurred? How could large-scale soot deposition on the ice cap cause a similar melting?

3. a) The total mass of carbon contained in fossil fuels that was burned in the world from 1860 to 1975 was 14.0×10^{16} g. It is known that the concentration of CO_2 in the atmosphere in 1975 was 330 ppm, corresponding to a total mass of 2.59×10^{15} kg of CO_2. If the concentration of CO_2 in 1860 was 295 ppm, calculate the percentage of burned carbon that has remained in the atmosphere.

   b) Plant studies indicate that the net primary production (NPP) of organic carbon by photosynthesis can increase with increasing CO_2 concentration in the atmosphere. It has been estimated that the increase in NPP of the biosphere is 0.27 of the percentage increase of atmospheric CO_2. Given that the total NPP of the biosphere is currently estimated to be 5.08×10^{16} g of carbon per year, how much more carbon is being absorbed per year into the biosphere compared with the amount that would be absorbed if the CO_2 concentration were 295 ppm? [Estimates from C. D. Keeling, "Impact of Industrial Gases on Climate," *Energy and Climate: Outer Limits to Growth*, Geophysics Study Committee, Geophysics Research Board (Washington, D.C.: National Academy of Sciences, 1976).]

   c) Currently 0.454×10^{16} g of fossil fuel carbon is burned annually. Assuming the value obtained in part b, what percentage of burned carbon added to the atmosphere would be taken away by increased absorption in the biosphere? The effect of human activities such as clearing of the forests is generally believed to be reducing the NPP. How does such a reduction affect the potential of the biomass to serve as a CO_2 sink?

4. Which of the molecules in the following table has the potential to cause a greenhouse effect similar to that predicted for CFMs (see Figure 2.11)? For polyatomic molecules, identify the specific vibration involved.

S—C—O (linear)	H—Cl	F_2	H_2S (nonlinear)	Cl_2O (nonlinear)
$\nu_1 = 11,641$ nm	$\nu = 3,465$ nm	$\nu = 11,211$ nm	$\nu_1 = 3,830$ nm	$\nu_1 = 14,706$ nm
$\nu_2 = 18,975$ nm			$\nu_2 = 7,752$ nm	$\nu_2 = 30,303$ nm
$\nu_3 = 4,810$ nm			$\nu_3 = 3,726$ nm	$\nu_3 = 10,277$ nm

5. Assume that the concentration of suspended particulates in a polluted atmosphere is 170 $\mu g/m^3$. The particulates contain adsorbed sulfate and hydrocarbons comprising 14% and 9% of the weight, respectively. An average person respires 8,500 l of air daily and retains 50% of the particles smaller than 1 μm in diameter in the lungs. How much sulfate and hydrocarbon accumulate in the lungs in one year if 75% of the particulate mass is contained in particles smaller than 1 μm? [Concentration data taken from S. I. Rasool, ed., *Chemistry of the Lower Atmosphere* (New York: Plenum Press, 1973), p. 85.]

6. a) The lapse rate of the atmosphere over a certain city is positive up to an altitude of 1,000 m, rising 1° C for each 100 m increase in altitude. At 1,000 m, the lapse rate becomes negative, decreasing by 1° C for each 100 m increase in altitude up to 10,000 m. Plot altitude versus temperature for the 10-km layer of atmosphere over the city. The surface temperature is 20° C.

   b) What climatologic phenomenon is occurring in the city? Describe the public health danger that can result from it.

7. For the conversion reaction of carbon monoxide to carbon dioxide:

$$CO(g) + \tfrac{1}{2}O_2(g) \rightarrow CO_2(g)$$

the equilibrium constant K (at 25° C) = 3×10^{45}. Given this enormous value, why doesn't carbon monoxide convert spontaneously to carbon dioxide in air? How does the use of platinum in the catalytic converter of automobiles facilitate the conversion to carbon dioxide? (Hint: Platinum contains unpaired electrons like iron and copper in biological systems; see Figure 2.26.)

8. Why is NO_2, unlike the higher oxides of carbon and sulfur (CO_2 and SO_3, respectively), unstable at 25° C in the presence of sunlight? Describe briefly how the reaction of NO_2 with sunlight plays a key role in smog formation and in the regeneration of NO_2 itself.

9. Examine the accompanying graph and Figure 2.36, and explain the basic dilemma in

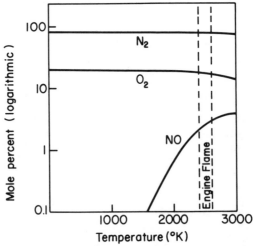

Equilibrium concentrations of nitric oxide in air as a function of temperature

automobile pollution control; i.e., more complete combustion leading to the reduction of unburned hydrocarbons and CO leads to increased formation of NO. How does the stratified charge engine serve to mitigate this dilemma?

10. The oxidation of SO_2 to SO_3 proceeds very slowly in purified air at ambient temperatures. In the presence of particles that contain iron, the oxidation rate is greatly increased. Why is this true (see Figure 2.26 and problem 7)? Since iron is a common constituent in coal soot, describe the link between burning of high-sulfur coal and sulfuric acid formation in urban atmospheres. Why is the removal of pyrites (iron sulfides) from coal relatively easy and effective in pollution abatement?

11. a) The concentration of cloud condensation nuclei (C_n) in polluted city air was found to be $2,000/cm^3$, while the concentration in the countryside was found to be $50/cm^3$. Assume clouds over the two areas have the same water content (W) per unit volume of cloud space. Calculate the ratio r_v/r_v', where r_v is the mean volume radius of a cloud droplet in the countryside and r_v' is the radius for the city cloud. Assume $W = 1$ g/cm^3. (Hint: Write the expression for W in terms of r_v and C_n.)

b) The loss of light due to scattering by the cloud can be expressed as:

$$\frac{I}{I_0} = e^{-2\pi r^2 C_n l}$$

where I_0 and I are the incident and transmitted light intensity, respectively, r and C_n are as defined in part a, and l is the light path length. Compare the loss of light through 10 m of cloud for each of the clouds described in part a.

c) How would you expect the clouds to differ in albedo and effects on visibility? From which cloud would you expect precipitation to occur most readily?

12. When an electron donor such as an organic radical R· or a heavy metal M· reacts with O_2 to form RO_2· or MO_2·, the O—O bond is weakened considerably. Use the molecular orbital diagram for the O_2 molecule (see page 143) to explain why this weakening occurs. Explain with at least two examples from atmospheric or biological chemistry how these electron donors can serve as catalysts for oxidation reactions at ambient temperatures.

13. Give two reasons why the stratosphere is more susceptible to chemical pollution than the troposphere.

14. What is the major natural process that leads to a 50% depletion in the ozone layer? How could a nuclear war lead to a similar process of depletion? Show relevant equations.

15. If the earth's average absolute temperature, T, is given by a balance between the absorbed solar energy, $\Omega (1 - a)/4$, and black body radiation, sT^4, what would be the direction and magnitude of the temperature change if:

a) Power is generated from fossil or nuclear fuels at a rate equivalent to 1% of the incident solar energy?

b) The albedo increases by 1%?

The solar flux, $\Omega = 2$ calories/minute/cm^2; the albedo, $a = 0.4$; and the radiation constant, $S = 1.43 \times 10^{-12}$ calories/sec/cm^2 per degree.

16. a) The atmosphere weighs $1,000$ g/cm^2 and is 20% oxygen and 80% nitrogen by volume. If all the air was at standard pressure (1 atm) and temperature (0° C), how high would the atmosphere extend? The radius of the earth is 6.4×10^6 m. The gas constant $R = 0.082$ atm-l/mol-degree.

b) It is estimated that the ozone layer would be 0.3 cm thick at standard temperature and pressure. What is the fraction of ozone in the atmosphere by volume? By weight?

17. Calculate the factor for converting parts per million by volume to micrograms per cubic meter at 1 atm pressure and (a) at $0°$ C and (b) at $25°$ C.

18. a) Calculate the molar concentration of oxygen in the atmosphere at sea level (1 atm, $25°$ C) and at an altitude of 30 km (0.015 atm, $-40°$ C).

b) What are the concentrations in units of molecules per cubic centimeter?

19. Write the rate expressions for reactions 1–4 of Figure 2.21 and set up the steady-state conditions for O and O_3 (assume that formation and destruction are equal for O and for O_3). Solve for the $(O_3)/(O_2)$ ratio. What is the value of the ratio at an altitude of 30 km, where the rate constants are $k_1 = 10^{-11}$, $k_2 = 10^{-32.7}$, $k_3 = 10^{-3}$, and $k_4 = 10^{-15}$? Also $(M) = 10^{17.7}$. (Units are molecules per cubic centimeter.)

20. Allow for reactions 5 and 6 of Figure 2.23 in the kinetics. Find the dependence of O_3 on NO_2 (include the rate terms for reactions 5 and 6 in the O and O_3 balances, and set up a steady-state condition for NO_2). What concentrations of nitrogen oxides are needed to reduce the O_3 concentration by a factor of three at an altitude of 30 km, where $k_5 = 10^{-14.4}$ and $k_6 = 10^{-11}$?

Notes

1. *Inadvertent Climate Modification. Report of the Study of Man's Impact on Climate (SMIC)*, C. L. Wilson, Director, sponsored by Massachusetts Institute of Technology (Cambridge, Mass.: MIT Press, 1971), p. 198.
2. R. D. Cadle, *Particle Size* (New York: Reinhold Publishing Corp., 1965), pp. 54–62.
3. J. R. Hodkinson, *Aerosol Science*, edited by C. N. Davies (New York: Academic Press, 1966), chap. X.
4. "Long-Term Worldwide Effects of Multiple Nuclear-Weapons Detonations" (Washington, D.C.: National Academy of Sciences, 1975).
5. "Effect of Increased Nitrogen Fixation on Stratospheric Ozone," Council for Agricultural Science and Technology, Report No. 53, January 1976.
6. M. J. Molina and F. S. Rowland, *Nature* 249 (1974):810.
7. For discussion of molecular obritals, see B. H. Mahan, *University Chemistry*, 3rd ed. (Reading, Mass.: Addison-Wesley Publishing Co., Inc., 1975), chap. 12.
8. For discussion of most stable electron configurations and spin alignments, see C. E. Mortimer, *Chemistry: A Conceptual Approach*, 3rd ed. (New York: D. Van Nostrand Company, 1975), pp. 45, 118.

Suggestions for Further Reading

Atmosphere

Heicklen, J. *Atmospheric Chemistry*. New York: Academic Press, 1976.
Rasool, S. I., ed. *Chemistry of the Lower Atmosphere*. New York: Plenum Press, 1973.

Barry, R. G., and Chorley, R. J. *Atmosphere, Weather and Climate*. New York: Holt, Rinehart and Winston, Inc., 1970.

Inadvertent Climate Modification. Report of the Study of Man's Impact on Climate (SMIC). Cambridge, Mass.: MIT Press, 1971.

"Understanding Climatic Change. A Program for Action." Washington, D.C.: National Academy of Sciences, 1975.

Schneider, S. H. *The Genesis Strategy. Climate and Global Survival*. New York: Plenum Press, 1976.

Baes, C. F., Goeller, H. E., Olson, J. S., and Rotty, R. M. "The Global Carbon Dioxide Problem," Oak Ridge National Lab (ORNL-5194), August 1976.

Kerr, J. A., Calvert, J. G., and Demerjian, K. L. "Free Radical Reactions in the Production of Photochemical Smog." In *Free Radicals in Biology*, edited by W. A. Pryor, Vol. II. New York: Academic Press, 1976.

"Environmental Impact of Stratospheric Flight." Washington, D.C.: National Academy of Sciences, 1975.

"Halocarbons: Environmental Effects of Chlorofluoromethane Release." Washington, D.C.: National Academy of Sciences, 1976.

Perera, F., and Ahmed, A. *Respirable Particles: Impact of Airborne Fine Particulates on Health and the Environment*. Cambridge, Mass.: Ballinger Publishing Company, 1979.

Pollution and Climate

Bryson, R. A. "A Perspective on Climatic Change." *Science* 184 (1974):753.

Prospero, J. M., and Nees, R. T. "Dust Concentration in the Atmosphere of the Equatorial North Atlantic: Possible Relationship to the Sahelian Drought." *Science* 196 (1977):1196.

Potter, G., Ellsaesser, H. W., MacCracken, M. C., and Luther, F. M. "Possible Climatic Impact of Tropical Deforestation." *Nature* 258 (December 25, 1975):697.

Houghton, H. G. "On the Annual Heat Balance of the Northern Hemisphere." *J. Meteorol.* 11 (February 1954):1.

Manabe, S., and Wetherald, R. T. "Thermal Equilibrium of the Atmosphere with a Given Distribution of Relative Humidity." *J. Atmos. Sci.* 24 (May 1967):241.

Broecker, W. S. "Climatic Change: Are We on the Brink of a Pronounced Global Warming?" *Science* 189 (1975):460.

Wong, C. "Atmospheric Input of Carbon Dioxide from Burning Wood." *Science* 200 (1978):197.

Adams, J. A., Mantorani, M. S., and Lundell, L. L. "Wood Versus Fossil Fuels As a Source of Excess Carbon Dioxide in the Atmosphere: A Preliminary Report." *Science* 196 (1977):54.

Stuiver, M. "Atmospheric Carbon Dioxide and Carbon Reservoir Changes." *Science* 199 (1978):253.

Woodwell, G. M., et al. "The Biota and the World Carbon Budget." *Science* 199 (1978):141.

Kerr, R. "Carbon Dioxide and Climate: Carbon Budget Still Unbalanced." *Science* 197 (1977):1352.

Woodwell, G. "The Carbon Dioxide Question." *Sci. Am.* 238 (January 1978):34.

Baes, C. F., Goeller, H. E., Olson, J. S., and Rotty, R. "Carbon Dioxide and Climate: The Uncontrolled Experiment." *Am. Sci.* 65 (May–June 1977):310.

Siegenthaler, U., and Oeschger, H. "Predicting Future Atmospheric Carbon Dioxide Levels." *Science* 199 (1978):388.

Kellogg, W. W. "Is Mankind Warming the Earth?" *Bull. Atom. Sci.* 34 (February 1978):10.

McLean, D. "A Terminal Mesozoic 'Greenhouse,' Lessons from the Past." *Science* 201 (1979):401.

Ramanathan, V. "Greenhouse Effect Due to Chlorofluorocarbons: Climatic Implications." *Science* 190 (1975):50.

Wang, W. C., Yung, Y. L., Lacis, A. A., Mo, T., and Hansen, J. E. "Greenhouse Effects Due to Man-Made Perturbations of Trace Gases." *Science* 194 (1976):685.

Tropospheric Air Pollution

Newell, R. E. "The Global Circulation of Atmospheric Pollutants." *Sci. Am.* 224 (January 1971):32.

Lee, R. E., and von Lehmden, D. J. "Trace Metal Pollution in the Environment." *J. Air Pollut. Control Assoc.* 23 (October 1973):853.

Shinn, J. H., and Lynn, S. "Do Man-Made Sources Affect the Sulfur Cycle of Northeastern States?" *Environ. Sci. Technol.* 13 (September 1979):1062.

Novakov, T., Chang, S. G., and Harker, A. B. "Sulfates As Pollution Particulates: Catalytic Formation on Carbon (Soot) Particles." *Science* 186 (1974):259.

Natusch, D. F., and Wallace, J. R. "Urban Aerosol Toxicity: The Influence of Particle Size." *Science* 186 (1974):695.

Kerr, J. A., Calvert, J. G., and Demerjian, K. L. "The Mechanism of Photochemical Smog Formation." *Chem. Br.* 8 (1972):252.

Pitts, J. N. "Keys to Photochemical Smog Control." *Environ. Sci. Technol.* 11 (May 1977):456.

Wilson, D. G. "Alternative Automobile Engines." *Sci. Am.* 239 (July 1978):39.

Cleveland, W. S., Kleiner, B., McRae, J. E., Warner, J. L., and Pasceri, R. E. "Geographical Properties of Ozone Concentrations in the Northeastern United States." *J. Air Pollut. Control Assoc.* 27 (April 1977):325.

Gillette, D. G. "Ambient Oxidant Exposure and Health Costs in the United States—1973." *Science* 199 (1978):329.

Williams, W. T., Brady, M., and Willison, S. C. "Air Pollution Damage to the Forests of the Sierra Nevada Mountains of California." *J. Air Pollut. Control Assoc.* 27 (March 1977):230.

Wolf, P. C. "Carbon Monoxide. Measurement and Monitoring in Urban Air." *Environ. Sci. Technol.* 5 (March 1971):212.

Sze, N. D. "Anthropogenic CO Emissions: Implications for the Atmospheric CO–OH–CH_4 Cycle." *Science* 195 (1977):673.

Carter, L. "Asbestos: Trouble in the Air from Maryland Rock Quarry." *Science* 197 (1977):237.

Stratospheric Pollution

Johnston, H. S. "Ground-Level Effects of Supersonic Transports in the Stratosphere." *Accounts Chem. Res.* 8 (1975):289.

Broderick, A. "Stratospheric Effects from Aviation." *J. Aircraft* 15 (October 1978):643.

Molina, M. J., and Rowland, F. S. "Stratospheric Sink for Chlorofluoromethanes: Chlorine Atom-Catalyzed Destruction of Ozone." *Nature* 249 (June 28, 1974):810.

Cutchis, P. "Stratospheric Ozone Depletion and Solar Ultraviolet Radiation on Earth." *Science* 184 (1974):13.

Johnston, H. "Newly Recognized Vital Nitrogen Cycle." *Proc. Nat. Acad. Sci. USA* 69 (1972):2369.

Council for Agricultural Science and Technology (CAST). "Effect of Increased Nitrogen Fixation on Stratospheric Ozone," Report No. 53. Ames: Iowa State University, 1976.

Other Readings

Brimblecombe, P. "Attitudes and Responses Towards Air Pollution in Medieval England." *J. Air Pollut. Control Assoc.* 26 (October 1976):941.

Garrels, R. M., Lerman, A., and Mackenzie, F. T. "Controls of Atmospheric O_2 and CO_2: Past, Present and Future." *Am. Sci.* 63 (May–June 1976):306.

PART III | HYDROSPHERE

1 | Water Resources

About 97% of the earth's water supply is in the oceans, but its high salt content makes it unfit for human consumption and most other uses. Everyday, however, the sun's rays evaporate a large quantity of the water in the oceans as well as on land and this water falls as rain, which provides us with our supply and reserves of freshwater. We treat water as if it were free and, in a sense, it is free—a by-product of the enormous flux of solar energy on the earth. As noted at the beginning of this book in Figure 1.1, one-third of the solar energy absorbed by the earth's surface goes into the hydrologic cycle. Yet we are using freshwater so fast that we are running into shortages of it from place to place and from year to year.

Table 3.1 shows the amounts of water present on the average in the United States, as atmospheric and soil moisture, and in rivers, reservoirs, and lakes. It also shows the total amount of water in aquifers under the ground. In the right-hand column these figures are translated into units of total annual water consumption in 1975. If water were nonreplenishable and if the hydrologic cycle stopped tomorrow, the United States would, in principle, have enough water available, particularly in groundwater supplies, to last almost 150 years. But, of course, water is recycled continuously through evaporation and precipitation and none of it is literally consumed; it is simply detoured through the various uses that we find for it.

The flow diagram in the top part of Figure 3.1 shows that of the annual precipitation, 70% is evaporated or transpired by plants while the remaining 30% goes into the streamflow. About a quarter of this streamflow is used for various purposes that can be broadly divided into irrigation, municipal water supplies, industrial uses, and electric utilities. Some of the water is evaporated during use, but most of it eventually finds its way to the ocean.

Historically irrigation for agricultural purposes has been the main use of water, but as shown in the lower part of Figure 3.1, the cooling of electric power plants has caught up and is now the chief consumer in the United States. While none of these uses actually destroys the water, the uses contaminate it with pesticides and

Table 3.1   U.S. Freshwater Reserves

Source of Water	Amount (10^{14} l)	Reserve Life*
Atmospheric moisture	2.18	0.4
Soil moisture	7.85	1.5
Rivers	0.56	0.1
Reservoirs	4.51	0.8
Lakes	160.77	30.2
Groundwater	587.43	110.4
Total	763.30	143.4

*Numbers represent units of 5.23×10^{14} l, which equals the total water consumption in the United States in 1975. They represent the number of years the source would last if all water needs were taken from that source alone.
Source: R. G. Bond, C. P. Straub, and R. Prober, eds., *Handbook of Environmental Control: Water Supply and Treatment,* Vol. III (Cleveland: Chemical Rubber Co., 1973), p. 5.

fertilizers, animal wastes, suspended soil particles, waste chemicals, and sewage. If the water is to be used again, it must be purified. This can be accomplished by natural means, through bacterial action or evaporation, or by chemical treatment. The use of water is increasing rapidly and, although water reserves are abundant, the amount accessible at a particular location may be quite limited. It will become more and more necessary to find efficient means for recycling wastewater for its immediate reuse. Another reason to insist on better treatment of the wastewater is that the pollutants carried into our rivers and lakes can cause disruptive effects on the ecologies of these water systems and on human health.

Properties of Water and Aqueous Solutions

Hydrogen bonding

Water is by far the most abundant liquid on the surface of the earth, and it is essential to all known forms of life. Its properties in the liquid state are, however, highly anomalous. This can be seen from a comparison of melting and boiling points for the hydrides of the elements in the first row of the periodic table, as shown in Table 3.2. Not only does water melt and boil at a higher temperature

Table 3.2

	CH_4	NH_3	H_2O	HF
Melting point (° C)	−182	−78	0	−83
Boiling point (° C)	−164	−33	100	20

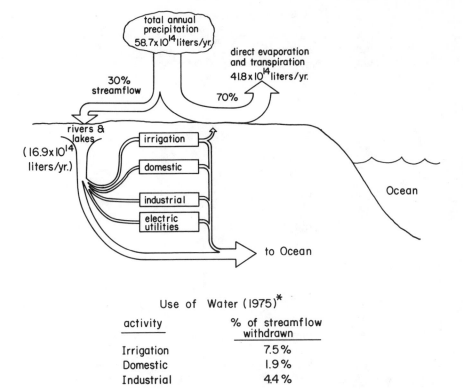

Figure 3.1 Average Distribution of Precipitation in the United States

*Streamflow supplied about 85% of U.S. demand in 1975; the balance was drawn from groundwater.
Source: Data from R. G. Bond, C. P. Straub, and R. Prober, eds., *Handbook of Environmental Control: Water Supply and Treatment,* Vol. III (Cleveland: Chemical Rubber Co., 1973), pp. 6, 131.

than any of its neighboring hydrides, but it also has a larger range of temperature over which it is a liquid. One characteristic that makes the planet earth uniquely suitable for the evolution of life is that its surface temperature, over most of its extent, lies within the liquid range of water.

Another anomalous property of water is that it expands on freezing, whereas almost all other substances contract on solidification. The reason that ice has an anomalously low density is that it has a very open molecular structure, as shown in Figure 3.2. The crystal structure consists of a hexagonal network of water molecules. It has much more empty space than the close-packed structures that are typical of most simple solids.

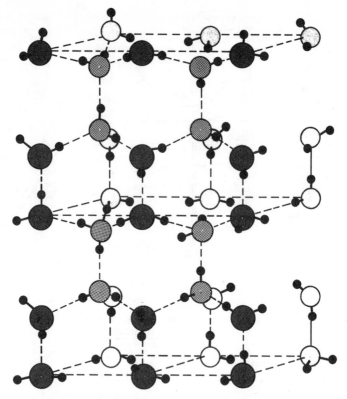

Figure 3.2 Structure of an Ice Crystal

The open network structure reflects the strong directional interactions between water molecules, which are attributable to hydrogen-bonding. Hydrogen bonds (H bonds) are formed between an electron pair donor and a hydrogen atom bonded to an electronegative atom:

$$\overset{\delta^-}{A} - \overset{\delta^+}{H} \cdots : B$$

We draw the H bond as a dotted line to indicate that it is not a new covalent bond, since the valence of the hydrogen atom is already satisfied by the bond to A. Since A is electronegative, however, there is a residual positive charge on H, which permits an electrostatic interaction with the electron pair on B. There are electrostatic interactions for all polar molecules, but they are particularly important when hydrogen is involved, since the hydrogen ion, being a bare proton, has a much higher charge density than any other ion. The strongest H bonds are formed when hydrogen is bound to nitrogen, oxygen, or fluorine, since these are the most highly electronegative elements. Even the strongest H bonds, however, are much weaker than covalent bonds to hydrogen. In the case of water, the intermolecular H- - -O bond energy is about 6 kcal/mol, while the covalent O−H bond energy is 119 kcal/mol. Nevertheless, the intermolecular H- - -O bonds are strong enough to establish the open packing of water molecules in ice.

The neighboring hydrides, NH_3 and HF, can also form quite strong intermolecular hydrogen bonds. However, they can form only one H bond per molecule; NH_3 has only one available electron pair, while HF has only one available H atom. Consequently these substances can form only H-bonded chains of molecules:

or

Only water has two H atoms and two available electron pairs per molecule and, therefore, the ability to form H-bonded networks. The elements directly below oxygen in the periodic table, sulfur, selenium, and tellurium, also have hydrides

with two H atoms and two electron pairs per molecule. They are much less electronegative than oxygen, however, and their intermolecular H bonds are weak. Consequently their melting and boiling points are lower and the temperature range of their liquid state is smaller than those of water.

Most substances expand upon melting because the molecules take up more room in the chaotic liquid state than they do in the close-packed solid. As the liquid is heated, it continues to expand because of the increased motion of the molecules. When ice melts, however, the open lattice structure collapses on itself and the density increases. While the long-range order of the lattice is lost, considerable short-range order remains in liquid water. X-ray scattering measurements have shown that the average number of nearest neighbors around each molecule is only slightly more than four.[1] H-bonded networks still exist, but they fluctuate very rapidly, allowing the individual water molecules to be mobile. As liquid water is heated from 0° C, it continues to contract, reflecting the further disruption of the H-bonded networks. A minimum density is found at 4° C, beyond which water slowly expands, reflecting the increasing thermal motion. H-bonding is important throughout the liquid range, however, as reflected by the high boiling point of water.

Nonpolar solutes; clathrates

Another manifestation of the ability of water molecules to hydrogen bond to each other is the existence of crystalline hydrates of nonpolar molecules called *clathrates*. Examples of these are compounds with the formula $8X·46H_2O$, where $X = Ar, Kr, Xe,$ or CH_4 (Cl_2 and Br_2 also form clathrates of the formula $6X·46H_2O$). The crystals consist of arrays of dodecahedra (Figure 3.3) formed from 20 water molecules H-bonded together (three H bonds per molecule), and the dodecahedra are connected by other H bonds. These extended arrays have relatively large voids in which the nonpolar molecules reside. The hydrates are stable to temperatures appreciably higher than the melting point of ice. (The methane hydrate, which melts at 18° C, caused clogging of natural gas pipelines until the problem was solved by removing water vapor before the gas was fed into the lines.) By filling the voids, the guest molecules stabilize the clathrate H-bond network.

Something similar probably happens when nonpolar molecules dissolve in liquid water. The entropy of solution is large and *negative*. Some examples are given in Table 3.3.

Since $\Delta G = \Delta H - T\Delta S$, a negative entropy means a positive, (unfavorable) ΔG, unless ΔH is negative. The table shows that ΔH is either zero (for aromatic compounds) or negative (for aliphatic compounds), but not negative enough to outweigh the negative entropy. This means that nonpolar substances are immiscible with water, not because the molecules are unattracted to one another, but because the entropy would decrease. A decrease in entropy implies an increase in order. It is reasonable to infer that when nonpolar molecules dissolve in liquid water, they induce the formation of clathrate-like H-bonded networks around themselves. Any such structures, however, are in rapid equilibrium with the bulk water.

Polar and ionic solutes

Water can also H-bond with amine, alcohol, carbonyl, and other polar groups of solute molecules. Such groups increase the solubility of molecules in water.

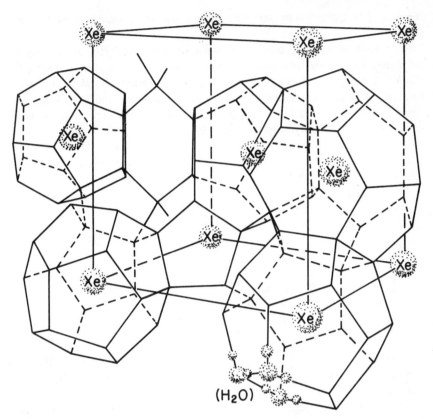

(H₂O)

Figure 3.3 The Structure of a Clathrate Crystal, Xenon Hydrate

The xenon atoms occupy cavities (eight per unit cube) in a hydrogen-bonded three-dimensional network formed by the water molecules (46 per unit cube).

Table 3.3 Free Energy, Enthalpy, and Entropy of Solution in Liquid Water

Process	ΔG (calories/ mol)	ΔH (calories/ mol)	ΔS (entropy units)
CH_4 in benzene $\rightarrow$ CH_4 in water	+2,600	−2,800	−18
C_2H_6 in benzene $\rightarrow$ C_2H_6 in water	+3,800	−2,200	−20
C_2H_4 in benzene $\rightarrow$ C_2H_4 in water	+2,920	−1,610	−15
C_2H_2 in benzene $\rightarrow$ C_2H_2 in water	+1,870	−190	−7
Liquid propane $\rightarrow$ C_3H_8 in water	+5,050	−1,800	−23
Liquid n-butane $\rightarrow$ C_3H_{10} in water	+5,850	−1,000	−23
Liquid benzene $\rightarrow$ C_6H_6 in water	+4,070	0	−14
Liquid toluene $\rightarrow$ C_7H_8 in water	+4,650	0	−16
Liquid ethyl benzene $\rightarrow$ C_8H_{10} in water	+5,500	0	−19

Source: W. Kauzmann, *Adv. Protein Chem.* 14 (1959): 39.

Because of its highly polar character, water is also an excellent solvent for ionic solids.

Such solids are held together by very strong electrostatic forces, which must be overcome upon dissolution. Water greatly assists this process by reducing the magnitude of these forces by a factor of about 80 (relative to air). This is the value of its *dielectric constant* (ϵ). On a molecular level, the large value of ϵ stems from the large value of the *dipole moment* (1.86 Debye) resulting from the partial charges on the hydrogen and oxygen atoms:[2]

Net dipole = 1.86 D

Several water molecules can couple by H-bonding and thus align their dipoles to oppose (and thereby weaken) the electric field that is generated by ions in solution.

Both positive and negative ions are effectively solvated, and the solvation energies are sufficient to overcome the electrostatic stabilization of the ionic lattice. The anions interact with water via H-bonding, while the cations interact with the oxygen electron pairs; e.g.:

The hydration energy increases with increasing charge density on the ions. Some estimates are given in Table 3.4.

Anions, being generally larger than cations, are less strongly hydrated. For a

Table 3.4   Estimated Heats of Hydration

Process	ΔH (kcal/mol)	Charge Ionic Radius
$Li^+(g) \rightarrow Li^+(aq)$	−228	1.47
$Na^+(g) \rightarrow Na^+(aq)$	−202	1.03
$K^+(g) \rightarrow K^+(aq)$	−182	0.75
$Mg^{2+}(g) \rightarrow Mg^{2+}(aq)$	−669	3.04
$Ca^{2+}(g) \rightarrow Ca^{2+}(aq)$	−590	2.02
$Sr^{2+}(g) \rightarrow Sr^{2+}(aq)$	−555	1.78
$F^-(g) \rightarrow F^-(aq)$	−18	0.75
$Cl^-(g) \rightarrow Cl^-(aq)^*$	+14	0.55
$I^-(g) \rightarrow I^-(aq)$	+31	0.45

*The larger anions have $\Delta H > 0$ due to large disruption of the structure of water with consequent breaking of H bonds between water molecules without compensatory strong H-bond formation between anion and water.

given charge type, the energy decreases with increasing ionic radius, while it increases markedly for multiply charged ions. Transition metal cations have well-defined first solvation shells of (usually) six water molecules arranged in an octahedron, e.g.:

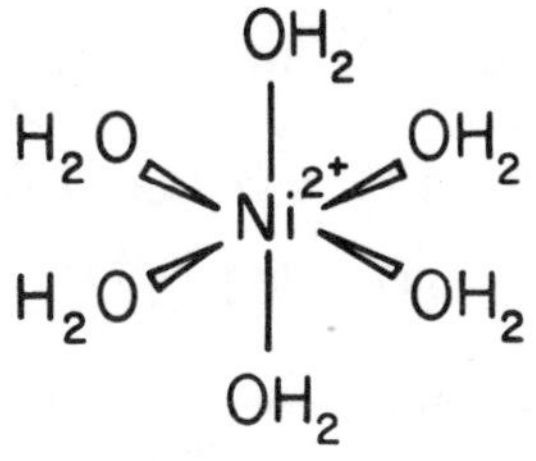

Additional water molecules interact more weakly with the Ni^{2+} ion, but the second solvation shell is not well defined. For anions and most other cations, the exchange of solvating water molecules with bulk water is so fast that even the first hydration shell is not well defined.

2 | Acidity

We will deal with the topic of water treatment after first considering the chemistry of natural waters and how it is affected by human use. The water molecule has an oxygen atom and two hydrogen atoms; in the liquid state there is a small tendency for the hydrogen-oxygen bonds to dissociate, producing a hydrogen ion and a hydroxide ion, as shown in the upper part of Figure 3.4. In pure water, the concentration of each of these ions is 10^{-7} mol/l. A mole is Avogadro's number, 6.02×10^{23}, of molecules, atoms, or ions. The product of the molar concentrations of the hydrogen and hydroxide ion is 10^{-14}. This is the equilibrium constant, K_w, for the ionization reaction of water shown in the

Ionization

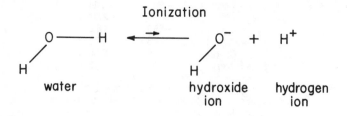

water   hydroxide   hydrogen
             ion   ion

equilibrium constant $K_W = 10^{-14}$

where $K_W = \left[H^+ \right] \times \left[OH^- \right]$

$\left[H^+ \right]$ and $\left[OH^- \right]$ are concentrations in units of moles per liter of solution (1 mole $= 6.02 \times 10^{23}$ molecules, atoms or ions)

Acidity and Basicity

$$pH = -\log \left[H^+ \right]$$

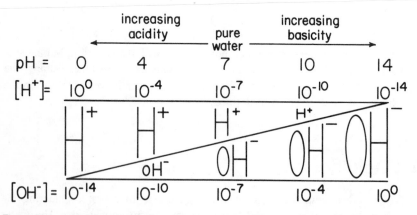

Figure 3.4 Properties of Water

Source: Lower graph designed by Professor Hubert Alyea, Department of Chemistry, Princeton University. Permission for reproduction courteously granted.

figure. The concentration of hydrogen ions can be increased by the addition of acids to water, such as sulfuric, nitric, or hydrochloric acids, and likewise the concentration of hydroxide ions can be increased by the addition of bases, such as sodium hydroxide or ammonia. As illustrated graphically in the lower part of Figure 3.4, the product of the hydrogen and hydroxide concentrations must remain constant, and thus they are reciprocally related; as one goes up, the other goes down. The acidity or basicity of a solution is expressed quantitatively by the pH scale. The pH is defined as the negative logarithm of the hydrogen ion concentration. Thus, as acidity increases, pH decreases. At neutrality, the pH is 7. Acid solutions have pH values less than 7, and basic solutions have pH values greater than 7.

While pure water should have a pH of 7, the water in the atmosphere is not neutral. As illustrated in Figure 3.5 and shown in equation 1, the water can react with carbon dioxide to form carbonic acid, H_2CO_3. Carbonic acid is a weak acid and dissociates to a slight extent, as indicated by equation 2, to form hydrogen ions and bicarbonate ions, HCO_3^-. The concentration of hydrogen ion and bicarbonate ion depend on the carbonic acid concentration, which in turn depends on the carbon dioxide concentration in the air. The current level of carbon dioxide is 325 ppm. As shown by the calculations in the lower part of the figure, saturated rainwater has a carbonic acid concentration of 10^{-5} mol/l and a pH of 5.7.

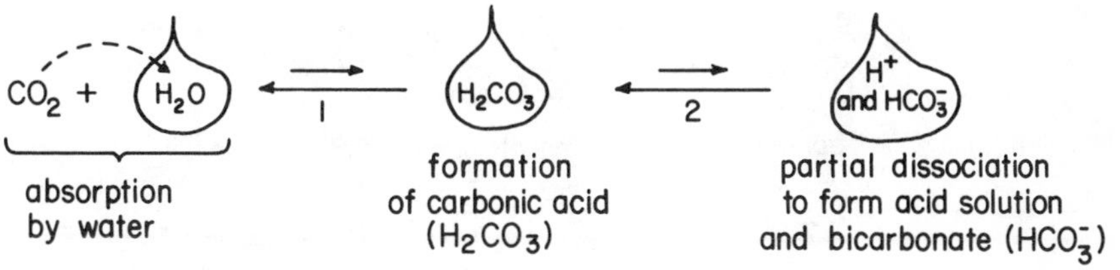

$$1. \quad CO_2 + H_2O \rightleftharpoons H_2CO_3 \qquad K_1 = \frac{[H_2CO_3]\ (mol/l)}{p_{CO_2}\ (atm)} = 10^{-1.5}$$

$$2. \quad H_2CO_3 \rightleftharpoons H^+ + HCO_3^- \qquad K_2 = \frac{[H^+][HCO_3^-]}{[H_2CO_3]}(mol/l) = 10^{-6.4}$$

Atmospheric concentration of CO_2 = 325 ppm
Hence, p_{CO_2} = 0.325 × 10^{-3} atm = $10^{-3.5}$ atm
Therefore, from equation 1:
   $[H_2CO_3]$ = $10^{-5.0}$ mol/l
From equation 2:
   $[H^+]$ = $[HCO_3^-]$
hence, $[H^+]^2$ = $(10^{-6.4})(10^{-5.0})$ = $10^{-11.4}$
   $[H^+]$ = $10^{-5.7}$
   $\boxed{pH = 5.7}$

Figure 3.5 Major Reactions with Carbon Dioxide Causing Natural Acidity of Rainwater

Once the rain has fallen, it percolates through the topsoil as diagrammed in Figure 3.6. The topsoil contains a large amount of carbon dioxide produced by bacterial action. Typically, the carbon dioxide concentration in topsoil is 100 times what it is in the atmosphere and the pH falls to about 4.7. Deeper in the soil there is less bacterial activity and here the carbonic acid can react with basic minerals, such as silicate clays or calcium carbonate, in the neutralization reactions shown in Figure 3.6. The result of these reactions is that carbonic acid is converted into bicarbonate ion and the acidity is lowered. Through these reactions, the pH may rise to neutrality and even a little higher. The pH values of many lakes lie between 7 and 8 and the pH of the oceans is about 8.

The acidity of rain can be significantly increased by industrial pollutants, as we discussed in the preceding part of this book. As shown in Table 3.5, the pH of rain in southern Norway and Sweden, which had a background value in 1956,

Rain (slightly acidic)

↓ ↓ ↓ ↓ ↓ ↓ ↓

TOPSOIL

Zone of intense bacterial action   → CO_2 produced in large amounts
rain (pH = 5.7) + CO_2 →   rain (pH ~ 4.7)

Some ion exchange with silicate clays that lower acidity

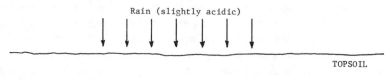

$$[M(SiO_4)]_x + H_2CO_3 \rightarrow \underbrace{M^{n+} + HCO_3^-}_{\text{water soluble}} + [H(SiO_4)]_x$$

$M^{n+} = K^+$, Na^+, Ca^{2+}, or Mg^{2+} and small amounts of Fe^{2+}, Sr^{2+}, and Mn^{2+}

SUBSOIL

Zone of lesser bacterial action → CO_2 produced in lesser amounts

Continued chemical action with clays, limestone particles

LIMESTONE BEDROCK
($CaCO_3$)

crevice

Zone of chemical neutralization reactions that lower acidity

$$CaCO_3 + H_2CO_3 \quad \rightarrow \quad Ca^{2+} + 2HCO_3^-$$

$$MgCO_3 + H_2CO_3 \quad \rightarrow \quad \underbrace{Mg^{2+} + 2HCO_3^-}_{\text{dissolved ions}}$$

Figure 3.6 Chemistry of Water Hardness

Table 3.5   Examples of Acid Rain Downwind from Industrial Areas

Average Changes in pH of Rain
in Southern Norway and Sweden, 1956–1975

Year	pH
1956	6.0–5.5
1961	5.0–4.5
1966	4.5–4.0
1975	4.6–4.3

Average pH of Rain at Selected Sites
in New England, 1970

Place	pH
Hubbard Brook, N.H.	4.03
Hubbardston, Mass.	4.29
Thomaston, Conn.	4.27
New Haven, Conn.	3.81

Ions Present in Rain at Hubbard Brook,
New Hampshire

Ion	Percent
H^+	69 (of cations)
SO_4^{2-}	62 (of anions)
NO_3^-	23 (of anions)
Cl^-	14 (of anions)

Source: pH values given in G. E. Likens, F. H. Bormann, and N. M. Johnson, *Environment* 14 (March 1972): 33. Percentage of ions given in G. E. Likens and F. H. Bormann, *Science* 184 (1974): 1176. Data for 1975 given in G. E. Likens, *Chem. Eng. News* (November 22, 1976), p. 29.

dropped quite dramatically in the succeeding decades. Similarly, pH values for rain falling in various locales in New England in 1970 were on the order of 4. Such low values imply the presence in the local atmosphere of acids that are significantly stronger than carbonic acid. Table 3.5 also shows an analysis of the ions present in rainwater at Hubbard Brook in New England. The fact that 62% of the negative ions are sulfate supports the view that acid rain results mainly from sulfuric acid transported downwind from urban and industrial areas. The particularly severe acid rain conditions encountered in New England and Scandanavia are thought to arise from the concentration of pollutants produced by the industrial cities of the northeastern United States and by the British and German industrial areas, respectively. As shown in the top graph of Figure 3.7, a suffi-

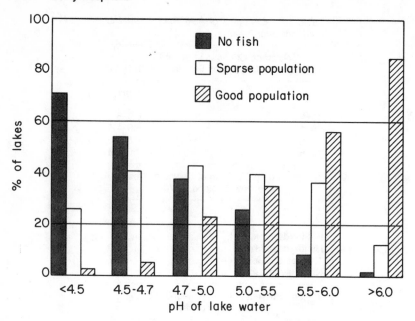

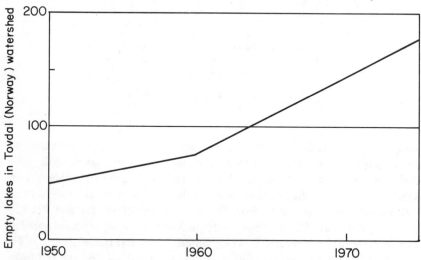

Figure 3.7 Population Declines As the Acidity of Lake Water Increases
Source: G. E. Likens, *Chem. Eng. News,* November 22, 1976, p. 29.

In coal mines, oxidation of sulfide in pyrite (FeS_2) occurs in the presence of water:

$$FeS_2 + \frac{7}{2} O_2 + H_2O \quad \rightarrow \quad Fe^{2+} + 2HSO_4^- \tag{1}$$

In streams, brown precipitate and acid form:

$$Fe^{2+} + \frac{1}{4} O_2 + \frac{1}{2} H_2O \quad \rightarrow \quad Fe^{3+} + OH^- \tag{2a}$$

$$Fe^{3+} + 3H_2O \quad \rightarrow \quad Fe(OH)_3 \downarrow + 3H^+ \tag{2b}$$
$$\text{brown precipitate}$$

Total reaction: (1) + (2a) + (2b) = (3)

$$\underset{\text{pyrite}}{FeS_2} + \frac{15}{4} O_2 + \frac{7}{2} H_2O \quad \rightarrow \quad Fe(OH)_3 \downarrow + \underbrace{2H^+ + 2HSO_4^-}_{\text{sulfuric acid}} \tag{3}$$

Stream pH is as low as 3; i.e. $[H_2SO_4] \approx 0.5 \times 10^{-3}$ M.

Figure 3.8   Acid Mine Drainage

cient drop in the pH in lakes can lead to the elimination of desirable kinds of fish, many of which have rather restricted tolerances for acidity. Lakes in Scandinavia and New York State have already shown marked declines in fish populations. The trend for southern Norway is shown in the bottom graph of Figure 3.7.

The increased acidity of runoff and stream water also increases leaching rates, since basic minerals are dissolved in acid. The effects of this on the ecosystem are not known at this time.

A condition somewhat related to acid rain is that of acid mine drainage. Coal mines, especially those that have been abandoned, are known to release substantial quantities of sulfuric acid as well as iron hydroxide into local streams through seepage. As shown in the reactions in Figure 3.8, these chemicals result from the oxidation of iron sulfide, which is present in large quantities in the underground seams that also contain coal. Iron sulfide is stable in the absence of air, but when the coal seams are exposed to air in mining operations, the oxidation reactions shown in Figure 3.8 take place, with the production of substantial quantities of acid. These reactions continue long after coal-mining operations have ceased. The resulting local pollution problem is quite severe, with many streams in coal-mining areas completely polluted by sulfuric acid. It is difficult to control since sealing up the mines effectively is arduous and expensive. It has been estimated that billions of dollars will be required for adequate cleanup of this problem.

Acids and Bases

The pH scale

The ions formed in the autoionization reaction,

$$H_2O \rightarrow H^+ + OH^- \tag{1}$$

are solvated. The hydrogen ion is believed to have three water molecules in its first solvation shell:

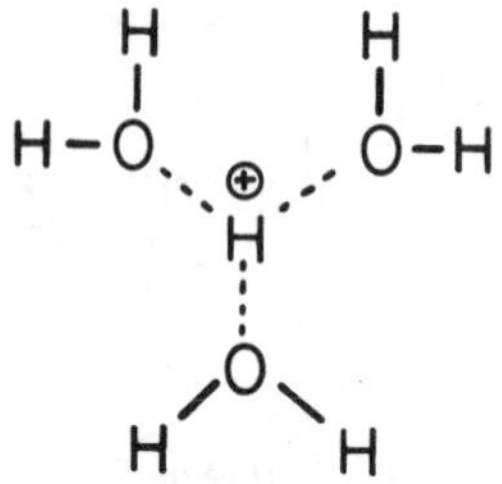

with other water molecules more loosely associated. The hydroxide ion is likewise hydrated. Reaction (1) represents an equilibrium that lies largely on the left. The equilibrium constant expression is:

$$K = \frac{(H^+)(OH^-)}{(H_2O)}$$

Since the concentration of water in water is a constant (55.5 mol/l), it is generally included in the equilibrium constant, which is then written

$$K_w = (H^+)(OH^-) \tag{2}$$

with the concentrations expressed in moles per liter (or molar, M). K_w has a value close to 10^{-14}. In pure water the concentrations of hydrogen and hydroxide ions must be equal, according to reaction (1). Consequently,

$$(H^+) = (OH^-) = \sqrt{K_w} = 10^{-7} \ M$$

   Strong acids are substances in which bonds to protons are sufficiently ionic so that they are split by the solvating action of water. Hydrochloric acid is a strong acid. Although hydrochloric acid is a stable gaseous molecule, it ionizes completely in water to form (solvated) H^+ and Cl^- ions. The concentration of H^+ ions is equal to the concentration of dissolved hydrochloric acid plus the contribution of the autoionization reaction, reaction (1). The latter is such a small quantity that it is usually completely negligible compared with the amount of dissolved acid. It is less than $10^{-7} \ M$ since the addition of acid supresses the autoionization reaction, shifting the equilibrium farther to the left. Since, according to equation (2),

$$(OH^-) = \frac{K_w}{(H^+)}$$

the hydroxide ion concentration [and therefore the contribution to (H^+) from the autoionization reaction] is 10^{-14} divided by the concentration of hydrochloric acid.

Strong bases are hydroxide salts, e.g., NaOH, or a substance that is able to remove a proton completely from water, e.g., sodium methoxide, $NaOCH_3$:

$$CH_3O^- + H_2O \rightarrow CH_3OH + OH^-$$

In a strong base solution the hydrogen ion concentration is given by the reciprocal relation: $(H^+) = K_w/(OH^-)$. A solution that is 10^{-3} M in NaOH has (H^+) $10^{-14}/10^{-3} = 10^{-11}$.

These relationships are expressed with the pH scale, $pH = -\log(H^+)$. Thus, pure water has a pH of $-\log 10^{-7} = 7$. A 1 M solution of a strong acid has a pH of $-\log(1.0) = 0$, whereas a 1 M solution of a strong base (hydroxide) has a pH of $-\log(10^{-14}/1.0) = 14$. Acidity and basicity for most solutions can be expressed on a scale from 0 to 14 using the pH. A pH of 7 defines neutrality.

Conjugate acids and bases

Strong acids transfer a proton completely to water, but with weak acids the proton transfer is only partial, and the degree of transfer is determined by an equilibrium constant:

$$HA \rightarrow H^+ + A^- \tag{3}$$

$$K_a = \frac{(H^+)(A^-)}{(HA)} \tag{4}$$

The value of the acidity constant K_a is often expressed as its negative logarithm, pK_a. When HA is dissolved in water, an equal number of H^+ and A^- ions are produced, so $(H^+) = (A^-)$. Then, from equation (4):

$$(H^+)^2 = K_a(HA) \tag{5}$$

[This expression is valid as long as the contribution to (H^+) from the autoionization of water, reaction (1), is negligible, as it usually is.] If the degree of proton transfer is small [specifically if $K_a \ll (HA)$], then very little HA is used up in reaction (3), and (HA) is essentially the same as the initial concentration of dissolved HA, which we label C_{HA} (sometimes called the analytical, stoichiometric, or total concentration). For example, the acidity constant of acetic acid, HAc, is: $K_a = 10^{-4.75}$ ($pK_a = 4.75$). If HAc is dissolved in water to a concentration of 0.10 M, then

$$(H^+)^2 \simeq K_a C_{HAc} = 10^{-4.75} \times 10^{-1.0} = 10^{-5.75}$$

$$(H^+) = 10^{-2.88} \ M \ \text{or pH} = 2.88$$

i.e., a 0.1 M solution of HAc has a pH close to 3.0. [Since the value of (H^+) is only 1% of the value of C_{HA}, the approximation that $(HA) \simeq C_{HA}$ is a good one in this case. When this approximation is poor, then allowance must be made for the loss of HA.] Since every molecule of HA that ionizes produces one H^+ ion, $C_{HA} = (HA) + (H^+)$, or $(HA) = C_{HA} - (H^+)$. Substituting this into equation (5) and rearranging, we have

$$(H^+)^2 + K_a(H^+) - K_a C_{HA} = 0$$

which may be solved with the quadratic formula.

Weak bases remove a proton partially from water, with the degree of transfer again being determined by an equilibrium constant:

$$B + H_2O \rightarrow BH^+ + OH^-$$

$$K_b = \frac{(BH^+)(OH^-)}{(B)}$$

(the concentration of water is included in the constant). The value of the basicity constant is often expressed as pK_b. When a weak base is dissolved in water, an equal number of HB^+ and OH^- ions are produced. Consequently

$$(OH^-)^2 = K_b(B) \simeq K_b C_B$$

as long as the extent of the reaction is slight ($K_b \ll C_B$). For example, ammonia, NH_3, has a pK_b of 9.25. For a 0.10 M solution of NH_3:

$$(OH^-)^2 = 10^{-9.25} \times 10^{-1.0} = 10^{-10.25}$$

$$(OH^-) = 10^{-5.12} \quad \text{or} \quad pOH = 5.12$$

Since pH = 14 − pOH [from equation (2)], the pH of 0.1 M ammonia is 14 − 5.12 = 8.88.

Buffers

When a weak acid is mixed with its conjugate base, the pH of the resulting solution is relatively insensitive to small additions of other acids or bases. It is said to be *buffered*. The reason for the buffer effect is that the conjugate base is available to react with any extra acid, while the conjugate acid is available to react with any extra base. For example, a solution that is 0.1 M in acetic acid and 0.1 M in sodium acetate has [from equation (4)]:

$$(H^+) = K_a \frac{(HAc)}{(Ac^-)} = 10^{-4.75} \frac{(0.1)}{(0.1)} = 10^{-4.75}$$

or a pH of 4.75. If a small amount of hydrochloric acid is then added, equivalent to 10% of the acetate present (i.e., 0.01 M), the new acetate concentration is 0.09 M, while the new acetic acid concentration is 0.11 M. Now

$$(H^+) = 10^{-4.75}\frac{(0.11)}{(0.09)} = 1.22 \times 10^{-4.75}$$

$$= 10^{0.09} \times 10^{-4.75} = 10^{-4.66}$$

The pH has decreased by only 0.09 units, from 4.75 to 4.66. The same amount of hydrochloric acid, 0.01 M, added to pure, unbuffered water would give a solution of 0.01 M (H^+). Thus the pH would be lowered by 5 units, from 7.0 to 2.0. Similar considerations apply to the addition of extra base.

A mixture of a conjugate acid-base pair is itself called a *buffer*. It controls the pH at a value close to that of its pK_a, as the acetic acid example shows. This pH can be changed by altering the acid-base ratio, but only within narrow limits. For example, a mixture of 0.1 M HAc and 0.01 M Ac$^-$ has:

$$(H^+) = 10^{-4.75}\frac{(0.1)}{(0.01)} = 10^{-3.75}M$$

or a pH of 3.75. However, it is no longer an effective buffer. Addition of 0.01 M hydrochloric acid, as in the previous example, would neutralize the acetate completely, leaving only HAc (0.11 M) with a pH of less than 3. Control of pH is important for many chemical and biochemical processes, and a large number of buffer systems, each having a different pH range, have been developed.

Acid-base mixtures

If there is more than one acid-base pair in solution, the algebra for calculating the pH can become fairly involved. It is best to write down explicitly the mass balances that account for the total concentration of any component. For a single acid-base pair, HA and A$^-$, there are two components, A$^-$ and H$^+$, and the mass balances are

$$C_A = (HA) + (A^-)$$
$$C_H = (HA) + (H^+) - (OH^-) \tag{6}$$

[The (OH$^-$) term in equation (6) accounts for the contribution of autoionization, reaction (1); it is negligible for pH values of less than 7, while (H$^+$) is negligible for pH values greater than 7.] Often C_A and C_H are known from the amounts of material added to pure water when making up the solution, so there are four unknown equilibrium concentrations. The two mass balances and the two equilibrium expressions:

$$K_a = \frac{(H^+)(A^-)}{(HA)}$$

and

$$K_w = (H^+)(OH^-)$$

provide the four equations needed for the solution. Usually approximations can be made to simplify the algebra, as in the examples above.

A second acid-base pair, HB and B^- (the charges are arbitrary; the new pair could as well be HB^+ and B), adds an additional mass balance:

$$C_B = (HB) + (B^-)$$

and adds an extra term to the H^+ mass balance:

$$C_H = (HB) + (HA) + (H^+) - (OH^-)$$

Each additional acid-base pair does likewise. The complexity of a general algebraic solution mounts rapidly, but simplifying approximations can usually be found. In particular the acid-base pair present in highest concentration will control the pH. In addition to the mass balances, logarithmic graphs of the species concentrations, which are easy to construct, are useful in keeping track of the amount of various species (see Figure 3.9).

Some bases have more than one binding site for H^+. Their conjugate acids are called *polyprotic acids*. Because of charge effects, the successive proton ionizations of such acids occur with quite different pK_a values unless the binding groups are far apart (e.g., two carboxylate groups widely separated on an organic polymer). For example, carbonic acid has two ionizable protons:

$$H_2CO_3 \rightarrow H^+ + HCO_3^- \qquad K_{a_1} = 10^{-6.35}$$
$$HCO_3^- \rightarrow H^+ + CO_3^{2-} \qquad K_{a_2} = 10^{-10.33} \qquad (7)$$

while phosphoric acid has three ionizable protons:

$$H_3PO_4 \rightarrow H_2PO_4^- + H^+ \qquad K_{a_1} = 10^{-2.15}$$
$$H_2PO_4^- \rightarrow HPO_4^{2-} + H^+ \qquad K_{a_2} = 10^{-7.21}$$
$$HPO_4^{2-} \rightarrow PO_4^{3-} + H^+ \qquad K_{a_3} = 10^{-12.36}$$

A polyprotic acid-base system has two components with two mass balances. For phosphoric acid, they are:

$$C_{PO_4} = (H_3PO_4) + (H_2PO_4) + (H_2PO_4^{2-}) + (PO_4^{3-})$$
$$C_H = 3(H_3PO_4) + 2(H_2PO_4^-) + (HPO_4^{2-}) + (H^+) - (OH^-)$$

However, if the pK_a values are far apart, as in the present case, then only two or three species can be important at a time. For example, a mixture of 0.1 M $H_2PO_4^-$ and HPO_4^{2-} controls the pH near 7, just as a monoprotic buffer with the same pK_a would; the concentrations of H_3PO_4 and PO_4^{3-} are negligible in this pH range.

Logarithmic Concentration Diagram for 0·1 M Acetic Acid (HAc)

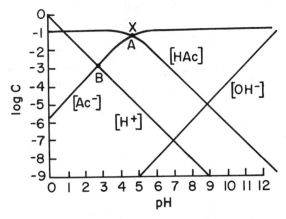

Figure 3.9 Logarithmic Concentration Diagram for 0.1 *M* Acetic Acid (HAc)

To construct such a graph, first locate point *x* at pH = pK_a and concentration *C*. *C* = 0.1 *M* for a 0.1 *M* solution of HAc or a buffered solution containing 0.05 *M* HAc and 0.05 *M* NaAc [total (Ac⁻) = 0.1 *M*]. Draw a horizontal line and lines of slopes +1 and −1 through point *x*. Join the appropriate lines with short curves crossing at a point 0.3 log units below *x*. The lines for (OH⁻) and (H⁺) have slopes of +1 and −1, crossing at pH = 7 and a concentration of 10^{-7}. No detailed numerical calculations are required, and such a diagram is very convenient for doing specific calculations on a system. In many cases, approximate calculations can be made by inspection. For example, point *A* corresponds to a buffered solution with (HAc) = (Ac⁻). We see immediately that the pH is 4.7. Point *B* is a 0.1 *M* solution of HAc where (Ac⁻) = (H⁺). The pH can be seen to equal approximately 2.8. For a system that contains multiple buffers, each buffer can be superimposed on the graph. Predominant components can be identified and negligible ones eliminated on inspection, thereby greatly simplifying the mass balance equations. In the simple diagram above, for example, we see immediately that (OH⁻) is negligible at points *A* and *B*, while at pH = 10, (H⁺) and (HAc) would be negligible.

Source: J. N. Butler, *Ionic Equilibrium, A Mathematical Approach* (Reading, Mass.: Addison-Wesley Publishing Co., 1964), chap. 5.

Likewise, the pH is near 2 for a mixture of H_3PO_4 and $H_2PO_4^-$, and near 12 for a mixture of HPO_4^{2-} and PO_4^{3-}.

3 | Hardness

In addition to its acidity, an important characteristic of natural water is the concentration of dissolved minerals—a condition known as *hardness*. The same neutralization reactions shown in Figure 3.6 that serve to raise the pH of water as it percolates through the soil also introduce appreciable quantities of calcium and magnesium ions and smaller amounts of strontium, iron, and manganese ions. These doubly charged positive ions become noticeable when we wash because they precipitate soap.

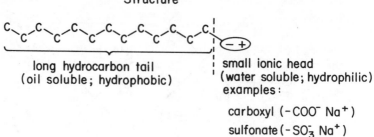

(i)

Structure

long hydrocarbon tail
(oil soluble; hydrophobic)

small ionic head
(water soluble; hydrophilic)
examples:

carboxyl (-COO⁻ Na⁺)
sulfonate (-SO₃⁻ Na⁺)
hydroxyl (-OH)

(ii)

Cleaning Action of Detergents in Water by Agglomeration
(Micelle Formation)

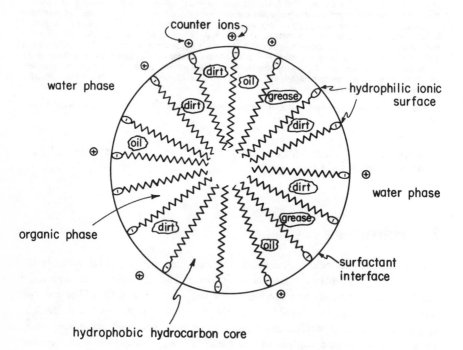

Figure 3.10 General Properties of Detergents

There is a wide variety of cleaning agents used to remove soil and dirt from clothes, dishes, and thousands of other commodities; they are classified under the general term "detergent." The upper part of Figure 3.10 shows that a detergent molecule contains two distinct parts: one part, called the *tail* of the molecule, is usually a long organic chain that is soluble in oil but not in water; the tail is called the *hydrophobic* part from the Greek word meaning "fear of water." In contrast, the head of the molecule is polar and readily soluble in water. This part is called *hydrophilic* from the Greek word meaning "love of water." It consists of carboxyl, sulfonate, or hydroxyl groups. This split personality of the molecule permits it to interact at the same time with both an organic phase and a water phase by concentrating at the surface between the two. The general name for such molecules is *surfactant*.

As illustrated in the lower part of Figure 3.10, detergents work by agglomerating at the interface between oil-soluble dirt particles and water. They surround these particles, with their hydrophobic parts sticking in and their hydrophilic parts sticking out. Such an agglomeration is called a *micelle*. These micelles float freely in the water and are prevented from aggregating with one another by the mutual repulsions of the polar hydrophilic head groups.

As shown in the first part of Figure 3.11, detergents are derived from both natural and synthetic sources. A natural soap is simply a sodium salt of a fatty acid obtained from the hydrolysis of animal fat. Also shown are synthetic deter-

---

Sources

a. Natural soaps—derived from animal fats
   Example:

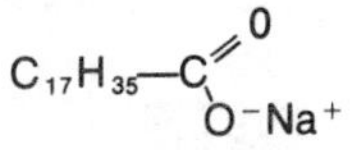

$$C_{17}H_{35}-C\underset{O^-Na^+}{\overset{O}{\lVert}}$$

   Sodium stearate

b. Synthetic detergents
   Example:

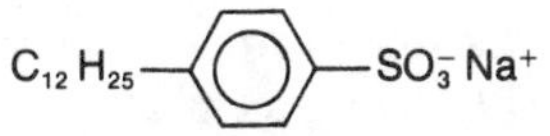

$$C_{12}H_{25}-\langle\bigcirc\rangle-SO_3^-\,Na^+$$

   Sodium alkylbenzene sulfonate

Precipitation of Detergents in Hard Water

$$2C_{12}H_{25}-\langle\bigcirc\rangle-SO_3^- + M^{2+} \longrightarrow (C_{12}H_{25}-\langle\bigcirc\rangle-SO_3^-)_2\,M^{2+} \downarrow$$
$$\text{Precipitate}$$

M^{2+} is mostly Ca^{2+}, some Mg^{2+}, and small amounts of Sr^{2+}, Fe^{2+}, and Mn^{2+}.

Figure 3.11 Sources of Detergents and Effect of Hard Water

gents such as sodium alkylbenzene sulfonate, which came into widespread use after World War II. They were found by detergent manufacturers to be cheaper and more effective than natural soaps. As shown in the lower part of Figure 3.11, all surfactants with a negative charge, whether natural or synthetic, share the same problem: They are precipitated by doubly charged positive ions such as calcium. They are then unavailable for solubilizing dirt and, moreover, the precipitates tend to be scummy and stick to the items being washed.

Consequently, detergent formulations contain other agents called *builders,* which are intended to eliminate precipitation by the positive ions. They can do this by tying the ions up, either in a soluble form or in a precipitate that can settle easily. Chemicals that tie up the ions in soluble form are called *chelating agents.* As illustrated in the upper part of Figure 3.12, these are molecules with several polar sites that can bind the ions through multiple points of attachment. The chelating agent in common use in commercial detergents is sodium tripolyphosphate (STP), which is shown bound to a Ca^{2+} ion at the top of the figure. This compound is relatively cheap and has the advantage that it rapidly breaks down in the environment to sodium phosphate, which is a naturally occurring mineral. Indeed, phosphate is a nutrient for plants, and it is for this reason that environmental groups have objected to its use in detergents on the grounds that natural bodies of water are being overfertilized as a result. Consequently, consumption of phosphate in detergents has decreased by 67% over the past ten years in the United States.

A variety of substitutes for STP have been explored, but none has been found to be fully satisfactory so far. One chelating agent, sodium nitrilotriacetate (NTA), whose structural formula is shown in Figure 3.12, has considerable promise, but there is concern that NTA can bind not only calcium but also heavy metals and could mobilize these toxic elements in the environment. NTA does not break down as readily as does STP and is, therefore, a more potent carrier of metals. Also, there is some evidence that its breakdown products may themselves be carcinogenic.

In the areas of the country where phosphates have been banned from detergent formulations, the substitutes have generally been sodium carbonate or sodium silicate. As shown in the lower part of Figure 3.12, these precipitate Ca^{2+} ions before they can precipitate the detergent. But the $CaCO_3$ or $CaSiO_3$ precipitates produce a scummy residue and are apparently detrimental to the operation of automatic washing machines. Moreover, there is a safety problem associated with these formulations because of the high alkalinity of sodium carbonate and sodium silicate. Both carbonate and silicate can form hydroxide ions in water as shown in equation 5 of Figure 3.12. The alkalinity may be dangerous if the material is accidentally lodged in the eyes or swallowed. A promising new candidate for detergent builders is zeolite, an aluminosilicate mineral, which, as indicated in equation 6 of Figure 3.12, can trap Ca^{2+} ions by exchanging them for its own Na^+ ions. Suspensions of zeolite are not alkaline.

Chelating Agents: Chemicals That Tie Up Positive Ions in Solution So They Can No Longer React with Detergents

1. Sodium tripolyphosphate (STP): $Na_5P_3O_{10}$

Ca^{2+} + STP →

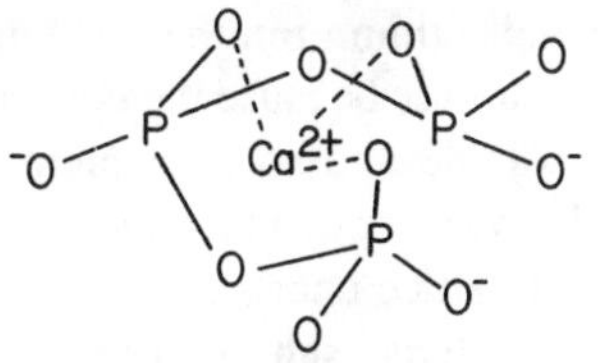

Ca^{2+} tied up in solution;
no further reaction with surfactant

2. Sodium nitrilotriacetate (NTA): $N(C_2H_2O_2)_3Na_3$

Ca^{2+} + NTA →

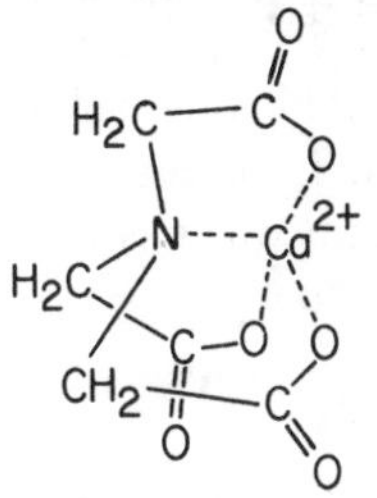

Precipitating Agents

3. Sodium carbonate: Na_2CO_3

$$Ca^{2+} + CO_3^- \longrightarrow CaCO_3 \downarrow$$

4. Sodium metasilicate: Na_2SiO_3

$$Ca^{2+} + SiO_3^{2-} \longrightarrow CaSiO_3 \downarrow$$

5. Hydrolysis of excess Na_2CO_3 or Na_2SiO_3 causes alkaline solution:

$$CO_3^{2-} + H_2O \longrightarrow HCO_3^- + OH_-$$
$$SiO_3^{2-} + H_2O \longrightarrow HSiO_3^- + OH^-$$

Strongly basic solution,
dangerous irritant

6. Zeolite exchange:

$$Ca^{2+} + Na_2 \cdot Al_2O_3 \cdot 2SiO_2 \cdot 4.5H_2O \rightarrow CaAl_2O_3 \cdot 2SiO_2 \cdot 4.5H_2O + 2Na^+$$

Zeolite   Suspension

Figure 3.12 Builders to Prevent Precipitation of Detergents in Hard Water

Two-Phase Interactions

Solubility; calcium carbonate

Although water is generally an excellent solvent for ions, many ionic compounds are only sparingly soluble because the forces that hold the ions together outweigh the ion-water forces. This happens when the ions can arrange themselves in an energetically favorable way in a crystalline lattice. Lattice energies are generally maximum when the positive and negative ions have equal size and charge. For example, lithium fluoride is less soluble than lithium iodide, because fluoride is closer in size to the small lithium ion than is iodide, whereas cesium iodide is less soluble than cesium fluoride because the cesium ion is closer in size to iodide. Sodium carbonate is soluble and so is calcium nitrate, but calcium carbonate is sparingly soluble because both the cation and anion are doubly charged and therefore have a large lattice energy.

The dissolution of a sparingly soluble salt is governed by an equilibrium constant, called the solubility product, K_{sp}. For barium sulfate,

$$BaSO_4 \rightarrow Ba^{2+} + SO_4^{2-} \tag{1}$$

$$K_{sp} = (Ba^{2+})(SO_4^{2-}) = 1.1 \times 10^{-10} \ M^2 \tag{2}$$

The equation is valid as long as there is solid barium sulfate in equilibrium with the solution. Barium sulfate will precipitate if the concentration product of Ba^{2+} and SO_4^{2-} exceeds the value of K_{sp}. If pure water is equilibrated with barium sulfate:

$$(Ba^{2+}) = (SO_4^{2-}) = K_{sp}^{1/2} = 1.0 \times 10^{-5} \ M$$

If either Ba^{2+} or SO_4^{2-} is present in excess, the concentration of its partner decreases in inverse proportion via equation (2).

Often the anion has an appreciable affinity for protons, and its basic character affects the solubility equilibrium. This is the case for the carbonate ion, which is a moderately strong base:

$$CO_3^{2-} + H_2O \rightarrow HCO_3^- + OH^- \qquad K_b = 10^{-3.67} \tag{3}$$

Reaction (3) is obtained by subtracting reaction (7) on page 204 from reaction (1) on page 200, and its equilibrium constant is obtained by dividing the constant for reaction (1) by the constant for reaction (7):

$$K_b = \frac{K_w}{K_{a2}} = \frac{10^{-14}}{10^{-10.33}} = 10^{-3.67}$$

The solubility product of calcium carbonate is $10^{-8.34}$. If calcium carbonate is equilibrated with water, i.e.,

$$CaCO_3 \rightarrow Ca^{2+} + CO_3^{2-} \tag{4}$$

its solubility would be $10^{-4.17}$, provided the calcium and carbonate ions are present in equal amounts. However, a large fraction of the carbonate is immediately converted to bicarbonate via the carbonate hydrolysis reaction (3), and this increases the solubility. In fact, a better approximation is given by

$$CaCO_3 + H_2O \rightarrow Ca^{2+} + HCO_3^- + OH^- \tag{5}$$

which is the sum of reactions (3) and (4). It is the main reaction taking place, with Ca^{2+}, HCO_3^-, and OH^- produced in a 1:1:1 proportion upon dissolution of calcium carbonate. Under this approximation,

$$(Ca^{2+})^3 = K'$$

where K' is the equilibrium constant for reaction (5), obtained by multiplying the equilibrium constants for reactions (3) and (4): $K' = K_b K_{sp} = 10^{-12.01}$. Then $(Ca^{2+}) = (HCO_3^-) = (OH^-) = 10^{-4.00}$, which is about 50% higher than the estimate made without considering carbonate hydrolysis ($10^{0.17} = 1.48$). An accurate calculation, taking account of both (CO_3^{2-}) and (HCO_3^-), gives a value that is 15% higher still.

Note that a saturated solution of calcium carbonate is basic, with a pH close to 10.00. If acid is added, the solubility of calcium carbonate increases further, as the OH^- ion generated by reaction (5) is neutralized. Moreover HCO_3^- can be converted to carbonic acid, H_2CO_3, if the pH drops to the region of the carbonic acid pK_a, 6.35. It is easy to calculate the solubility as a function of pH. We only have to recognize that the calcium ion concentration must remain equal to the total concentration of carbonate in all its protonation states:

$$(Ca^{2+}) = (CO_3^{2-}) + (HCO_3^-) + (H_2CO_3)$$

Substituting the equilibrium expressions:

$$K_{a_1} = \frac{(H^+)(HCO_3^-)}{(H_2CO_3)} \qquad (6)$$

and

$$K_{a_2} = \frac{(H^+)(CO_3^{2-})}{(HCO_3^-)} \qquad (7)$$

$$(Ca^{2+}) = (CO_3^{2-})[1 + (H^+)K_{a_2}^{-1} + (H^+)^2 K_{a_1}^{-1} K_{a_2}^{-1}]$$

and since $(CO_3^{2-}) = K_{sp}/(Ca^{2+})$, we have

$$(Ca^{2+}) = [K_{sp}(1 + (H^+)K_{a_2}^{-1} + (H^+)^2 K_{a_1}^{-1} K_{a_2}^{-1})]^{1/2}$$

With the equilibrium constants given above, $K_{SP} = 10^{-8.34}$, $K_{a_1} = 10^{-6.35}$, and $K_{a_2} = 10^{-10.33}$, this equation gives $(Ca^{2+}) = 10^{-3.0}$ at pH 8 and $10^{-0.82}$ (0.15 M) at pH 5.

If calcium carbonate is equilibrated with carbonic acid, then the dissolved CO_3^{2-} reacts with H_2CO_3 to form HCO_3^-, and the main reaction is

$$CaCO_3 + H_2CO_3 \rightarrow Ca^{2+} + 2HCO_3^-$$

It is obtained by adding reaction (4) to reaction (6) and subtracting reaction (7). Its equilibrium constant is $K_{SP} K_{a_1} K_{a_2} = 10^{-4.36} = (Ca^{2+})(HCO_3^-)^2/(H_2CO_3)$. Since two HCO_3^- ions are produced for every Ca^{2+} ion,

$$(HCO_3^-) = 2(Ca^{2+}) \qquad (8)$$

At equilibrium,

$$(Ca^{2+})(HCO_3^-)^2 = 4(Ca^{2+})^3 = 10^{-4.36}(H_2CO_3)$$

or

$$(Ca^{2+}) = 10^{-1.65}(H_2CO_3)^{1/3} \qquad (9)$$

If the solution is open to the atmosphere, then the equilibrium concentration of carbonic acid depends on the partial pressure of carbon dioxide in the atmosphere,

$$CO_2(g) + H_2O \rightarrow H_2CO_3(s) \qquad (10)$$

The equilibrium constant for the dissolution reaction is $K_s = 10^{-1.50} = (H_2CO_3)/p_{CO_2}$. *The current average of CO_2 content of the atmosphere is 325 ppm, and at sea level $p_{CO_2} = 325 \times 10^{-6}$ atm. This gives $(H_2CO_3) = 10^{-5}$ M and a calcium carbonate solubility, $(C^{2+}) = 10^{-3.32}$ M from equation (9). Also, the bicarbonate concentration, from equation (8), is $(HCO_3^-) = 10^{-3.02}$ M. The pH can be calculated from the equilibrium expression for reaction (6):

$$pH = pK_a - \log \frac{(H_2CO_3)}{(HCO_3^-)} = 6.35 + 1.98 = 8.33$$

Thus, calcium carbonate in equilibrium with air-saturated water is predicted to have a pH of 8.33 and a calcium concentration of $10^{-3.32}$ M. The weathering of limestone, which is mainly calcium carbonate, is a major source of calcium ions and of alkalinity in rivers and lakes.

Ion exchange; clays

Many solids have ions that are loosely held at fixed charge sites. These can be exchanged with ions that are free in solution. The exchanging ions can be either positively charged (cations) or negatively charged (anions):

---

*Actually, dissolved CO_2 is mostly unhydrated; only a small fraction exists as H_2CO_3 molecules:

$$CO_2(s) + H_2O = H_2CO_3(s) \qquad K_h = \frac{(H_2CO_3)}{(CO_2)} = 10^{-2.81}$$

The total concentration of dissolved CO_2 is:

$$(CO_2)_T = (CO_2) + (H_2CO_3) = (H_2CO_3)(1 + K_h^{-1}) = 10^{2.81}(H_2CO_3)$$

Most equilibrium measurements are made with respect to total dissolved CO_2, and in the equilibrium expressions for reactions (6) and (10), (H_2CO_3) is to be understood as $(CO_2)_T$. This works perfectly well as long as $CO_2(s)$ and $H_2CO_3(s)$ are themselves in equilibrium. The intrinsic values of K_{a_1} and K_s are larger than the values given by the factor $10^{2.81}$, since only one molecule of dissolved CO_2 in $10^{2.81}$ actually exists as H_2CO_3. This factor cancels in calculations with the apparent equilibrium constants, if (H_2CO_3) is taken as total dissolved CO_2.

$$R^-M_2^+ + M_2^+ \rightarrow R^-M_2^+ + M_1^+ \qquad \text{cation exchange}$$

$$R^+X_1^- + X_2^- \rightarrow R^+X_2^- + X_1^- \qquad \text{anion exchange}$$

In these reactions R represents a fixed charge site. It attracts ions of the opposite charge with strengths that are proportional to the charge/radius ratio. (Multiply charged ions occupy more than one ion exchange site.) Ion exchange resins are organic polymers with charged groups that are covalently attached. Cation exchangers commonly have sulfonate groups, $-OSO_3^-$, whereas anion exchangers commonly have quaternary ammonium groups, $-N(CH_3)_3^+$. Some anionic groups, such as carboxylate, $-COO^-$, have especially high affinities for protons and are called *weak acid cation exchangers,* while some cationic groups, such as ammonium, $-NH_3^+$, have especially high affinity for hydroxide and are called *weak base anion exchangers.* Cation and anion exchange resins are widely used together to deionize water:

$$R^-H^+ + M^+ - X^- \rightarrow R^-M^+ + H^+ + X^-$$

$$R^+OH^- + H^+ + X^- \rightarrow R^+X^- + H_2O$$

The spent resins can be regenerated by washing them with strong acids and bases.

Nature's chief ion exchangers are silicate minerals. Silicon dioxide, or silica, is a polymeric solid with a three-dimensional network of silicon atoms bound tetrahedrally to four oxygen atoms, which are in turn bound to two silicon atoms each.

In highly alkaline solution, silica is broken down to silicate ions, SiO_4^{4-}. Neutralization produces silicic acid, $Si(OH)_4$, which is a weak acid. The concentration of monomeric silicic acid is very low, however, because of the strong tendency of the silicate units to repolymerize, with loss of water:

$$2Si(OH)_4 \rightarrow (HO)_3Si-O-Si(OH)_3 + H_2O$$

Polymers of varying size and structure are formed, depending on the solution

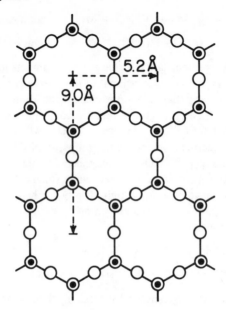

Figure 3.13   Diagram of Phyllosilicate Sheet (top view)

The black circles represent silicon atoms and the open circles represent oxygen atoms. Each silicon atom is tetrahedrally bound to four oxygen atoms. The oxygen atoms shown superimposed on the silicons are directed upward and bound to a second parallel layer.

conditions. Their surfaces contain the weakly acidic Si—OH groups, which can exchange protons for ions in solution.

Many silicate minerals contain sheets of polymerized silicate tetrahedra arranged in layers. Figure 3.13 shows a structural diagram of a silicate sheet. Three of the oxygen atoms around each silicon atom are linked to neighboring silicon atoms in the sheet, while the fourth oxygen atom sticks up out of the sheet. Often the fourth oxygen atom is bound to an aluminum ion, Al^{3+}. This is the case for the common aluminosilicate clay mineral, kaolinite, whose structural diagram is shown in Figure 3.14. Aluminum prefers octahedral coordination by six oxygen atoms. In kaolinite, two of these are provided by neighboring silicate groups, while the remainder are hydroxide groups. The aluminum hydroxide octahedra complete the layer. The next layer is held to the first one by hydrogen bonds between the aluminum hydroxyl groups and the silicate oxygen atoms.

Figure 3.15 shows another common aluminosilicate mineral, pyrophyllite, with a triple-layer structure. In this case the aluminum octahedra are sandwiched between two silicate sheets. The next triple layer is held only weakly to the first one, since the facing silicate oxygen atoms lack protons with which to form hydrogen bonds. The interlayer space can be filled with water molecules, and pyrophyllite swells considerably in water.

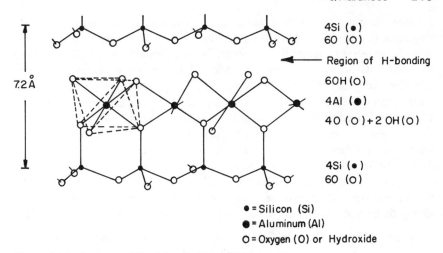

4Si (•)
6O (O)

←——— Region of H-bonding

6OH (O)
4Al (•)
4O (O) + 2 OH (O)

4Si (•)
6O (O)

7.2 Å

• = Silicon (Si)
● = Aluminum (Al)
O = Oxygen (O) or Hydroxide

Figure 3.14   Structure of Kaolinite, $Al_4Si_4O_{10}(OH)_8$

Figure shows phyllosilicate and octahedral layers. The distance between two successive plates is 7.2 Å. Dashed lines show sixfold coordinate positions in octahedral layer. Note that six oxygen atoms are associated with four silicon atoms in the phyllosilicate layer since silicon shares each of its three oxygens with another silicon. Hence, each Si is bonded to 3/2 oxygen atoms.

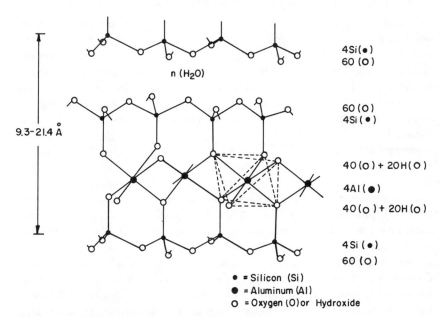

4Si(•)
6O (O)

n (H₂O)

6O (O)
4Si (•)

4O (o) + 2OH(O)
4Al(•)
4O (o) + 2OH (o)

4Si (•)
6O (O)

9.3–21.4 Å

• = Silicon (Si)
● = Aluminum (Al)
O = Oxygen (O) or Hydroxide

Figure 3.15   Structure of Pyrophyllite, $Al_2Si_4O_{10}(OH)_2$

Figure shows octahedral layer sandwiched between two phyllosilicate layers. The distance between the plates can vary up to 21 Å, depending on the amount of water present between plates. Dashed lines show sixfold coordinate positions in octahedral layer.

Other aluminosilicates have kaolinite or pyrophyllite structures, but with aluminum or silicon substituted by metal ions of lower charge. Thus, the common clay mineral montmorillonite has the pyrophyllite structure, but about one-sixth of the Al^{3+} ions are replaced with Mg^{2+}. Likewise, the illite clays share this structure, but with Al^{3+} replacing some of the Si^{4+} ions in the silicate sheet. The substitution of cations with lower charge produces an excess negative charge, which is balanced by the adsorption of cations, commonly Na^+, K^+, Mg^{2+}, or Ca^{2+}, in the medium between the aluminosilicate layers. It is this feature that makes clay particles good ion exchangers, since the adsorbed cations are readily exchanged for other cations in solution. If the solution is acidic, then the adsorbed cations are replaced by protons, and both the pH of the solution and its metal ion concentration increase. Furthermore, the aluminosilicate structure can slowly be broken down upon acidification, with the production of silicic acid

$$cation-Al-silicate + H_2CO_3 + H_2O \rightarrow HCO_3^- + cation + Si(OH)_4 + \\ Al-silicate$$

This type of reaction is important in the weathering of rocks and soil, as well as in the alkalinizations of natural waters.

Ocean chemistry and the size of the carbon dioxide sink

The oceans as well as the atmosphere are thought to have formed from the outgassing of the primitive earth. As the earth evolved, large quantities of gases such as H_2, H_2O, CO, CO_2, N_2, and HCl were released at the surface by volcanic action. The H_2 escaped into outer space or reacted with the carbon oxides and N_2 to form CH_4, NH_3, and more complex organic molecules, from which life eventually evolved. The N_2 formed the bulk of the atmosphere, with O_2 arising as a major constituent much later with the development of photosynthesizing organisms.

As the earth cooled, the H_2O condensed to form the oceans. The strong acid HCl reacted with the basic aluminosilicates of the earth's crust via the ion-exchange processes described in the preceding section, producing salt water. Today's oceans contain 0.55 mol/l of chloride ion. The principal cation is Na^+ (0.47 M), followed by Mg^{2+} (0.054 M), Ca^{2+} (0.010 M), K^+ (0.010 M), and many others in trace concentrations. Anions of importance are SO_4^{2-} (0.038 M), HCO_3^-, and CO_3^{2-}.

Most of the earth's CO_2 was precipitated as calcite, $CaCO_3$, and dolomite, $CaMg(CO_3)_2$. Some of it was reduced through photosynthesis and buried in the earth's crust. A small fraction of the total CO_2 circulates among the atmosphere, biosphere, and the oceans. The amounts contained in these reservoirs are given in Table 3.6. By burning fossil fuels, we are adding to the total amount of circulating CO_2. The atmospheric CO_2 concentration has been rising significantly in recent years, but at a rate only about half that expected if all the CO_2 from fossil

Table 3.6   Major Carbon Reservoirs*
(pool sizes in 10^9 tons carbon)

Atmosphere	702
Terrestrial biosphere	
Live	680
Dead (humus, new peat)	1,080
Total	1,760
Oceans	
Surface layer (0–70 m)	580
Deep layers	38,420
Total	39,000
Yearly production from burning of fossil fuels	5

*Table does not include deposits of organic shale and lime-
stone whose quantities dwarf any given in the table. They are
not included because they are essentially immobile. Table
also does not include total fossil fuel reserve, which is 10^{13}
tons carbon.
Source: C. F. Baes, H. E. Goeller, J. S. Olson, and R. M.
Rotty, "The Global Carbon Dioxide Problem," Oak Ridge
National Laboratory Report No. 5194, August 1976, p. 2.

fuels stayed in the air. It is important to know where the CO_2 has gone and
whether it is likely to be distributed similarly in the future if the effect of

From the atmosphere, CO_2 can enter the biosphere or the hydrosphere. Although CO_2 cycles continuously between the biosphere and the atmosphere, the
net flux is zero unless the mass of reduced carbon in the biosphere is changing.
There is much uncertainty about whether the biomass is shrinking or expanding.
It is known that green plants can respond to increasing CO_2 concentration by
increasing their growth, but under most natural conditions it is likely that plant
growth is limited by the amounts of sunlight, water, or other nutrients, rather
than by the CO_2 concentration. Agricultural activities are expected to produce a
net decrease in the biomass through forest clearing and soil erosion. But quantitative estimates of biomass reductions or accretions are extremely difficult to
make, and neither the magnitude nor the size of the net flux between the biosphere and the atmosphere is known.

The net flux between the atmosphere and the oceans should be much more
predictable, since the solution chemistry is straightforward. The average pH of
ocean water is 8.15. This is the value maintained by the ion-exchange
mechanisms of the silicate minerals that line the ocean floor. If the pH is held
constant, then the relative concentrations of H_2CO_3, HCO_3^-, and CO_3^{2-} are also
held constant via the equilibrium:

$$H_2CO_3 \rightarrow H^+ + HCO_3^- \qquad K_{a_1} = \frac{(H^+)(HCO_3^-)}{(H_2CO_3)} \qquad (6)$$

$$HCO_3^- \rightarrow H^+ + CO_3^{2-} \qquad K_{a_2} = \frac{(H^+)(CO_3^{2-})}{(HCO_3^-)} \qquad (7)$$

If the total dissolved carbonate is C_c,

$$C_c = (H_2CO_3) + (HCO_3^-) + (CO_3^{2-})$$

or

$$C_c = (H_2CO_3)F$$

where

$$F = [1 + K_{a_1}(H^+)^{-1} + K_{a_2}K_{a_1}(H^+)^{-2}]$$

This expression is obtained by substitution of the equilibrium equations (6) and (7). F is constant if (H^+) is constant. In this case, the equilibrium ratio of the total dissolved carbonate to the atmospheric CO_2 content is also constant:

$$CO_2(g) + H_2O \rightarrow H_2CO_3(s) \qquad K_s = \frac{(H_2CO_3)}{p_{CO_2}}$$

$$\frac{C_c}{p_{CO_2}} = \frac{(H_2CO_3)F}{p_{CO_2}} = K_sF$$

This means that an increase in the amount of atmospheric CO_2 is followed by transfer to the ocean to keep the equilibrium ratio constant. According to Table 3.6, the ocean contains about 56 times more carbon than does the atmosphere. Consequently a doubling of the atmospheric CO_2 content would require transfer to the ocean of 56 times as much CO_2 as is presently in the atmosphere in order to maintain a constant value of C_c/p_{CO_2}.

The ocean is therefore a large-scale sink for CO_2. The time it takes for the whole ocean to reach equilibrium is very long, however. The top layer of the ocean, about 75 m deep, is well mixed and exchanges CO_2 with the atmosphere fairly rapidly. Below this, the temperature drops rapidly. The stratification of the water is therefore stable and mixing with the surface layer is slow. It is estimated to take thousands of years for complete mixing of the ocean.[3,4]

The surface layer is not in equilibrium with the silicate minerals at the bottom, and its pH is regulated by the carbonate system itself. Of the total dissolved carbonate, about 87% exists as HCO_3^- and 13% as CO_3^{2-}, H_2CO_3 being less than 1%. When more CO_2 dissolves in the surface layer, it reacts with CO_3^{2-} to produce more HCO_3^-:

$$CO_2(g) + CO_3^{2-} + H_2O \rightarrow 2HCO_3^- \qquad (11)$$

This reaction is obtained by adding reactions (6) and (10) and subtracting reaction (7); its equilibrium expression:

$$K = K_s K_{a_1} K_{a_2}^{-1} = \frac{(HCO_3^-)^2}{(CO_3^{2-})p_{CO_2}}$$

can be rearranged to

$$(CO_3^{2-})p_{CO_2} = \frac{(HCO_3^-)^2}{K} \qquad (12)$$

Since $(CO_3^{2-})/(HCO_3^-)$ is only 0.15, a substantial depletion of (CO_3^{2-}) via reaction (11) produces little change in (HCO_3^-). The right side of equation (12) is essentially constant, and (CO_3^{2-}) and p_{CO_2} are reciprocally related. However, there is relatively little (CO_3^{2-}) for the CO_2 to react with. According to Table 3.6, the surface layer of the ocean contains 83% more carbon than does the atmosphere. Of this, 13% is CO_3^{2-}, corresponding to 11% of the atmospheric reservoir. If p_{CO_2} doubles, then (CO_3^{2-}) is halved, but this requires the transfer of only ½(11%) or 5.5% of the incremental CO_2 to the surface layer. The remaining 94.5% of the incremental CO_2 remains in the atmosphere.

It is evident that the rapidly equilibrating surface layer has very little capacity for absorbing CO_2, whereas the ocean as a whole has a very large capacity but equilibrates only slowly. The response of the air-ocean system to increasing CO_2 inputs therefore depends sensitively on the rate of mixing of the surface with the deeper layers. This can be determined from the vertical distribution of radioisotopes that have half-lives on the scale of years and that exchange with the atmosphere, such as $^{14}CO_2$ and ^{222}Rn. The mixing can be represented with a diffusion equation; the process is called *eddy diffusion*, as opposed to *molecular diffusion*, which would be much too slow a mechanism. It has recently been shown that a model with a rapidly mixed surface layer and eddy diffusive deeper layers gives a satisfactory account of the observed atmosphere increase over the past 20 years.[5] The fraction of the injected CO_2 that remains in the atmosphere is indeed calculated to be around 50%. A similar fraction is predicted for further modest injections, but the fraction is predicted to increase appreciably for large CO_2 increments. According to the model, the value of p_{CO_2} is expected to double in about 200 years, even if the CO_2 production rate is held at the 1975 level, assuming that the biosphere makes no net contribution. If the CO_2 production rate continues to grow at 5% a year, as it did between 1960 and 1970, p_{CO_2} would double by the year 2020 and would increase very rapidly thereafter.

If the p_{CO_2} doubles, then the pH of the surface water at equilibrium would be decreased by about 0.3 units. This can be seen from the equilibrium expression for reaction (7):

$$K_{a_2} = \frac{(H^+)(CO_3^{2-})}{(HCO_3^-)}$$

$$pH = pK_a + \log \frac{(CO_3^{2-})}{(HCO_3^-)}$$

Since (CO_3^{2-}) would be halved, with no significant increment in (HCO_3^-) the change in pH would be about $\log 2 = 0.30$. Each additional doubling of p_{CO_2} would produce an additional 0.3-unit drop in the pH, as the buffer ratio $(CO_3^{2-})/$

(HCO_3^-) continues to decrease. The equilibrium would be disturbed, however, by the steady mixing with the deeper ocean layers, which would limit the pH drop. In the very long run, the pH would be restored to its initial value by equilibration with the silicate minerals.

Another interesting fact about the surface layer is that it is supersaturated with respect to calcite and even more saturated with respect to dolomite. The solubility products in seawater at atmospheric pressure are estimated to be

$$CaCO_3 \rightarrow Ca^{2+} + CO_3^{2-} \quad K_{sp} = (Ca^{2+})(CO_3^{2-}) = 10^{-6.8}$$

$$CaMg(CO_3)_2 \rightarrow Ca^{2+} + Mg^{2+} + 2CO_3^{2-} \quad K_{sp} = (Ca^{2+})(Mg^{2+})(CO_3^{2-})^2$$
$$= 10^{-14.3}$$

Seawater contains $0.010\ M\ Ca^{2+}$, and $0.054\ M\ Mg^{2+}$. If it were in equilibrium with calcite, the carbonate concentration would be:

$$(CO_3^{2-}) = \frac{10^{-6.8}}{(Ca^{2+})} = 10^{-4.8} = 1.6 \times 10^{-5}$$

while in equilibrium with dolomite, it would be:

$$(CO_3^{2-}) = \left[\frac{10^{-14.3}}{(Ca^{2+})(Mg^{2+})} \right]^{1/2} = 10^{-5.5} = 3.2 \times 10^{-6}$$

The measured carbonate concentration is 2.6×10^{-4}, which is a factor of 16 greater than the calcite equilibrium value and a factor of 80 greater than the dolomite equilibrium value. If equilibrium with the more stable mineral, dolomite, were established, the carbonate concentration would decrease by a factor of 80 and so would the atmospheric p_{CO_2}. Both calcite and dolomite are known to form very slowly, and equilibrium is not established at ambient pressure and temperature within the circulation time of the ocean. In fact, the main mechanism of calcium carbonate sedimentation is via the biological deposition of sea shells. The solubility of calcium carbonate increases with increasing pressure, and seawater becomes undersaturated at depths of about 4,000 m. At greater depths sea shells gradually dissolve, and no limestone deposits are found.

Amphiphilic solutes; surfactants, lipids and proteins

Many molecules contain both a nonpolar and a polar or ionic part. Such a molecule reacts with water in two ways and is called *amphiphilic*. The nonpolar part is hydrophobic, whereas the polar or ionic part is hydrophilic. An amphiphilic molecule concentrates at the interface between water and a nonpolar liquid; one part of it is in contact with each phase. It is a surfactant, reducing the surface tensions between the two phases.

Surfactants whose hydrophobic parts are long-chain hydrocarbons form micelles when mixed with water, as illustrated in the lower part of Figure 3.10. The aggregation of the hydrocarbon chains is sometimes referred to as *hydrophobic bonding*; it reflects entropic exclusion of hydrocarbons from water, as discussed above.

The shape of the micelle depends on the size of the hydrocarbon chains. The hydrophobic bonding favors close packing of the tails, whereas the head groups are electrostatically repelled from one another. There is, therefore, an optimum surface area occupied by each head group, reflecting this balancing of opposing forces. The shape of the micelle reflects the surface-to-volume ratio. It is twice as big for a sphere as it is for a cylinder. Surfactant micelles are ellipsoids that vary in shape between these two extremes. Short tails produce small micelle volumes and favor spherical shapes, while long tails produce large volumes and favor cylindrical shapes.

Another possible shape is the bilayer, shown in Figure 3.16. This has half the surface-to-volume ratio of a cylinder. Surfactants with single tails do not form bilayers, but phospholipids, which have two hydrocarbon tails, do form bilayers. Phospholipids are biological molecules in which two long-chain fatty acids are esterified with glycerol. The third glycerol-hydroxyl group is linked to a phosphate group with an additional polar substituent. In the case of lecithin, whose molecular structure is shown in Figure 3.16, the polar group is the quaternary ammonium derivative choline. (Lecithin belongs to the class of lipids called phosphatidylcholine.) The two hydrocarbon chains produce twice the micellar volume per head group of a single chain, thereby stabilizing the bilayer structure. The membranes of all biological cells are based on the lipid bilayer.

Proteins are also amphiphilic molecules. They consist of long polypeptide chains,

$$\cdots-\overset{\overset{\text{O}}{\|}}{\text{C}}-\text{NH}-\underset{\underset{\text{R}}{|}}{\text{CH}}-\overset{\overset{\text{O}}{\|}}{\text{C}}-\text{NH}-\underset{\underset{\text{R}'}{|}}{\text{CH}}-\overset{\overset{\text{O}}{\|}}{\text{C}}-\text{NH}\cdots$$

folded up into specific three-dimensional structures, which are essential to the protein's function. The only thing that distinguishes one peptide unit from the next is the nature of the side chain, R, of which there are 20. Some of these are hydrophobic, while others are hydrophilic. In soluble proteins, those that function in biological fluids, the hydrophobic side chains are generally found on the interior of the folded structure in contact with other hydrophobic groups, whereas the hydrophilic side chains generally stick out into the aqueous solution. In effect, the protein forms its own micelle, with an oily inner region and a generally polar surface. The actual structures are, of course, much more complex, with clefts and channels whereby water and substrate molecules can reach interior regions of the protein.

Lecithin

$$\overset{+}{N}-(CH_3)_3$$
$$|$$
$$CH_2$$
$$|$$
$$CH_2$$
$$|$$
$$O$$
$$|$$
$$O=P-O^-$$
$$|$$
$$O$$

$$CH_2-CH-CH_2$$
$$|\qquad\quad|$$
$$O\qquad\quad O$$
$$|\qquad\quad|$$
$$C=O\quad\;\; C=O$$
$$|\qquad\quad|$$
$$CH_2\quad\;\;\; CH_2$$
$$|\qquad\quad|$$
$$(CH_2)_{15}\;(CH_2)_{15}$$
$$|\qquad\quad|$$
$$CH_3\quad\;\;\; CH_3$$

Polar head

Hydrocarbon tails

Cross Section of a Lipid Bilayer Containing Two Planar Sheets

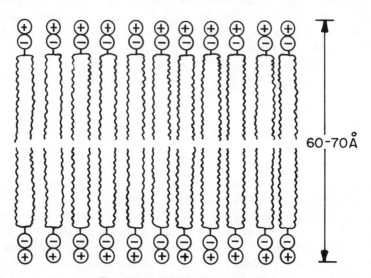

60-70Å

Figure 3.16 The Lipid Bilayer

It is believed that hydrophobic bonding is important in maintaining the native folding patterns of proteins. This is supported by the observation that high concentrations of substances like urea, NH_2—$\overset{\overset{O}{\|}}{C}$—$NH_2$, can denature proteins, causing them to unfold. (High temperatures also denature proteins; cooked egg white is denatured albumin.) The urea molecule is effective at H-bonding; it has both positive hydrogen atoms and electron pair acceptors. At high concentrations it can compete with water for H bonds, disrupting the H-bonded network of water itself. This would be expected to reduce the entropic driving force for hydrophobic bonding. (The solubility of nonpolar solutes increases when urea is added to the solution.)

Many proteins are bound to biological membranes. They generally consist of two regions; one of these sticks into the solution (there are two such regions if the protein spans the entire membrane) and has many hydrophilic side chains, while the other is anchored among the hydrocarbon chains of the lipid bilayer and has mostly hydrophobic side chains. The only way to extract such proteins from their membranes without disrupting their structure is to add surfactants, which can form a micelle around the hydrophobic portion of the protein. Even when highly purified, membranous proteins inevitably have a substantial amount of surfactant attached. They can be transferred to artificial but pure lipid bilayers for studies of their function.

4 | Eutrophication

Overnutrition of bodies of water caused by inputs of phosphates or other nutrients is commonly called *eutrophication*. Technically, eutrophication is simply the natural process of providing a body of water with the nutrients for the aquatic life it supports. As diagrammed in Figure 3.17, the process leads to filling in of lakes with sediment. A lake starts its life cycle as a clear body of water, which is described as *oligotrophic*. Then, as nutrients enter the lake through land runoff and as aquatic life grows and dies, the water acquires a high content of organic debris. At this stage the lake is described as *eutrophic*. Eventually it fills in completely, forming a marsh and then dry land.

As illustrated at the top of Figure 3.18, the natural aging process in lakes and coastal areas is slow because algae and other phytoplankton depend on sunlight and are productive only in the surface layer, called the *euphotic zone*. Nutrients are lost as dead biomass and other organic debris sink into the deeper waters, where sunshine cannot penetrate. Growth is limited by the nutrient balance between surface inputs and losses to the deeper layers. The physical mixing of the deeper layers with the surface is prevented by thermal stratification, since the surface is warmed by the sunlight. As shown at the right side of the first diagram

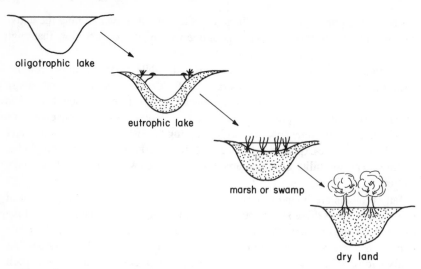

oligotrophic lake

eutrophic lake

marsh or swamp

dry land

Figure 3.17 Eutrophication and the Aging of a Lake by Accumulation of Sediment

of Figure 3.18, the temperature decreases sharply near the bottom of the euphotic zone. Since warm water is less dense than cold water, this stratification is stable and there is little mixing.

In temperate zones the layers mix in the winter, as diagrammed in the second part of Figure 3.18. When the surface cools down, the temperature and hence the density become uniform. Wind and waves easily induce mixing, which brings nutrient-rich waters to the surface. Productivity is now limited, however, by the low solar intensity in winter.

Of current concern is the enormous acceleration of the eutrophication process in lakes and estuaries brought about by the year-round injection of large quantities of phosphates and other nutrients from human sources, thus upsetting the natural balance of the nutrient cycle.

As shown schematically in Figure 3.19, the rate of eutrophication establishes the balance between the production of aquatic life and its destruction by bacterial decomposition. Under natural conditions the rate of decomposition is nearly equal to the rate of production, and little sedimentation occurs. Where there are large inputs of nutrients from human sources, bacterial decomposition cannot keep pace with productivity and sedimentation increases.

As is also shown in Figure 3.19, the primary producers in a lake require specific proportions of various nutrients for growth. They require sources of carbon, nitrogen, and phorphorus in the atomic ratios of 106:16:1 and a large number of other elements in relatively small amounts. These minor elements are usually available at sufficient concentration in the natural environment to provide for the needs of aquatic organisms, although in particular cases the deficiency of

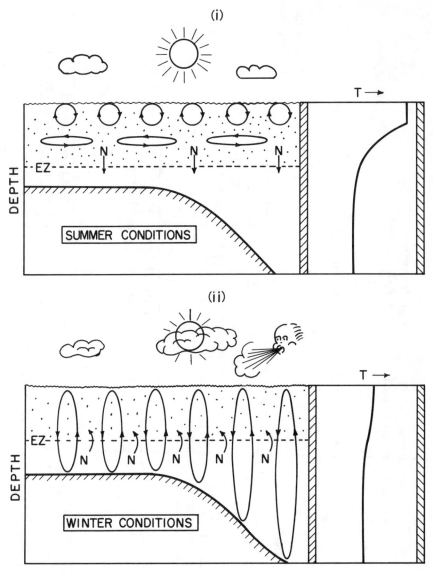

EZ = euphotic zone
stipple represents phytoplankton growth
N → signifies direction of nutrient flow
enclosed arrows indicate circulation of waters

Figure 3.18   Natural Cycling of Nutrients for Controlled Growth of Aquatic Life in Lakes and Coastal Areas

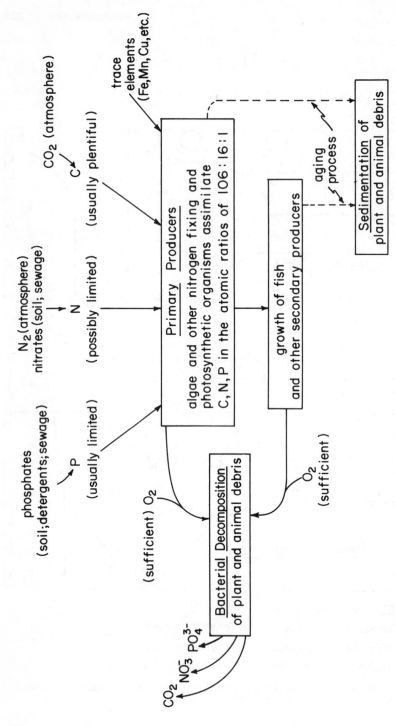

Figure 3.19 Factors That Affect Aquatic Production, Decomposition, and Sedimentation

one or more of these trace elements may limit growth and determine the nature of the organisms present.

With respect to the major nutrient elements, carbon, nitrogen, and phosphorus, there has been considerable debate about which one limits growth. The nutrient that is present in lowest quantity in relation to the proportions required by the organisms is the one that determines and limits the growth rate.

Carbon is the element required in the largest amounts. Carbon dioxide from the atmosphere is utilized directly by algae and aquatic plants, and bacterial decomposition of organic matter produces more carbon dioxide. Only dissolved carbon dioxide can be used directly by algae. Under conditions of very rapid growth, as may occur in algal blooms, it is possible that the concentration of dissolved carbon dioxide might fall low enough to limit growth. Under normal growing conditions, however, it appears that ample carbon dioxide is available from the atmosphere to prevent carbon from being the limiting nutrient.

Nitrogen is needed by plants to synthesize protein and a variety of other essential constituents. It is available as nitrate, which enters the water in runoff and sewage. Also, a number of species of algae are able to use atmospheric nitrogen directly, thereby providing a sufficient supply of nitrogen to the local water environment. If these algae are absent and nitrate levels are very low, nitrogen can become the limiting nutrient.

Phosphorus is required by all organisms in substantial quantities. It is the only one of the major nutrient elements that does not have any atmospheric source; that is, there is no gaseous form of phosphorus that occurs naturally and forms a part of the biological cycle. Phosphorus has to be obtained from soluble phosphate compounds that enter the water from runoff and sewage. While much of the phosphorus injected into lakes and streams from land runoff is in an insoluble form, detergent phosphates are very soluble and, hence, are readily available for biological assimilation. Presently, in regions of the United States that do not have a detergent phosphate ban in effect, approximately one-third of the phosphorus in domestic wastewater is derived from detergents. Due to increasingly strict regulations, this amount has been decreasing steadily since the early 1970s, when half the phosphorus in sewage effluent stemmed from detergent use. There is substantial evidence that for relatively unpolluted bodies of water, phosphorus is indeed the limiting nutrient. As is shown in Figure 3.20, for nine lakes in Oregon, the biological productivity correlates quite well with the phosphorus levels in the water but not with the nitrogen or carbon levels.

The availability of phosphorus for biological growth in oceans and lakes depends both on the inputs of external sources and on the rate of mobilization of phosphorus from bottom sediments. In the temperate zone, the winter overturn diagrammed in Figure 3.18 brings to the surface the phosphorus dissolved in the deep layers. Figure 3.21 shows schematically that the cycling of phosphorus between the sediments and the water above is controlled by chemical factors.

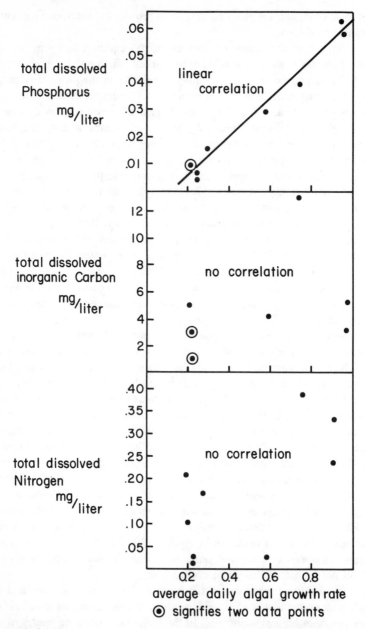

Figure 3.20 Evidence for Phosphorus As the Limiting Nutrient in Algal Growth: An Analysis of Nine Oregon Lakes

Source: G. E. Likens, ed., "Nutrients and Eutrophication, the Limiting-Nutrient Controversy," Proceedings of the Symposium on Nutrients and Eutrophication, Michigan State University, 1971, p. 139.

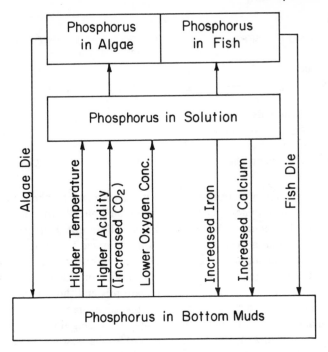

Figure 3.21 Chemical Factors That Affect Phosphorus Equilibria in Lakes

Source: H. R. Jones, *Detergents and Pollution, Problems and Technical Solutions* (Park Ridge, N.J.: Noyes Data Corporation, 1972), p. 8.

Fish and algae die and settle into the sediment, carrying an appreciable part of their phosphorus with them. Also metal ions, particularly calcium and iron, form insoluble phosphates, which settle to the bottom. The solubility of these sedimentary phosphate deposits depends on the conditions in the bottom water. The solubility increases with increasing temperature and also with decreasing pH, since hydrogen ions form soluble complexes with phosphate. The amount of dissolved oxygen is also important because under oxygen-free conditions, tripositive iron ions, called *ferric ions,* are reduced to dipositive iron ions, called *ferrous ions,* and it appears that ferrous phosphates are substantially more soluble than ferric phosphates.

This chemistry makes a quantitative evaluation of the dependence of biological growth rates on phosphorus inputs difficult, and modeling of this complex pro-

Removal by lime:

$$5Ca^{2+} + 4OH^- + 3HPO_4^{2-} \longrightarrow Ca_5(PO_4)_3(OH)\downarrow + 3H_2O$$
$$\text{Hydroxyapatite}$$

Removal by alum:

$$Al_2(SO_4)_3 + 2PO_4^{3-} \longrightarrow 2AlPO_4\downarrow + 3SO_4^{2-}$$

Removal by ferric chloride:

$$FeCl_3 + PO_4^{3-} \longrightarrow FePO_4\downarrow + 3Cl^-$$

Figure 3.22 Precipitation of Phosphate by Lime, Alum, or Ferric Chloride

cess is an active area of current research. It seems that a number of lakes and streams in the United States are sufficiently polluted already so that eliminating phosphorus in detergents would have relatively little effect on the biological productivity. Growth in these lakes is no longer limited by phosphorus. It will take a long time and substantial control measures to restore them to the conditions of relative purity required for phosphorus limitation. Removing phosphorus from detergents would be a contribution toward this end, however.

An alternative approach is to introduce phosphate removal at the sewage treatment plant. This can be done fairly simply by adding lime, calcium oxide, alum (aluminum sulfate), or ferric chloride to the sewage. The calcium, aluminum, or ferric ions precipitate the phosphate quite effectively via the reactions shown in Figure 3.22. This procedure has the advantage that all phosphates from human waste as well as from detergents are removed and prevented from entering the hydrosphere.

Bioactivity of Lakes

Figure 3.23 illustrates the yearly cycle of biological productivity in lakes in the temperate zone. There is a sharp peak in the phytoplankton population in late spring. As plant growth increases, the water becomes depleted in nutrients, and photosynthetic activity in the summer is low. The decomposition of organic matter gradually replenishes the nutrient supply and leads to another peak in photosynthetic activity in the autumn. Finally, the dropping temperatures and light levels shut down photosynthesis for the winter. The winter turnover brings nutrients from the deeper layers that are ready to support intense photosynthesis when sunlight and temperature increase again in the spring.

Figure 3.23 also shows the relationship between the phytoplankton population and the phosphate and nitrate levels. If large quantities of phosphate and nitrate are fed into the lake, via agricultural runoff or urban waste disposal, for example, then much higher populations of phytoplankton can be supported. The limit on growth may then switch to another factor, the availability of trace minerals, for

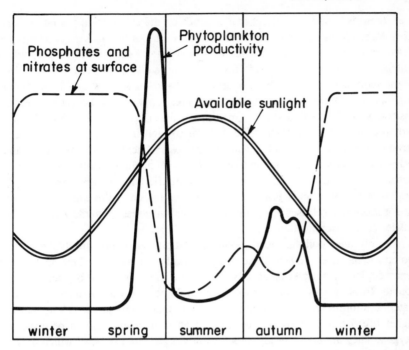

Figure 3.23 Seasonal Phytoplankton Productivity As a Function of Sunlight and Nutrient Concentration

Source: Adapted from W. D. Russell-Hunter, *Aquatic Productivity* (New York: Macmillan Publishing Co., Inc., 1970), p. 43. Copyright © 1970. Reprinted with permission.

example, or the availability of sunlight, since the phytoplankton may increase sufficiently to reduce the transparency of the water. It is even possible for carbon to become the limiting nutrient since the plankton growth rate may surpass the rate at which carbon dioxide can be transferred from the atmosphere or generated from decomposing bacteria. The consumption of carbon dioxide in explosive algal blooms can drive the pH of the water to values as high as 9 or 10 due to the depletion of carbonate:

$$CO_3^{2-} + 2H^+ \rightarrow H_2O + CO_2$$

The increase in pH can in turn alter the nature of the algal growth, selecting for high-pH resistant varieties.

Whatever the new limiting factor is under these conditions, the plankton population is much greater than it would be in the absence of overfertilization by phosphates and nitrates. The rate of sedimentation is greatly increased. Moreover, there is a snowball effect that depends on the structure of the lake. Deep lakes form sediment more slowly than shallow lakes because they have more dissolved oxygen per unit of surface area. The rate of decomposition per unit of biological production is therefore faster and the rate of sedimentation is slower. As the sediment builds up, the lake becomes shallower and the rate of sedimentation increases. Moreover, an overfertilized lake supports a higher rate of decomposition as well as sedimentation, and this has the effect of increasing the level of carbon dioxide and decreasing the level of oxygen in the sediment. Increased carbon dioxide (i.e., carbonic acid) increases the acidity, whereas decreased oxygen increases the reduction potential of the medium. Both effects act to dissolve an oxidized microzone consisting of iron(III) and manganese(III and IV) oxides, phosphates, and carbonates, which often line the sediments. The dissolution of this lining releases nutrients from the sediment back into the water, further accelerating eutrophication.

Not only does pollution lead to eutrophication, but it also upsets the natural biological balances. When algae grow in explosive blooms, their subsequent decay depletes the water of dissolved oxygen. Direct injection of organic compounds from wastes also increases the biological oxygen demand. Polluted waters are turbid with undecomposed organic matter and are unable to support higher life forms such as fish because of an insufficient amount of dissolved oxygen. They are breeding grounds for microorganisms, some of which may be pathogenic. At sufficiently low levels of oxygen, anaerobic bacteria take over, releasing noxious gases.

5 | The Oceans

In addition to the problem of overnutrition of bodies of water, an area of increasing concern is pollution of the world's water systems by toxic materials, and the subsequent lethal effects on plant and animal life. Figure 3.24 shows the pattern of distribution for the primary production of photosynthetic organisms in the world's oceans. The pattern for secondary production, that is, the animals and fish that feed on the primary producers, corresponds closely to that for primary production. One can see that the regions of greatest marine productivity, the estuaries, upwellings, coral reefs, and continental shelf areas, which provide most of the fish we eat, lie close to the continental areas. Large quantities of hazardous wastes can be injected directly into these high-productivity areas by river flow, runoff from the land, or direct discharge. The concern is that these toxic inputs will have serious effects on the entire marine ecosystem and on the fish population that it supports.

Some effects on the oceans have already been observed. One of the more

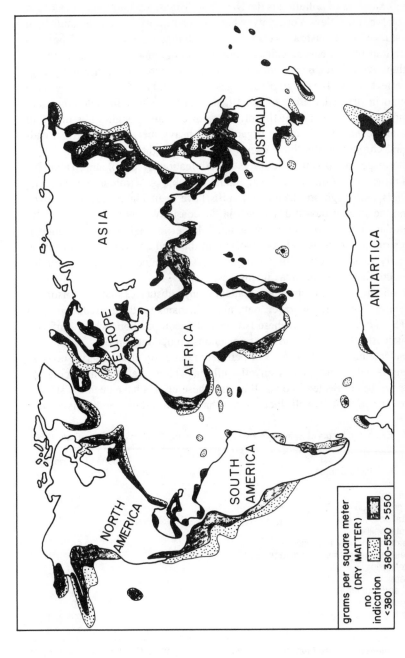

Figure 3.24 Distribution of Annual Production of Plant Biomass (Primary Production) in the World's Oceans

Source: *Productivity of World Ecosystems* (Washington, D.C.: National Academy of Sciences, 1975), p. 22. Reproduced with the permission of the National Academy of Sciences.

notorious examples of pollution is the New York Bight, a 50,000-km² area of the ocean not far from New York City where an enormous amount of municipal sewage sludge and industrial wastes has been dumped continuously. The high concentrations of nutrients actually support a level of aquatic productivity that is higher than average for ocean coastal regions, but there has been a noticeably adverse effect on fish life. High percentages of dead and abnormal fish eggs have been found in particular areas of the Bight, and the winter flounders have an uncommonly high incidence of fin rot. These effects are thought to be linked to the elevated levels of chlorinated organics and heavy metals (lead, silver, cadmium, and chromium) that have been found in the Bight.

Another aspect of ocean pollution is contamination by petroleum. Table 3.7 shows a projection of the sources and annual amounts of petroleum inputs in the early 1980s. Although spectacular oil spills have been highly publicized over the years, the smaller day-to-day inputs in the coastal waters and harbors of the world produce chronic pollution that is much larger in total volume. Municipal and industrial effluents as well as runoff from the land and rivers all contribute significantly. Offshore oil drilling will be increasingly important as the search for oil in the continental shelf areas intensifies.

Crude oil and petroleum products contain many substances that are poisonous to marine life. There are, however, natural mechanisms for the degradation of oil at sea. The most important of these is bacterial decomposition, which, unfortunately, is least effective for the most poisonous compounds in oil.

Our understanding of the effects of petroleum pollution on the marine ecosystem stems largely from studies on oil spills in which relatively high concentrations have been injected into small areas. These effects have been the subject of controversy, but it is well documented that under certain conditions even a

Table 3.7　Estimated Inputs of Petroleum Hydrocarbons in the Oceans during the Early 1980s

Input Source	Millions of Metric Tons Per Year
Natural seeps	0.60
Offshore production	0.20
Transportation	
Accidental spills	0.25
Losses during normal operation	0.55
(bilges bunkering, tanker washings, etc.)	
Coastal refineries	0.02
Atmosphere	0.60
Municipal and industrial	0.45
Urban runoff	0.30
River runoff	1.60
Total	4.57

Source: *Petroleum in the Marine Environment* (Washington, D.C.: National Academy of Sciences, 1975), p. 14.

relatively small oil spill can devastate the local marine ecosystem. For example, shellfishing was still forbidden in Buzzard's Bay, Massachusetts, in 1978, nine years after 700 tons of oil had been washed up into the salt marshes and pounded into the sediment of the shallow bay by storm waves. A really large oil spill can release as much as 100,000 tons of oil.

The impact of an oil spill depends on many factors. It is ameliorated if winds or currents push the oil out into the high seas. Another determinant is the amount of clay suspended in the seawater. The clay tends to adsorb onto the spilled oil, making it heavier and causing it to sink and concentrate in the sediment before it is dispersed in the ocean.

We are just beginning to learn about the effects of petroleum on marine ecology, especially chronic exposure to low-level concentrations. A reliable assessment will require studies of the effects on the lower organisms in the food chain as well as on fish.

6 | Sewage Treatment

Abatement of water pollution from overnutrition or toxic chemicals depends largely on the efficacy of wastewater treatment. It is becoming increasingly apparent that the treatment of hazardous industrial wastes should be separated from that of nonhazardous organic wastes from domestic sewage. Let us now take a closer look at how sewage wastewater can be purified.

Domestic sewage treatment

Conventional sewage treatment plants have been designed to deal solely with nontoxic organic wastes by utilizing bacteria to decompose them, as shown in the reaction of Figure 3.25. The key feature of the process is an abundance of oxygen, a condition called *aerobic*. The solubility of gaseous oxygen in water is not very high—about 9 mg/l at 20° C and less at higher temperatures. The oxidation of 1 mg of carbon requires 2.67 mg of dissolved oxygen. Organic hydrogen, sulfur, and nitrogen are also oxidized and use up additional oxygen.

Thus, the purity of water depends primarily on the rate of transport of oxygen

$$(C, H, O, N, S)^* + O_2 \xrightarrow[\text{bacteria}]{\text{aerobic}} CO_2 + H_2O + H_2SO_4 + NH_4^+ + NO_3^{-\dagger}$$

Figure 3.25 Bacterial Action in Water Containing Organic Wastes

*(C, H, O, N, S) are the major elements in wastewater.
†Bacteria needed to oxidize NH_4^+ to NO_3^- grow slowly in wastewater and generally do not compete well with carbon-feeding bacteria.

by aeration and on the total load of organic material that must be oxidized. As shown in the upper part of Figure 3.26, this load is expressed as the biological oxygen demand (BOD), the number of milligrams of oxygen needed to carry out the overall oxidation reaction in one liter of water. This biological oxygen demand is very high for sewage and the waste products of various industries, as seen by the numbers in the seond part of Figure 3.26. Domestic sewage on the average requires 165 mg of oxygen per liter and manufacturing wastewater requires about 200 mg/l. Obviously, this load would overwhelm the capacity of most natural bodies of water, so sewage treatment is necessary to maintain water quality.

Definition

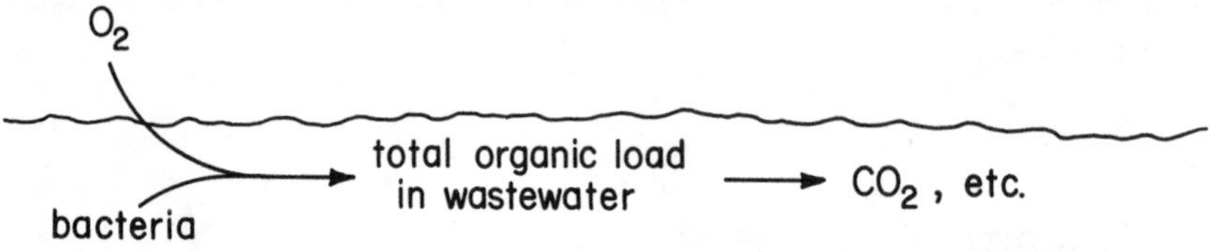

O$_2$

bacteria → total organic load in wastewater → CO_2 , etc.

(solubility of O$_2$ in water = 9mg/liter)

BOD = milligrams of oxygen which must be removed from the water to decompose the organic material contained in one liter of wastewater.

Typical BOD's for Various Processes[*]

type	BOD (mg O$_2$/liter waste water)
Domestic sewage	165
All manufacturing	~200
Chemicals and allied products	314
Paper	372
Food	747
Metals	13

Figure 3.26 Biological Oxygen Demand (BOD)

Source of lower table: "Intermedia Aspects of Air and Water Pollution Control," U.S. Environmental Protection Agency (600/5-73-003), August 1973, p. 76.

Figure 3.27 is a diagram of the processes that are most commonly used today for domestic sewage. Primary treatment consists of removing solid wastes from the water by screening, scum removal, and settling of sludge. The remaining liquid is then subjected to secondary treatment, which is a method of greatly accelerating natural biological respiration. The medium for doing that is called *activated sludge,* which is essentially a bed of microbes that are allowed to grow rapidly and feed on the organic solutes in the wastewater under well-aerated conditions. The effluent from such a tank has a much lower biological oxygen demand due to the action of the microbes in the sludge. As the volume of the sludge increases through growth of the microbes, excess sludge is removed and thickened for disposal along with the primary sludge. Most sewage treatment, then, consists of removal of solids and then biological oxidation of soluble organic materials.

Sludge disposal is one of the major problems of sewage treatment. The sludge can be spread on soil or landfills, although available land for this method of disposal is becoming scarce. For communities that are close to the shore, the sludge commonly has been dumped into the ocean. Because of the fragility of the ocean's ecosystem, however, all ocean dumping will be stopped in the United States in the 1980s.

In principle, sludge could be used as fertilizer on crop lands, and some experiments in this are being carried out. However, the problem of toxic materials in the sludge is again the major stumbling block, and methods need to be developed for their removal. The incineration or pyrolysis of sludge is being considered in many areas. This method also suffers from the presence of toxic pollutants in the sludge, which can be emitted into the atmosphere. An alternative is to use the sludge in the production of methane gas using anaerobic digestion, as mentioned in the first part of this book.

The liquid effluent from secondary treatment plants has a considerably reduced biological oxygen demand. After being treated by chlorination to kill pathogenic microorganisms, it is often mixed directly into lakes and streams. Figure 3.27 shows the composition of typical secondary effluent—a BOD of 25 mg/l, an ammonium concentration of 20 mg/l, and a phosphate concentration of 25 mg/l. For clear lakes, these concentrations can enhance the rate of eutrophication. Removal of the dissolved materials requires further steps, which come under the heading of tertiary treatment. A flow diagram for one type of tertiary treatment plant, originally designed to maintain the purity of Lake Tahoe, California, is shown in Figure 3.28.

Secondary effluent enters a flocculation tank where lime, calcium hydroxide, is added to remove phosphates as calcium phosphate. From there the water moves to an ammonia stripping tower. The nitrogen present in the wastewater exists mainly as ammonium ions, which are converted to gaseous ammonia at the high pH values produced by the addition of the lime. Finally, the remaining

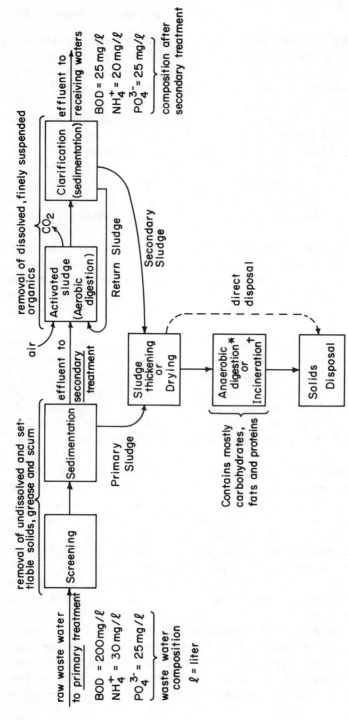

Figure 3.27 Primary and Secondary Treatment of Municipal Wastewater

*Typically, 50% of the sludge can be digested anaerobically to produce methane gas by a method similar to that shown in Figure 28.
†Dried sludge can be burned as low-quality fuel with a typical heat value of about 3,200 calories/g.
Source: Adapted from *Cleaning Our Environment, the Chemical Basis for Action* (Washington, D.C.: American Chemical Society, 1969), p. 107.

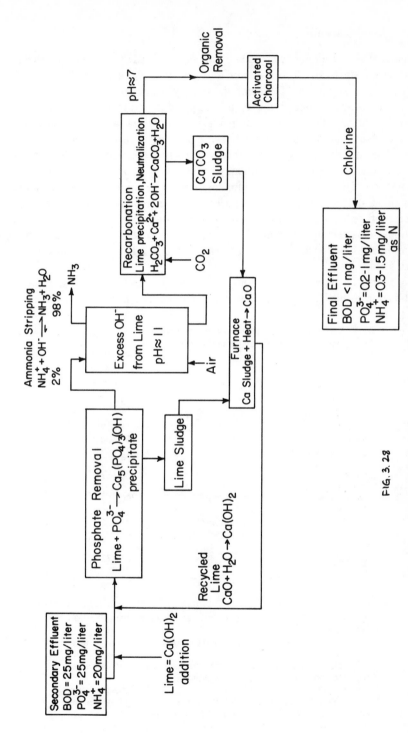

Figure 3.28 Tertiary Treatment of Municipal Wastewater

FIG. 3. 28

239

organic materials are removed by adsorption on activated carbon, and chlorine is added as a disinfectant. The levels of nitrogen, phosphorus, and dissolved organic carbon are quite low following the tertiary treatment.

Phosphorus and nitrogen removal are not practiced presently on a wide scale because of the added cost of the required tertiary treatment facilities. Such plants are expensive to run as well as build, because of their high energy requirements.

The data in Table 3.8 show the relative energy requirements of the various steps indicated in the tertiary treatment process diagrammed in Figure 3.28. The combination of lime treatment and ammonia stripping requires substantially more energy than does secondary treatment. The main energy costs are for recycling the calcium oxide via heating and running the ammonia stripping tower. An additional disadvantage of ammonia stripping is that its efficiency decreases markedly at low temperatures, and ceases to work at all at temperatures below freezing.

An alternative method for nitrogen removal is conversion to N_2, using a combination of nitrifying and denitrifying bacteria. The former use NH_4^+ as an

Table 3.8   Energy Requirements for Secondary and Advanced Wastewater Treatment Processes (100 million gallons per day plant)

Process		Energy Requirement (kwh/day)
Secondary treatment		154,282*
Lime treatment		
Lime addition		5,613
Recalcining		182,860
Recarbonation		29,133†
	Total	217,606
Ammonia stripping		186,587
Nitrification/denitrification		
Nitrification		60,259
Denitrification		1,020
Purification and transport of methanol		35,826
	Total	97,105
Activated carbon		
Operation		23,773
Regeneration		31,620‡
	Total	55,393
Chlorination		607

*Of this, 61,000 kwh/day can be recovered as methane through sludge digestion.

†Does not include energy for carbon dioxide production and transportation.

‡Does not include energy for carbon production and transportation needed to replace carbon lost in regeneration.

Source: Data extracted from R. M. Hagan and E. B. Roberts, *Water Sewage Works* 123, No. 12 (1976): 52; and D. G. Argo and G. M. Wesner, *Water Wastes Eng.* 13, No. 5 (1976): 24.

energy source, metabolizing it to NO_2^- and then to NO_3^-, in an aerobic environment. Denitrifying bacteria, on the other hand, use NO_3^- as an oxidant to metabolize organic carbon. The overall products are N_2 and CO_2. The energy requirement for this process is only half that for ammonia stripping, although care must be taken to maintain the right growth conditions for the bacteria.

Another concept for tertiary wastewater treatment that consumes minimal energy is to use the land as a natural filter. Soil particles efficiently absorb phosphate ions and, to a lesser extent, ammonium and nitrate ions. The soil also harbors microbes that can biologically oxidize carbon and nitrogen. One concept is to spread effluents on the ground itself. In this case, the filtering capacity of the soil is the crucial variable. Another possibility, shown in Figure 3.29, is to spray secondary effluents onto forest or crop land. An experiment of this type has been carried on for a number of years at the Pennsylvania State University, where the effluent from the sewage treatment plant that serves the town of University Park has been sprayed onto agricultural and forest land. The results have shown essentially complete removal of phosphorus and nitrogen from the water before it

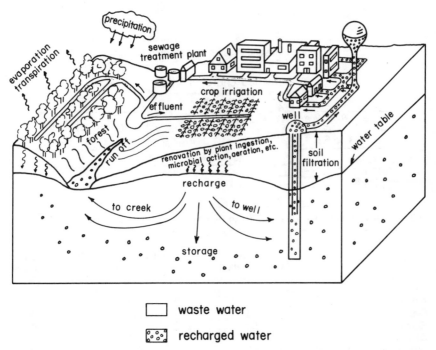

☐ waste water

▨ recharged water

Figure 3.29 Tertiary Treatment by Spraying the Effluent from Secondary Treatment on Forest and Crop Land

Source: "Renovation of Secondary Effluent for Reuse As a Water Resource," U.S. Environmental Protection Agency (660/2-74-016), February 1974, p. 8.

enters the water table. At the same time, crop and forest productivity has increased. Methods of this type obviously depend on the availability of sufficient land and on the absence from the effluent of toxic materials and pathogenic microorganisms.

The complexity of the problem of toxic materials arises from the multiplicity of sources of the sewage treated by municipal treatment plants. These include households and offices but also hospitals and a variety of industries. Runoff from the city streets or adjacent agricultural areas is also carried to the treatment plants, as storm drains and sewer lines are usually interconnected. Under increasingly strict government regulations, large industries have installed their own waste treatment facilities, and recycling of the wastewater is increasing. Nevertheless, industrial effluents form a substantial fraction of the wastewater treated by municipal plants. As a result, these plants must often deal with toxic materials that they are not designed to handle. Clearly the ultimate solution to the toxic waste problem is separate treatment for each type of waste product at the point where it is produced.

Filtering Industrial Wastes by Activated Charcoal

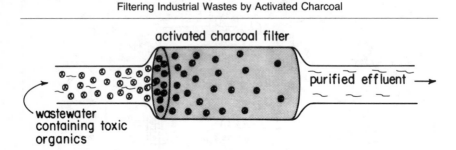

Effectiveness of Activated Charcoal in the Removal of Some Toxic Chlorinated Organics

Compound	Initial Concentration (μg/l)	Concentration after Carbon Treatment (μg/l)	Orgaic Reduction (%)
Aldrin	48	<1.0	99+
Dieldrin	19	0.05	99+
Endrin	62	0.05	99+
DDT	41	0.1	99+
Arochlor 1242 (PCB)	45	<0.5	99+

Source of lower table: D. G. Hager, *Chem. Eng. Prog.* 72, No. 10 (1976): 57.

Figure 3.30 Activated Charcoal Filtration

Industrial wastewater treatment

There are two basic methods for purifying wastewater of toxic, nonbiodegradable chemicals: filtration and membrane techniques. Figure 3.30 shows that activated charcoal, which has a large surface area and readily adsorbs organic molecules, is an effective filter medium. The table gives data that show more than 99% reduction in the concentration of several chlorinated hydrocarbons in the effluent stream. As illustrated in Figure 3.31, synthetic resins are also being used for filtering. The figure shows a styrene-divinylbenzene copolymer that is also effective in removing chlorinated pesticides by adsorption to its surface. Also shown are cationic and anionic ion-exchange resins that have successfully removed ionic dyes from the wastewater from textile manufacturing.

Figure 3.32 illustrates a major membrane technique for toxic waste removal by ultrafiltration or reverse osmosis. In ultrafiltration the solution is forced through a membrane that contains pores of controlled size. These can be anywhere from 2 to 10,000 nm (20–10^5 Å). Molecules that are too big to pass through the pores are

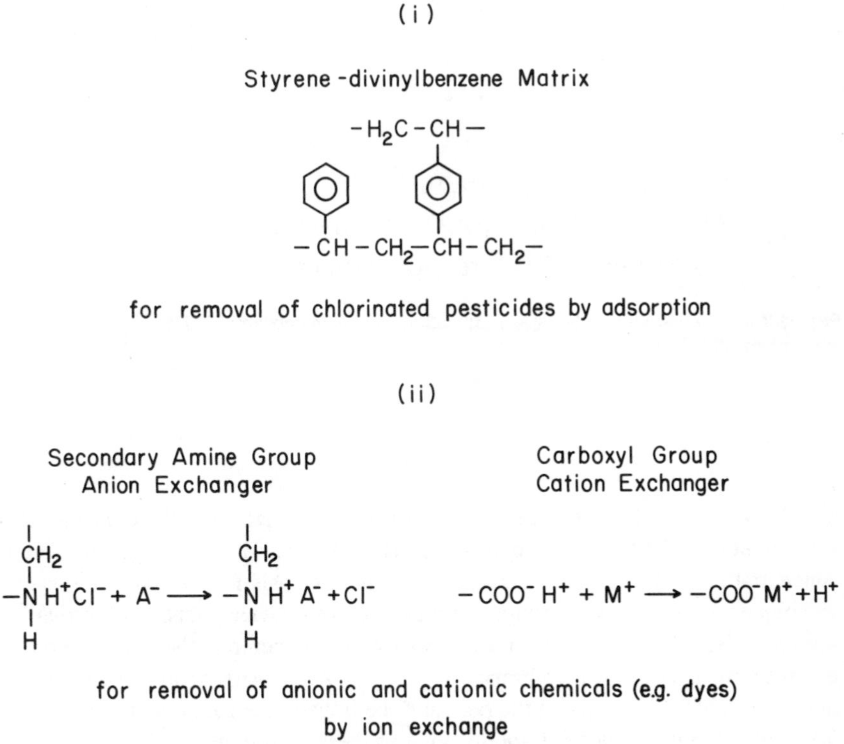

(i)

Styrene -divinylbenzene Matrix

for removal of chlorinated pesticides by adsorption

(ii)

Secondary Amine Group
Anion Exchanger

Carboxyl Group
Cation Exchanger

for removal of anionic and cationic chemicals (e.g. dyes)
by ion exchange

Figure 3.31   Filtering Industrial Wastes by Synthetic Resins

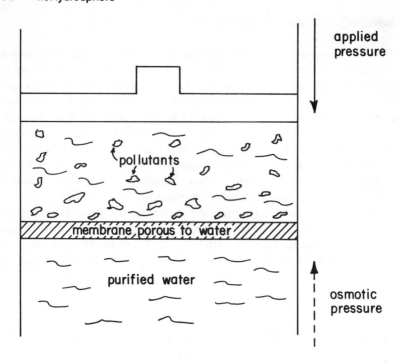

applied
pressure

pollutants

membrane porous to water

purified water

osmotic
pressure

range of pore size
ultrafiltration: 2 to 10,000 nanometers
reverse osmosis: 0.04 to 600 nanometers

Figure 3.32   Industrial Wastewater Purification by the Membrane Technique of Ultrafiltration or Reverse Osmosis

held back. The effluent is free of molecules of this size, and the concentrated solution behind the membrane can be led off to another filtration stage for further concentration and finally for disposal. Reverse osmosis is essentially the same technique (*osmosis* is the thermodynamically driven passage of solvent through a semipermeable membrane from a less to a more concentrated solution), except that the pore sizes of the membrane are generally smaller, from about 0.04 to 600 nm. Also, charged groups on the pore surface impede the passage of ions. Table 3.9 contains a list of current applications of these techniques.

Another membrane technology, electrodialysis, is appropriate for the concen-

Table 3.9   Applications of Reverse Osmosis and Ultrafiltration

---

Metal Industry
  Recovery of gold, silver, platinum, nickel, chrome, zinc, aluminium, and cadmium from
    plating wastes
  Reuse of rinse waters
  Recovery of metal salts: nickel sulfamate, copper sulfate, copper pyrophosphate, zinc
    chloride
  Recovery of detergent for reuse in cleaning operations in metal phosphating; oil concen-
    tration
  Removal of sulfates from acid mine drainage
Textile Industry
  Recovery of polyvinyl alcohols and mineral oils
  Removal of dyes
Paper and Pulp
  Color removal
  Solids concentration from white liquor
  Cleaning of water from black liquor
Food Industry
  Concentration of whey from dairy wastes
  Sugar recovery in candy manufacture
Miscellaneous
  Desalting
  Chromate removal from cooling tower blowdowns
  Concentration of radioactive wastes
  Removal of emulsified oils

Source: Adapted from T. J. Mulligan and R. D. Fox, *Chem. Eng.* 83, no. 22 (1976): 49.

tration of ions. The process is depicted in Figure 3.33. An applied voltage causes anions to migrate toward the anode (positive electrode) on the right, and cations to migrate toward the cathode (negative electrode) on the left. The cell contains membranes with fixed charges that are either negative or positive and that render the membranes impermeable to either anions or cations. These are arranged alternately, so that every other compartment gradually becomes more concentrated in electrolyte (sodium chloride in this illustration), while the remaining compartments become less concentrated. After a time the freshwater can be separated from the brine and the entire operation can be run continuously. The method can be used to obtain freshwater in arid coastal regions. Japan obtains its entire salt supply by electrodialysis of seawater. In the United States electrodialysis is widely used for desalting cheese whey, which is a major additive in processed food. Other anticipated uses are for the treatment of industrial discharges from metal plating, battery manufacture, glass etching, and wood pulp washing, and of saline effluents generally.

Although the removal of toxic chemicals from the wastewater from industrial facilities is expensive and energy-consuming, many of the trapped chemicals can be recycled or used in other processes. The purified water may also be suitable for further use in manufacturing. Both of these factors cut down the overall cleanup cost.

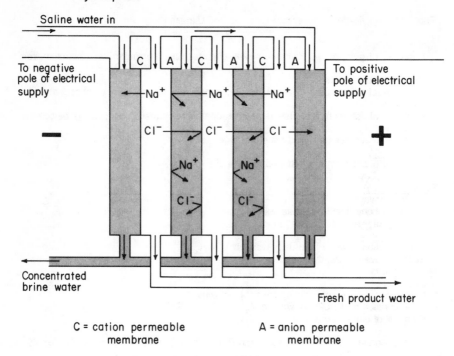

C = cation permeable
membrane

A = anion permeable
membrane

Figure 3.33   The Electrodialysis Process

7 | Drinking Water Supplies

Thus far we have dealt with the purification of sewage and industrial wastewater. Drinking water supplies must also be treated to ensure public safety. Potable water treatment plants are generally simpler than sewage treatment plants. The biological oxygen demand is very low and no bacteria digesters are needed. The major steps involve disinfection and, where necessary, the removal of unpleasant physical characteristics such as turbidity, color, and bad taste.

Small particles that cause turbidity and discoloration can be removed by coagulating them into larger particles that are heavy enough to precipitate out. The coagulating agents commonly used are aluminum sulfate, or alum, and iron chloride. These are the same chemicals used to precipitate soluble phosphates from sewage effluents, as was shown in the reactions in Figure 3.22.

Disinfection is carried out in the United States by chlorination. Other countries such as France and Switzerland use ozone to kill bacteria. Chlorination is less expensive in terms of energy use, since ozone is produced in an electric discharge. Also, ozone is unstable and rapidly converts to oxygen, so chlorine is a longer-lasting disinfectant. The usefulness of chlorination was unquestioned for

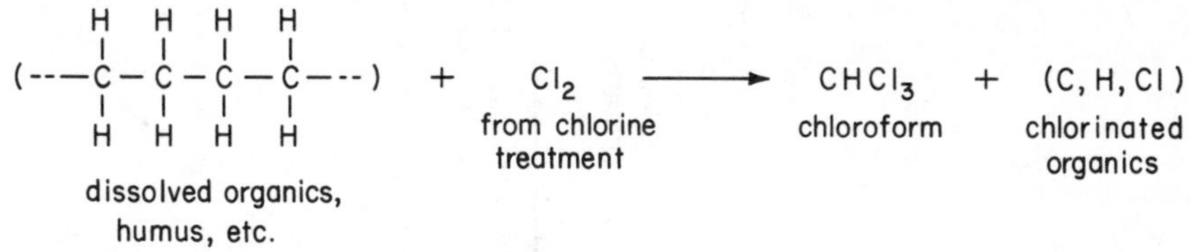

Figure 3.34 Generation of Chlorinated Hydrocarbons in Drinking Water by Reaction of Chlorine with Natural Organics

decades until recently. As shown in Figure 3.34, it has been discovered that chlorine plays a role in generating toxic chlorinated compounds by reacting with organic material that is naturally present in the water.

Virtually every water system investigated in a nationwide survey by the U.S. Environmental Protection Agency showed trace levels of chloroform contamination. As a result, the EPA has proposed regulations that would limit chloroform concentration in drinking water to 100 parts per billion. The most effective way to meet this standard is to install activated carbon treatment as shown in Figure 3.30 as a final step after chlorination. Not only chloroform but also other halogenated organics from various industrial and agricultural sources can be removed simultaneously.

8 | Agricultural Pollution

While much attention is focused on municipal and industrial water supplies, problems associated with agricultural water pollution are increasingly coming to the fore. Table 3.10 tabulates the four main sources: erosion of crop land, animal wastes, commercial fertilizers that contain nitrates and phosphates, and pesticides.

Erosion leads to the silting of waterways and the loss of good topsoil. In the United States, the Agriculture Department's Soil Conservation Service estimates that 3 billion tons of topsoil are lost every year. One major abatement strategy involves the planting of a legume such as alfalfa or clover in late summer to serve as a cover crop for winter when wind and rain cause the most severe soil losses. As we will see in the next section, this technique has the added advantage of supplying nitrogen to the soil, which can be plowed under in the spring. There are severe erosion problems when sloped land is cultivated as it often is in poor, overpopulated countries where arable land is scarce. In such cases erosion can be reduced by terracing the land or building diversion ditches to slow down the runoff that carries suspended soil particles.

Erosion is becoming an increasingly severe worldwide problem as arable land

Table 3.10 Water Pollution from Agriculture

Source	Soil Erosion	Feedlot Animal Wastes	Fertilizers	Pesticides
Effect on Water Quality	Silting of waterways	Leaching of nitrates into groundwater; increasing biological oxygen demand	Leaching of nitrates into groundwater; runoff of nitrates and phosphates into river flow	Leaching into groundwater; runoff into natural bodies of water
Abatement Strategy	Cover cropping; terracing of sloped land; abundance of freshwater supplies	Production of methane gas by bacterial action	More conservative application; more use of legumes, manure, and mulch	Biodegradable substitutes; alternative techniques

dries up when irrigation water is diverted to supply growing needs for water in cities. Furthermore, as water supplies become more scarce, groundwater with high salt content will be used increasingly for irrigation. With time the soil becomes salty and unfit for agricultural purposes. When the land is abandoned, it is especially vulnerable to the ravages of wind erosion.

With respect to pollution from animal wastes, it has been estimated that farm animals in the United States produce about 20 times more wastes than does the human population. As long as this is spread over the land as fertilizer, it constitutes a resource rather than pollution, but increasingly the production of animals is being concentrated in feedlots and poultry farms, and the animal wastes are concentrated along with them. The biological oxygen demand of the wastewater from a feedlot with 10,000 cattle is equivalent to that of the sewage from a city of about 45,000 people. As mentioned early in this book, this animal waste could be converted into an energy source by methane digestion.

Of particular concern is the seepage of nitrate through the soil and into water tables. Nitrate is produced by microbial oxidation of ammonia associated with animal wastes. The problem is even more acute in farming areas that rely on heavy use of commercial fertilizer, which is essentially ammonium nitrate. Plants often cannot absorb the applied nitrogen fast enough, and nitrates tend to be washed through the soil to aquifers or carried away in runoff. As a result, drinking water in many agricultural areas has increasingly high levels of nitrate. While nitrate itself is relatively innocuous, biologically speaking, it can be reduced to nitrite by microbes in the human intestines, particularly in the intestines of small children. There has been concern that nitrites can react with amines in the digestive system to produce nitrosamines, which are known to be carcinogenic, a subject we will examine more closely in the next section.

Pesticide pollution in our water systems has created much concern. Strategies for reducing this problem also will be discussed in detail in the next section.

9 | Summary

The chemistry of the hydrosphere is dominated by dissolved oxygen and dissolved ions, including hydrogen ions, metal ions, and negatively charged ions such as carbonate, nitrate, and phosphate. Together, they determine the nature and level of the biological activity in water. The problem of water pollution is largely one of misplaced resources. The wastes that are flushed into streams, lakes, and oceans can easily overwhelm the biological capacities of the receiving waters. The same wastes applied to the land, with its much higher level of aeration, could significantly increase biological productivity. The main obstacle is the presence in wastes of toxic chemicals and pathogens, which have to be removed, preferably close to the source.

Problem Set

1. Given that the concentration of O_2 in water is only 9 milligrams per liter, why should water be a last resort for dumping of organic wastes and biodegradable chemicals? Why is the soil a more efficient medium?

2. Why is a soap micelle an effective cleansing agent for hydrophobic substances such as grease and oil? How does a builder foster micelle growth?

3. Assume algae need carbon, nitrogen, and phosphorus in the atomic ratios 106:16:1. What is the limiting nutrient in a lake that contains the following concentrations: total $C = 20$ mg/l, total $N = 0.80$ mg/l, and total $P = 0.16$ mg/l? If it is known that half the phosphorus in the lake originates from the use of phosphate detergents, will banning phosphate builders slow down eutrophication?

4. Five hundred kilograms of n-propanol ($CH_3CH_2CH_2OH$) is accidentally discharged into a body of water containing 10^8 l. By how much is the BOD (in milligrams per liter) of this water increased? Assume the following reaction:

$$C_3H_8O + \tfrac{9}{2}O_2 \rightarrow 3CO_2 + 4H_2O$$

5. In tertiary wastewater treatment, nitrogen is sometimes removed by stripping off gaseous NH_3 after the pH has been raised by the addition of lime. If the pH is raised to 10.0, what fraction of the NH_4^+ is converted to NH_3 (for NH_4^+, the pK_a is 9.25)? Imagine that the stripping process consists of complete removal of the NH_3, followed by reequilibration of the NH_4^+, with the pH held constant. What fraction of the nitrogen would be removed after three such stripping stages?

6. A 10-ml sample of wastewater is diluted to 500 ml. The initial concentration of dissolved oxygen in the dilute sample is found to be present at 7.3 mg/l. The sample is then treated with bacteria and incubated for five days. The oxygen concentration after that time is 1.8 mg/l. What is the BOD of the original sample after five days? (Such a measurement is called BOD_5, which is a common parameter in wastewater engineering.)

7. The density difference between water at 30° C and at 29° C is 0.000298 g/ml, and the density difference between water at 5° C and at 4° C is 0.000008 g/ml. Using this information, can you explain why the wind circulates nutrients in lake water most readily in early spring and autumn when the temperature of the water is around 4° C, rather than in summer when the surface temperature is generally higher than 20° C?

8. a) A lake with a cross sectional area of 1 km² and a depth of 50 m has a euphotic zone that extends 15 m below the surface. What is the maximum weight of the biomass (in grams of carbon) that can be decomposed by aerobic bacteria in the region of the lake below the euphotic zone during the summer when there is no circulation with the upper layer? The reaction is:

$$(CH_2O)_n + nO_2 \xrightarrow{\text{bacteria}} nCO_2 + nH_2O$$

The solubility of oxygen in pure water saturated with air is 8.9 mg/l; 1 m³ = 1,000 l.

b) Sugarcane, one of the most efficient converters of photosynthetic energy, yields about 3,600 g carbon/m² per year. If the lake had the same level of productivity, how deep would it have to be to completely digest the biomass aerobically?

9. a) Assume that an electrodialysis plant for desalting seawater removes 60% of the salt each time the water is passed through an electrodialysis stack (see Figure 3.33 for a schematic). The electrical energy requirement in kilowatt-hours per cubic meter of product water for a single pass through the stack is

$$E = \frac{I \times V}{1,000 \times W}$$

where I (current) = 74 a, V (voltage) = 1,000 v, and W is the product flow rate = 30 m³/hour. Since seawater contains about 35,000 ppm of total dissolved salts, through how many stacks must the water be passed to obtain water that contains 1,000 ppm—the maximum salinity permissible for human consumption? How many kilowatt-hours of energy are needed per cubic meter of potable water?

b) What is the efficiency of the process if the theoretical minimum energy expenditure for potable water is 0.71 kwh/m³?

10. A wastewater effluent contains dust, bacteria, viruses, glucose, and proteins. Using membrane filter technology, devise a way to separate the glucose and proteins from the rest of the material. The diameter of dust particles is on the order of 1 μm, the bacteria is 5 μm, viruses are 20 nm, glucose is 0.5 nm, proteins are 5 nm, and water is 0.2 nm.

11. Why do negatively charged sites exist in silicate clays? Would you expect a plant nutrient such as Ca^{2+} to be held tighter by the clay than nutrients such as NO_3^-, PO_4^{3-}, and K^+? Can you thus explain why nitrate, phosphate, and potassium are the most commonly added chemical fertilizers?

12. Estimate the average height by which the oceans would be raised if half the ice caps and glaciers in the world melted. The total surface area of the oceans is 3.61×10^8 km²; the total volume of water in the oceans is $1,320 \times 10^{18}$ l; and the amount trapped in glaciers and ice caps is $29,148 \times 10^{15}$ l (melted volume).

13. H_2S boils at $-61°$ C, H_2Se at $-42°$ C, and H_2Te at $-2°$ C. Based on this trend, at what temperature would one expect water to boil? Why does water boil at a much higher temperature?

14. A 100 million gallon per day sewage treatment plant serves a population of 500,000. The energy needed to run the plant is 200,000 kwh/day. During sludge digestion methane gas is produced in a quantity equal to 150,000 calories per capita per day. What percentage of the energy needs of the treatment plant is provided by methane gas production?

15. a) Phosphate removal for a 100 million gallon per day sewage treatment plant requires 217,606 kwh/day of energy. Typically, 6,000 lb of phosphorus is removed per day. Compare this with the amount of sulfur emitted as sulfur dioxide by a coal-burning power plant that supplies the extra energy needed for phosphorus removal. Assume that this plant, which uses bituminous coal, produces 3,260 kwh of electrical energy per ton of coal burned. Further assume the coal contains 2% sulfur and that half the sulfur is emitted as sulfur dioxide. How many pounds of pollutants are produced by the plant if the cumulative weight of other air pollutants (i.e., fly ash, nitrogen oxides, unburned hydrocarbons, and carbon monoxide) equals that of sulfur dioxide?

b) Since phosphorus is an essential plant nutrient, whereas sulfur dioxide and other air pollutants are dangerous to public health, under what conditions could you justify the removal of phosphorus from sewage wastewater?

16. Raw river water used for a public drinking supply was found to contain no Cl_2 and 0.9 $\mu g/l$ (ppb) of chloroform ($CHCl_3$), a suspected carcinogen. Upon treatment with chlorine, the water contained ppm Cl_2 and 22.1 $\mu g/l$ of $CHCl_3$. After the water settled for three days, it contained 2 ppm of Cl_2 and 60.8 $\mu g/l$ of $CHCl_3$. Give a possible explanation for these observations. Cite at least two ways in which chlorinated hydrocarbon can be eliminated from finished drinking water supplies. [Data from T. A. Bellar, J. J. Lichtenberg, and R. C. Kroner, "The Occurrence of Organohalides in Chlorinated Drinking Waters," *Am. Water Works Assoc. J.* 66 (1974):703.]

17. What are the pH and the Ca^{2+} concentration of a lake with pure water in equilibrium with both its limestone ($CaCO_3$) lining and the atmospheric carbon dioxide, whose partial pressure is 3.0×10^{-4} atm. The dissolution reaction is

$$CaCO_3(s) + H_2CO_3 = Ca^{2+} + 2HCO_3^-$$

The following equilibrium constants are applicable:

$$
\begin{aligned}
CO_2 + H_2O &= H_2CO_3 & K_p &= 10^{-1.5}\ M/atm \\
H_2CO_3 &= H^+ + HCO_3^- & K_{a_1} &= 10^{-6.4} \\
HCO_3^- &= H^+ + CO_3^{2-} & K_{a_2} &= 10^{-10.2} \\
CaCO_3(s) &= Ca^{2+} + CO_3^{2-} & K_{sp} &= 10^{-0.5}
\end{aligned}
$$

18. Lead pipes that are used to carry drinking water often become coated with a lead carbonate film if the water contains appreciable amounts of CO_3^{2-}. Assume drinking water is taken from the lake described in problem 17 and passed through a $PbCO_3$ coated pipe. What is the concentration of Pb^{2+} (in micrograms per liter) in the drinking water? If the acidity of the water increases to pH = 6, what is the new Pb^{2+} concentration?

$$PbCO_3(s) = Pb^{2+} + CO_3^{2-} \qquad K_{sp} = 1 \times 10^{-13}$$

19. If rainwater has a Ph of 3.0 because of contamination by H_2SO_4, what concentration of SO_4^{2-} and HSO_4^- should it have? The first proton of H_2SO_4 dissociates completely, whereas the second dissociation has a pK_a of 2.0.

20. Usually results of water analyses are given in units of milligrams per liter, whereas molar (or millimolar) units are more instructive for chemical purposes. Consider the following concentrations in milligrams per liter given for the effluent of a sewage treatment plant: Na^+ 135, K^+ 15, NH_4^+ 20, Ca^{2+} 60, Mg^{2+} 25, Cl^- 130, No_3^- 15, HCO_3^- 300, SO_4^{2-} 100, HPO_4^{2-} 25, hardness (as $CaCO_3$) 270.
    a) Does the hardness value match the sum of Ca^{2+} and Mg^{2+}?
    b) Do all the charges balance?

21. If the concentration of carbon dioxide in the atmosphere doubles as a result of burning fossil fuels, what is the predicted *change* in the pH of (unpolluted) rainwater?

22. Describe how deforestation, conversion of forest land for agricultural use, and diversion of water supplies for growing cities and industries can lead eventually to desert conditions without proper water and land management.

Notes

1. A. Ben-Naim, *Water and Aqueous Solutions: Introduction to a Molecular Theory* (New York: Plenum Press, 1974), pp. 233–38.
2. For a discussion of dipole moments, refer to any good elementary chemistry text; for example, B. H. Mahan, *University Chemistry*, 3rd ed. (Reading, Mass.: Addison-Wesley Publishing Co., Inc., 1975), pp. 518–20.
3. W. S. Broecker and Y.-H. Li, *J. Geophys. Res.* 75, no. 18 (1970):3545.
4. H. Oeschger, U. Siegenthaler, U. Schotterer, and A. Gugelmann, *Tellus* 27, no. 2 (1975):168.
5. U. Siegenthaler and H. Oeschger, *Science* 199 (1978):388.

Suggestions for Further Reading

Aqueous Solutions

Eisenberg, D., and Kauzmann, W. *The Structure and Properties of Water.* New York: Oxford University Press, 1969.

Frank, H. S. "The Structure of Ordinary Water." *Science* 169 (1970):635.

Frank, H. S., and Wen, W. Y. "Ion-Solvent Interactions: Structural Aspects of Ion-Solvent Interactions in Aqueous Solutions—A Suggested Picture of Water Structure." *Discus. Faraday Soc.* 24 (1957):133.

Meites, L., Pode, J., and Thomas, H. C. "Are Solubilities and Solubility Products Related?" *J. Chem. Educ.* 43 (1966):667.

Hydrophobic Bonding in Micelles and Biological Systems

Kauzmann, W. "Some Factors in the Interpretation of Protein Denaturation." *Adv. Protein Chem.* 14 (1959):1.

Tanford, C. "Micelle Shape and Size." *J. Phys. Chem.* 76 (1972):3020.

Tanford, C. *The Hydrophobic Effect: Formation of Micelles and Biological Membranes.* New York: J. Wiley & Sons, Inc. 1973.

Lehninger, A. L. *Biochemistry*, 2nd ed. New York: Worth Publishers, 1975, pp. 287–307.

Acid Rain

Likens, G., Wright, R., Galloway, J., and Butler, T. "Acid Rain." *Sci. Am.* 241 (October 1979):43.

Likens, G. "Acid Precipitation." *Chem. Eng. News,* November 22, 1976, p. 29.

Vermeuler, A. "Acid Precipitation in the Netherlands." *Environ. Sci. Technol.* 12 (September 1978):1016.

Johnson, N. "Acid Rain: Neutralization within the Hubbard Brook Ecosystem and Regional Implications." *Science* 204 (1979):497.

Lakes and Oceans

Ruttner, F. *Fundamentals of Limnology,* 3rd ed. Toronto: University of Toronto Press, 1963.

Russell-Hunter, W. D. *Aquatic Productivity.* New York: Macmillan Publishing Co., Inc., 1970.

Cole, G. A. *Textbook of Limnology.* St. Louis: The C. V. Mosby Company, 1975.

Beeton, A. M. "Eutrophication of the St. Lawrence Great Lakes." *Limnol. Oceanogr.* 10 (1965):240.

Rogatzkie, R. A. "The Great Lakes Rediscovered." *Am. Sci.* 62 (July–August 1974):454.

Hutchinson, G. E. "Eutrophication." *Am. Sci.* 61 (May–June 1973):269.

Lee, G., Rast, W., and Jones, R. "Eutrophication of Water Bodies: Insights for an Age-Old Problem." *Environ. Sci. Technol.* 12 (August 1978):900.

MacIntyre, F. "Why the Sea Is Salt." *Sci. Am.* 223 (November 1970):104.

Herring, P. J., and Clarke, M. R., eds. *Deep Oceans.* New York: Praeger Publishers, Inc., 1971.

Mueller, J. A., Anderson, A. R., and Jeris, J. S. "Contaminants in the New York Bight." *J. Water Pollut. Control Fed.* 48 (1976):2309.

Dewling, R. T., and Anderson, P. W. "New York Bight I: Ocean Dumping Policies." *Oceanus* 19, no. 4 (1976):2.

Gross, M. G. "New York Bight II: Problems of Research." *Oceanus* 19, no. 4 (1976):12.

Olexsey, R. A. "After Ocean Disposal, What?" *Water Wastes Eng.* 13, no. 9 (1976):59.

Travers, W. B., and Tuney, P. R. "Drilling, Tankers, and Oil Spills on the Atlantic Outer Continental Shelf." *Science* 194 (1976):791.

Harwood, M. "Oil and Water: In the Wake of the Argo Merchant." *Harper's,* September 1978:43.

"Petroleum in the Environment." Washington, D.C.: National Academy of Sciences, 1975.

Wastewater Treatment

Keith, L. H., and Telliard, W. A. "Priority Pollutants—A Perspective View." *Environ. Sci. Technol.* 13 (April 1979):416.

Westman, W. E. "Problems in Implementing U.S. Water Quality Goals." *Am. Sci.* 65 (March–April 1977):197.

Argo, D. G., and Wesner, G. M. "Advanced Waste Treatment: Energy Needs a Prime Concern." *Water Wastes Eng.* 13, no. 5 (1976):24.

Hagan, R. M., and Roberts, E. B. "Energy Requirements for Waste-water Treatment." *Water Sewage Works* 123, no. 12 (1976):52.

Dean, R. B., and Forsythe, S. L. "Estimating the Reliability of Advanced Waste Treatment." *Water Sewage Works* 123, no. 6 (1976):87.

Mulligan, T. J., and Fox, R. D. "Treatment of Industrial Wastewaters." *Chem. Eng.* 83 (October 18, 1976):49.

Bush, K. E. "Refinery Wastewater Treatment and Reuse." *Chem. Eng.* 83 (April 12, 1976):113.

Behrman, B. W. "Nitrogen Removal Depends on Form Nutrient Takes." *Water Wastes Eng.* 13, no. 2 (1976):27.

Stover, E. L., and Kincannon, D. F. "One- Versus Two-Stage Nitrification in the Activated Sludge Process." *J. Water Pollut. Control Fed.* 48 (1976):645.

Hayes, D. G. "Waste Water Treatment Via Activated Carbon." *Chem. Eng. Prog.* 72, no. 10 (1976):57.

Suffet, I., McGuire, M., Josephson, J., and Ember, L. "Activated Carbon Cleanup: That Old Black Magic Works Again!" *Environ. Sci. Technol.* 12 (October 1978):1138.

Kim, B. R., Snoeyink, V. L., and Saunders, F. M. "Adsorption of Organic Compounds by Synthetic Resins." *J. Water Pollut. Control Fed.* 48 (1976):120.

Fisher, S. A., and McGarvey, F. X. "Ion Exchange for Water Recycle." *Ind. Water Eng.* 13, no. 2 (1976):14.

Sammon, D. C., and Stringer, B. "Application of Membrane Processes in the Treatment of Sewage." *Process. Biochem.* 10 (March 1975):4.

Leitz, F. B. "Electrodialysis for Industrial Water Cleanup." *Environ. Sci. Technol.* 10 (1976):136.

Westbrook, G. T., and Wirth, L. F. "Water Reuse—By Electrodialysis." *Ind. Water Eng.* 13, no. 2 (1976):8.

Stover, R. C., Sommers, L. E., and Silviera, D. J. "Evaluation of Metals in Wastewater Sludge." *J. Water Pollut. Control Fed.* 48 (1976):2165.

"Application of Sewage Sludge to Cropland: Appraisal of Potential Hazards of the Heavy Metals to Plants and Animals." Council for Agricultural Science and Technology (CAST), Report No. 54. Ames, Iowa, 1976.

Hyde, H. C. "Utilization of Wastewater Sludge for Agricultural Soil Enrichment." *J. Water Pollut. Control Fed.* 48 (1976):77.

Varanka, M. W., Zablocki, Z. M., and Hinesly, T. D. "The Effect of Digested Sludge on Soil Biological Activity." *J. Water Pollut. Control Fed.* 48 (1976):1728.

Crites, R. W., and Pound, C. E. "Land Treatment of Municipal Wastewater." *Environ. Sci. Technol.* 10 (1976):548.

Harvey, W. B. "Spray Irrigation Solves Disposal Problem." *Water Wastes Eng.* 13, no. 10 (1976):31.

Woodwell, G. W. "Recycling Sewage through Plant Communities." *Am. Sci.* 65 (September–October 1977):556.

Rehlberger, G. W. "Chlorination: The Current Dilemma." *Water Sewage Works* 122, no. 11 (1975):62.

Hoehn, R. C. "Comparative Disinfection Methods." *J. Am. Water Works Assoc.* 68 (1976):302.

Furr, A. K., et al. "Multielement and Chlorinated Hydrocarbon Analysis of Municipal Sewage Sludges of American Cities." *Environ. Sci. Technol.* 10 (1976):683.

Drinking Water, Conservation, and Water Resources

Agino, E., Wixson, B., and Smith, I. "Drinking Water Quality and Chronic Disease." *Environ. Sci. Technol.* 11 (July 1977):660.

Shoji, K. "Drip Irrigation." *Sci. Am.* 237 (November 1977):62.

Ambroggi, R. P. "Underground Reservoirs to Control the Water Cycle." *Sci. Am.* 236 (May 1977):21.

Eckholm, E., and Brown, L. "Spreading Deserts—The Hand of Man." *Bull. Atom. Sci.* 34 (January 1978):10.

PART IV | BIOSPHERE

1 | Nitrogen and Food Production

The final part of this book concerns the biosphere—the realm of living organisms and their interactions. We have already touched on several aspects of the biological world in connection with energy flows and air and water chemistry, but we now focus more directly on biological processes, particularly as they affect human welfare.

The first topic we will consider is food production and the important role of the nitrogen cycle. The main process in the production of biological energy is the carbon cycle. However, as we saw in the preceding section, organisms need more than carbon dioxide and water as nutrients. They also require nitrogen, phosphorus, and several other elements in smaller amounts. Most of these elements are available in the soil in sufficient quantities to support plant growth, although some of them may need to be supplemented for intensive agriculture. The main limitation to plant productivity is the supply of nitrogen. While 80% of the atmosphere consists of molecular nitrogen, it is in an extremely stable and unreactive form, as observed in our discussion of atmospheric chemistry. In order to participate in biological reactions, nitrogen must be fixed; that is, it must be combined with other elements.

The upper part of Figure 4.1 contains a schematic diagram of the nitrogen cycle. We have already seen that at sufficiently high temperatures, such as in combustion or during lightning, nitrogen and oxygen can combine to form nitrogen oxides. These eventually are converted to nitric acid, which is washed out by rain. Nitric acid is a strong acid and readily dissociates in water to hydrogen ion and nitrate ion.

Plants, but not animals, can utilize nitrate in the production of protein as well as other essential organic nitrogen compounds. But the pathway through nitrogen oxides and nitrate is insufficient to support the abundant plant life we know. Most nitrogen fixation goes via the pathway shown on the left-hand side of the figure, in which certain bacteria and algae combine molecular nitrogen with hydrogen to produce ammonia, NH_3, or its acid form, ammonium ion, NH_4^+. This unique class of organisms possesses a specialized biochemical apparatus

The Nitrogen Cycle

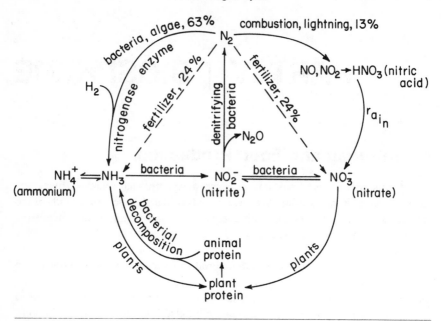

Fertilizer Production

1. $3H_2 + N_2 \xrightarrow[\text{high}\{\text{pressure}]{\text{Fe} \atop \text{temperature}} 2NH_3$ (Haber process)

2. $NH_3 + 2O_2 \xrightarrow[\text{high temperature}]{\text{catalyst}} HNO_3 + H_2O$

3. $NH_3 + HNO_3 \longrightarrow NH_4NO_3$ (fertilizer)

4. $2CH_4 + \text{air} + H_2O \longrightarrow 5H_2 + 2N_2 + 2CO$ (hydrogen production)
   Methane

Figure 4.1

called the *nitrogenase enzyme system,* which can form ammonia rapidly at ambient temperatures. Plants can use ammonia directly for their nitrogen source.
When plants and animals die, their protein is decomposed by another type of
bacteria to produce ammonia again.

In the middle of the diagram we find nitrite ion, NO_2^-, which represents an
oxidation level of nitrogen intermediate between ammonia and nitrate. Some
kinds of bacteria oxidize ammonia to nitrite and then nitrite to nitrate. Still other
bacteria, called *denitrifying bacteria,* can convert nitrite back to molecular nitrogen, thus completing the nitrogen cycle. A by-product of this denitrification

reaction, accounting for an estimated 5–10% of the total, is nitrous oxide, N_2O. As we saw in our consideration of the ozone layer, this gas is important in the ozone balance. It is inert in the lower atmosphere but can be converted to nitric oxide in the stratosphere, thereby accelerating the destruction of ozone. There is some concern currently that the rate of production of nitrous oxide might be increasing as a result of the use of artificial fertilizers, but we do not yet know enough about the quantitative aspects of the denitrification reaction to tell whether this is a serious problem.

The main natural sources of nitrogen for agriculture are the nitrogenase-containing bacteria, which grow in symbiosis with a limited variety of food plants, most notably those of the legume family. The nodules of legumes, such as beans, peas, alfalfa, and clover, contain these bacteria. When the plants die, nitrogen is returned to the soil in fixed form, where it is available for other kinds of plants, except for the fraction that is returned to the atmosphere via the denitrification reaction. For this reason, crop rotation, in which legumes are planted alternately with cereals, grains, and other vegetables, is an ancient agricultural practice designed to maintain the productivity of the nonlegume plants. In the absence of crop rotation, plants that do not fix nitrogen quickly deplete the soil of its nitrogen stores, unless they are replaced by the addition of fertilizer. Animal manure can be used for this purpose, but in recent years it has been increasingly supplanted by artificial fertilizers produced industrially.

This industrial supplementation of nature's nitrogen fixation is indicated by the dashed lines in the first part of Figure 4.1. The commercial production of fertilizer is shown by the four reactions in the lower part of Figure 4.1. The first step is the Haber process, in which nitrogen is combined directly with molecular hydrogen to form ammonia. This reaction releases energy and therefore should occur spontaneously, but because of the very strong bond that connects the two nitrogen atoms, the reaction is extremely slow except at very high temperatures, unless a catalyst is used to lower the activation energy. In the Haber process, iron is used as a catalyst, and the reaction runs efficiently at 500° C and 100 atm pressure. As shown in reactions 2 and 3, the ammonia is then partially oxidized to ammonium nitrate, which is the main form of nitrogen in commercial fertilizer. As we have seen, plants use both ammonia and nitrate. The Haber process requires hydrogen gas. Currently, the most economic process for obtaining hydrogen is the partial oxidation of methane, shown in reaction 4 of Figure 4.1.

Table 4.1 summarizes present estimates of worldwide nitrogen fixation through the natural pathways and by industrial production. Industry now accounts for about one-quarter of the total production of fixed nitrogen, and its contribution is increasing rapidly.

The application of fertilizer can dramatically improve agricultural yields. The graphs in Figure 4.2 demonstrate the correlation between increased fertilizer use and increased crop yields in the Iowa cornbelt over the past few decades. The

Table 4.1 Estimates of Total Nitrogen Fixation for 1974

	Nitrogen Fixed	
Mechanism of Fixation	MT/year	Percent of Total
Bacteria and algae	150	63.3%
Lightning	10	4.2
Combustion	20	8.4
Industrial ammonia production	57	24.1
Total	237	100.0%

Source: "Effect of Increased Nitrogen Fixation on Stratospheric Ozone," Council for Agricultural Science and Technology, Report No. 53, January 19, 1976, p. 13.

tripling of yields for corn and certain other grains between 1940 and 1975 has made the U.S. and Canadian Midwest the breadbasket of much of the world.

When sufficient fertilizer has been added to support plant growth at its maximum rate, then further additions either have no effect or actually inhibit growth. The curve of diminishing returns for corn is shown in Figure 4.3. The dashed curve shows that the total yield of corn begins to decrease after about 200 pounds of nitrogen per acre is added. The solid curve is the ratio of the energy contained in the corn produced per unit of energy required to grow it in the United States. This curve peaks between 100 and 120 pounds of nitrogen per acre.

Fertilizer is the highest energy consumer in U.S. corn production, accounting for nearly one-third of the total energy used. The main reason for the high energy cost is that, as we saw in reaction 4 of Figure 4.1, methane gas must be utilized to produce hydrogen. The Haber process is quite efficient, but the hydrogen required to reduce nitrogen is high-quality stored energy. The cost of ammonia production is therefore tied directly to the price of natural gas, which has been escalating steeply since the fuel crunch of 1973. Hydrogen can also be produced from coal, or by any of the other energy sources discussed in the first part of this book. The cost of any of these alternative sources is higher than that of natural gas, even at today's prices, but that situation may change in the future. The low price of fossil fuels until 1973 was a major factor in the rapid increase in fertilizer use during the preceding 30 years.

The vertical lines in Figure 4.3 show the rates of current fertilizer application for U.S. cornfields. This range corresponds to a region of the productivity curve where the total yield is still increasing but the energy output/input ratio has leveled off. No doubt increasing prices will provide an incentive to conserve fertilizer and in some measure to reintroduce traditional agricultural practices such as crop rotation and the use of animal manure. This economic incentive reinforces recent interest in organic farming, whose proponents claim that the use

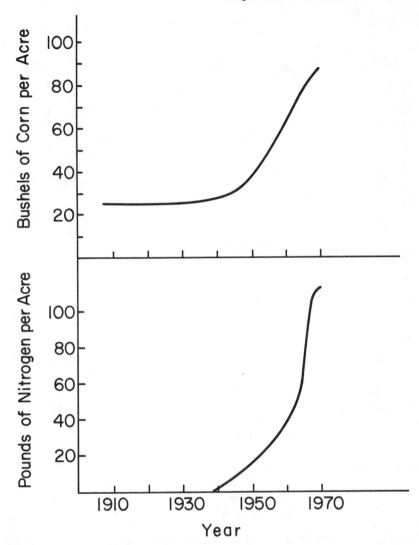

Figure 4.2 Effect of Fertilizer Use on Corn Yields in the United States

Source: Adapted from D. Pimentel, L. E. Hurd, A. C. Bellotti, M. J. Forster, I. N. Oka, O. D. Sholes, and R. J. Whitman, *Science* 182 (1973):445.

of natural fertilizers, as opposed to ammonium nitrate, helps to build up the humus of the soil and maintain it in a more productive state.

Increased fertilizer prices are more critical for poor countries, which are trying hard to expand their agricultural production to meet the hunger of their growing and ill-fed populations. Considerable progress in this very difficult task was

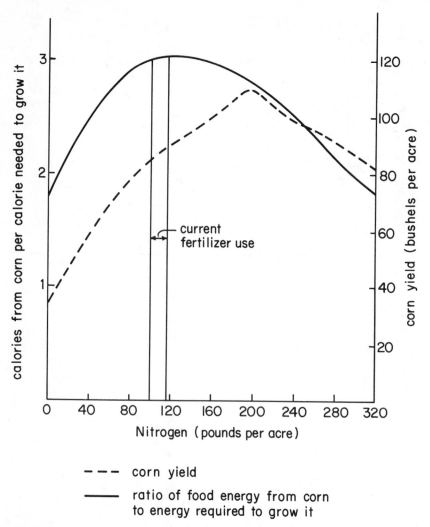

Figure 4.3 Corn Yield and Energy Return Versus Fertilizer Use
Source: D. Pimentel, et al., *Science* **182** (1973):445.

achieved in the 1960s through what has become known as the Green Revolution. This involved the development by plant scientists, working in research institutes in Mexico and the Philippines, of new strains of wheat and rice that produce high yields when fertilized. As shown in Figure 4.4, traditional varieties of grain indigenous to tropical and subtropical countries do not respond well to fertilizer. They grow too tall and fall over in winds and heavy rain. The new strains are

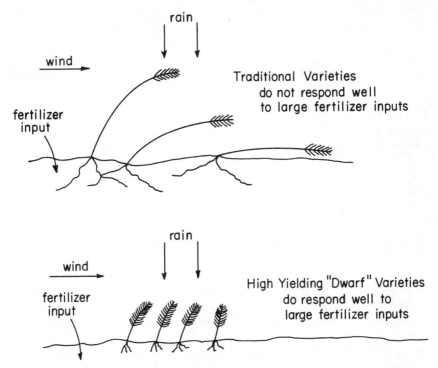

Figure 4.4   The Green Revolution: High-Yielding Variety Grains for Use in the Developing World

dwarf plants, with stalks that remain short while the grain matures. A larger number of plants can be sown per unit area for the dwarf varieties than for the less compact traditional varieties, which have large leaves and extended root networks to absorb the small amounts of nutrients and water often found in tropical soil.

During the six years between 1965 and 1972, the developing countries increased their food production by 23%, as more than 70 million acres in Asia and North Africa were planted with high-yielding varieties of grain. The years 1972 and 1974 produced a severe setback to the Green Revolution, however, with significant production declines and widespread famine. The main causes were bad weather and the petroleum crisis. Not only was industrial fertilizer too expensive for third-world farmers, but so was the fuel for operating irrigation pumps. Many farmers elected to return to the traditional plant varieties, which are hardier and more resistant to drought than the high-yielding varieties.

This experience produced much discouragement about the concept of the Green Revolution, but the real problem appears to be overreliance of the world

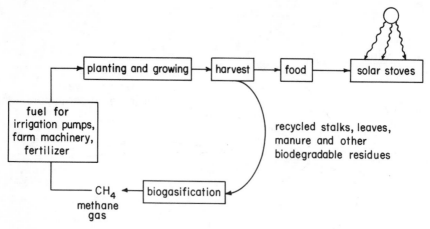

Figure 4.5 Appropriate Technology for Achieving Energy Self-Sufficiency in Agriculture in the Developing World

agricultural system on petroleum and natural gas deposits. For poor countries in particular, the development of alternative, domestically available energy sources is a critical need. One plan for achieving energy self-sufficiency in agriculture is shown in Figure 4.5. A number of sources that seem relatively insignificant in the context of the U.S. energy supply could make an important contribution in developing countries. A good example is biogasification, the process shown earlier in Figure 1.36, by which farm wastes, nonwoody plants, and sewage can be converted to methane in simple microbial digesters. Even in the United States, it has been estimated that enough energy is available from this resource, at a conversion efficiency of 40%, to supply all farm energy needs, including fuel, electricity, fertilizer production, and irrigation. Since agriculture is much less energy-intensive in most developing countries, a much lower conversion efficiency would still allow the fulfillment of energy needs. Community-sized biogasification plants could produce methane for making fertilizer, driving irrigation pumps, and running simple farm machinery. Engines that now operate on liquid fuels could readily be adapted to run on gaseous fuel.

Direct solar energy could also be an important resource for poor countries in tropical areas that have abundant sunshine. The widespread adoption of solar stoves for cooking would be particularly desirable. At present, wood and cow dung are used as cooking fuels in most rural areas of poor countries. These fuels are inefficient and in short supply, however. Cooking with them expends as much energy as is required to grow the food being cooked. Cow dung would be better utilized as fertilizer or in the production of methane gas, and the use of wood for fuel has produced serious deforestation in many tropical areas, with attendant erosion and loss of arable land. Solar stoves have been developed that are surprisingly effective. One model with a parabolic collector is capable of cooking a kilogram of rice in 15 minutes, a rate comparable to that of a small coal stove.

Much current agricultural research is aimed at improving the rates of natural nitrogen fixation as well as photosynthesis. One avenue of investigation involves experiments in plant breeding designed to produce symbiotic association between nitrogen-fixing bacteria and cereal plants such as wheat and rice. If this work is successful, it opens the door to freeing the production of important cereal crops from the current dependence on nitrogen supplementation.

Bioenergetics

From a chemical point of view, the most fundamental characteristic of living things is that they require a continual flow of chemical energy. This flow is needed to operate the complex biochemical machinery and maintain vital functions. In most cases, the energy is provided by the oxidation of reduced carbon compounds, although some microorganisms can extract energy from the oxidation of reduced nitrogen or sulfur compounds. In higher organisms, the oxidant is molecular oxygen:

$$C_6H_{12}O_6 + 6O_2 \rightarrow 6CO_2 + 6H_2O \qquad \Delta G^0 = -686 \text{ kcal/mol} \qquad (1)$$

In reaction (1), $C_6H_{12}O_6$ is the six-carbon sugar, glucose, the main constituent of carbohydrates. In many microorganisms, energy is obtained from internal disproportionations into reduced and oxidized forms, e.g.,

$$C_6H_{12}O_6 \rightarrow 2CH_3CH_2OH + 2CO_2 \qquad \Delta G^0 = -43.2 \text{ kcal/mol} \qquad (2)$$
$$\text{ethanol}$$

which is the fermentation reaction, or

$$C_6H_{12}O_6 \rightarrow 2CH_3CH(OH)CO_2^- + 2H^+ \qquad \Delta G^0 = -47.0 \text{ kcal/mol} \qquad (3)$$
$$\text{lactate}$$

The amount of free energy released by reactions (2) and (3) is much less than that released by reaction (1), since no external oxidant is used. The much larger energy flow available through respiration presumably allowed the evolution of life forms that are more complex than microorganisms.

None of the reactions (1), (2), or (3) proceeds spontaneously at an appreciable rate at ordinary temperatures. If they did, they would be of no use to living things, which must extract and use the energy *before* it is dissipated to the surroundings as heat. The lack of spontaneous reaction despite favorable free energies reflects the existence of large kinetic barriers. In the case of reaction (1), we observed on pages 143–144 that the barrier is largely due to the special electronic structure of O_2, with its two unpaired electrons. For reactions (2) and

(3), the barriers reflect the need to break and rearrange several covalent bonds to arrive at the products. As a result of these barriers, glucose can remain unreacted for a long time, with its free energy unexpended. Organisms lower these barriers selectively, feeding the energy into their various biochemical processes as required to maintain their integrity and functions. This process is called *metabolism*. It is carried out by dividing the redox reactions into many subsidiary reactions.* The barrier to each of these is lowered by a specific enzyme, a protein that is tailored to bind the reactants and catalyze the reaction.

ATP, the energy currency

The energy released by the redox reactions is channeled into useful processes by coupling subsequent reactions. For example, a reaction that requires energy

$$X + Y = X—Y \qquad \Delta G > 0$$

can be driven by one that releases energy:

$$A—B = A + B \qquad \Delta G < 0$$

by a coupling mechanism such as:

$$A—B + X = X—B + A \qquad \Delta G < 0 \qquad (4)$$

$$X—B + Y = X—Y + B \qquad \Delta G < 0 \qquad (5)$$

$$A—B + X+Y = A+B + X—Y \qquad \Delta G < 0 \qquad (6)$$

as long as the sum of the two reactions, (6), has a negative value of ΔG. Reactions (4) and (5) are examples of group transfer reactions, which are very common in biochemistry. The group B is transferred from A to X and then to the solvent (water), in order to drive the desired production of X—Y. The latter may involve the formation of a chemical bond, or it may involve a change in the structure of a protein that allows the transmission of a force (e.g., muscle contraction) or the transport of molecules across membranes.

Nature has chosen a single molecule to channel most of the biological energy flow. It is adenosine triphosphate (ATP); its structural formula is shown in Figure 4.6. It has three chemically distinct parts linked by single covalent bonds: a heterocyclic base, adenine; a five-carbon sugar, ribose; and a linear triphosphate group. The adenine-ribose portion is called adenosine. The phosphate groups of ATP can be split off successively to form adenosine diphosphate, ADP, and adenosine monophosphate, AMP. AMP is a member of the class of nucleotides, which are the repeating units of nucleic acids (see pages 334–337). The splitting

---

*"Redox" is a contraction of reduction-oxidation. Both processes always occur together. Thus while glucose is oxidized in reaction (1), oxygen is reduced. In reaction (2) glucose is simultaneously oxidized (to CO_2) and reduced (to CH_3CH_2OH). Use of the term *redox* avoids singling out one partner or the other in the overall reduction-oxidation reaction.

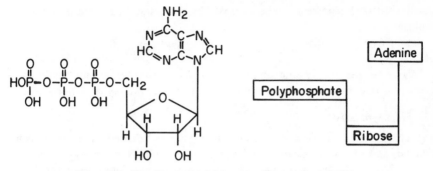

Figure 4.6   The Structure of Adenosine Triphosphate (ATP)

of phosphate from ATP by water (called *hydrolysis*) releases energy:

$$ATP + H_2O \rightarrow ADP + P_i \qquad (7)$$

P_i stands for an inorganic monophosphate ion, which in neutral solution is a mixture of mono- and diprotonated forms HPO_4^- and $H_2PO_4^-$. (The pK_a of $H_2PO_4^-$ is 6.7.) ATP and ADP are both monoprotonated at neutral pH ($pK_a = 6.50$ and 7.20, respectively) and they bind to Mg^{2+} ions (through the negatively charged phosphate groups), which are always present inside biological cells. It is the Mg^{2+} complex of ATP that is biologically active.

At a pH of 7 and the ionic concentration found in cells, the free energy of reaction (7), at hypothetical $1.0\,M$ concentrations of ATP, ADP, and P_i, is $\Delta G^{0'} = -7.4$ kcal/mol (the prime denotes that the standard state is a solution of the stated composition rather than pure water). This free energy is used to drive a wide variety of biochemical processes, including ion transport and muscle contraction, via coupled reactions like (4) and (5), in which A—B is ATP and the group B being transferred is phosphate. It is important for the success of this scheme that the uncatalyzed hydrolysis of ATP is slow, since the P—O—P bonds are relatively inert to attack by water. This kinetic barrier permits the phosphate transfer to be directed toward the proper target, X, by a specific enzyme. The function of the adenosine part of the ATP is to bind to an appropriately tailored binding site on the enzyme, thereby giving the enzyme a handle on the phosphate group.

An alternative mode of ATP hydrolysis is:

$$ATP + H_2O \rightarrow AMP + PP_i$$

where PP_i is the pyrophosphate ion, which is present at neutral pH in its diprotonated form $H_2P_2O_7^{2-}$. The free energy is similar to that of reaction (7), $\Delta G^{0'} = -7.5$ kcal/mol. A number of biosynthetic reactions, including the synthesis of nucleic acids, are driven by a coupling scheme in which AMP is the group transferred from ATP to X (e.g., the growing end of a nucleic acid). The energy available for this process can be increased by the further hydrolysis of pyrophosphate:

$$PP_i \rightarrow 2P_i \qquad \Delta G^{0'} = -8.0 \text{ kcal/mol}$$

This extra energy may sometimes be needed to ensure that group transfer proceeds in one direction only, thereby maintaining the fidelity of the process.

Photosynthesis

The conversion of sunlight to biochemical energy is carried out by green plants and by some kinds of bacteria. In the case of green plants, the energy of the light is used to transfer electrons from water to carbon dioxide, with the production of oxygen and carbohydrates. This occurs in chloroplasts, which are specialized organelles found in the leaves of plants. Inside the chloroplast is a highly folded membrane, called the *thylakoid membrane,* that contains the plant's chlorophyll. The structure of chlorophyll and its absorption spectrum were shown earlier in Figure 1.31. There we saw that chlorophyll is an excellent collector of visible radiation.

Most of the chlorophyll molecules in the thylakoid membrane, called *antennae* chlorophyll, simply capture photons and funnel them to special sites, called *reaction centers.* The chlorophyll molecules in the centers are in a unique environment and are excited to a reactive state by the photons. The essence of this excitation, which is currently under active study in research laboratories, is a separation of charge at the reaction center. The excited electrons are passed on to carbon dioxide during many intervening steps, while the positive holes are refilled with electrons drawn from water.

The energy required for this overall electron transfer is sufficiently large that plants have evolved two separate photoprocesses, called *photosystems I and II,* which operate in series to accomplish the task. These processes are carried out at physically distinct sites and have different wavelength dependencies. Photosystem I is excited by photons with wavelengths shorter than 700 nm, while photosystem II is excited by photons with wavelengths shorter than 680 nm. As illustrated in Figure 4.7, excitation of photosystem II generates a high-energy hole (large positive redox potential), capable of extracting an electron from water. (This has to happen four times in succession to produce oxygen. The molecular apparatus required for this has not yet been elucidated, but it is known to require manganese ions, which probably catalyze the combination of nascent oxygen atoms to O_2.) The electron is transferred to plastoquinone (labeled Q in Figure 4.7 and shown in Figure 4.8). The quinone portion of this molecule is reduced to the semiquinone form, which is a mild reducing agent. It provides the electron needed to replenish photosystem II, which has meanwhile been excited by another photon. This excitation yields a high-energy electron (large negative redox potential). It is captured by an as yet uncharacterized molecule called

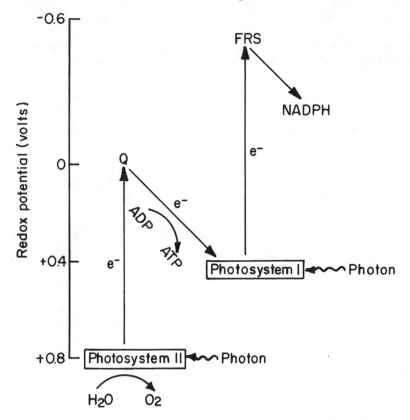

Figure 4.7 The Flow of Electrons in Photosystems I and II of Green Plants

ferredoxin reducing substance (FRS in Figure 4.7), and then passed on, via the iron-sulfur protein ferredoxin, to the molecule nicotinamide adenine dinucleotide phosphate (NADP).

The structure of NADP is shown on the left-hand side of Figure 4.9. Its reducible portion is the pyridine ring. Addition of two electrons and a proton

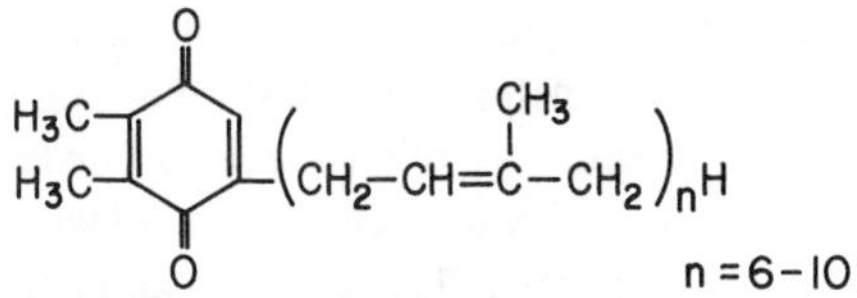

Figure 4.8 Structure of Plastoquinone

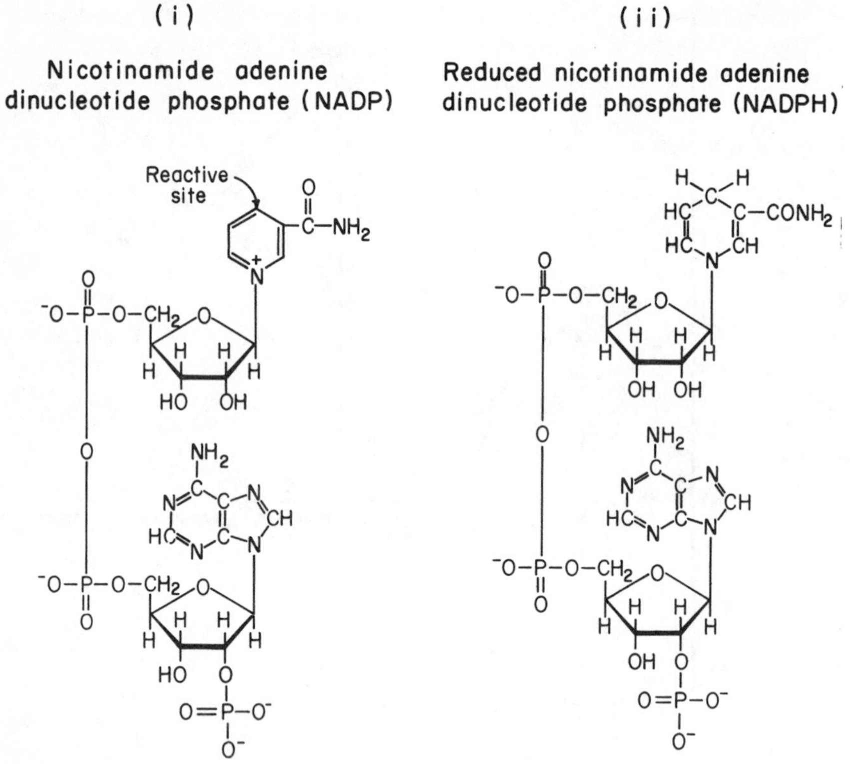

(i)

Nicotinamide adenine dinucleotide phosphate (NADP)

(ii)

Reduced nicotinamide adenine dinucleotide phosphate (NADPH)

Figure 4.9 Structures of NADP and NADPH

produces the hydride, NADPH, shown on the right in Figure 4.9. NADP, and its close analog NAD, which lacks the phosphate group at the bottom of the structure, are two of nature's universal electron carriers. NADP is found in all cells and participates in a large variety of enzymatic redox reactions. It is well suited for this since the uncatalyzed oxidation of its reduced form is slow in the presence of oxygen. In the chloroplast, NADPH diffuses away from the thylakoid membrane and participates in the enzymatic reduction of carbon dioxide to carbohydrates in a complex cycle of reactions elucidated by Melvin Calvin and his colleagues.[1] These are the "dark reactions" of photosynthesis, which do not require light but only a supply of NADPH and ATP.

Plastoquinone has a hydrocarbon tail (see Figure 4.8), which anchors it in the thylakoid membrane. Electron transfer from plastoquinione to photosystem I is not a simple process but proceeds via other electron carriers, including cytochromes (see the next section) and a copper protein, plastocyanine. There is a substantial decrease in energy between plastoquinone and photosystem I, and the electron flow is used to drive the synthesis of ATP from ADP and inorganic phosphate. This process is called *photophosphorylation*. Thus the photoreaction centers convert light to two forms of chemical energy, NADPH and ATP. If the transfer of an electron from the excited photosystem I to NADP is blocked (e.g., if all the available NADP is reduced), then the electron can flow back via the same electron transport system leading from plastoquinone, and can participate in the production of ATP.

Respiration

The overall chemistry of respiration is the reverse of photosynthesis, and the mitochondrion, in which this chemistry is carried out, resembles the chloroplast in several respects. As in the chloroplast, the electron transfer components of the mitochondrion are held in a highly folded membrane called the *inner membrane,* which is the site of energy transduction. Transduction consists of generating ATP from ADP and phosphate, utilizing the energy released by the oxidation of reduced carbon compounds. This is accomplished by separating the redox processes spatially. As illustrated in Figure 4.10, oxygen is reduced at the outside surface of the inner membrane, while carbon is oxidized to carbon dioxide in the inner space, called the *matrix*. This oxidation is carried out enzymatically via the citric acid cycle. Carbon from various sources is fed into the cycle in the form of acetyl groups, CH_3COO-, attached to a shuttle molecule, coenzyme A (see Figure 4.11). Two carbon atoms are oxidized per turn of the citric acid cycle, and this is accompanied by the reduction of NAD to NADH and also by the reduction of FAD to $FADH_2$. FAD is another electron-carrying molecule that is found widely in nature. Its structure is shown in Figure 4.12. The reducible part of the molecule is the tricylic flavin ring.

Electrons are transferred from NADH and $FADH_2$ to oxygen via several elec-

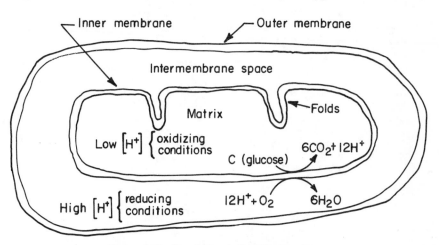

Figure 4.10   Respiration in the Mitochondrion

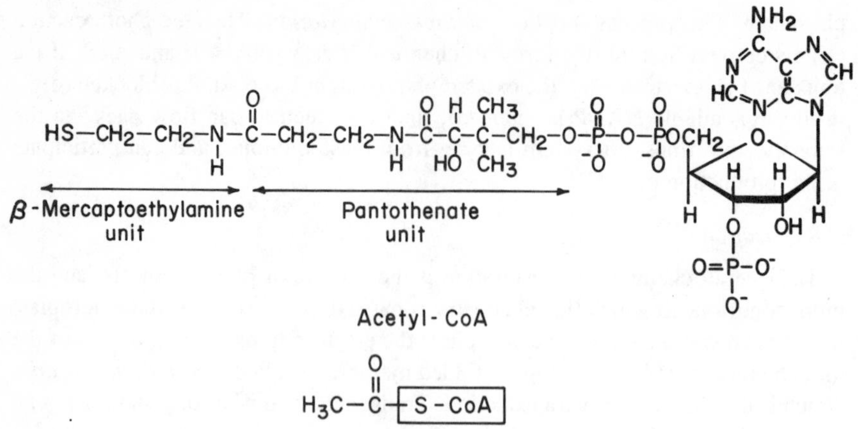

β-Mercaptoethylamine unit / Pantothenate unit

Acetyl- CoA

$$H_3C-\overset{\overset{O}{\|}}{C}\!-\!\boxed{S-CoA}$$

Figure 4.11 Structure of Coenzyme A (CoA)

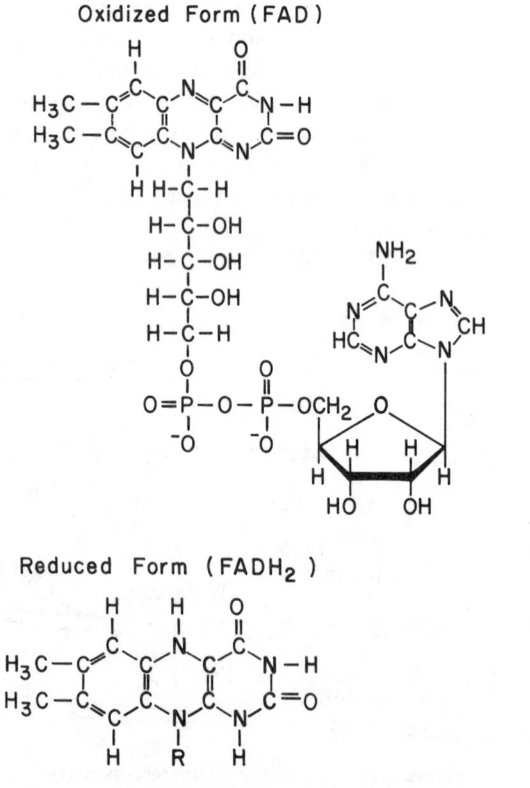

Oxidized Form (FAD)

Reduced Form (FADH$_2$)

Figure 4.12 Structure of Flavin Adenine Dinucleotide (FAD)

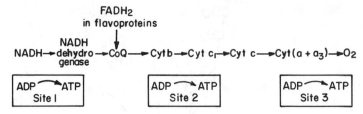

Figure 4.13 Sequence of Electron Carriers in the Respiratory Assembly

tron transfer molecules localized in the membrane. The steps are shown schematically in Figure 4.13. The large energy difference between NADH and oxygen is used to generate three ATP molecules. This process, called *oxidative phosphorylation,* is carried out at three distinct sites, which are organized protein assemblies that contain electron transfer molecules with redox potentials spaced between those of NADH and oxygen (see Table 4.2). The first of these, NADH dehydrogenase, contains flavin and iron-sulfur complexes. It transfers electrons from NADH to coenzyme Q. Like the plastoquinone of chloroplasts, coenzyme Q is a lipid-soluble quinone. It is free to move around within the membrane and transfers electrons to the next protein assembly, at site 2, which contains two kinds of cytochromes, b and c_1. Cytochromes are proteins that contain iron-porphyrin complexes, often called *hemes* (see Figure 4.14). Hemes are similar in structure to chlorophyll which is a magnesium-porphyrin molecule. Electron transfer takes place via the iron atom at the center of the ring. From site 2, electrons are transferred to cytochrome c, a small water-soluble protein bound at the membrane surface. Finally, cytochrome c transfers electrons to the last protein assembly, at site 3, called *cytochrome oxidase.* It contains two iron-porphyrin complexes in cytochromes a and a_3 and also two copper ions. All four metal ions are probably involved in the concerted addition of four electrons to oxygen, thus reducing it directly to two molecules of water. $FADH_2$ has a less negative redox potential than NADH and enters the electron transport chain at coenzyme Q. Its oxidation generates two ATP molecules rather than three.

Table 4.2 Standard Redox Potentials of Transfer Molecules in the Generation of ATP

Reductant	Oxidant	E' (volts)*
NADH	NAD$^+$	-0.32
NADH dehydrogenase (reduced)	(oxidized)	-0.11
Coenzyme Q (reduced)	(oxidized)	$+0.10$
Cytochrome b Fe($+2$)	Fe($+3$)	$+0.07$
Cytochrome c_1 Fe($+2$)	Fe($+3$)	$+0.22$
Cytochrome c Fe($+2$)	Fe($+3$)	$+0.26$
Cytochromes ($a + a_3$) Fe($+2$), Cu($+1$)	Fe($+3$), Cu($+2$)	$+0.28$
H_2O	$\frac{1}{2}O_2 + 2H^+$	$+0.82$

*E' is the standard oxidation-reduction potential (pH 7, 25° C).

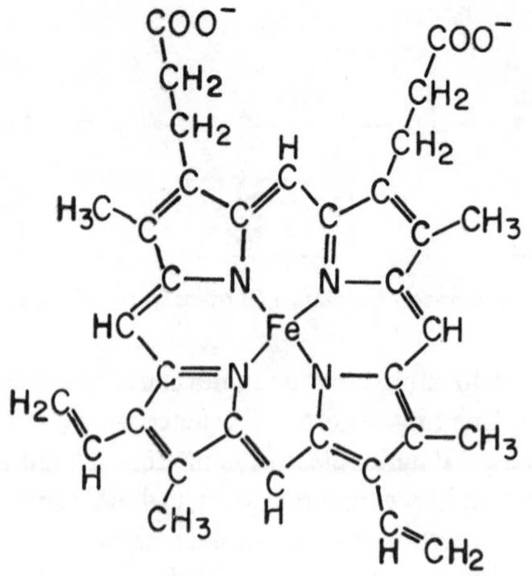

Heme
(Fe - protoporphyrin IX)

Figure 4.14 Structure of Heme

The mechanism for coupling electron transfer to ATP generation is not yet fully understood. It involves additional protein assemblies, called *coupling factors* or *ATPases* (separated from the mitochondria, these proteins catalyze the hydrolysis of ATP back to ADP and phosphate), which stick out from the membrane into the matrix. It seems very likely that the coupling mechanism involves proton, as well as electron, transport. The widely accepted chemiosmotic theory, propounded chiefly by Peter Mitchell, gives a central role to the difference in the concentration of protons and other ions on either side of the inner membrane.[2] A gradient is believed to be generated by the spatial arrangement of the electron transfer proteins in the membrane, which effects the passage of protons from the inner to the outer side as the proteins are successively oxidized and reduced. The proton gradient in turn somehow provides the driving force for ATP generation via the coupling factors.

Ion gradients across membranes are important for many other biological processes, including the transmission of nerve impulses, muscle contraction, and the transport of molecules into and out of cells.

Nitrogen Cycle Enzymes

Nitrogenase

Although most of the energy flow in the biosphere is carried on by the reduction and reoxidation of carbon compounds, a significant fraction passes through the nitrogen cycle. Organisms incorporate nitrogen from ammonia into amino acids, nucleotides, and other organic molecules. Ammonia is the thermodynamically stable form of nitrogen in a reducing environment. The stable form in the presence of O_2 is N_2. A large kinetic barrier inhibits the direct reduction of N_2 because of its very strong bond (226 kcal/mol). This barrier was overcome early in the evolution of life via the enzyme nitrogenase (N_2-ase).

The overall chemistry of nitrogenase is illustrated schematically in Figure 4.15. The enzyme is a complex of two different proteins. The smaller of these (Fe protein) contains an iron-sulfur complex, whereas the larger (Mo-Fe protein) contains iron, sulfur, and molybdenum in the ratio 14:16:1. The molecular arrangement of these inorganic atoms is not yet known. It seems likely that N_2 binds to the molybdenum atom in the first step of the reduction reaction. Molybdenum has a variety of oxidation states available to it, so that it is capable of engaging in multiple electron transfers. Inorganic complexes of Mo have been shown to bind N_2, and under some conditions, the bound N_2 can be reduced to NH_3 and also to intermediate reduction products that remain bound to the Mo, such as $-N_2H$, $-H_2H_2$, and $-N_2H_3$.[3,4] It seems likely that the six electrons needed to reduce N_2 to two NH_3 molecules are added in stages, perhaps in two-electron steps, to produce $HN=NH$ and H_2H-NH_2 prior to $2NH_3$. (The needed protons are obtainable from the aqueous environment.) A stepwise pro-

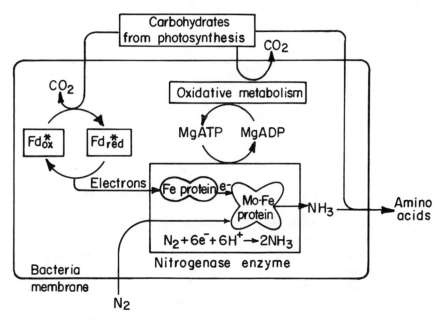

*Fd = ferredoxin

Figure 4.15   The Chemistry of the Nitrogenase Enzyme System in Algae and Bacteria

cess would then avoid breaking N≡N triple bonds all at once and would demand less energy. If intermediates are formed, however, they remain tightly bound to the enzyme, as they have never been detected in solution during the nitrogenase reaction.

The role of the iron and sulfur atoms in both the Mo-Fe protein and the Fe protein is probably to deliver electrons to the active site at the appropriate potential. Iron-sulfur proteins are used widely in nature for transferring electrons. The supplier of electrons to the nitrogenase complex is still another Fe-S protein, ferredoxin, which has a strongly negative redox potential. It obtains electrons either from the photosynthetic apparatus, as in nitrogen-fixing algae, or from the metabolism of carbon compounds. In addition to the supply of electrons, the nitrogenase reaction requires ATP, which binds to the Fe protein and is hydrolyzed to ADP during the reduction of N_2.

The nitrogenase reaction is therefore expensive in terms of energy. It requires the generation of a strong reductant and also consumes ATP. This may be the reason that nitrogenase was not retained by higher organisms during their evolution. Only microorganisms, certain algae and bacteria, possess nitrogenase, and before the advent of the Haber process, the entire biosphere was dependent on them for its supply of reduced nitrogen. These microorganisms are widespread in nature. Some of them colonize the root nodules of legumes, where they live in symbiosis, obtaining their energy from the plant and providing the plant with ammonia.

Nitrification

Other bacteria, called *nitrifying bacteria,* have evolved to use reduced nitrogen as a fuel source. Some of them (organisms of the genus *Nitrosomonas*) oxidize ammonia to nitrite

$$NH_4^+ + \frac{3}{2}O_2 \rightarrow NO_2^- + H_2O + 2H^+ \qquad \Delta G^0 = -66 \text{ kcal/mol}$$

while others (*Nitrobacter*) oxidize nitrite further to nitrate

$$NO_2^- + \frac{1}{2}O_2 \rightarrow NO_3^- \qquad \Delta G^0 = -17.5 \text{ kcal/mol}$$

These bacteria belong to the class of chemoautotrophs, meaning that they utilize the energy of these chemical reactions to reduce carbon dioxide by mechanisms similar to those of carbon reduction in photosynthetic organisms (photoautotrophs). (The word autotroph is Greek for "self-feeder.")

The oxidation of ammonia apparently proceeds via the formation of an intermediate, hydroxylamine (NH_2OH), as shown schematically in Figure 4.16. This first step is catalyzed by a copper protein. The subsequent oxidation of NH_2OH to nitrite proceeds by two steps and is mediated by a protein complex that

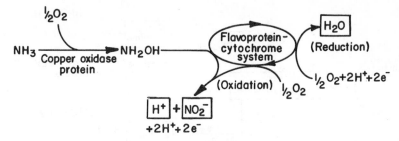

Figure 4.16 Oxidation of Ammonia to Nitrite by *Nitrosomonas* Bacteria

contains both flavin and heme. The ocidation of nitrite to nitrate in *Nitrobacter* organisms proceeds in a single step, catalyzed by cytochromes, as illustrated in Figure 4.17.

Denitrification

The nitrogen cycle is completed by denitrifying bacteria that convert nitrate back to N_2. These are also chemoautotrophs, but they use reduced carbon compounds as fuel, and nitrate instead of oxygen as oxidant. Nearly as much energy is available from oxidation by NO_3^- as by O_2, as illustrated by the following reactions:

$$CH_3OH + \frac{3}{2} O_2 \rightarrow CO_2 + 2H_2O \qquad \Delta G = -168 \text{ kcal/mol}$$

$$CH_3OH + \frac{5}{2}NO_3^- \rightarrow CO_2 + \frac{7}{5}H_2O$$
$$+ \frac{6}{5}OH^- + \frac{3}{5}N_2 \qquad \Delta G = -147 \text{ kcal/mol}$$

As shown in Figure 4.18, the bacterial reduction of NO_3^- to N_2 occurs in stages. The reduction of NO_3^- to NO_2^- is catalyzed by another Mo-Fe protein, nitrate reductase. The further reduction of NO_2^- to N_2 is catalyzed by nitrite reductase,

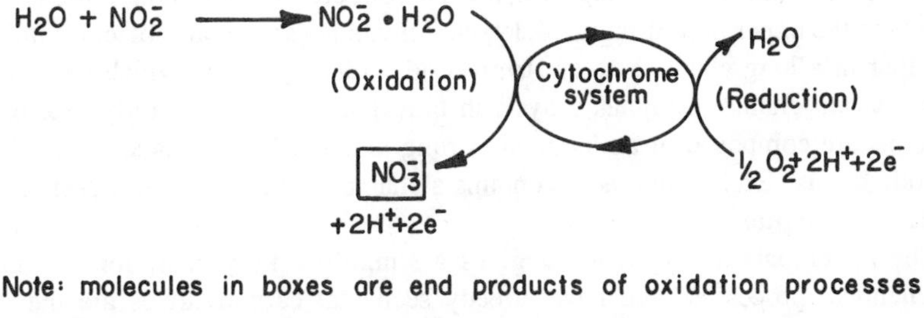

Note: molecules in boxes are end products of oxidation processes

Figure 4.17 Oxidation of Nitrite to Nitrate by *Nitrobacter* Bacteria
Note: Molecules in boxes are end products of oxidation processes.

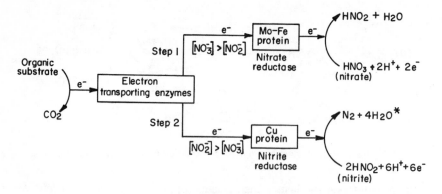

*small amount of NO, N_2O also produced

Figure 4.18 Reduction of Nitrate to Nitrogen by Denitrifying Bacteria

which is apparently a copper protein. NO and N_2O are produced as secondary products of this reaction.

Plants have an enzyme system for reducing nitrate or nitrite all the way to ammonia in order to meet their reduced nitrogen requirements. This is the reason that from the point of view of the biosphere, it is the total amount of *fixed* nitrogen that counts, whatever its chemical state. N_2 is the only form of nitrogen that cannot be directly assimilated by plants.

2 | Nutrition

Having looked at the essential energy and nitrogen requirements for plant growth, let us turn our attention to the biochemical pathways whereby the food we eat keeps us functioning. This is the chemistry of biological metabolism.

The major nutritional categories are carbohydrates, fats, and protein. As shown in the upper part of Figure 4.19, carbohydrates are sugar molecules linked together in a long chain. Fats are triglycerides of fatty acids, which have long hydrocarbon chains, designated by R in the figure, bonded to a glycerol unit. Proteins are composed of amino acids strung together like beads and joined by peptide bonds. Each amino acid contains a characteristic side chain, designated by R in the figure.

The lower part of Figure 4.19 gives a simplified flow chart for the main biochemical processes. We have already seen that carbohydrates are the immediate product of photosynthesis and also the immediate source of biological energy in the process of respiration. Most of the energy that we need to keep our

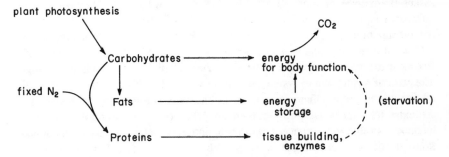

(i)
Chemical Structures

Carbohydrates are sugar polymers

e.g.

... n units

Fats are triglycerides of fatty acids

e.g.

$$CH_2O-\overset{O}{\underset{||}{C}}-R$$
$$CHO-\overset{O}{\underset{||}{C}}-R'$$
$$CH_2O-\overset{O}{\underset{||}{C}}-R''$$

glycerol unit

$R-\overset{O}{\underset{||}{C}}-$, etc. are fatty acids
R is a hydrocarbon chain

Proteins are polypeptides

e.g.

—peptide link between two amino acids

one amino acid unit   second amino acid unit

R is an amino acid side chain.

(ii)
Biochemical Functions

plant photosynthesis

fixed N_2

Carbohydrates ⟶ energy for body function ⟶ CO_2

Fats ⟶ energy storage

Proteins ⟶ tissue building, enzymes

(starvation)

Figure 4.19 Major Nutritional Categories

various bodily functions going is obtained from the oxidation of carbohydrates.

Fats represent a form of biological energy storage. In comparison with carbohydrates, fats contain less oxygen and more carbon and hydrogen, whose oxidation is the source of our energy. The energy content of fats is 9 calories/g, compared with 4 calories/g for carbohydrates. Also, fats are immiscible with water, whereas carbohydrates are hydrophilic. Carbohydrates are usually found in association with a quantity of water that is approximately four times their weight. Consequently, the conversion of carbohydrates to fats represents a concentration of energy in lightweight portable form. A person who weighs 70 kg, which is about 154 pounds, contains about 16% fat. This represents enough energy for bodily requirements for 30 days. If this amount of excess energy were stored as carbohydrate with its associated water, the body weight would have to be 160 kg, or 350 pounds. When we eat more food than we require for our energy needs, the excess calories are stored as fat. The biological oxidation of fat is slower than that of carbohydrates. When we need energy, we burn off our carbohydrate supply first and then call upon the fat stores.

Aside from an energy supply, we need to maintain the biochemical machinery of the body itself. This is the realm of protein chemistry. Proteins make up most of the body's structural tissues and also the myriad enzymes, the biological catalysts that carry out the thousands of reactions that are necessary for the maintenance of life. There are 20 different kinds of amino acids, each with a different chemical side chain. Their chemical structures are given in Figure 4.20. Each kind of protein molecule is made up of a fixed sequence of these amino acids. Most of the amino acids can be synthesized by the body from a variety of starting materials as long as there is an adequate supply of protein nitrogen in the diet. There are, however, eight amino acids, shown in the box in Figure 4.2, that the body cannot synthesize. They are valine, leucine, isoleucine, threonine, lysine, methionine, phenylalanine and tryptophan. These essential amino acids must be obtained directly from the diet. They occur with different frequencies in different proteins. Table 4.3 shows these frequencies for the average of all protein matter in the body. For example, tryptophan represents 0.6 out of every 100 amino acids, while lysine represents 2.6 out of every 100. We need to maintain a proper balance of the essential amino acids in our diet. The ratio of tryptophan to lysine needs to be 0.6 to 2.6. If this ratio is exceeded, the amount of protein that can be made by the body is limited by the lysine, and the extra tryptophan is simply burned up. The notion of essential amino acid balance is similar to the concept of limiting nutrients that we discussed in connection with the growth of algae in water. Whichever amino acid is present in the lowest amount relative to the frequency with which it is used is the one that limits the total amount of protein produced.

Different food sources contain different amounts of protein; but also the amino acid composition of their protein is variable. As you might expect, animal protein

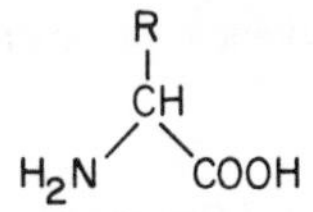

R
|
CH
H₂N   COOH

General formula

Amino Acid*	R (side chain)
1. Glycine	—H
2. Alanine	—CH_3
3. Serine	—CH_2OH
4. Aspartic acid	—CH_2COOH
5. Glutamic acid	—CH_2CH_2COOH
6. Asparagine	—CH_2CONH_2
7. Glutamine	—$CH_2CH_2CONH_2$
8. Arginine	—$CH_2CH_2CH_2NHC(NH)NH_2$
9. Cysteine	—CH_2SH
10. Tyrosine	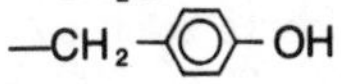 —CH_2—⟨O⟩— OH

11. Proline   (H₂C ⟨CH₂ CH₂⟩ HN—C–H COOH)   { general formula including R group

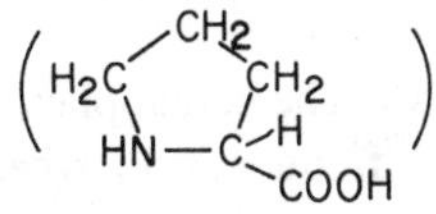

12. Histidine $-CH_2$— (imidazole ring) N N H

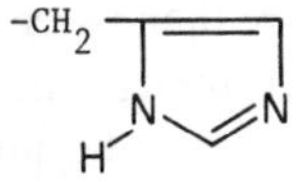

Essential Amino Acids	
13. Valine	—$CH(CH_3)_2$
14. Leucine	—$CH_2CH(CH_3)_2$
15. Isoleucine	—$CH(CH_3)CH_2CH_3$
16. Threonine	—$CH(OH)CH_3$
17. Lysine	—$CH_2CH_2CH_2CH_2NH_2$
18. Methionine	—CH_2CH_2-S-CH_3
19. Phenylalanine	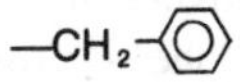 —CH_2—⟨O⟩
20. Tryptophan	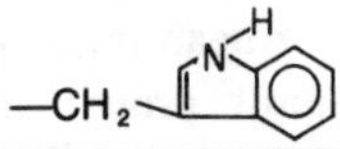 —CH_2—(indole ring)

Figure 4.20 The 20 Common Amino Acids—The Building Blocks of Protein

*1–12 can be synthesized by the human body if sufficient protein nitrogen is present in the diet. 13–20 cannot be synthesized and must be obtained directly from food.

is fairly close to human protein in its amino acid composition. For this reason, milk, eggs, and meat provide us with a rather close approximation to the amino acid balance we need. This is demonstrated in Table 4.3, where we see that the amino acid frequencies for cow's milk and meat are fairly close to the human average. Plant protein, on the other hand, is farther from the human composition,

Table 4.3 Essential Amino Acid Content in Common Foods

Essential Amino Acid	Average Frequency of Occurrence in Human Protein (out of 100 amino acids)	Out of 100 Amino Acids Number Present in:			
		Cow's Milk	Meat	Beans	Wheat
Tryptophan	0.6	0.5	0.5	0.4	0.6
Phenylalanine	3.1	3.8	2.7	2.8	2.8
Lysine	2.6	3.3	3.4	2.8	1.1
Threonine	2.0	2.0	2.0	1.6	1.3
Methionine	3.5	2.8	3.3	2.2	3.2
Leucine	4.0	4.2	3.3	3.1	3.1
Isoleucine	2.5	2.8	2.3	2.2	1.6
Valine	3.2	3.6	2.7	2.5	2.0

Source: Extracted from data in F. E. Deathrage, *Food for Life* (New York: Plenum Press, 1975), pp. 74, 84; and President's Science Advisory Committee, *The World Food Problem*, Report of the Panel on World Food Supply, Vol. II (Washington, D.C.: 1967), p. 315.

as the table also shows. The cereal plants, particularly wheat, are quite deficient in lysine. The lysine frequency in wheat is less than half that of the human average. It would take more than twice as much wheat protein as milk protein to supply human needs. Even though the remaining amino acids are closer to the correct proportions, they cannot be utilized without sufficient lysine. For this reason, wheat protein is often referred to as low-quality protein in comparison with the high-quality protein contained in meat, eggs, and milk.

We can also see from Table 4.3 that different plants show different patterns of deviation from the ideal amino acid balance. Thus, whereas wheat is deficient in lysine, beans have lysine in abundance. However, beans are deficient in methionine, which wheat has in abundance. In this respect, wheat and beans are complementary. As shown in Figure 4.21, if we mix the two together, the amino acid balance is greatly improved. It takes less total vegetable protein for the mixture than for either one alone to provide the human requirements. A diet of half wheat protein and half bean protein provides a protein mixture that is only 10% less efficient than milk protein in providing the right balance. It is no accident that beans and rice or wheat products are traditionally eaten together in many parts of the world. In order to be effective complements, the different proteins must be mixed in the same meal, so that they are digested together. Thus, vegetarians must pay close attention to balancing different protein sources.

Although meat is an important component in the diets of relatively prosperous nations, most people in the world cannot afford to eat meat, and it is possible to do without meat altogether and still remain healthy. While it is a high-quality source of protein, meat represents a considerable waste of biological energy, since animals typically store only 10% of the food they consume in the form of meat. It takes 10 g of plant protein to produce 1 g of meat protein. Most countries

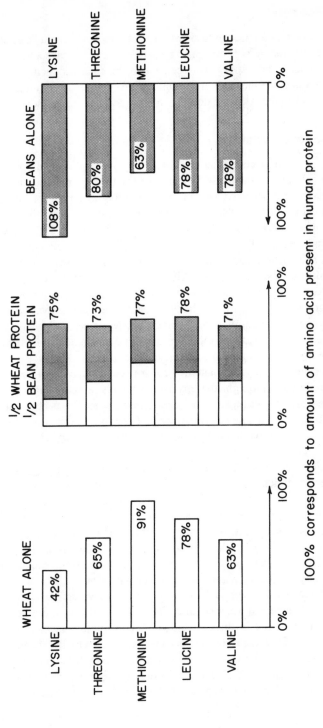

Figure 4.21 Protein Complementarity

100% corresponds to amount of amino acid present in human protein

do not have enough plant protein to spare for meat production on a large scale. If there is sufficient grass to support grazing animals, they can make a net contribution to the human food supply. In recent years in meat producing countries, however, it has become increasingly common to feed animals high-quality plant food, cereals and soybeans, for example, in order to fatten them more quickly.

Diet Components; Vitamins

The human diet must contain an adequate supply of reduced carbon (usually measured in calories) to maintain ATP production through respiration. In addition it must contain a balanced assortment of building materials for maintaining the biochemical machinery. The needed elements must be present in the correct proportions. They are H, C, N, O, P, S, Na, K, Mg, Ca, Fe, Zn, Cu, Co, Cr, Mo, Se, I, and perhaps other elements in exceedingly small amounts. Moreover the elements must be in assimilable chemical forms. We are unable to use carbon as CO_2 or nitrogen as NO_3^-, although plants do so. Also, ferric hydroxide is useless as a dietary source of iron because of its insolubility, and many soluble ferric salts are also ineffective, probably because they are converted to ferric hydroxide in the alkaline milieu of the intestine. Microbes and plants produce chelating agents, which extract iron from the ferric hydroxide in their vicinity, but these are not present in animal biochemistry.

Once the elements are assimilated, they are incorporated into the required biological molecules through the myriad biosynthetic pathways that have evolved. There are, however, some molecules that are needed as building blocks and that the body is incapable of synthesizing. These include the essential amino acids, which must be provided in the proper portions by dietary protein, and the vitamins.

The vitamins have been discovered through the disease states induced when they have been deficient in the diet. In 1747 James Lind discovered that citrus fruit was effective in treating British sailors who suffered from scurvy. In 1932 the active ingredient in citrus fruit was found by Albert Szent-Györgyi and by Charles King to be ascorbic acid, vitamin C. Thirteen vitamins are known today. The last one (vitamin B_{12}) was discovered 30 years ago, and it is unlikely that any more will be found. Many people have lived for years on intravenous solutions that contain only the known vitamins and other nutrients.

Figure 4.22 shows the chemical structures of the 13 vitamins. They fall into two classes: fat soluble and water soluble. The water-soluble vitamins are enzyme cofactors or are required in their synthesis. For example, niacin provides the pyridine end of NAD, while riboflavin is incorporated into FAD. The roles of the fat-soluble vitamins are more complex. Vitamin A, retinol, is incorporated into the visual pigment, rhodopsin. Vitamin D is required for the proper deposition of calcium in bones. Vitamin E appears to be a natural antioxidant, protecting

Figure 4.22 Vitamins: Structures, Dietary Sources, and Deficiency Symptoms

Vitamin	Structural Formula	Dietary Sources	Deficiency Symptoms

Fat-soluble vitamins

Vitamin	Structural Formula	Dietary Sources	Deficiency Symptoms
Vitamin A	Retinol	Fish liver oils, livr, eggs, fish, butter, cheese, milk. A precursor, β-carotene, is present in green vegetables, carrots, tomatoes, squash	Night blindness, eye inflammation
Vitamin D	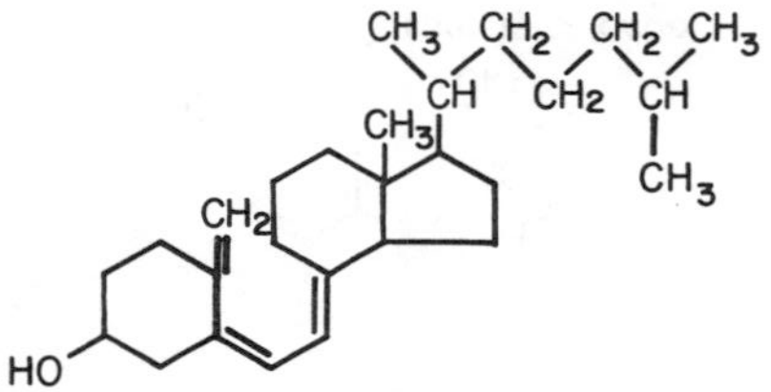 Vitamin D$_3$	Fish liver oils, butter, vitamin-fortified milk, sardines, salmon. Body also obtains this compound when ultraviolet light converts 7-dehydrocholesterol in the skin to vitamin D	Rickets, osteomalacia, hypoparathyroidism
Vitamin E	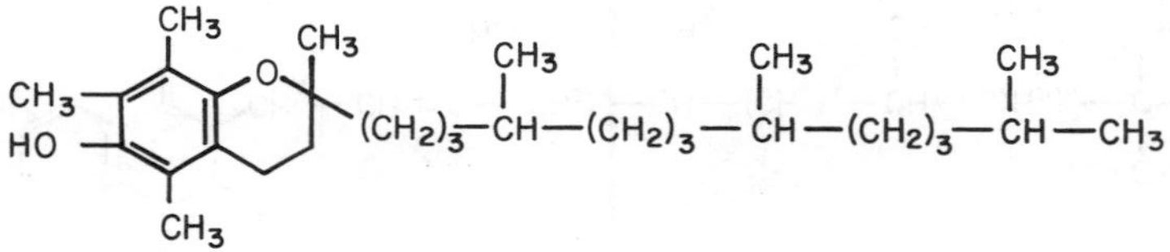 α-Tocopherol	Vegetable oils, margarine, green leafy vegetables, grains, fish, meat, eggs, milk	Anemia in premature babies fed inadequate infant formulas

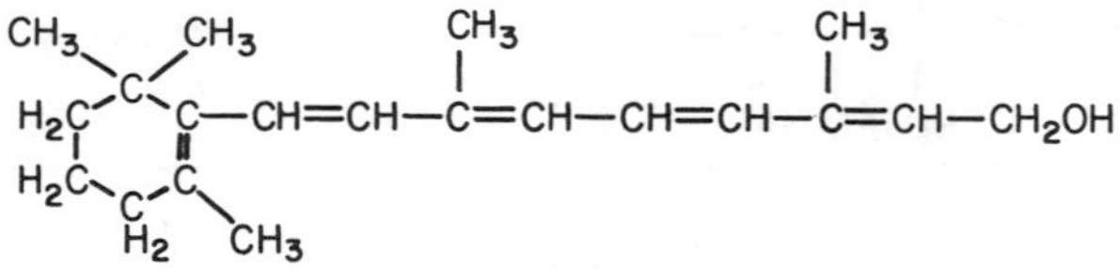

(continued)

Figure 4.22 *(continued)*

Vitamin	Structural Formula	Dietary Sources	Deficiency Symptoms
Vitamin K	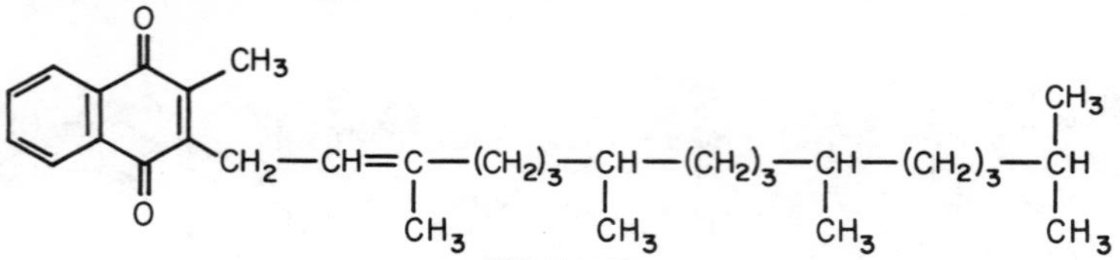 Vitamin K₁	Spinach and other green leafy vegetables, tomatoes, vegetable oils	Increased clotting time of blood, bleeding under skin and in muscles

Water-soluble vitamins

Vitamin	Structural Formula	Dietary Sources	Deficiency Symptoms
Thiamine (vitamin B₁)	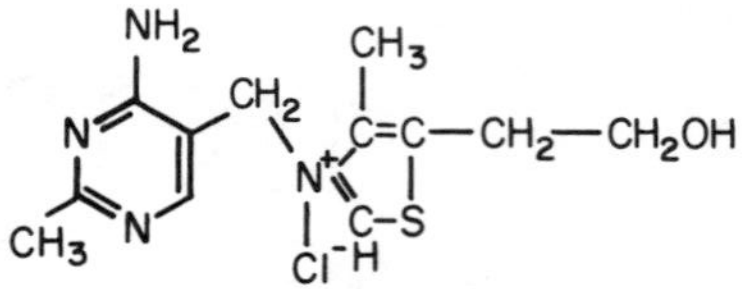 Thiamine chloride	Cereal grains, legumes, nuts, milk, beef, pork	Beriberi
Niacin (nicotinic acid)	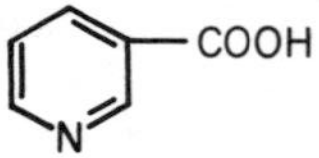	Red meat, liver, turnip greens, fish, eggs, peanuts	Pellagra
Riboflavin (vitamin B₂)	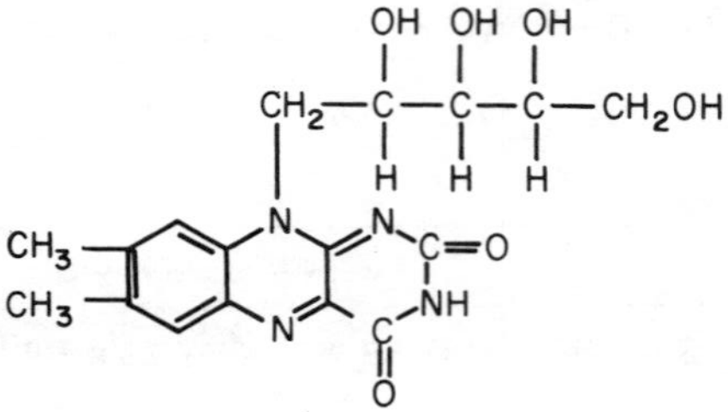	Milk, red meat, liver, green vegetables, whole wheat flour, fish, eggs	Dermatitis, glossitis (tongue inflammation), anemia

Vitamin	Structure	Sources	Deficiency symptoms
Pyridoxine (vitamin B_6)	CH_2OH ... CH_2OH, HO, CH_3, N, CH_3 — Pyridoxol	Eggs, meat, liver, peas, beans, milk	Dermatitis, glossitis, increased susceptibility to infections, irritability, convulsions in infants
Pantothenic acid	$H-C-C-N-C-C-COOH$ with OH, CH_3, OH, O, H, H, H, H and CH_3, H, CH_3, H, H	Liver, beef, milk, eggs, molasses, peas, cabbage	Gastrointestinal disturbances, depression, mental confusion
Folic acid (pteroylglutamic acid)	NH_2-C ... N, CH, C, N, C, C, N, OH, CH_2-NH ... $C-NH-CH-COOH$ with O, $COOH$, CH_2, CH_2	Liver, mushrooms, green leafy vegetables, wheat bran	Anemias, gastrointestinal disturbances
Biotin	H H $(CH_2)_4COOH$, $C-C$, S, $C-C$, H H, N, N, H H, C, O	Beef liver, kidney, peanuts, eggs, milk, molasses	Dermatitis

(continued)

Figure 4.22 (continued)

Vitamin	Structural Formula	Dietary Sources	Deficiency Symptoms
Vitamin B$_{12}$ (cyanocobalamine)	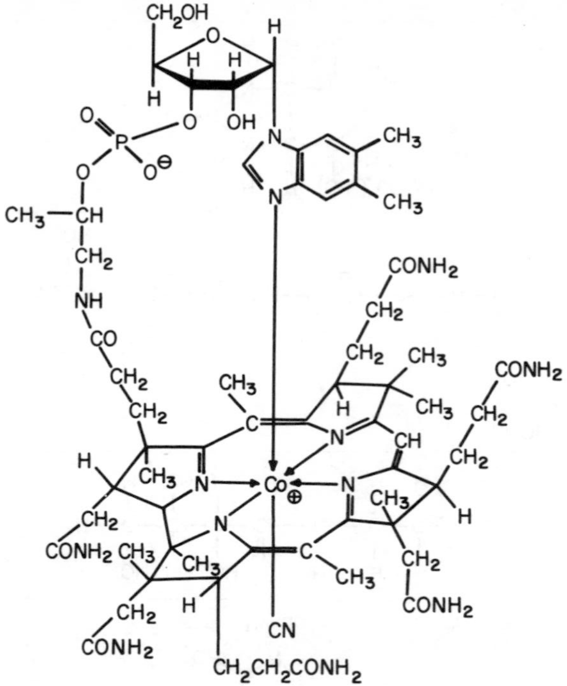	Liver, meat, fish, eggs, milk, oysters, clams	Pernicious anemia, retarded growth, glossitis spinal cord degeneration
Ascorbic acid (vitamin C)	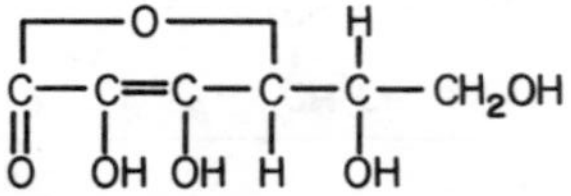	Citrus fruit, tomatoes, green peppers, straw-berries, potatoes	Scurvy

Source: H. J. Sanders, *Chem. Eng. News*, March 26, 1979, p. 30.

membranes from damage by molecular oxygen. And vitamin K is involved in the blood clotting mechanism. The vitamins may well have additional biochemical roles that have yet to be defined.

Minimum required doses of the vitamins have been set by examing the levels below which deficiency diseases set in. There is no agreement, however, on the optimum levels of dietary vitamins. There have been numerous claims of the beneficial health effects of vitamin supplements. The most illustrious proponent of vitamin therapy is Linus Pauling, who has argued forcefully that the optimum level of vitamin C is much higher than the minimum level, and that large doses can prevent colds and even cancer.[5] Well-controlled clinical studies have so far failed to support these claims. Although there may be beneficial effects of large doses of various vitamins, they are extremely difficult to demonstrate. Most of the available evidence is anecdotal or based on poorly controlled chemical trials. On the other hand, large doses may have deleterious effects. Vitamin A is quite toxic in excessive amounts, and less obvious harmful effects might result from a high intake of other vitamins over an extended period.

3 | Insecticides

Another limitation on the human food supply is that we must share plant foods with insects. It has been estimated that the weight of the world's insect population exceeds that of its human inhabitants by a factor of 12. Only a small fraction of the insect species, about 500 species out of the world total of 5 million, actually feed on human crops, but these have the potential of doing enormous damage. Moreover, there are other insect species, such as the mosquito, flea, and tsetse fly, that are carriers of devastating human diseases. Insect invasions, sometimes on a massive scale, have been a recurrent part of human history.

Attempts to combat insect pests were relatively ineffective until the development of modern chemical pesticides. The first of these was DDT, whose chemical structure is shown in Figure 4.23. Introduced as a pesticide for the first time during World War II, DDT saved millions of lives through malaria control programs. It won for its discoverer, the Swiss chemist Paul Müller, the Nobel Peace Prize in 1948. After the war, DDT was the first pesticide to come into widespread agricultural use.

The reason for DDT's effectiveness as a pesticide is still not completely understood. Being oil soluble, it is readily absorbed by the waxy outer coating of insects. Once inside, the chemical quickly paralyzes the insect. Evidently it acts on the nervous system, and it is thought to block specific channels for the flow of the sodium and potassium ions that carry the nerve impulses. The shape of the molecule is quite important. Some chemical changes can be made, as shown for

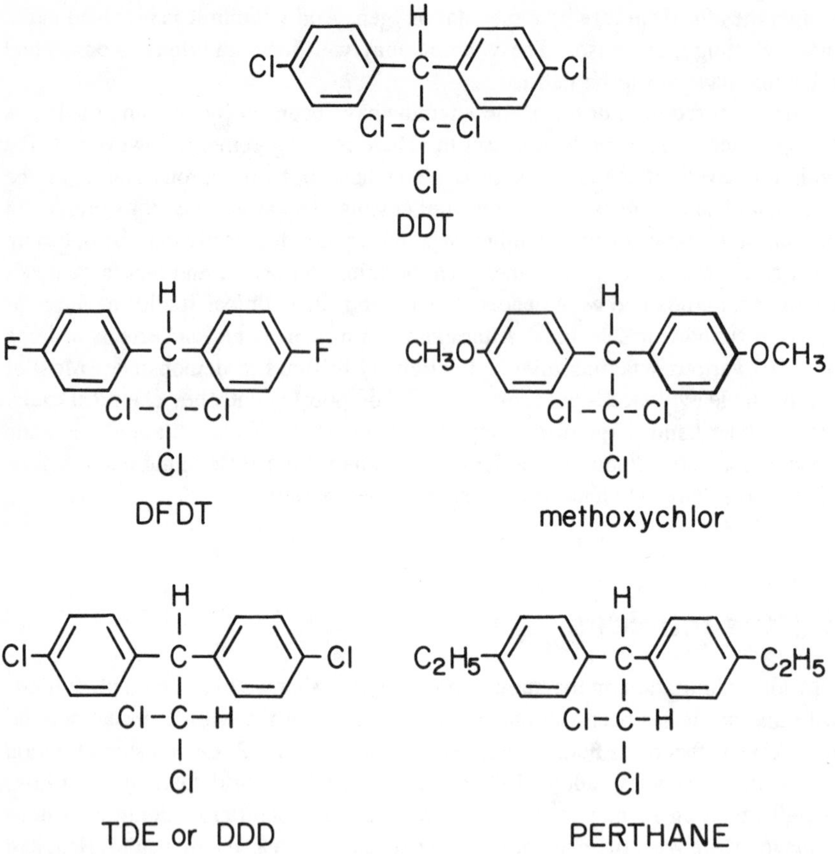

Figure 4.23   DDT and Analogs

the DDT analogs in Figure 4.23, all of which are effective insecticides. But other chemical substitutions, the replacement of the chlorine atoms at the ends of the molecule by hydrogen, for example, greatly decrease the insecticide activity.

Despite its useful service to humanity, DDT was banned for most applications in the United States because of concern about its long-term health effects. It is not that DDT is known to be directly toxic; substantial quantities of DDT have been consumed by individuals accidentally or in voluntary tests without any observable symptoms. Apparently DDT does not act directly on the human nervous system in the way that it does on insects. The concern is about the possibility of long-term effects that are much more difficult to determine. DDT is a persistent chemical; that is, it breaks down very slowly in the environment. Consequently, the DDT already produced and discharged will circulate in the environment for many years.

Because DDT is oil soluble, it accumulates in fat tissues; moreover, DDT builds up in the food chain. As one animal eats another, it stores the accumulated DDT in its own body fats. This is shown for an aquatic food chain in Figure 4.24. The numbers given for the different organisms are the concentrations of DDT in parts per million in the tissues. Plankton contain 0.04 ppm, but the clams that feed on plankton have ten times as much, while the fish that feed on the clams can have up to 2 ppm and the birds that feed on the fish are found to have up to 75 ppm in their muscles. Similar concentrations occur in the terrestrial food chains that provide us with our meats and milk. As a result, all of us have DDT stored in our bodies. The levels vary from country to country depending on the use of DDT. Residents of the United States and most of Western Europe had about 7 ppm stored in their fat tissues in 1975, whereas residents of India, for example, had levels several times higher.

We do not know whether DDT has adverse effects over the long term. There is at least a possibility that DDT might upset hormone balances. This is because DDT, along with other fat-soluble substances, can induce the body to produce enzymes that convert these substances to water-soluble chemical forms so that they are more readily eliminated. These same enzymes are involved in the transformation of hormones from active to inactive forms, and vice versa. It is known that many species of hunting birds are threatened with extinction because the eggs they lay have shells that are too thin and fragile, probably because of interference with the hormones that control calcium deposition. These birds have high levels of DDT, as we saw in Figure 4.24, and there is strong evidence linking DDT with eggshell fragility, although other pollutants may also be involved. The potential long-term effects of a chemical stored in body fat were enough to persuade the U.S. Environmental Protection Agency that most uses of DDT should be banned. The situation is different elsewhere in the world. Particularly where malaria is still endemic, it would be unreasonable to expect DDT to be banned, since no adequate substitute for mosquito control has been developed.

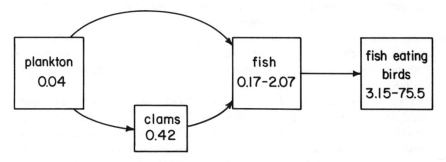

Figure 4.24   Accumulation of DDT in Aquatic Food Chain (ppm)

Source: C. A. Edwards, *Persistent Pesticides in the Environment,* 2nd ed. (Cleveland: CRC Press, 1973), p. 80.

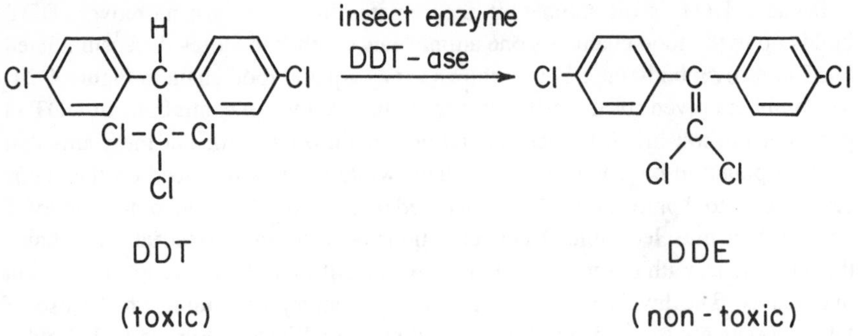

Figure 4.25 Insect Resistance to DDT

Although DDT was banned in the United States in 1973, its use had been declining since 1959. The reason for this has nothing to do with its potential health hazards, but rather with the fact that DDT has become much less effective than it originally was. The chemical itself has remained the same but the insects have changed by evolving a resistance to the insecticide. Because individual insects that are relatively resistant to DDT are more likely to survive than those that are susceptible, the new generations that are born have a steadily higher incidence of resistant characteristics. The resistance factor for DDT is an enzyme called *DDTase,* which carries out the chemical transformation shown in Figure 4.25. The product, DDE, has lost a hydrogen atom and a chlorine atom and has a new double bond in the middle. This molecule is no longer toxic to the insect. It is, however, as persistent as DDT in the environment and also builds up in fat tissue. The levels of DDT recorded usually include the contribution of DDE.

Although the level of DDT used has been declining since 1959, the total amount of chemical insecticides in use has been increasing. The DDT has been replaced by other chemicals that have been developed. Figure 4.26 shows some other organochlorine chemicals that are effective pesticides. These share with DDT the characteristic of environmental persistence and they also build up in fat tissues. Moreover, some of them are distinctly more toxic than DDT and cause at least as much concern about health effects. In 1974, the U.S. Environmental Protection Agency stringently regulated the application of aldrin and dieldrin, which had come into widespread use.

Meanwhile, some nonpersistent classes of insecticides have been developed; they degrade quite rapidly in the environment. Figure 4.27 shows representatives of the two major classes, organophosphates and carbamates. The organophosphates all have a phosphorus atom, connected by a double bond to either sulfur or oxygen, and by single bonds to oxygen or sulfur atoms with attached organic groups. Carbamates have a chemical structure in which a carbon atom is connected by a double bond to an oxygen atom and by single bonds to oxygen on one

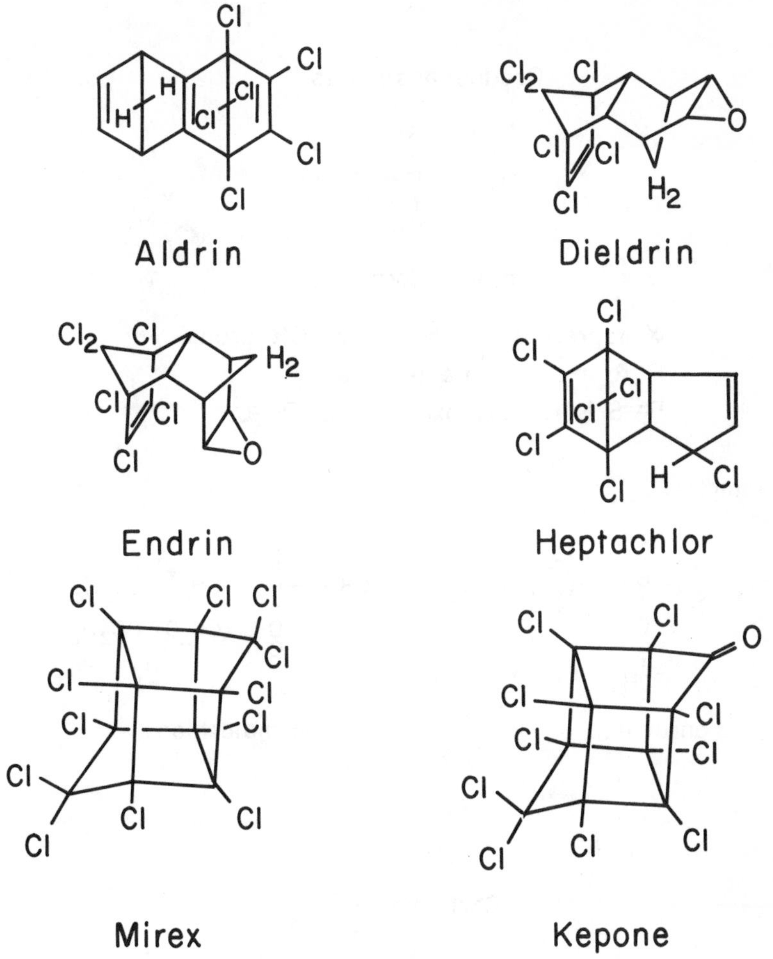

Aldrin

Dieldrin

Endrin

Heptachlor

Mirex

Kepone

Figure 4.26   Other Effective Organochlorine Pesticides

side and nitrogen on the other, each with attached organic groups. As shown in Figure 4.28, both organophosphates and carbamates react with oxygen and water to decompose within a few days in the environment. The products are not toxic; they are phosphates and alcohols in the case of the organophosphates, and carbon dioxide, alcohols, and amines in the case of the carbamates. The mechanism of action of these insecticides is that they inhibit a vital enzyme, acetylcholinesterase, as shown in Figure 4.29. Acetylcholine is a neurotransmitter; it serves as the signal for a nerve cell to fire. The space between nerve cells, called a *synapse,* contains both acetylcholine and the enzyme, acetylcholinesterase, which breaks acetylcholine down and stops the nerve cell from firing. As shown

(i)

Organophosphates

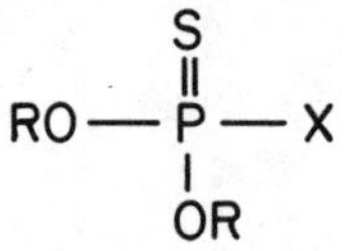

general formula

X represents an SR′ or an OR′ group
R, R′ are organic groups
P=S is rapidly oxidized to P=O

examples:

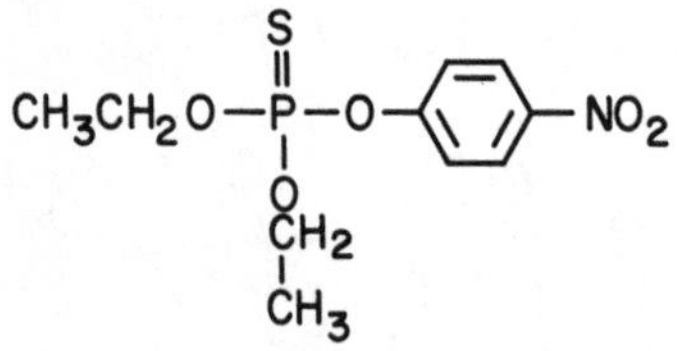

parathion 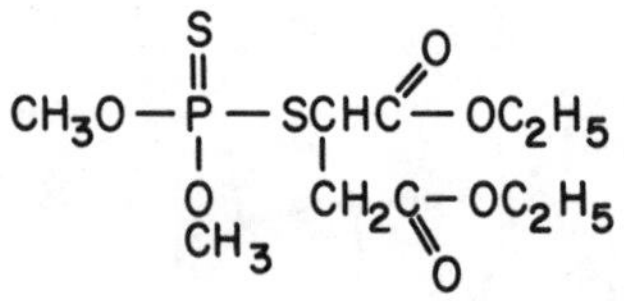   malathion

(ii)

Carbamates

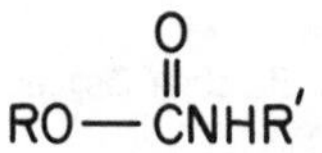

general formula

example:

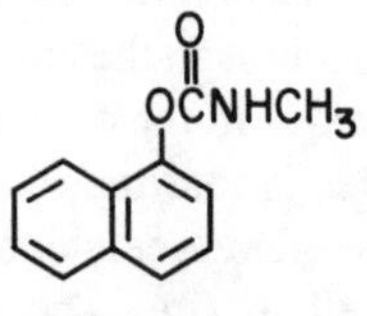

carbaryl

Figure 4.27 Insecticides That Do Not Persist in the Environment

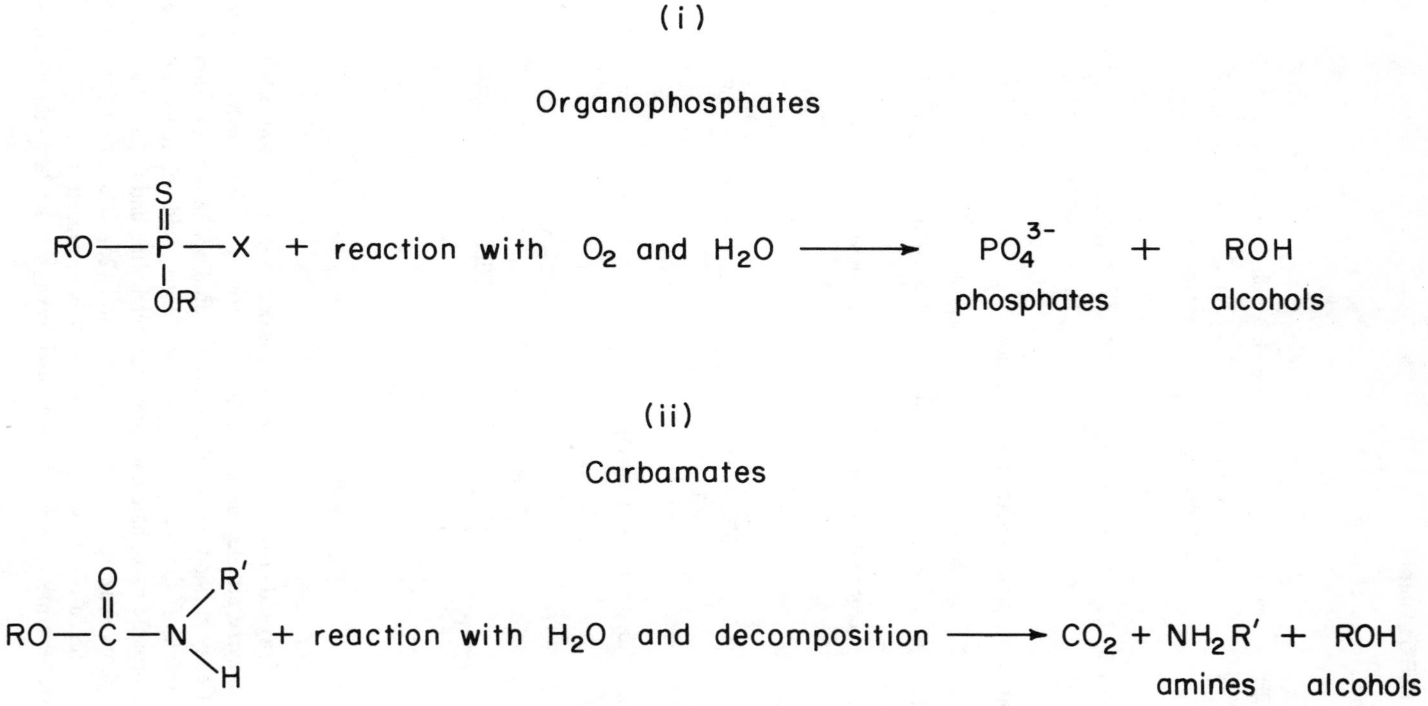

(i)

Organophosphates

$$RO-\underset{\underset{OR}{|}}{\overset{\overset{S}{\|}}{P}}-X \; + \; \text{reaction with } O_2 \text{ and } H_2O \longrightarrow \underset{\text{phosphates}}{PO_4^{3-}} \; + \; \underset{\text{alcohols}}{ROH}$$

(ii)

Carbamates

$$RO-\underset{}{\overset{\overset{O}{\|}}{C}}-\underset{\underset{H}{\diagdown}}{\overset{\overset{R'}{\diagup}}{N}} \; + \; \text{reaction with } H_2O \text{ and decomposition} \longrightarrow CO_2 + \underset{\text{amines}}{NH_2R'} + \underset{\text{alcohols}}{ROH}$$

Figure 4.28 Decomposition of Nonpersistent Insecticides in the Environment

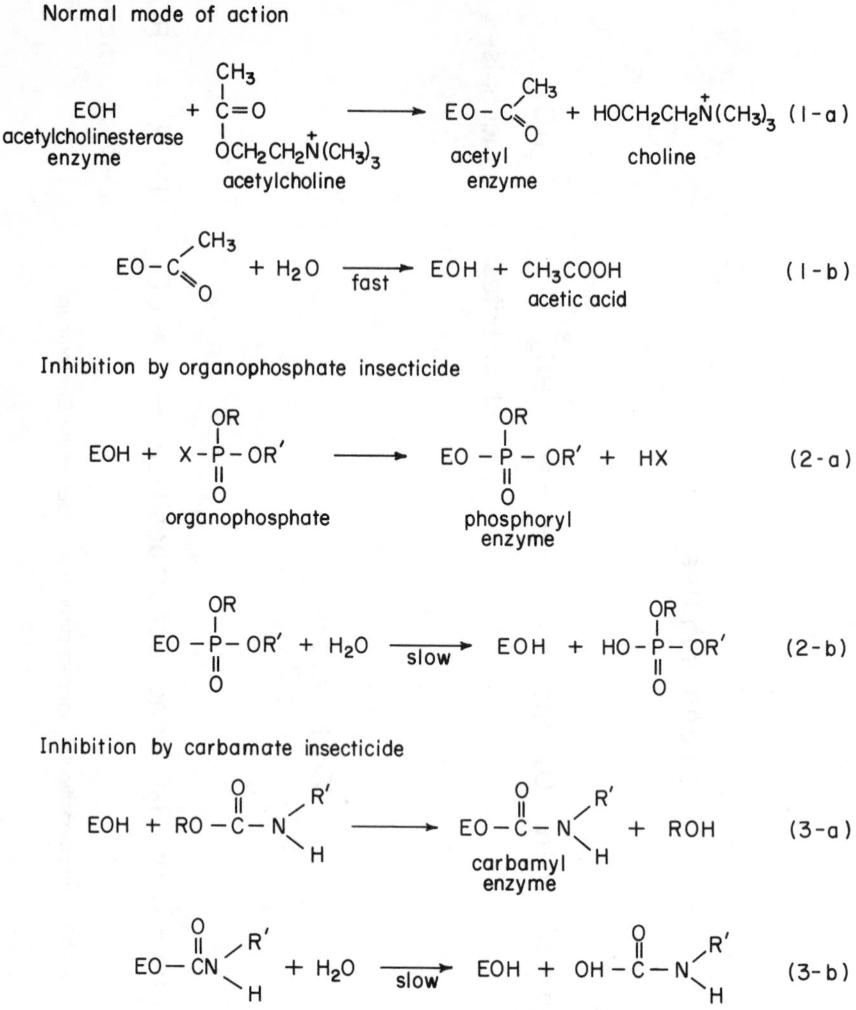

Normal mode of action

$$EOH + \underset{\substack{\text{acetylcholine}}}{\underset{\substack{OCH_2CH_2\overset{+}{N}(CH_3)_3}}{\overset{\substack{CH_3 \\ | \\ C=O \\ |}}{}}} \longrightarrow \underset{\substack{\text{acetyl} \\ \text{enzyme}}}{EO-C\overset{CH_3}{\underset{O}{}}} + HOCH_2CH_2\overset{+}{N}(CH_3)_3 \quad (1\text{-}a)$$

acetylcholinesterase enzyme

$$EO-C\overset{CH_3}{\underset{O}{}} + H_2O \xrightarrow{\text{fast}} EOH + \underset{\substack{\text{acetic acid}}}{CH_3COOH} \quad (1\text{-}b)$$

Inhibition by organophosphate insecticide

$$EOH + \underset{\substack{\text{organophosphate}}}{X-\overset{\overset{\displaystyle OR}{|}}{\underset{\underset{\displaystyle O}{\|}}{P}}-OR'} \longrightarrow \underset{\substack{\text{phosphoryl} \\ \text{enzyme}}}{EO-\overset{\overset{\displaystyle OR}{|}}{\underset{\underset{\displaystyle O}{\|}}{P}}-OR'} + HX \quad (2\text{-}a)$$

$$EO-\overset{\overset{\displaystyle OR}{|}}{\underset{\underset{\displaystyle O}{\|}}{P}}-OR' + H_2O \xrightarrow{\text{slow}} EOH + HO-\overset{\overset{\displaystyle OR}{|}}{\underset{\underset{\displaystyle O}{\|}}{P}}-OR' \quad (2\text{-}b)$$

Inhibition by carbamate insecticide

$$EOH + RO-\overset{\overset{\displaystyle O}{\|}}{C}-N\overset{R'}{\underset{H}{}} \longrightarrow \underset{\substack{\text{carbamyl} \\ \text{enzyme}}}{EO-\overset{\overset{\displaystyle O}{\|}}{C}-N\overset{R'}{\underset{H}{}}} + ROH \quad (3\text{-}a)$$

$$EO-\overset{\overset{\displaystyle O}{\|}}{C}N\overset{R'}{\underset{H}{}} + H_2O \xrightarrow{\text{slow}} EOH + OH-\overset{\overset{\displaystyle O}{\|}}{C}-N\overset{R'}{\underset{H}{}} \quad (3\text{-}b)$$

Figure 4.29 Acetylcholinesterase Inhibition

in reactions (1a) and (1b) of Figure 4.29, this occurs in two chemical steps. In the first, the enzyme attacks the acetylcholine, forming an intermediate molecule, the acetyl enzyme, and one of the products, choline. In the next step, a water molecule splits off the acetyl group to form acetic acid and regenerate the enzyme. An organic phosphate can mimic acetylcholine and induce the formation of a phosphoryl enzyme, as shown in reaction (2a). The rate of the reaction depends on the ease with which the group X is displaced from the phosphorus atom by the enzyme. The subsequent breakdown of this intermediate, shown in reaction (2b), is much slower than that of the acetyl enzyme shown in reaction (1b). Consequently, the amount of phosphoryl enzyme builds up and the level of active enzyme drops. The acetylcholine is no longer broken down rapidly enough, and the nerve continues to fire uncontrollably. This leads to the rapid death of the organism. Reactions (3a) and (3b) show that the carbamates act in a very similar fashion.

The potency of the organophosphates or carbamates in inhibiting acetyl-cholinesterase depends on the nature of the chemical substituents in the phosphate or carbamate group. Toxicity can be varied over wide limits by chemical substitutions. At one extreme are the deadly nerve gases, developed during World War II, which are organophosphates with fluorine attached to phosphorus. Fluorine is an easily displaceable leaving group X in reaction (2a). At the other extreme is malathion shown, in Figure 4.27, a relatively mild insecticide that is safe for home use. The more powerful organophosphates and carbamates are quite toxic, and there have been many fatalities as well as less severe episodes of poisoning since their introduction into agricultural use. The organophosphate and carbamate insecticides, therefore, alleviate one problem, namely, the buildup associated with the organochlorine chemicals, but at the expense of accidental deaths associated with acute poisoning.

Increasingly, the main problem associated with all the general classes of chemical insecticides is that they become decreasingly effective as insect resistance builds up. Not only DDT but any chemical insecticide provides pressure for the selection of insects that have natural defenses, usually enzymes that quickly detoxify the chemicals. Not only do the chemicals become progressively less effective, but they also sometimes remain more effective against the natural enemies of the target pest, thereby actually making the problem worse than it was at the beginning. This is because the predator species are usually slower to reproduce than the prey, and so it takes longer for resistance to develop among them. A fairly common pattern is that the introduction of a new pesticide causes an immediate decline in the population of the pest to be controlled, followed a few years later, however, by a population explosion of a strain of the same pest against which the insecticide is no longer effective.

For this reason, increasing attention has been given to the development of pest control methods that operate more selectively. Research on the biochemistry of insects has led to the discovery of hormones that control their growth and sexual behavior. If applied at the right time, these chemicals can disrupt the insect's life cycle. The upper part of Figure 4.30 shows the chemical structures of some juvenile hormones that regulate growth. If these are applied externally, the synchronization of metamorphosis is disrupted and the insects cannot develop.

Shown in the lower part is the set of chemicals that make up the sex attractant of the boll weevil. Sex attractants come under the general heading of *pheromones*—molecules that act as messengers between insects, guiding them to

(i)

Juvenile hormones: natural insect growth regulators
Ex.

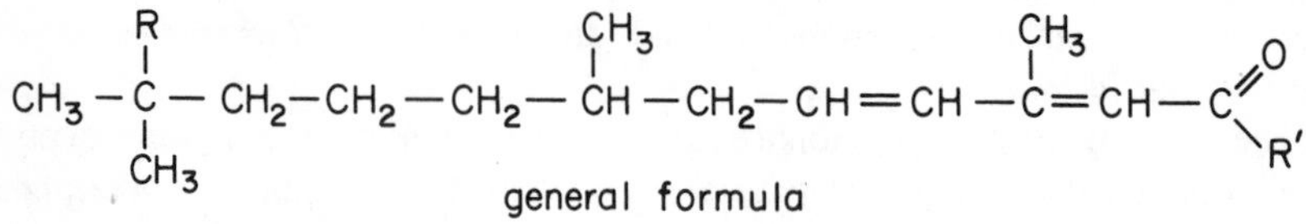

$$CH_3 - \underset{\underset{CH_3}{|}}{\overset{\overset{R}{|}}{C}} - CH_2 - CH_2 - CH_2 - \underset{\overset{CH_3}{|}}{CH} - CH_2 - CH = CH - \underset{\overset{CH_3}{|}}{C} = CH - C \overset{O}{\underset{R'}{\diagdown}}$$

general formula

specific formula	controls stages of growth in:
$R = H$, $R' = OCH_2 CH_3$	potato aphid, cockroach, grain-eating beetles
$R = H$, $R' = OCH_2C \equiv CH$	green peach aphid, pea aphid, citrus mealybug
$R = OCH_3$, $R' = OCH(CH_3)_2$	mosquito, apple maggot, mediterranean fruit fly

(ii)

Pheromones: natural insect sex attractants
Ex.

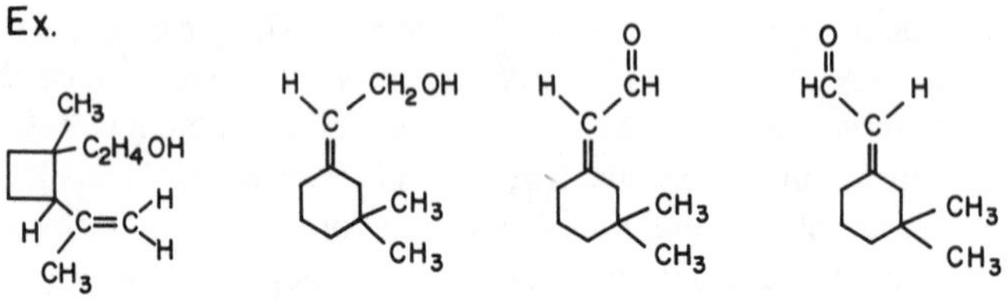

I   II   III   IV

mixture of molecules emitted by male
boll weevil as sex attractant

Figure 4.30 Use of Juvenile Hormones and Pheromones in Insect Control

Source: Upper part: C. A. Henrick, W. E. Willy, and G. B. Staal, J. Agric. Food Chem. 24 (1976):207.
Lower part: R. D. Henson, D. L. Bull, R. I. Ridgway, and G. W. Ivie, J. Agric. Food Chem. 24 (1976):228.

each other or to their food supply. Application of sex attractants can confuse the insects and prevent them from finding mates. It is also feasible to use pheromones to bait insect traps that contain high concentrations of toxic chemicals and are much more effective in killing the insects than is broad-scale spraying.

Another technique of insect control is to sterilize large numbers of male insects, which are bred for the purpose, using chemicals or radiation. When these sterile insects are released, they mate with the native population but no offspring are produced. The result is a substantial reduction in the total insect population. The Mediterranean fruit fly, for example, has been controlled in this fashion in California. It is also possible to artificially introduce predators to control the population of pests and insects. This solution is dangerous, however, since the predator can become so well adapted that it becomes a bigger pest than the target insect.

These new methods of controlling specific insect species are still under development. They require careful planning and timing and are much more sophisticated than simply spraying a field with chemical insecticide. Because they are effective against only one species at a time, however, they are costlier than applying the broad-spectrum insecticides. Nevertheless, with the increasing environmental costs and decreasing effectiveness of the traditional insecticides, pressure is mounting for their development and use.

Membranes and Receptors

Transport

Membrane function   The basic, self-replicating unit of biology is the cell. A diagram of an animal cell is shown in Figure 4.31. At its center is the *nucleus,*

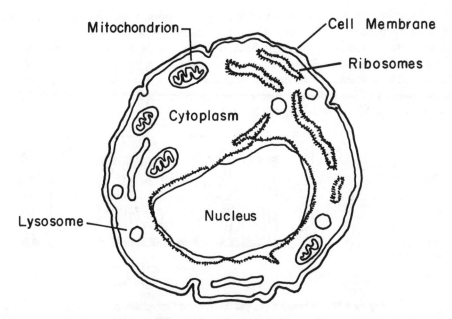

Figure 4.31   The Animal Cell

which contains the genetic material, DNA, and its associated proteins. The fluid medium surrounding the nucleus is called the *cytoplasm.* It contains dissolved proteins and smaller molecules and ions and also a number of subcellular particles, or organelles. These include the *mitochondria,* where ATP is manufactured via respiration; the *ribsomes,* where proteins are synthesized; and the *lysosomes,* which play a role in the breakdown of cellular products and foreign substances.

The integrity of a cell is maintained by the membrane in which it is enveloped. The structural elements of biological membranes are lipid molecules, which were illustrated in Figure 3.16. Like soaps, lipids are surfactant molecules with hydrophilic and hydrophobic ends. While soaps have a single hydrocarbon tail, however, lipids have two. Because of this, lipids spontaneously form bilayers between two aqueous phases, rather than forming the micelles characteristic of soaps. As shown in Figures 3.16 and 4.32, the lipid molecules line up perpendicular to the plane of the bilayer, with the hydrocarbon chains pointing in and the phosphate head groups pointing out. The hydrocarbon interior of the membrane is fairly fluid; it can readily take up fat-soluble molecules such as cholesterol. It forms an impermeable barrier to water and water-soluble substances, however, thereby sealing the aqueous contents of the cytoplasm inside the cell. Nevertheless the cell must maintain a constant but controlled exchange of solutes with its external surroundings in order to remain alive. This is accomplished by transport proteins that are embedded in the lipid bilayer, as diagrammed in Figure 4.32.

These proteins bind the solutes selectively and transport them across the membrane by mechanisms that are not yet fully understood. In some cases the solute flows down a concentration gradient, and the protein simply facilitates the diffusion—a process called *passive transport.* However, the cell must also pump some solutes against the concentration gradients in order to maintain its internal environment. This process, called *active transport,* requires the expenditure of energy, which is provided by the hydrolysis of ATP.

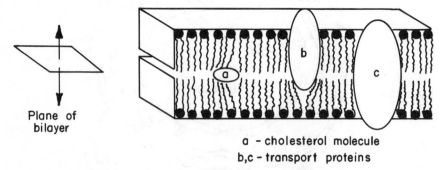

Plane of
bilayer

a – cholesterol molecule
b,c – transport proteins

Figure 4.32 Schematic of Lipid Bilayer and Embedded Molecules

Na$^+$ $-$K$^+$ pump   Most animal cells have a high concentration of K$^+$ ions and a low concentration of Na$^+$ ions compared with the external medium. These ion gradients are maintained by actively transporting K$^+$ into the cell and Na$^+$ out of the cell. The two processes are carried out in concert by a single protein assembly, called the Na$^+$ $-$K$^+$ "pump," which has been studied in considerable detail. It is known that in the presence of Na$^+$ and Mg^{2+} (the cell also maintains a relatively high concentration of Mg^{2+}), ATP reacts with the pump, transferring its phosphate to E, a particular amino acid residue (glutamate):

$$E + ATP \xrightarrow{\text{Na}^+, \text{Mg}^{2+}} E\text{---}P + ADP$$

When K$^+$ is present, the enzyme-bound phosphage is hydrolyzed:

$$E\text{---}P \xrightarrow{\text{K}^+} E + P_i$$

The sum of these two reactions is the hydrolysis of ATP. When the pump is in a cell membrane, it is activated only if Na$^+$, Mg^{2+}, and ATP are present inside the cell and K$^+$ is outside the cell. The hydrolysis of ATP is then coupled to the transport of K$^+$ into and Na$^+$ out of the cell. It is reasonable to suppose that the mechanism is something like the one shown schematically in Figure 4.33: Na$^+$ binds to a protein site in the interior of the membrane, inducing the phosphorylation reaction, which then alters the conformation of the protein in such a way that the Na$^+$ ion and the phosphorylated site are exposed to the exterior of the membrane. K$^+$ replaces Na$^+$ at the site and induces the dephosphorylation reaction, which reverses the conformation change and exposes the unphosphorylated site, now containing K$^+$, to the interior. Na$^+$ then replaces K$^+$, thus starting the cycle again. The mechanism must be more complicated than this, however, since it is known that three Na$^+$ ions and two K$^+$ ions are transported for every molecule of ATP hydrolyzed.

Neurochemistry

Ion conductance   The Na$^+$ and K$^+$ gradients, which are established by all cells, provide the mechanism for electrical conduction along the specialized cells of the nervous system. A diagram of a typical neural cell is given below.

The neural cell

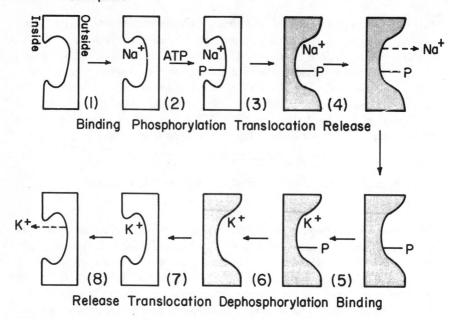

Figure 4.33 Schematic Diagram of a Proposed Mechanism for the Na$^+$–K$^+$ Pump.
The forms are shown here as having very different conformations. The actual conformational change may be quite small.

Electrical impulses flow into the cell body through the dendrites and out along the axon. The impulses consist of traveling waves of Na$^+$ and K$^+$ ion currents moving across the cell membrane (i.e., perpendicular to the direction of travel of the impulse).

In the resting nerve cell, the high K$^+$ and low Na$^+$ concentrations inside as compared with those outside produce an electrical potential difference of about 70 mv. This can be measured with suitably placed microelectrodes. When the cell fires, there is a sudden depolarization of this potential, as Na$^+$ ions move into the cell and K$^+$ ions move out of the cell. This occurs via channels, or pores, that form temporarily in the nerve cell membrane. Depolarization at one location in the membrane apparently activates the channels adjacent to it. This accounts for the traveling wave character of the depolarization (called the *action potential*). Once the wave has passed, the channels are deactivated and the resting potential is restored.

The physical nature of the ion channels is unknown. They are difficult to study because their concentration in nerve membranes is quite low. This is known from studies of the binding of a specific inhibitor, tetrodotoxin, a poison from the puffer fish. Tetrodotoxin binds very tightly to the nerve membrane and blocks the ion movement, thereby inhibiting the action potential. DDT is also thought to act

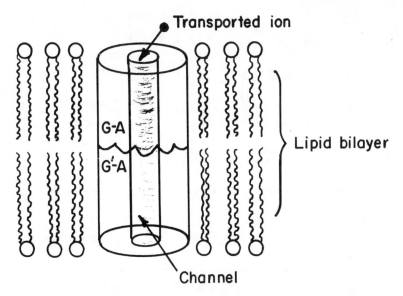

Transported ion

Lipid bilayer

Channel

G-A and G'-A are gramicidin A molecules

Figure 4.34   Schematic Diagram of a Channel-Forming Antibiotic

on insect nerves by blocking the ion channels.[6,7] A possible model for nerve channels is gramicidin A, an antibiotic that forms artificial ion channels in lipid bilayers. It is a polypeptide consisting of 15 amino acid residues, many of them hydrophobic, so that the molecule can insert itself into a lipid bilayer. As illustrated in Figure 4.34, it is believed that channels are formed when two gramicidin A molecules on opposite sides of the bilayer form a complex, which allows ions to pass through a central pore.

Neurotransmitters   The firing of nerve cells is induced by the binding of neurotransmitter molecules to specific receptor proteins embedded in the nerve membrane. For many nerves, including those that control the voluntary muscles, the neurotransmitter is acetylcholine (see Figure 4.29). The end of the axon contains a number of vesicles, each containing about 10,000 acetylcholine (Ach) molecules. As diagrammed in Figure 4.35, when the nerve impulse reaches the end of the axon, these vesicles release their acetylcholine molecules, which then diffuse across the synapse and bind to the acetylcholine receptors in the postsynaptic membrane of the next nerve cell, which then fires. Apparently the binding of acetylcholine induces a change in the conformation of the receptor protein, which results in the opening of adjacent ion channels and initiates depolarization. Repolarization then requires depletion of the acetylcholine. This

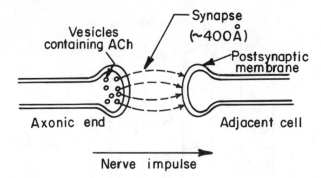

Figure 4.35   Transmission of Nerve Impulses Between Nerve Cells

is accomplished by the enzyme acetylcholinesterase, which is also embedded in the postsynaptic membrane.

Organophosphate and carbamate insecticides block the transmission of nerve impulses by inhibiting acetylcholinesterase (see Figure 4.29). Enough is known about the nature of the covalent intermediate formed by acetylcholinesterase to permit the design of a drug that relieves the inhibition. This is 2-pyridine aldoxime methiodide (PAM), which is used as an antidote to poisoning by acetyl-

Pyridine aldoxime methiodide
(PAM)

cholinesterase inhibitors. The $-$NOH group displaces the phosphoryl or carbamyl group from the covalent intermediate by nucleophilic attack, thereby accelerating the regeneration of the active enzyme. The role of the pyridinium group, analogous to the quaternary ammonium group of acetylcholine, is to bind to the active site of the enzyme and correctly position the $-$NOH group for attack. Consequently, PAM is effective at low concentrations.

Other neurotoxins act by binding directly to the acetylcholine receptor, again blocking the transmission of nerve impulses. An example is d-tubocurarine, the

d- tubocurarine

active ingredient of curare. Although far from evident from the structural formula, this complex molecule must have a three-dimensional structure, a portion of which closely resembles the active conformation of acetylcholine. The theme of receptor or active-site binding by natural or synthetic molecules that mimic the true substrate is important and pervasive in both pharmacology and toxicology. The biochemical mechanisms underlying the effects of many toxic chemicals will probably turn out to involve specific binding to receptor protein and enzymes.

Other neurotransmitters; opiates   There are neurotransmitters other than acetylcholine. The nerves that control involuntary (smooth) muscles, for example, use norepinephrine as their neurotransmitter. The brain is rich in norepinephrine and other neurotransmitters of the catecholamine class: dopamine and epinephrine. These are all derived from the amino acid tyrosine:

Norepinephrine   Dopamine   Epinephrine

The phenol group of tyrosine is also found in the structure of morphine:

CH$_3$

N

HO   O   OH

Morphine

The powerful narcotic effects of morphine and other opiates have long been known, but the recent development of sensitive binding assays has led to the discovery that the brain has specific opiate receptors.[8,9] They are located in the thalamus and in the connected spinal neurons, a part of the nervous system associated with the transmission of low-level pain. Subsequent work led to the discovery of the body's own opiates, the endorphins, which bind to the same receptors.[10-12] These turn out to be short polypeptides. One well-studied example, methionine-enkephalin, has the sequence NH_2-tyrosine-glycine-glycine-phenylalanine-methionine-COOH. It is likely that the orientation of the tyrosine side chain in the active conformation of methionine-enkephalin is similar to that of the phenol ring of morphine, and that this structural feature is important for binding to the receptors.

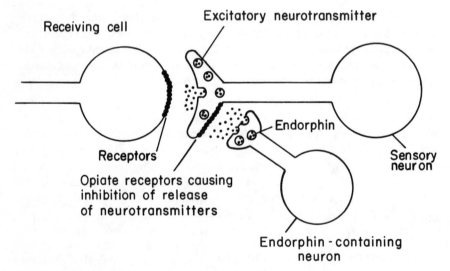

Figure 4.36 Proposed Mechanism of Opiate Activity

Source: S. H. Snyder, *Chem. Eng. News*, November 28, 1977, p. 26.

The mechanism of opiate activity is still under intensive study. One effect of an opiate is to inhibit neurotransmitter release from excited nerve cells. There may be special neurons that release endorphins near the synapse, thereby providing a means of inhibiting nerve impulse transmission, as diagrammed in Figure 4.36.

4 | Inadvertent Contamination by Toxic Organic Chemicals

Although pesticides may be toxic, their danger to human health can be minimized by judicious application. More dangerous is the inadvertent release of toxic chemicals through accident or lack of foresight. Much publicity was generated, for example, by the discovery that the insecticide kepone had been contaminating Chesapeake Bay as a result of unsafe practices in a small manufacturing plant in Virginia. Kepone washings from the plant's wastewater had killed the bacteria in the digesters of the local municipal sewage system, and the contaminated sewage effluent had been discharged into the river that empties into Chesapeake Bay. Fish and shellfish in the river and estuary were discovered to have kepone concentrations of about one part per million, exceeding allowable health limits, and commercial and sport fishing was prohibited in the affected areas. Worse effects were suffered by the workers in the plant, who inhaled exceedingly high levels of kepone, up to 3 g/m^3 in air, and experienced a variety of illnesses. These conditions led to the closing of the plant in July 1975, 16 months after it had begun operations.

Worrisome sources of chemical contamination are the dump sites for industrial wastes, many of them abandoned and buried close to developed communities. A notorious example is Love Canal in Niagara Falls, New York, which had been used to hold chemical and municipal wastes during the period 1930–53. In 1953 the site was covered with earth and sold to the City Board of Education, which built an elementary school there. Houses were constructed on the periphery of the site. Over the years the residents complained of bad odors and a variety of health problems. They were found to be subject to a significantly higher incidence of spontaneous abortions and congenital birth defects than would normally be expected. In 1978, state and federal officials, monitoring air samples in the basements of houses adjacent to the former dump site, identified 26 toxic organic compounds, some of which are listed along with the highest levels found in Table 4.4. The total concentration of organic compounds reached 12.9 mg/m^3 in the dining room of one of the homes. This value approaches the limits set for workers in the chemical industry, which vary from about ten to several hundred milligrams per cubic meter, depending on the compound, for a 40-hour work-

Table 4.4   Concentrations of Some Toxic Organic Chemicals Found
in Houses near Love Canal Dump Site

Chemical	Highest Concentration Observed (μg/m³)*
Chloroform	24
Benzene	270
Trichloroethylene	73
Toluene	570
Perchloroethylene	1,140
Chlorobenzene	240
Chlorotoluene	6,700
Xylene (meta + para)	140
Xylene (ortho)	73
1,3,5-Trichlorobenzene	74
Total organics (one sample, dining room)	12,919 (12.9 mg/m³)

*Except as noted for total organics, concentrations were measured in the basements of homes.
Source: "In the Matter of the Love Canal Chemical Waste Landfill Site," Report of the Commissioner of Health of the State of New York, August, 1978; and *Chem. Eng. News.* August 7, 1978, p. 6.

week. As a result of these findings, the state of New York declared a health emergency in the area and relocated more than 300 families who were potentially affected.

The buildup of the organic chemicals can be traced to the characteristics of the dump site itself, diagrammed in Figure 4.37. The overlying soil is relatively porous, but the stratum under the wastes consists of silt and clay of low permeability, which acts as a barrier to penetration of the waste into deeper ground. When the soil is wet, volatile organics rise to the surface and infiltrate the basements of the surrounding homes.

No one knows how many similar trouble spots exist. The U.S. Environmental Protection Agency has identified 638 chemical dumps that may contain significant quantities of toxic materials, and there are literally thousands of other dump sites in the United States alone that have not yet been examined.

Perhaps the most dramatic recent incident of chemical contamination occurred in the Italian town of Seveso, where a chemical plant accidentally released about 2 kg of the toxic chemical TCDD in a cloud that settled in the surrounding area. Some 250 of the residents were affected by skin disorders of varying severity, and many of the animals in the area died. There was extensive damage to plants, primarily burning and browning of trees. About 1,000 persons were evacuated from two affected areas covering 123 acres.

TCDD stands for 2,3,7,8-tetrachlorodibenzo-*p*-dioxin, and its structure is highlighted in the center of Figure 4.38. As illustrated there, TCDD, a member of the dioxin family of molecules, is produced as a by-product from 2,4,5-

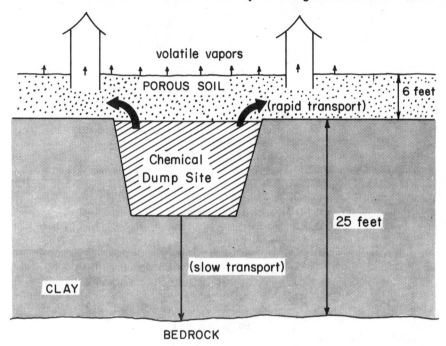

Figure 4.37 Transport of Toxic Organic Chemicals from Love Canal Dump Site into Surrounding Homes

trichlorophenol in the manufacture of the herbicide 2,4,5-trichlorophenoxy-acetate (usually abbreviated 2,4,5-T) or of the germicide hexachlorophene. A similar chlorinated dioxin, which is also highlighted in the figure, is made as a by-product of pentachlorophenol, a widely used wood preservative.

TCDD is a flat molecule, which fits into a rectangle about 10 Å long and 3 Å wide, as illustrated in Figure 4.39. There are chlorine atoms at each of the four corners of the rectangle. These aspects of molecular structure seem to be the important ones associated with the toxicity of TCDD. If two or more of the chlorine atoms are removed or placed in other positions, or if the molecule is changed so that it is no longer flat, its toxicity decreases markedly. Other molecules with similar shape produce the same kind of toxicity. An example is tetrachlorodibenzofuran, which is also shown in Figure 4.39. It differs from dioxin only in having a direct bond between the two benzene rings replacing one of the dioxin oxygen atoms. Chlorinated dibenzofurans are by-products in the formation of polychlorinated biphenyls (PCBs); an example of a PCB is also shown in the figure. Chlorinated dibenzofurans can also be formed from PCBs on exposure to high temperatures, as in an incinerator. PCBs themselves share some of the toxicity of dibenzofurans and dioxins, since they have a similar molecular

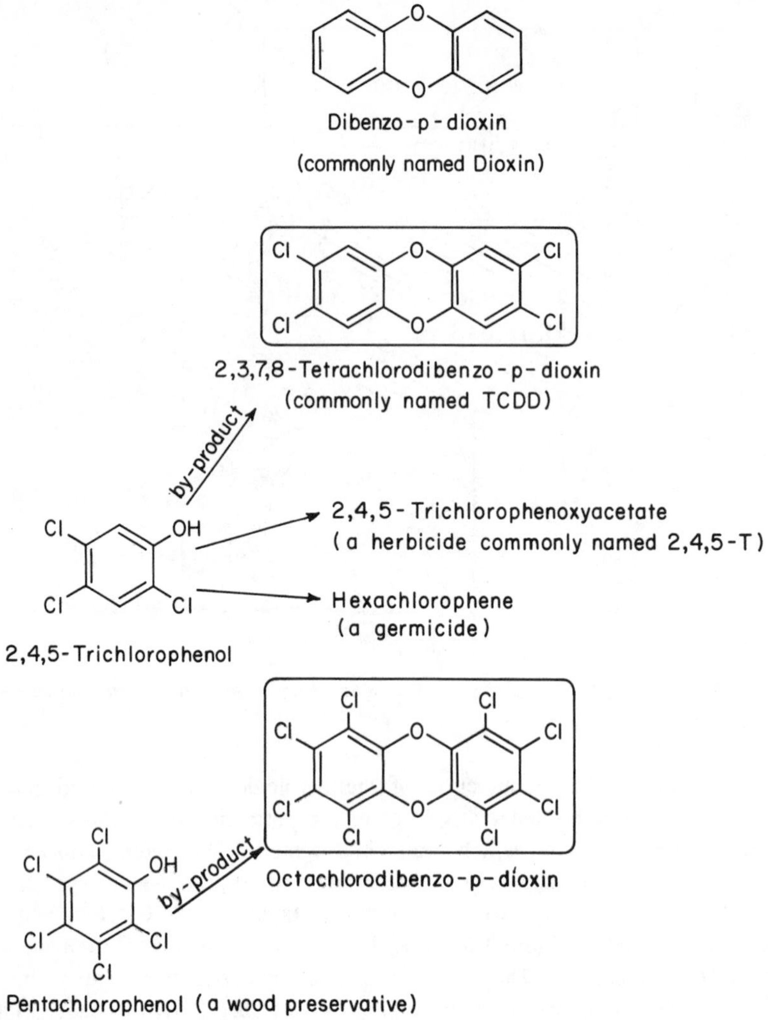
O
O
Dibenzo-p-dioxin
(commonly named Dioxin)
Cl
Cl
Cl
Cl
2,3,7,8-Tetrachlorodibenzo-p-dioxin
(commonly named TCDD)
by-product
Cl
OH
Cl
Cl
2,4,5-Trichlorophenoxyacetate
(a herbicide commonly named 2,4,5-T)
Hexachlorophene
(a germicide)
2,4,5-Trichlorophenol
Octachlorodibenzo-p-dioxin
by-product
Pentachlorophenol (a wood preservative)

Figure 4.38 The Formation of Chlorinated Dioxins As By-products of Manufactured Chemicals

Source: A. Poland and A. Kende, *Fed. Proc.* 35 (1976):2404.

shape, as shown in the figure. PCBs have been used widely in a variety of manufacturing processes. Although their application is now restricted to insulating fluids in high-voltage transformers, large quantities have already been dispersed in the environment.

The biochemistry of these compounds is not fully understood at present and is a subject of active research. In laboratory animals, TCDD produces birth defects,

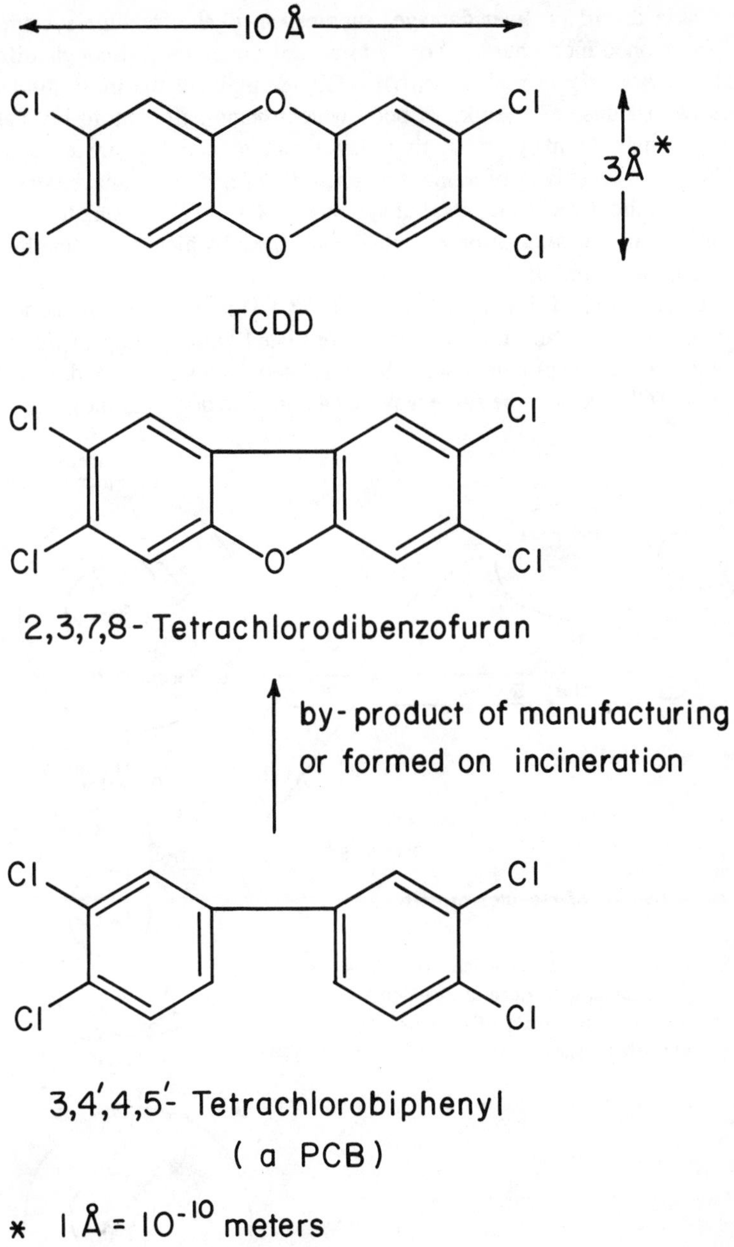

Figure 4.39   Structural Similarity Between TCDD and Other Toxic Chlorinated Organics

Source: A. Poland, Department of Pharmacology, University of Wisconsin, private communication, February 1979.

cancer, skin disorders, liver damage, suppression of the immune system, and death from undefined causes. Toxic doses are quite low, although different animals vary widely in their sensitivity. Guinea pigs are the most susceptible species, with a dose of 1 µg/kg of body weight being sufficient to kill half the affected animals. Monkeys are 70 times less sensitive, and dogs are less sensitive still. The exact sensitivity of humans is not well defined. There have been a few deaths due to industrial accidents, but symptoms of TCDD exposure have mostly been limited to the skin disorder called *chloracne,* which can sometimes be long-lasting and painful.

At the cellular level, it is now known that TCDD induces the production of a number of enzymes, and this activity is correlated with binding of the TCDD molecule to a specific protein that has been isolated from various kinds of cells. It seems that TCDD acts in the same way that a hormone does. As shown in Figure

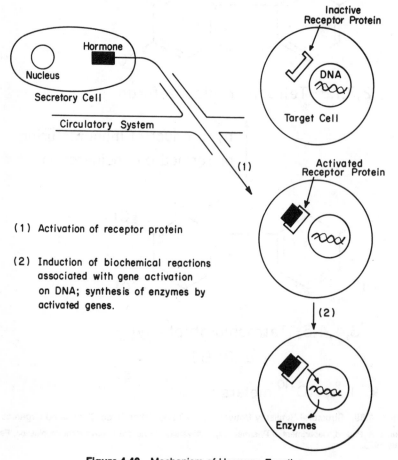

(1) Activation of receptor protein

(2) Induction of biochemical reactions associated with gene activation on DNA; synthesis of enzymes by activated genes.

Figure 4.40 Mechanism of Hormone Function

4.40, many hormones work by binding to a receptor protein in a specific target cell. The receptor becomes activated upon attachment of the hormone and causes genes on the DNA strand to initiate the production of various enzymes. Presumably, the toxic symptoms of TCDD are caused by mimicking hormonal activity that alters the cell's biochemical apparatus for enzyme production. It is likely that the binding site of the receptor protein imposes the structural requirements that are needed for a molecule to possess TCDD-like toxicity.

The concern about TCDD and similar molecules is not limited to dramatic accidents. Because they are present as by-products in a variety of large-volume industrial chemicals, they are widely distributed in the environment. Moreover they can be formed when the chemicals or products that contain them are burned. Recent studies indicate that effluents from incinerators can spread detectable amounts of dioxins around the countryside. No one knows whether low-level environmental contamination causes a significant hazard to human health. Part of the problem is that toxic doses are so low that we do not have methods sensitive enough to monitor the buildup of these chemicals in human beings at subtoxic levels.

Hormonal Function

Hormones are messenger molecules, excited by various glands, that circulate in the bloodstream and powerfully influence the biochemistry of specific tissues. This mechanism for transmitting biochemical instructions is another important strand in the theme of molecular recognition; hormone activity is initiated by binding to receptor proteins in the target cells.

There are basically two kinds of hormones with entirely different mechanisms of actions; they can be classed as water soluble and lipid soluble. The water-soluble hormones include amino acid derivatives, such as epinephrine (see page 305, and large polypeptides, such as insulin. In either case the hormone binds to a receptor protein embedded in the target cell membrane, analogous to the neurotransmitter receptors (see Figure 4.35). This binding induces the activation of an enzyme inside the cell, which catalyzes the synthesis of an interior messenger molecule, called a *second messenger*. The second messenger of many hormones is cyclic AMP, which is derived from ATP by the action of the enzyme adenyl cyclase:

Cyclic AMP has profound effects on the biochemistry of many cells. It acts by binding to and activating a class of enzymes called *protein kinases*. These are control enzymes that turn metabolic enzymes on and off by phosphorylating them at specific sites, using ATP as the source of phosphate.

The lipid-soluble hormones are all steroids, derivatives of cholesterol. Some

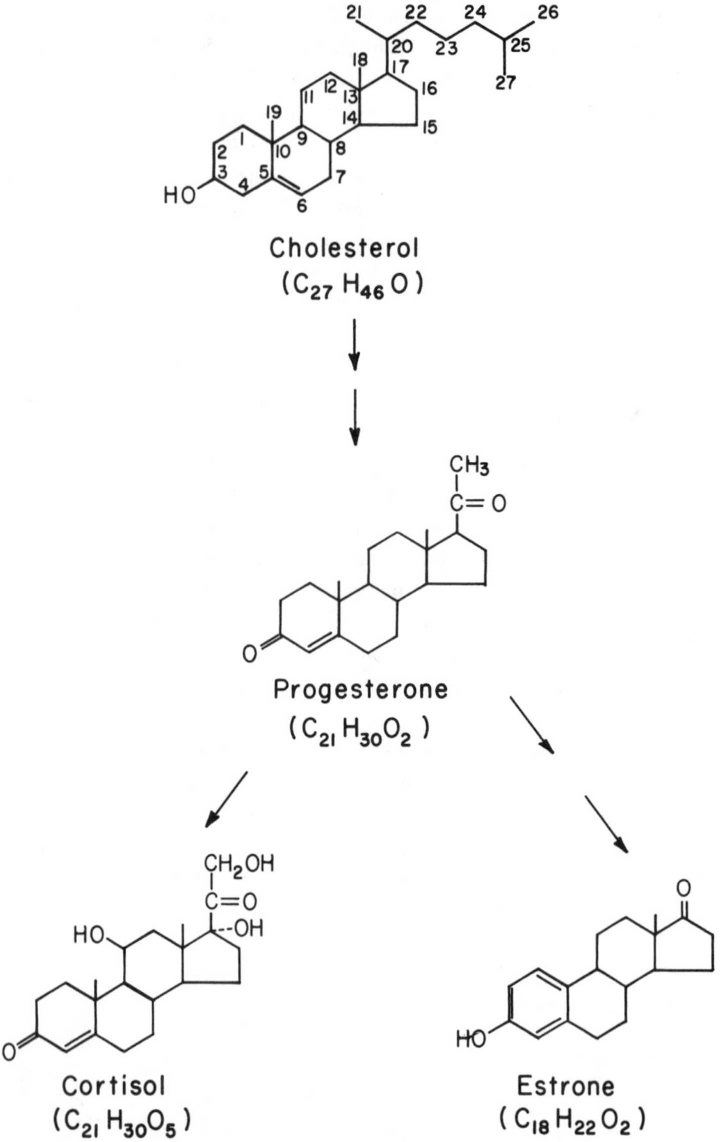

Cholesterol
$(C_{27} H_{46} O)$

Progesterone
$(C_{21} H_{30} O_2)$

Cortisol
$(C_{21} H_{30} O_5)$

Estrone
$(C_{18} H_{22} O_2)$

Figure 4.41   Steroid Derivatives of Cholesterol

examples are given in Figure 4.41. They diffuse through cell membranes and are picked up at the inside surface by specific receptor proteins that are dissolved in the interior fluid (cytosol) of the target cell. Hormone binding changes the shape of the receptor protein and enables it, after diffusion to the nucleus, to turn on specific genes. This is the mechanism illustrated in Figure 4.40. Thus the steroid hormones act by inducing the synthesis of enzymes by controlling the levels present in the cells. It is this activity that the toxicant TCDD appears to mimic. Other lipid-soluble toxic chemicals may behave similarly.

Environmental Decomposition of Toxic Organic Chemicals

In an aerobic world, the stable form of carbon is CO_2. When exposed to air, all organic compounds are unstable with respect to oxidation. As we saw earlier, however, the rate of oxidation is slow because of the special electronic structure of O_2, with its unpaired electrons. The oxidation rate can be greatly accelerated by sunlight if the organic molecule absorbs light in the visible or near-ultraviolet region, since light absorption often leads to the unpairing of electrons. The activated "triplet" molecules (two unpaired electrons) react rapidly with triplet O_2. The overall process is called *photooxidation*. Even if the organic molecule does not absorb sunlight, it can still undergo photooxidation in the presence of a sensitizer. This is a molecule that does absorb the light and reacts with O_2 to form a reactive product that attacks and oxidizes nearby molecules. There are a number of complex biological molecules in the environment that can serve as sensitizers, including chlorophyll, riboflavin, and a variety of quinones.[13] Photooxidation is a major pathway for the eventual decomposition of persistent organic chemicals.

An equally important pathway is biological oxidation. Soil microorganisms have a wide range of mixed-function oxygenase enzymes that catalyze the insertion of one of the oxygen atoms of O_2 into C−H bonds.[14] They also have dioxygenase enzymes, which insert both atoms of O_2 into organic molecules. This is an important mechanism for the cleavage and decomposition of aromatic rings.[15]

Reaction with water, hydrolysis, can break key bonds in toxic molecules and, thus, render them nontoxic. This is the pathway for the degradation of the nonpersistent organophosphate and carbamate insecticides.

When oxygen is not available, as in lake and ocean sediments or in water-laden soils or sewage, organic compounds are more stable. They are subject to the action of anaerobic microorganisms, however, which can metabolize them to CH_4, NH_3, H_2S, and other reduced molecules. These reactions are generally slower than aerobic ones, and many organic molecules are resistant to attack by anaerobes. An important anaerobic reaction is dehalogenation, the replacement of a carbon-bound halogen atom by a hydrogen atom. This appears to be the main mechanism for the degradation of organochlorine molecules, which are generally resistant to microbial oxidation. It has been found that DDT, heptachlor, and methoxychlor persist in well-aerated soil but are readily degraded in flooded soils.[16] Studies of DDT degradation under anaerobic conditions have shown DDD to be the initial product.[17]

$$\left(Cl - \langle\!\!\!\!\bigcirc\!\!\!\!\rangle\right)_2 CH - CCl_3 \longrightarrow \left(Cl - \langle\!\!\!\!\bigcirc\!\!\!\!\rangle\right)_2 CH - CHCl_2$$

DDT   DDD

5 | Contamination by Toxic Metals

Another environmental concern is that metallic elements that are toxic to human beings are being spread around increasingly as a result of industrial production and use. We have all read news stories about the problem of lead poisoning, particularly among city children, contamination of fish by mercury, and the possibility that cadmium may be harmful to our health. These elements occur naturally in the earth's crust and humans have been living with them throughout evolutionary history. However, the amounts of them that are being stirred up and spread around have been increasing greatly with the advance of industrialization.

Many metallic elements are essential to life. The amounts of them that we need, however, are highly variable, and in some cases are extremely small. For these trace elements, it has been difficult to establish that they are indeed essential. Moreover, even the essential elements are toxic if the amount is too high. This is indicated in Figure 4.42, which shows a schematic dose-response curve for an essential element. At zero concentration, the organism for which the curve is plotted cannot grow at all. As the concentration increases, growth increases rapidly but then levels off and starts to decline at concentrations where the organism can no longer handle the amounts of the element to which it is exposed. The peak of the curve represents the optimum concentration of that element for that particular organism. The dashed curve represents the response of the organism to a nonessential element. Growth declines continuously as the concentration increases from zero. At first the response curve may be fairly flat since the organism may be equipped with mechanisms for eliminating the element in question. But as the machinery for elimination gets overloaded, the toxicity rises and growth diminishes rapidly.

The optimum concentration of the essential elements is highly variable. In the case of iron, for example, the optimum concentration is relatively large. We all carry about 5 g of iron in our body, and it is difficult, although by no means

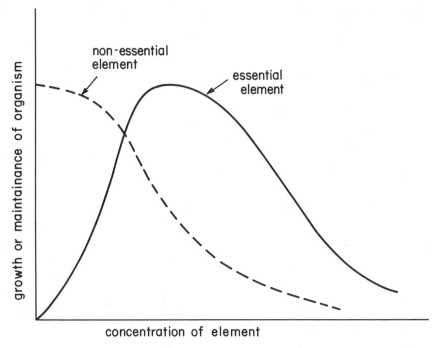

Figure 4.42   Dose-Response Curves for Essential and Nonessential Elements in Metabolic Processes

impossible, to take in too much iron. For copper, which is also essential, the optimum level is much lower. We carry only about 80 mg of this element, and copper is quite toxic even at relatively low levels.

For some elements that are known to be toxic, it has only recently been demonstrated that they are also essential. This is true for the element selenium, for example. Selenium has long been known to be poisonous, and cattle that feed on grass that grows in selenium-rich areas become ill. However, it has recently been discovered that selenium provides the body with essential protection against oxidation reactions, and it has been associated with depressed levels of cancer. But the concentrations needed for this protection are very low.

Lead

In the case of lead, we have no indication that the metal fills any essential role in biology and we do know that it is toxic. The physiological effects of lead are outlined in Table 4.5. Lead specifically interferes with the biochemical reactions that lead to the synthesis of the heme group, the iron complex responsible for the binding of oxygen to the transport protein hemoglobin. This interference can be detected at relatively low lead levels, about 0.3 ppm in the blood, because of the

Table 4.5   Physiological Effects of Lead Poisoning

Symptom	Blood Lead Level (ppm)
1. Interference with heme biosynthesis	
a) Metabolites in urine (δ-aminolevulinic acid)	>0.3
b) Reduced red blood cell production	>0.5
c) Anemia	>0.8
2. Kidney dysfunction	
a) Minimal disorder	>0.5
b) Severe dysfunction	>0.8
3. Permanent nerve and brain damage	>0.8

Source: J. J. Chisholm, *Sci. Am.* 224 (February 1971): 15.

buildup of metabolites, substances that are required for the synthesis of heme and cannot be utilized because of the inhibition of key reactions by the lead. The chemical detection of these metabolites, particularly δ-aminolevulinic acid (ALA), provides a sensitive test for lead in the body. At higher levels of lead in the blood, symptoms of anemia can set in due to the deficiency of hemoglobin. More serious is kidney dysfunction, which is also associated with elevated levels of lead. The most serious effects of lead are interferences with nervous tissue. This can lead to brain damage that is permanent unless the lead is quickly removed from the body.

Removal can be accomplished with the help of chelating agents—molecules with several binding sites for the metal ion. We discussed these agents earlier in connection with the problem of water hardness and detergents. The upper part of Figure 4.43 shows structural diagrams for some chelating agents that have been found to be particularly effective in binding lead. These are fed to the victim of lead poisoning as the calcium chelate. If they were given as the free chelating agent, they would bind calcium in the body and produce calcium depletion. As shown in the lower part of Figure 4.43, lead binds chelating agents more strongly than calcium, and displaces the calcium. The lead chelate is then rapidly excreted in the urine.

At greatest risk from lead poisoning are children in the inner cities. Many older buildings have lead-based paint, which peels from the walls in time. The paint chips are picked up and eaten by infants, particularly those who are under-nourished. A good-sized paint chip can provide an infant with a toxic dose of lead. In response to this situation, some communities have set up programs to measure the levels of lead in the blood of ghetto children and to paint over old walls with nonleaded paint.

The problem for city children is not limited to lead-based paints, however. The dust of city streets can sometimes be as rich in lead as are some lead ores. Table 4.6 shows some figures for the industrial city of Manchester, England. High levels of lead were found not only on major roads but on lightly traveled streets

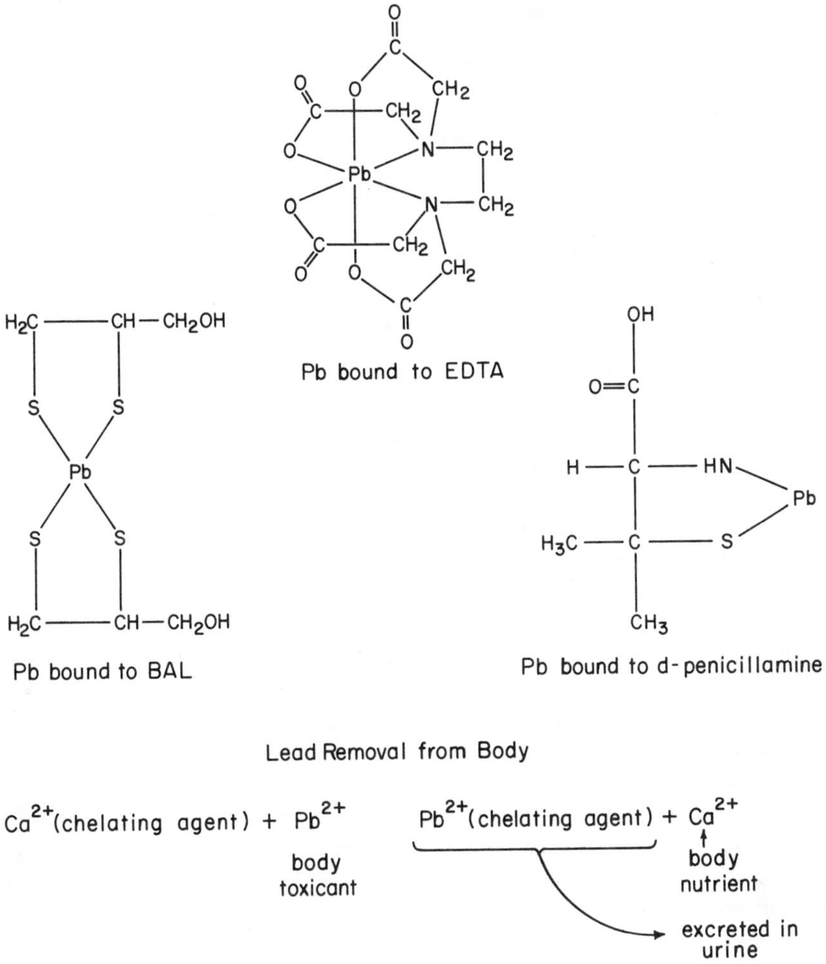

Pb bound to EDTA

Pb bound to BAL

Pb bound to d-penicillamine

Lead Removal from Body

$$Ca^{2+}(\text{chelating agent}) + Pb^{2+}$$

body
toxicant

$$Pb^{2+}(\text{chelating agent}) + Ca^{2+}$$

body
nutrient

excreted in
urine

Figure 4.43 Lead Chelating Agents

as well. Dust in urban playgrounds was found to contain about 1,000 ppm of lead, compared with a concentration of 85 ppm for playgrounds in the country. It is reasonable to expect that children who play in city dust will accumulate substantial amounts of lead. Indeed, a recent study has shown that in some cities 6–8% of preschool children have elevated levels of lead in their blood.

Moonshiners also bear a special risk of lead poisoning. Often backyard stills use old car radiators as condensers, and the hot alcohol vapors gradually dissolve the lead in the solder. Thus, illicit whiskey can contain toxic amounts of lead.

Another source of frequent lead poisoning is pottery that is inadequately fired.

Table 4.6   Lead in Urban and Rural Locations (Manchester, England, 1974)

Type of Locality*	Average Lead Concentration (ppm)
Major roads; moderate/heavy traffic	1,001
Minor roads; light/moderate traffic	888
Streets with very light traffic only	933
Children's playgrounds in urban areas	1,014
Children's playgrounds and parks in rural areas	85

*First four localities are urban areas.
Source: J. P. Day, M. Hart, and M. S. Robinson, *Nature* 253 (January 31, 1975): 343.

Pottery glaze contains lead compounds to give it the proper flow characteristics. If the glaze is baked on at a high enough temperature in a properly operating kiln, the lead is immobilized and does not easily leach out. If the temperature of the firing is not high enough, however, the lead leaches out into liquids contained in the pottery. Even a hot cup of coffee from a poorly glazed mug can contain significant concentrations of lead. Particularly dangerous are acidic liquids stored in crockery. The acid in fruit juices or soft drinks greatly accelerates the leaching of lead and there have been tragic cases of lead poisoning from this source.

While the dangers of lead poisoning are clear enough, there is controversy about the possible hazards associated with subacute levels of lead. The average concentration of lead in the blood of city dwellers is about 0.2 ppm. This is only a factor of four less than the level at which acute physiological symptoms of lead poisoning can be observed, and to many people a factor of four seems a small margin of safety. Moreover, it is not known whether there may be more subtle effects of chronic exposure to subtoxic amounts of lead. On the other hand, there is no clear evidence that the average lead concentration in blood has been increasing. Table 4.7 shows that there is an association between the amount of lead in

Table 4.7   Respiratory Exposure to Lead and Mean Blood Lead Levels as a Function of Job and Environment

Population	Lead in Air (ppm)	Mean Blood Lead Level (ppm)
Rural United States	0.4	0.16
Urban United States	0.8	0.21
Downtown Philadelphia	1.9	0.24
Cincinnati police officers	1.7	0.25
Cincinnati traffic police	3.0	0.30
Los Angeles traffic police	4.2	0.21
Boston automobile-tunnel employees	5.0	0.30

Source: J. J. Chisholm, *Sci. Am.* 224 (February 1971): 15.

blood and exposure to lead in the air. However, the association is fairly weak. The difference in exposure between people who work in the country and those who work in the Boston automobile tunnel is more than a factor of ten, but the difference in the lead levels of blood is only a factor of about two.

The concentration of lead in the blood depends on the rate of excretion as well as on the exposure. Also, lead is deposited in bones, where it replaces calcium. The measured levels of lead in blood do not reflect the amount of lead that is stored in this way. The stored lead can, however, reenter the bloodstream. For example, calcium is mobilized from bone during illnesses that are accompanied by fever. Lead is mobilized along with calcium, and if enough has been stored, lead poisoning can result.

Lead has been spread far and wide in recent years. This is shown graphically in Figure 4.44, which plots the lead content of successive layers of Greenland snow

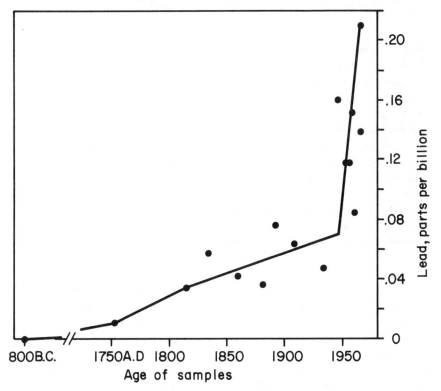

Increase of lead in snow at Camp Century, Greenland, since 800 BC.

Figure 4.44 Lead in the Ecosystem

Source: *Airborne Lead in Perspective* (Washington, D.C.: National Academy of Sciences, 1972), p. 7.

Table 4.8   Lead Emission in the United States, 1968

Emission Source	Lead Emitted (tons/year)
Gasoline combustion	181,000
Coal combustion	920
Fuel oil combustion	24
Lead alkyl manufacturing	810
Primary lead smelting	174
Secondary lead smelting	811
Brass manufacturing	521
Lead oxide manufacturing	20
Gasoline transfer	36
Total	184,316

Source: *Airborne Lead in Perspective* (Washington, D.C.: National Academy of Sciences, 1972), p. 13.

which have been deposited year after year and whose dates are accurately known. There has clearly been a sharp increase in the lead content since 1950. This correlates with the accelerated increase in the lead content of gasoline additives at around the same time. We know that lead emission comes almost entirely from gasoline combustion, as shown in Table 4.8. Therefore, the worldwide spread of airborne lead is quite clearly associated with the use of tetraethyl lead in gasoline. As mentioned earlier, this additive is needed to prevent knocking in gasoline engines. When gasoline is burned, the lead is emitted in fine particles. Most of these settle out rapidly giving city dust its high lead content, but the finest particles travel widely and are also small enough to penetrate the air passages of the lung. As mentioned before, there is considerable pressure to remove lead from gasoline because it poisons the platinum catalysts that are used for the removal of pollutants in automotive exhausts. The health problems posed by lead provide additional pressures in the same direction.

Mercury

Another toxic metal that has been well publicized is mercury. As indicated in Table 4.9, the toxicity of mercury depends very much on its chemical state. We know elemental mercury as the liquid quicksilver, which is fairly inert and nontoxic if swallowed. The liquid has a significant vapor pressure, however, and the vapor is highly toxic if inhaled. For this reason, liquid mercury should not be handled except in well-ventilated areas, and spills should be quickly cleaned up. The second entry in the table is the mercurous ion, which has two mercury atoms, each with a single positive charge. Mercurous ion forms a rather insoluble compound with chloride ion, and since our stomachs contain a high concentration of chloride, mercurous ion is not very toxic. The mercuric ion, with a double

Table 4.9 Chemical Forms of Mercury

Molecular Form	Chemical and Biochemical Properties
Hg	Elemental mercury. The liquid is relatively inert and nontoxic. The vapor is highly toxic when inhaled.
Hg_2^{2+}	Mercurous ion. Insoluble as the chloride; low toxicity.
Hg^{2+}	Mercuric ion. Toxic but not easily transported across biological membranes.
RHg^+	Organomercurials. Highly toxic, especially CH_3Hg^+ (methyl mercury); causes irreversible nerve and brain damage; easily transported across biological membranes; stored in fat tissue.
R_2Hg	Diorganomercurials. Low toxicity but can be converted to RHg^+.
HgS	Mercuric sulfide. Highly insoluble and nontoxic. Mercury is trapped in soil in this form.

positive charge, is quite toxic. It has a high affinity for sulfur atoms and attaches itself to the sulfur-containing amino acids of proteins. However, it does not move across biological membranes readily and therefore does not easily get inside biological cells. Far more toxic are the organomercury ions, particularly methyl mercury, which are fat soluble and can move across membranes. The diorganomercurials are not themselves toxic, but they can be converted to mono-organomercurials in the envrionment.

The most serious symptom of mercury poisoning is nerve and brain damage, which can easily become irreversible. These symptoms set in at blood levels of about 0.5 ppm for methyl mercury, somewhat lower than the corresponding level for lead. Cases of mercury poisoning have been associated with the consumption of seed grains that have been coated with organomercurial fungicides. If the seeds are planted as they are intended to be, there is no danger of toxicity, since the organomercurial chemicals are broken down in the soil and the mercury is trapped as highly insoluble mercuric sulfide. The danger arises from the misuse of the treated seed grains. In one incident, seed grains shipped from the United States to Iraq were inadvertently diverted to flour mills and baked into bread, leading to many fatalities. In another incident, a New Mexico family fed its pigs treated feed grain. When the slaughtered pig was cooked and eaten by the family, the children suffered brain damage from mercury poisoning. A successful court action brought by the family led to the banning of organomercurials for seed treatment by the U.S. Environmental Protection Agency.

The infamous case of mass mercury poisoning in Minamata, Japan, had a different origin. In this fishing village, a strange disease broke out in the mid-1950s, first among the cats of the village and then among the people. It took some time for the nervous disorders to be traced to mercury poisoning. It was then discovered that the fish in the bay were heavily contaminated with methyl mercury. The Minamata Chemical Company is located on the shore of the bay, and subsequent investigation showed that it was discharging large amounts of mercury but no methyl mercury compounds. The missing link between the discharge of inorganic mercury and the presence in the fish of the organic mercury derivative, methyl mercury, was later filled in by chemical researchers, who discovered that microbes that live in the absence of air and produce methane—the same ones we described earlier in connection with methane digesters—can also convert mercury to methyl mercury. It is the methyl mercury that is passed on up the food chain, as shown in the upper diagram of Figure 4.45. At each level of the aquatic food chain, the mercury concentration builds up strongly, as illustrated in the lower part of the figure. This is true even in uncontaminated waters. Mercury has always been part of our environment, and the biological

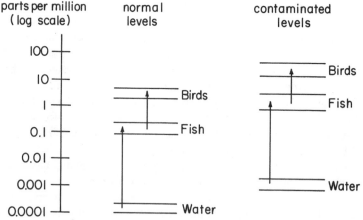

(i)

Mechanism of Propagation

(ii)

Levels of Mercury

Figure 4.45 Propagation of Mercury in Food Chain

mercury cycle evolved long before the advent of modern industry. Large fish that were preserved in museums many years ago have been found to contain significant concentrations of mercury. However, mercury pollution markedly increases the concentrations found in each level of the food chain.

The chief sources of mercury pollution have been paper mills and chloralkali plants, which generate chlorine gas by electrolysis using electrodes made of mercury pools. The effluents from these industries leave substantial quantities of mercury in the sediment of nearby lakes and bays. The sediments often contain the methane-producing bacteria that slowly convert the mercury deposits to methyl mercury, which quickly enters the food chain. In these circumstances, the fish in the area can have mercury concentrations higher than 20 ppm in their tissues. The victims of the Minamata disease had diets consisting mainly of fish taken from the polluted bay. These fish were subsequently found to have mercury concentrations of 27–102 ppm. Soon after the Minamata disaster, it was discovered that many fish in the Great Lakes had high levels of mercury, and important commercial fisheries had to be closed as a result. Since then new technology has been introduced in almost all mercury-using plants, and this has eliminated most of the mercury in their effluents. However, in many localities the damage has already been done, since the large amounts of mercury already dumped in sediments will continue to be a source of methyl mercury for many years to come. No effective way of cleaning up these sediments has yet been found.

Cadmium

A third heavy metal of current environmental concern is cadmium. At elevated levels, cadmium is known to cause kidney problems, anemia, and bone marrow disorders, and it has been implicated as a cause of hypertension and possibly cancer. Again, cadmium is a natural part of our environment. Indeed, the body seems to have a natural defense against cadmium in the form of a small protein called *metallothionein,* which is found in the kidneys and binds cadmium quite effectively. Most cadmium that is ingested is, therefore, trapped in the kidney and eliminated, as shown in Figure 4.46. A small fraction of the cadmium normally ingested is stored in the body, however, and gradually accumulates with increasing age. In its chemical properties, cadmium is similar to zinc, which is an essential element found at the active sites of many enzymes. It seems likely that when an excessive amount of cadmium is ingested so that the metallothionein-binding capacity is exceeded, cadmium then competes with zinc at key enzymatic sites.

Because of its chemical similarity, cadmium occurs naturally in association with zinc minerals. Zinc mining and smelting operations disperse a substantial amount of cadmium into the environment. Growing plants have a requirement for zinc, and many of them take up and concentrate cadmium with the same biochemical apparatus. The only known outbreak of environmental cadmium

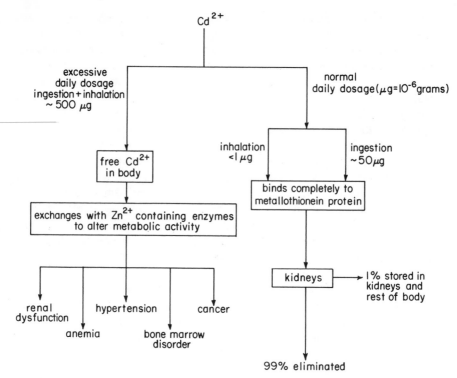

Figure 4.46   Metabolism of Cadmium

Source: Dose data abstracted from L. Friberg, M. Piscator, and G. Nordberg, *Cadmium in the Environment* (Cleveland: CRC Press, 1971), pp. 25, 26.

Table 4.10   Effect of Effluents from Zinc Mines and Smelting Works on the Concentration of Cadmium in Vegetables (Sasu River Basin, Japan)

Type of Vegetable	Mean Cadmium Concentration (ppm)	
	Control Area	Sasu-Shiine Basin
Rice	0.08	0.37
Bean paste	0.04	0.27
Mushroom	0.1	0.37
Carrot	0.15	0.44
Eggplant	0.1	0.3
Spinach	0.4	0.85
Potato	0.08	0.14
Onion	0.1	0.15

Source: L. Friberg, M. Pisacator, and G. Nordberg, *Cadmium in the Environment* (Cleveland: CRC Press, 1971), pp. 129–32.

poisoning also occurred in Japan, in the Sasu River Basin. Many people in the area developed a painful condition called the "itai itai," or "ouch ouch," disease, in which their bones became fragile and subject to numerous fractures. As shown in Table 4.10, it was found that the crops in the area had greatly elevated levels of cadmium as a result of irrigation with river water that contained effluents from a variety of mining and smelting operations. While no other outbreaks of this type have been observed elsewhere, with the increasing use of zinc and cadmium in industry, the levels of cadmium in the environment have been increasing and are a cause for concern.

6 | Cancer

While there are numerous toxic effects, both acute and long-term, associated with different chemicals, the most dreaded is cancer. This disease is now responsible for almost one-fifth of all deaths in the United States. Only heart disease takes more lives. Moreover, there is a strong likelihood that most cancers have environmental causes. The most striking evidence for this comes from the patterns of the incidence of cancer in different parts of the body in different countries. Figure 4.47 shows that Japanese people have much higher death rates from stomach and liver cancer and lower rates from colon and prostate cancer than do white residents of California. These differences are much less pronounced in Japanese immigrants to California, while their children show a pattern still closer to that of native Californians. Since genetic factors are the same for Japanese immigrants to California and for Japanese people who remain in Japan, these differences clearly indicate an environmental origin. One presumes that there are some factors in the living arrangements, possibly in the diet or the drinking water or the atmosphere, that are different in Japan than in California and account for the observed changes. At the moment, we have no idea what these factors are.

We do know the most probable cause of lung cancer, which is currently the most common form of cancer and accounts for one-fifth of all cancer deaths. Figure 4.48 shows the marked correlation between the increase in cigarette smoking among men early in the century and the incidence of lung cancer some 20 years later. A similar correlation is now emerging among women who started smoking later and whose incidence of lung cancer is now on the rise. The time delay is a characteristic of cancer and is one of its most insidious properties. It often takes 20 years or longer for a cancer to develop, making it difficult to trace the cause. This also means that if we are exposing ourselves to a new cancer-causing agent, we might not know about it for more than 20 years.

Many chemicals are capable of causing cancer. Laboratory tests show wide differences in the carcinogenicity of various chemical agents when applied to

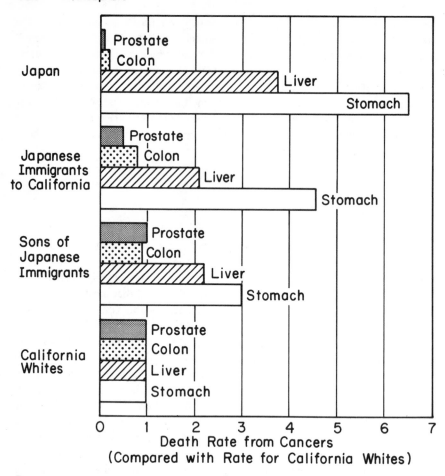

Figure 4.47 Change in Incidence of Various Cancers with Migration from Japan to the United States

animal species such as mice and rats. Similar patterns probably apply to humans, although extrapolations from laboratory studies to predictions about human beings is one of the most troublesome questions in cancer research. In other cases we know that chemicals can cause cancer in humans from tragic experience. Epidemiologic studies can implicate chemicals as cancer-causing agents either because of a high incidence of cancer observed in an occupationally exposed group, or because the chemical causes a specific and rare type of cancer that can be traced back to the source of exposure. Table 4.11 gives a list of chemical carcinogens along with the types of cancer they produce. The chemicals cover a wide range of types, with a few obvious similarities. Some are industrial chem-

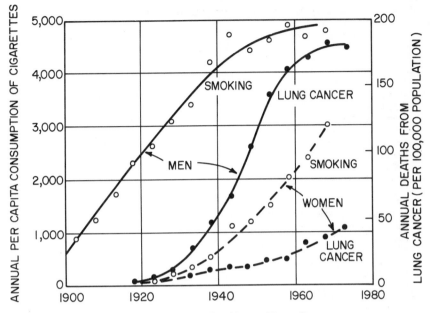

Figure 4.48 Cigarette Smoking and Lung Cancer

icals, some are drugs, and other occur naturally. For example, the aflatoxins, which are found naturally in peanuts that are infested with certain molds, are highly carcinogenic.

We do not know in detail how chemical carcinogens produce cancer, but as shown in Figure 4.49, it is likely that they attack the genetic material in the nuclei of cells, the DNA molecules. The DNA contains the genetic code, which specifies the chemical sequence of proteins as well as other DNA molecules. Cells reproduce by duplicating their DNA and then dividing in two. Damage to the DNA can result in a mistake in the genetic code. Most often this results in the death of the cell, but if the cell survives, the mistake can be passed on to the daughter cells when the DNA is copied. This is called a *mutation*. If a mutation occurs in a germ cell that gives rise to an offspring of the organism, all the progeny will carry the same coding error, which may be expressed as an alteration in some functions of the organism.

Cancer is a condition in which a cell grows and divides uncontrollably, invading normal body tissues. The mechanisms that control its growth are evidently impaired, and this is thought to result from damage to the DNA. It is known from laboratory studies on insects and bacteria that chemicals that are known to induce cancer usually are effective at producing mutations as well. In fact, tests for mutagenicity in bacteria are coming to play an important role in screening chemicals as potential carcinogens.

Table 4.11   Chemicals Recognized as Human Carcinogens

Chemical Mixtures	Site of Cancers
Soots, tars, oils	Skin, lungs
Cigarette smoke	Lungs
Industrial chemicals	
2-Naphthylamine	Urinary bladder
Benzidine	Urinary bladder
4-Aminobiphenyl	Urinary bladder
Chloromethyl methyl ether	Lungs
Nickel compounds	Lungs, nasal sinuses
Chromium compounds	Lungs
Asbestos	Lungs
Arsenic compounds	Skin, lungs
Vinyl chloride	Liver
Drugs	
N,*N*-bis(2-chloroethyl)-2-naphthylamine	Urinary bladder
Bis(2-chloroethyl)sulfide (mustard gas)	Lungs
Diethylstilbestrol	Vagina
Phenacetin	Renal pelvis
Naturally occurring compounds	
Betel nuts	Buccal mucosa
Aflatoxins	Liver
Potent carinogens in animals to which human populations are exposed	
Cyclamates	Bladder
Sterigmatocystis	Liver
Cycasin	Liver
Safrole	Liver
Pyrrolizidine alkaloids	Liver
Nitroso compounds	Esophagus, liver, kidney, stomach

Source: C. Heidelberger, "Chemical Carcinogenesis," *Annu. Rev. Biochem.* 44 (1975): 81.

Most cancer-producing chemicals have to be activated in the organism to express their carcinogenic properties. This is illustrated in Figure 4.50 for the compound benzanthracene. This is a member of the class of polycyclic aromatic hydrocarbon compounds that are found in tars and on fossil fuel soot and are known to be highly effective in producing cancers. Yet benzanthracene by itself is not particularly effective at inducing mutations in bacteria. It becomes mutagenic, however, if it is activated by enzymes from animals. Apparently the chemical must first be oxidized, probably to the epoxide intermediate shown in brackets in the figure. This intermediate can react through two different pathways. It may react with DNA to induce mutations or cancer. Alternatively, the epoxide may react to form the phenol product shown, which has an oxygen atom bonded to the aromatic ring. This oxygen atom is the point of attachment for making another derivative called a *glucuronide sulfate,* which the body is able to excrete. This biochemical reaction scheme represents an enzymatic detoxification mechanism for benzanthracene and for many other foreign organic com-

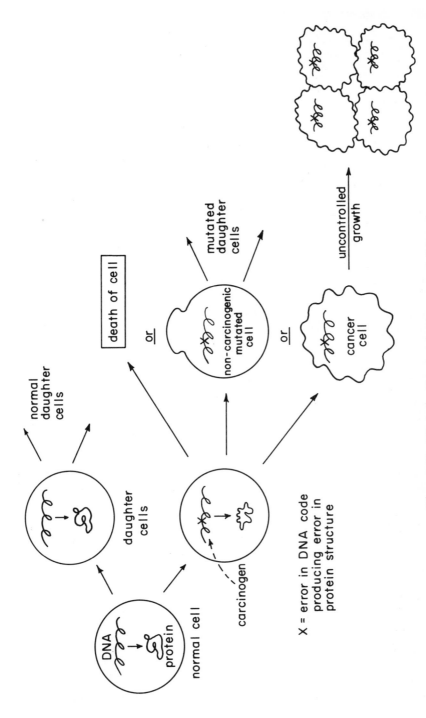

Figure 4.49 Effect of a Chemical Carcinogen on Cell Growth

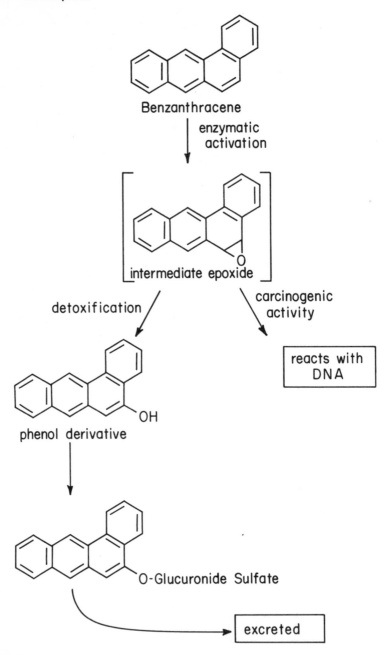

Benzanthracene

enzymatic
activation

intermediate epoxide

detoxification

carcinogenic
activity

reacts with
DNA

phenol derivative

O-Glucuronide Sulfate

excreted

Figure 4.50 Activation of Polycyclic Aromatic Hydrocarbons

Source: C. Heidelberger, "Chemical Carcinogenesis," *Annu. Rev. Biochem.* **44** (1975):87.

pounds as well. Such compounds are not soluble in water and are stored in the fat until they can be activated in this manner to produce a water-soluble derivative that can be excreted. It is one of nature's ironies that the same activation mechanism can produce cancer if the activated molecule first reacts with DNA.

The upper part of Figure 4.51 shows a similar activation scheme for dimethylnitrosamine. Again, reaction with oxygen produces an intermediate, which in this case can transfer a positively charged methyl group, called a *methyl cation,* to the DNA. Nitrosamines are powerful carcinogens and are of increasing concern because of the possibility that they can be formed in the stomach from common constituents of the diet. The lower part of Figure 4.51 shows that sodium nitrite can react with dimethylamine and hydrochloric acid to produce dimethylnitrosamine. Dimethylamine and other similar amines are present in meats and fish, and hydrochloric acid is a natural constituent of gastric juice. Sodium nitrite is a widely used preservative, particularly in bacon, hot dogs, and other cured meats. While no direct link has been established between these products and cancer, there is clearly cause for concern, and the use of sodium nitrite is currently under review.

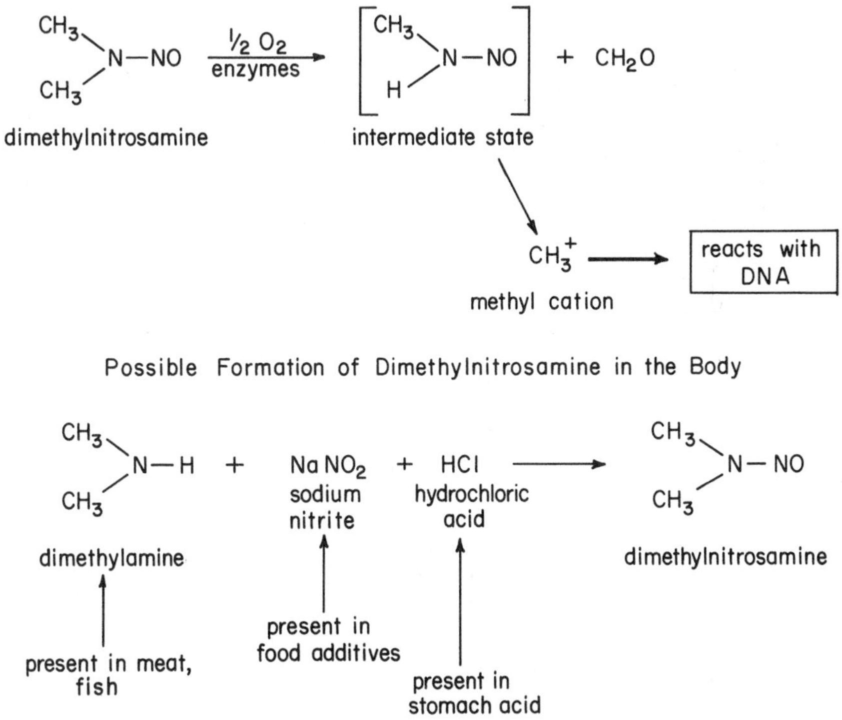

Figure 4.51   Activation of Dimethylnitrosamine in the Body

Genetic Mechanisms and Chemical Carcinogenesis

DNA replication and protein synthesis

Deoxyribonucleic acid (DNA) is the macromolecule that carries the genetic information necessary for the functioning and reproduction of the cell. A diagram of a single DNA strand is shown in Figure 4.52. The strand has a backbone of alternating phosphate and sugar (deoxyribose) groups. Attached to each sugar is an organic base, either a purine or a pyrimidine. The purines are adenine (A) and guanine (G), the pyrimidines are cytosine (C) and thymine (T). The DNA of the cell is arranged in a double helix; two strands are twisted about each other, with the backbones on the outside and the bases pointing inward and their planes perpendicular to the helix axis. The bases on opposing strands are linked by hydrogen bonds. The hydrogen-bond possibilities are restricted by the helical structure. Two pyrimidines are too small to span the space between the strands, while two purines would bump into one another; a purine and pyrimidine pair have just the right size. The possibilities are further restricted to just two by the arrangement of

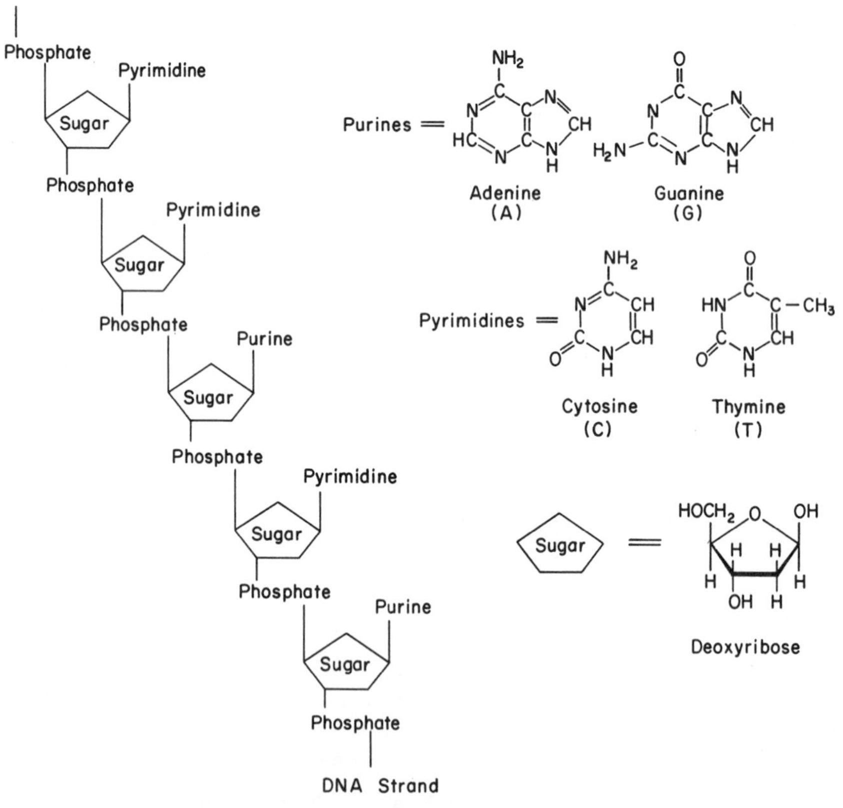

Figure 4.52   The Generalized Structure of a DNA Strand

functional groups on the bases. As shown in Figure 4.53, adenine is always joined to thymine, and guanine is always bonded to cytosine. Consequently, the organic bases along the two chains are complementary: A matching T and G matching C, and vice versa. If the sequence of one chain is known, that of its partner is automatically known. It is the sequence that carries the genetic information.

Cellular replication of DNA occurs with the two strands separate. As shown below, the single strands act as templates for the formation of daughter strands:

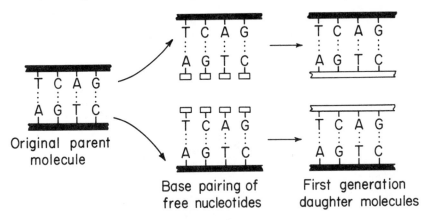

Base pairing of free nucleotides   **First generation daughter molecules**

Monomeric nucleotides (the phosphate-sugar-base units) are added stepwise to the complementary strand and are joined into a polymer by DNA polymerase enzymes. Selection of the correct nucleotides by hydrogen-bonding to the template bases is a very accurate process. The average probability of an error in the insertion of a new nucleotide under optimal conditions may be as low as 10^{-8} or 10^{-9}.

Each strand of DNA contains the complete information for synthesis of all the proteins in the cell. A gene is a small fraction of the strand that contains the information for the synthesis of one protein. The information is transferred from the genes to the ribosomes, where protein synthesis is carried out by ribonucleic acid (RNA). As shown in Figure 4.54, RNA differs from DNA in two aspects: the sugar of RNA is ribose instead of deoxyribose, and one of the major bases is uracil (U) instead of thymine. U differs from T only by the addition of a methyl group to the ring of T. The complementarity is unaffected; U hydrogen-bonds to A. Unlike DNA, RNA usually functions as a single-stranded unit.

The process for protein synthesis is shown in Figure 4.55. Messenger RNA (mRNA) is synthesized in the nucleus, using the gene as a template. The process is quite similar to DNA replication. The transfer of information from DNA to mRNA is called *transcription* because both are nucleic acids and the change is comparable to a change of script. mRNA then migrates to the cytoplasm and ribosomes become attached to it.

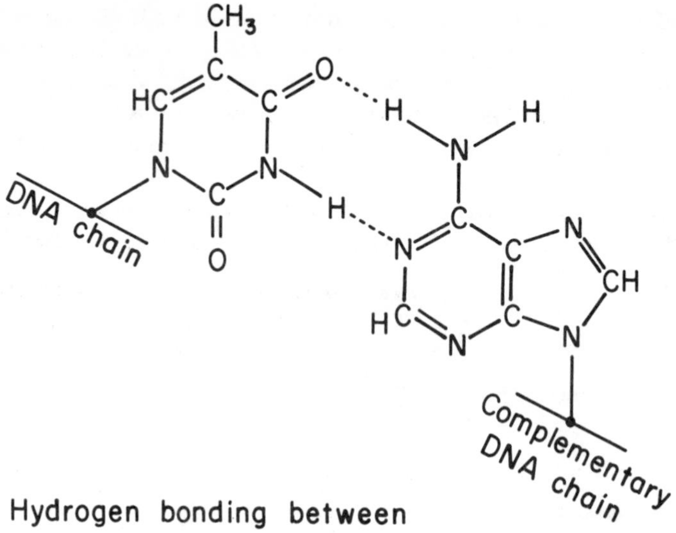

Hydrogen bonding between
thymine and adenine
(shown by dots)

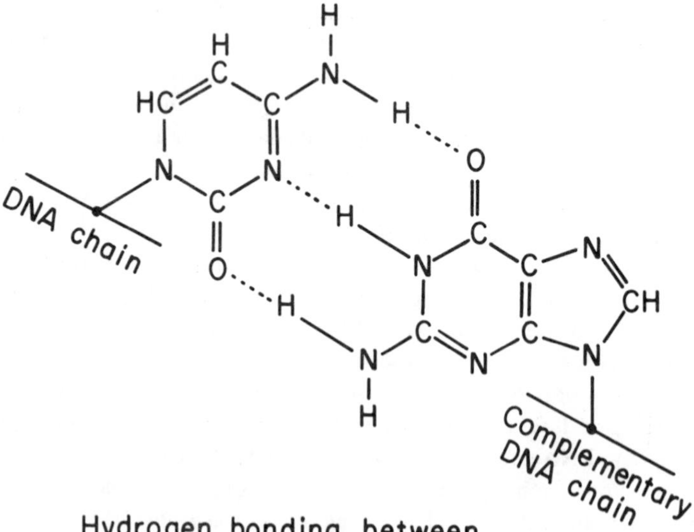

Hydrogen bonding between
cytosine and guanine

Figure 4.53 Base Pairing in DNA

(i)

Strand structure

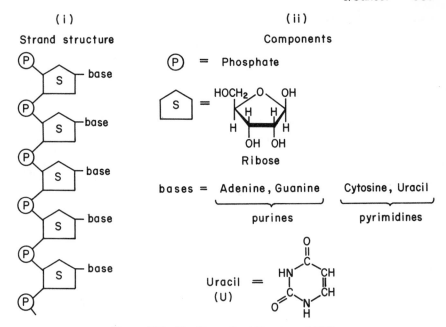

(ii)

Components

Figure 4.54   The Generalized Structure of RNA

Translation of the nucleotide sequence into an amino acid sequence is carried out via small RNA molecules, called transfer RNA (tRNA). Each amino acid is assigned to one or several specific tRNAs. The assignment process is mediated by different activating enzymes called aminoacyl-tRNA synthetases, which recognize the proper amino acid and the corresponding tRNA. The nucleotide sequence of tRNA is organized such that intramolecular hydrogen-bonding causes the molecule to assume a cloverleaf structure:

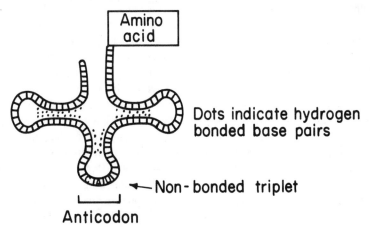

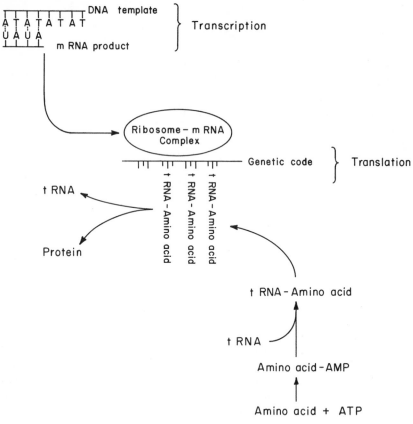

Figure 4.55 Protein Synthesis

The point of attachment of the amino acid occurs at the stem of the cloverleaf. At the opposite loop of the cloverleaf there is a group of three non-hydrogen-bonded nucleotides, which form the *anticodon*. At the ribosome, the anticodon nucleotides form base pairs with a complementary triplet of nucleotides on mRNA called the *codon*. Amino acids are brought to the ribosome surface by the appropriate tRNA-mRNA base-pair interactions. Each successive amino acid is joined to the polypeptide protein chain by enzymatic action, with the concurrent release of the associated tRNA. The matching of the codon with the complementary anticodon is the *translation* mechanism. The language of the genetic code has been deciphered, as shown in Table 4.12. Since there are four bases and a codon is formed from three of them, there are $4^3 = 64$ different codons. Three of them are to stop protein synthesis, and each of the remaining 61 is an instruction to incorporate one of the 20 amino acids into the protein chain. The code is said to be *degenerate* because a particular amino acid can be signaled by more than one codon.

Table 4.12   The Genetic Code

First Positions	Second Position				Third Position
	U	C	A	G	
U	Phe	Ser	Tyr	Cys	U
	Phe	Ser	Tyr	Cys	C
	Leu	Ser	Stop	Stop	A
	Leu	Ser	Stop	Trp	G
C	Leu	Pro	His	Arg	U
	Leu	Pro	His	Arg	C
	Leu	Pro	Gln	Arg	A
	Leu	Pro	Gln	Arg	G
A	Ile	Thr	Asn	Ser	U
	Ile	Thr	Asn	Ser	C
	Ile	Thr	Lys	Arg	A
	Met	Thr	Lys	Arg	G
G	Val	Ala	Asp	Gly	U
	Val	Ala	Asp	Gly	C
	Val	Ala	Glu	Gly	A
	Val	Ala	Glu	Gly	G

Given the position of the bases in a codon, it is possible to find the corresponding amino acid. For example, the codon AUG on mRNA specifies methionine, whereas CAU specifies histidine. UAA, UAG, and UGA are termination signals. AUG is part of the initiation signal, in addition to coding for internal methionines.

Mutations

Mutations are changes in the sequence of base pairs in DNA. Some mutations are single base pair replacements at a definite location; others involve insertions or deletions of one or several nucleotide pairs. Replacement of a single base pair by another may result naturally from base *tautomerizations* during replication. The tautomers are alternate molecular structures, occurring with low but finite frequency, that have different arrangements of hydrogen bond donor and acceptor sites and therefore can induce mispairing of the DNA, or RNA, bases. For

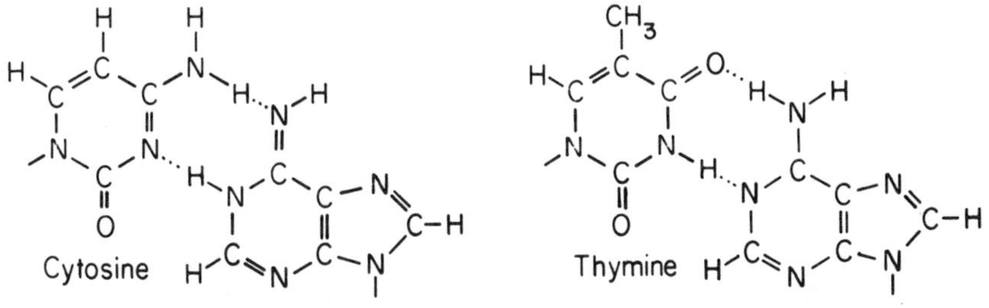

Cytosine   Imino Tautomer of Adenine

Thymine   Normal Adenine

example, adenine can exist in a rare imino tautomeric form that binds to cytosine rather than thymine. In the next round of replication, the mislocated cytosine pairs with guanine. Thus, one of the daughter molecules will contain a G-C pair in place of an A-T pair.

Chemical modification can also produce structures that induce mutations. For example, nitrous acid reacts with bases that contain amino groups and converts them to keto functions. Cytosine is converted to uracil, so a C-G pair is replaced by a U-A pair. Adenine is converted to hypoxanthine, a molecule that resembles guanine and pairs with cytosine. Guanine itself is converted to xanthine, which still pairs with cytosine.

Cytosine HNO_2 Uracil

Adenine HNO_2 Hypoxanthine

Guanine HNO_2 Xanthine

Certain chemicals that contain planar aromatic rings cause mutations by their ability to slip in between base pairs in the DNA double helix. The process, known as *intercalation,* is thought to stabilize a mispairing in the DNA during replication or repair synthesis by causing errors of insertion or deletion of one or more nucleotides. Deletions can also occur during exposure to high-energy radiation, which leads to breaks in the DNA strand. Enzymes can repair the strands, but there is a high probability, especially in multiple breaks, that two ends may be joined that were not previously connected. Mutations that result from the addition or deletion of nucleotides are known as *frame-shift* mutations because they interfere with the decoding of the genetic message by throwing the decoding out of register. The genetic message is read as if it were a continuous sequence of three-letter words, with each word corresponding to a particular amino acid in the desired protein product. At the point of the first deletion or addition, the message will be one letter out of register and the resulting protein will be completely nonfunctional.

Other chemicals cause mutations by binding strongly to DNA nucleotides. Such chemicals have electrophilic functional groups that interact with the electron-rich nucleotide bases. Some of the most potent carcinogens known contain both aromatic rings and electrophilic side chains.

Repair mechanisms

The cell possesses various repair mechanisms to correct for mismatched nucleotides in the DNA double helix. One of these operates during the DNA replication process. DNA polymerase, the enzyme that catalyzes the synthesis of the daughter DNA chain during replications, also has the ability to catalyze the removal of mismatched nucleotides. In the unlikely event that a noncomplementary nucleotide is added to a daughter chain during synthesis, it will be excised from the chain and replaced by the correct monomer:

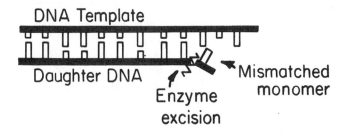

Thus the fidelity of DNA replication is increased because DNA polymerase checks the result of each polymerization it catalyzes before going on to the next.

Other types of repair mechanisms occur during DNA exposure to ultraviolet

1. A distortion in the DNA molecule caused by an ultraviolet light-induced thymine dimer.

2. A specific endonuclease breaks the backbone of one chain near the dimer.

3. The excision of a small region containing the thymine dimer by an exonuclease.

4. Synthesis of new strand. The correct bases are inserted by base pairing with those on the intact strand.

5. Polynucleotide ligase joins up the two ends of the strand and the "repaired" molecule is complete.

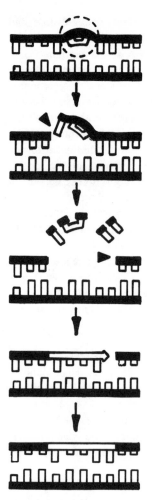

Figure 4.56 Some of the Enzymatic Steps Involved in the Repair of DNA Molecules Containing Thymine Dimers

light. The best understood case is the excision of pyrimidine dimers formed during ultraviolet irradiation. As shown schematically in Figure 4.56, two adjacent thymines in the DNA chain fuse together, forming a dimer structure that does not fit properly into the double helix. The affected strand cannot serve as a faithful template for the production of progeny DNA strands. Several enzymes participate in the repair process. An endonuclease recognizes the damaged region and cuts the strand near the dimer. Then an exonuclease digests away the nucleotides adjacent to the cut. This is followed by the synthesis of a new strand in the excised region, with the intact complementary strand serving as the template.

The newly synthesized strand and the original DNA chain are joined by a ligase enzyme.

Xeroderma pigmentosum, a rare skin condition in humans, appears to be caused by a defect in the endonuclease enzyme that initially breaks the DNA backbone near the pyrimidine dimer. The skin is extremely sensitive to sunlight and fatal skin cancers commonly develop.

There is evidence that repair processes for ultraviolet light damage exist in all forms of life, from bacteria to high plants and animals. The evolution of enzyme systems capable of repairing ultraviolet light damage may in fact have been a necessary prerequisite for the development of the higher forms, which have much more DNA that is also much more complex than that of microorganisms.

Regulation

Not all the cell's DNA is coded for transcription. Some regions are known to bind *regulatory* proteins, which switch transcription on and off, thereby regulating protein synthesis. As shown in the first part of Figure 4.57, control sites called the *operator* (*o*) and *promoter* (*p*) are associated with genes on the DNA chain. The genes for protein synthesis (*structural* genes) may be grouped together for a series of proteins involved in a particular cellular function. The set of genes and associated control sites is called an *operon*. Physically separated from the operon is a protein called a *repressor*. As shown in the second part of Figure 4.57, the repressor serves as an on-off switch for operon activity. It accomplishes this by its ability to exist in an active or inactive form. In the active form (part A of the figure), the repressor blocks the synthesis of the proteins coded in the operon by binding to the operator site. This binding prevents transcription of the operon mRNA, which begins at the promoter site. In the inactive form (part B), the repressor does not bind to the operator, and mRNA transcription and protein synthesis occur without interruption.

In biosynthesis, repressors are often activated by the presence of the end products. For example in *Escherichia coli,* the operon for the synthesis of tryptophan (the trp operon) is repressed by tryptophan. On a molecular level, tryptophan binds with the repressor and activates it. Tryptophan is an example of a *corepressor*. In food metabolism, the opposite effect may occur; the repressor may be deactivated by the presence of a nutrient molecule. For example, the operon for the metabolism of lactose (the lac operon) in *E. coli* is deactivated by a lactose derivative. This derivative, which is an example of an *inducer,* binds to the repressor and causes it to be released from the operator site.

Chemical carcinogenesis

Carcinogenic chemicals react in cells to cause an irreversible change in the genetic expression for controlled cell growth. Although the exact mechanism is not known for any chemical, it is generally believed that the carcinogen acts by

(i)

Map of the Operon Region

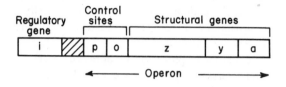

(ii)

Repressor Function

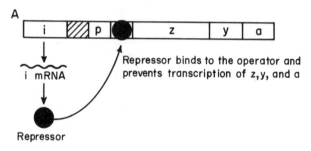

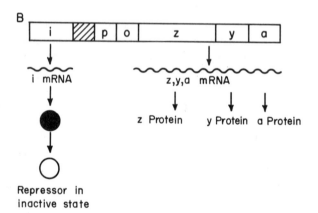

Figure 4.57   Protein Regulation in DNA

binding strongly with a critical information molecule in the cell. Binding to DNA is probably the key initial step, but this hypothesis has not been proved unequivocally. Cancer may also be caused by binding to RNA or to specific proteins, particularly DNA polymerases.

Carcinogens are almost always *electrophilic*; i.e. they are deficient in electrons. Such chemicals are thus strongly attracted to *nucleophilic* (electron-rich) sites. Oxygen, nitrogen, and anionic forms of sulfur or carbon are electron-rich atoms that are ubiquitous in the nucleic acids of DNA and RNA and in the amino acids of proteins. Figure 4.58 illustrates many of the electrophilic-nucleophilic interactions that may occur between an information molecule and a carcinogen.

Generally carcinogens are not active in their native forms. Ironically, the body's metabolic enzyme may inadvertently convert an inherently inactive chemical (procarcinogen) into an active carcinogen (ultimate carcinogen) (see Figure 4.59). One of the major activating systems is the mixed-function oxygenase enzymes in the liver, discussed earlier in connection with the metabolism of pesticides and PCBs. These enzymes oxidize fat-soluble organics by any one of several possible pathways. In carcinogen metabolism, at least one of these path-

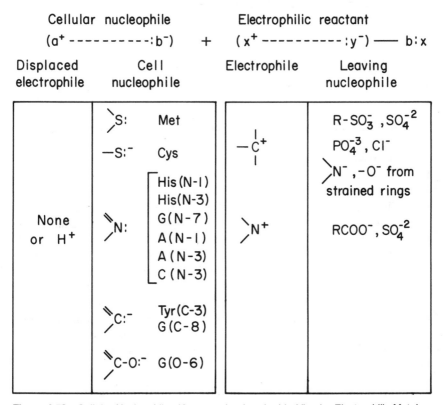

Figure 4.58 Cellular Nucleophiles Known to be Attacked in Vivo by Electrophilic Metabolites of Chemical Carcinogens

Source: E. C. Miller and J. A. Miller, *Molecular Biology of Cancer*, edited by H. Busch (New York: Academic Press, 1974), p. 391.

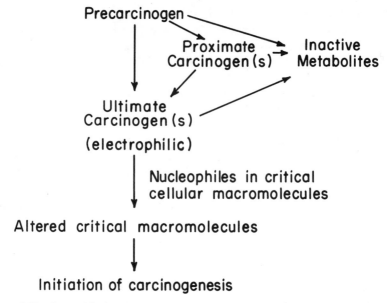

Figure 4.59 General Pathways in the Activation and Deactivation of Chemical Carcinogens

ways produces metabolites with the ability to bind to a critical information molecule.

The metabolic activation of some carcinogens has been studied extensively. Benzo(a)pyrene, one of the most widely dispersed carcinogens, can be converted by multiple pathways into electrophilic metabolites. These are shown in Figure 4.60. The formation of an epoxide, free radical, or ester yields species that may readily attack nucleophilic targets on macromolecules. Aromatic amines, carcinogens that had been widely used in the dye industry, are also metabolized to electrophilic products. As shown in Figure 4.61 for N-methyl-4-aminoazobenzene (MAB), liver enzymes may oxidize the amino group to the N-hydroxy form. If this metabolite is esterified, the N—O bond is easily broken, forming a positively charged nucleophilic site on the amine. Aflatoxin, a fungus associated with peanuts, is a highly potent naturally occurring carcinogen. In a fashion similar to benzo(a)pyrene (see Figure 4.62), it is oxidized to the epoxide form in the liver. Cleavage of the C—O bond occurs quite readily to form a highly reactive cationic carbon atom (C^+).

Carcinogen testing

Since 500 new chemicals are marketed every year, a primary concern in cancer control is singling out the potentially carcinogenic ones. Detection schemes are greatly hindered by the lack of concrete knowledge about the carcinogenic

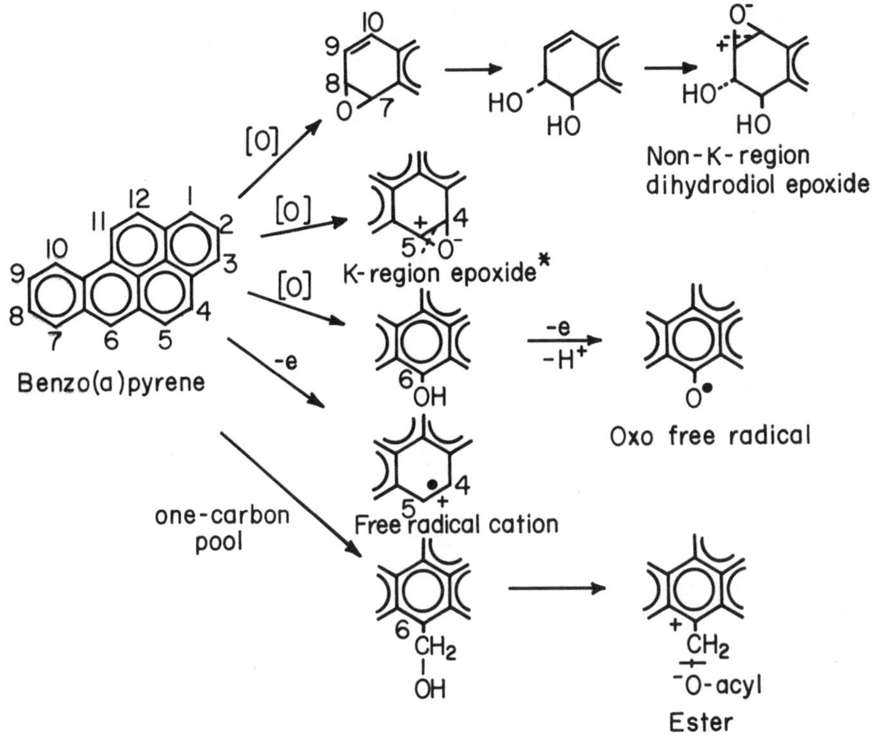

* K-region is between carbons 4 and 5. Activation at this site leads to particularly potent carcinogens.

Figure 4.60 Multiple Enzymatic Pathways for the Metabolism of Benzo(a)pyrene to Electrophilic Reactants

Source: E. C. Miller and J. A. Miller, "A.C.S. Monograph Series, No. 173—Chemical Carcinogens," edited by C. E. Searle, 1976, chap. 16.

mechanism. Studying the effects of chemicals on rats has proved to be the most valuable screening method to date; however, the results are often inconclusive. In a sample of several hundred rats, each animal is a surrogate for approximately a million people. To compensate for the small sample size, the rats are usually fed doses much higher than those to which humans are subjected. The assumption that a smaller dose administered to a larger sample would yield the same result cannot be checked. Furthermore, the effects of chemicals on rats may be different from the effects on humans. Apart from these difficulties, testing a single chemical takes up to three years and is very expensive. There are strong incentives for developing evaluations that are more sensitive, simpler, and less time-consuming.

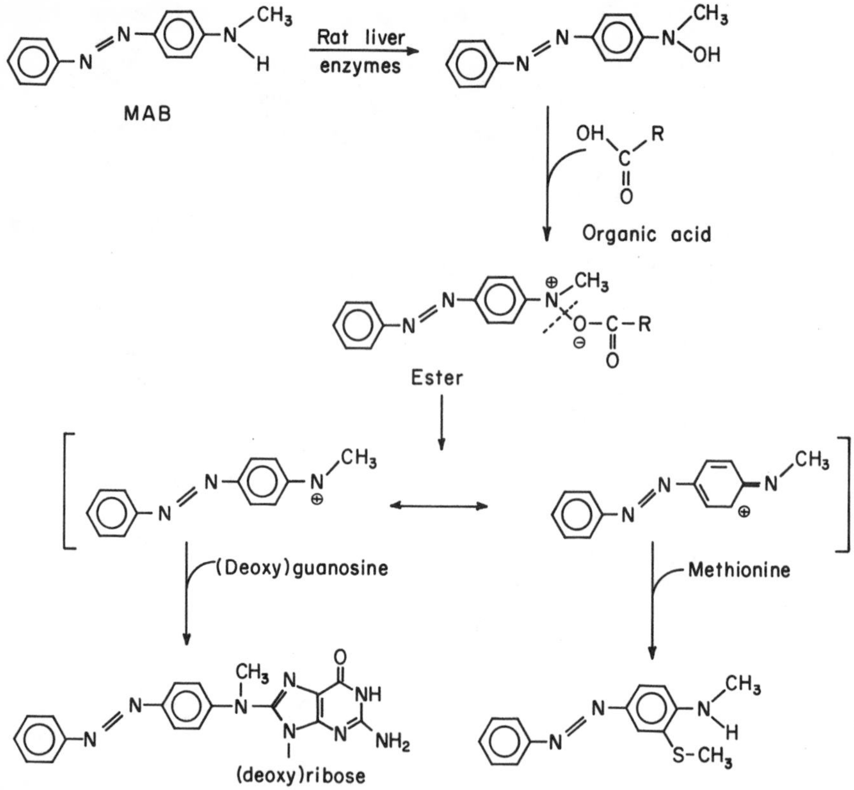

Figure 4.61 Metabolic Conversion of MAB

The metabolic conversion of *N*-methyl-4-aminoazobenzene (MAB) to guanine- and methionine-bound derivatives in nucleic acids and proteins, respectively.

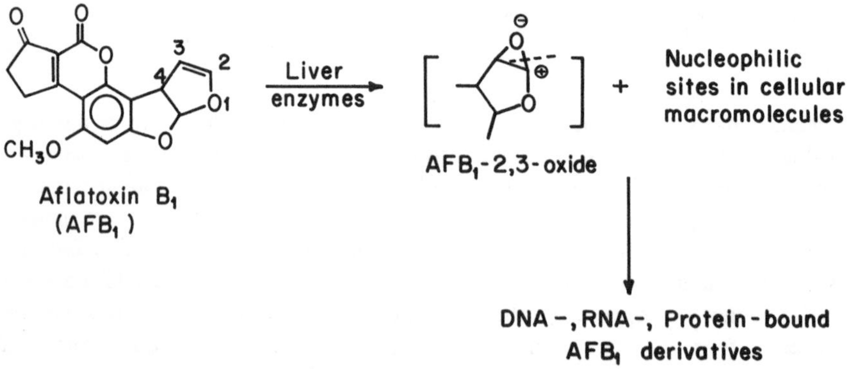

Figure 4.62 The Metabolic Activation of Aflatoxin B₁

Source: J. A. Miller and E. C. Miller, *Biology of Radiation Carcinogenesis*, edited by J. M. Yuhas, et al. (New York: Raven Press, 1976), p. 157.

The most widely known of the new tests is that developed by Professor Bruce N. Ames.[18] The Ames test exploits the fact that, with few exceptions, carcinogens are also mutagens.* The test is inexpensive, takes days rather than years to complete, and can detect a mutagenic response in microgram amounts of chemical. It is performed in a Petri dish on various strains of *Salmonella typhimurium* bacteria that have been developed for detecting and classifying mutagens. Each tester strain has a specific mutation in one of the genes of the operon for histidine synthesis, which causes it to require added histidine for growth. A chemical with mutagenic activity can cause a back-mutation in the operon, which restores the capacity for histidine synthesis. A positive result is indicated by growth of the revertent bacteria around the spot where the chemical was applied. In order to simulate carcinogen activation to the ultimate form, a mixed-function oxygenase system from rat or human liver is usually added. In addition to the histidine mutation, each tester strain contains two additional mutations that greatly increase its sensitivity to mutagens: one causes loss of the excision repair system and the other loss of the lipopolysaccharide barrier that coats the surface of the bacteria.

Some strains with frame-shift mutations in the histidine operon are designed for detecting frame-shift mutagens. Aflatoxin and benzo(a)pyrene, among others,[18] have been identified as frame-shift mutagens after liver activation. The mode of reaction is believed to be through intercalation of the aromatic rings with the DNA strand, coupled with attack of the electrophilic group on an active nucleophilic site on DNA. Another strain with a base-pair change in a histidine gene was developed to detect mutagens that cause base-pair substitutions. Propylsulfone and β-propiolactone are examples of chemicals that revert this strain. Some carcinogens such as nitroquinoline-N-oxide cause both types of mutations.

The Ames test has already proved to be a valuable tool in detecting cancer. In Japan a food additive, furylfuramide, had been tested on rats and mice with no apparent carcinogenic effect. The compound was widely used for about a decade starting in 1965. In 1972 Japanese scientists found it to be a potent mutagen in bacteria. Further animal testing verified that it is also carcinogenic.

Because of the simplicity and low cost of the Ames test, it is being used to pinpoint carcinogens in complex mixtures. This is accomplished by its use as an assay in purifying mutagenic components from the mixture. Recently, considerable mutagenic activity has been found in many commercial oxidative-type hair dyes, and several of the individual mutagenic components in the hair dyes have been identified.[19] Used in conjunction with animal testing, the Ames test and other cellular assays that are currently being developed will greatly increase the accuracy of carcinogenic prediction.

---

*Testing to date has shown the correlation between carcinogenicity and mutagenicity to be nearly 90%.

7 | Conclusion

We have sen that the biosphere too has its natural balances, which can be upset by human intervention. World agricultural production has become precariously tied to fossil fuel energy, and it needs to be weaned away from this dependence through less energy-intensive practices and alternate energy forms. The widespread application of chemical pesticides has produced ecological imbalances, and the need for more selective methods of pest control is increasingly recognized. The human organism is a marvelously balanced biochemical system that can maintain itself in the face of substantial environmental fluctuations. Over the long term, however, it does require a nutritionally balanced diet, and it is endangered by the buildup of toxic substances, by-products of industrial activity, which threaten to overwhelm its defenses. A particularly insidious danger is the loss of control of cellular division, leading to the growth of cancerous tissue. We need to know much more about how chemicals induce cancer in order to arrive at preventive measures.

This brings us to the end of the book, although we have certainly not exhausted the subject. Much more could be written and much more needs to be learned about all the environmental issues we have touched on. We hope we have given some concept of the scope of these issues and of the many interrelationships among them in the setting provided by the chemistry of the natural world that we inhabit.

Problem Set

Problems 1 and 2 refer to the following table:

Grams of Proteins of Corn and Beans Required to Give Daily Requirement of Essential Amino Acids

	Corn	Beans
Tryptophan	70.0	47.9
Lysine	72.2	33.0
Threonine	37.5	44.3
Leucine	27.4	44.8
Isoleucine	49.0	39.3
Valine	38.8	44.9
Phenylalanine	35.0	39.3
Methionine	33.3	56.4

1. Given that corn consists of 7.8% protein and only 60% of it is absorbed by the digestive tract, calculate the number of grams of corn that must be ingested for an adequate protein intake. There are 368 kilocalories in 100 g of corn. How many calories must be consumed daily in order to get adequate protein? Given that the average American consumes 2,000–3,000 kcal daily, can an all-corn diet supply the proper balance of protein and energy?

2. Given that beans are 24% protein and 78% of the protein is absorbed by the digestive tract, calculate the number of grams of corn and beans that must be consumed to supply adequate protein for a person whose diet is half corn and half beans. If there are 338 kcal in 100 g of beans, calculate the number of calories consumed in this diet. (see problem 1 for additional data for corn.)

3. In 1970 a total of about 2.9 million kilocalories were consumed by farmers to raise an acre of corn (equivalent to 80 gallons of gasoline). This amount includes energy for labor, fuel, seeds, and chemicals. If the average solar flux during the growing season (100 days) is 245 w/m², how much solar energy reaches an acre of corn during this time? About 1.26% of this is converted into corn and about 0.4% into corn grain (at 100 bushels per acre). What is the total amount of energy stored in the corn? If half the energy of the corn residue is retrieved by biogasification, is there enough energy for the farmer to raise the crop?

4. Assume a pesticide company dumps 10 tons of pesticide wastes into an approved 50-acre landfill site once a year. The maximum buildup of wastes at the site can be expressed as:

$$\frac{N_n}{N_0} = e^{-\lambda}\left(\frac{1}{1 - e^{-\lambda}}\right)$$

where N_0 is the initial concentration of wastes, N_n is the maximum concentration. and $\lambda = 0.693/t_{1/2}$, where $t_{1/2}$ is the half-life expressed in years. What is the maximum buildup of the wastes at the site if the half-life of the pesticide is ten years? What is the maximum if the half-life is one year? If it is two weeks?

5. a) In 1975 the United States produced 27.1 million metric tons (1 metric ton = 1,000 kg) of vegetable protein suitable for human use. Of this, 91% was fed to livestock to produce 5.3 million metric tons of animal protein. Calculate the efficiency of conversion of vegetable protein to animal protein.
   b) Assuming that humans need 60 g of protein per day, how many people could have been fed in 1975 on the surplus vegetable protein, if Americans decreased their meat consumption by 10%.

6. a) Assume that the industrial process for nitrogen fixation requires the breaking of the triple bond in $N{\equiv}N$ by the reaction:

$$N{\equiv}N + 3H_2 \rightarrow 2NH_3 \qquad (1)$$

Assume further that the natural process utilizing nitrogenase occurs by the sequential breaking of single bonds in $N{\equiv}N$ by the reactions:

$$N{\equiv}N + H_2 \rightarrow HN{=}NH \qquad (2a)$$
$$HN{=}NH + H_2 \rightarrow H_2N{-}NH_2 \qquad (2b)$$
$$H_2N{-}NH_2 + H_2 \rightarrow 2NH_3 \qquad (2c)$$

Reaction (1) requires an activation energy of 226 kcal to break the triple bond. The most energy-demanding step in process (2) is reaction (2a), which requires an activation energy of about 126 kcal to break $N{\equiv}N$ to form $HN{=}NH$. Calculate the ratio of the rate constants (k_{2a}/k_1) at 27° C for reaction (1) and reaction (2a) using the relationship:

$$k \propto e^{-Ea/RT}$$

where E_a is the activation energy, $R = 1.99$ calories/°K/mol, and T is measured in degrees Kelvin.

b) From the value of (k_{2a}/k_1), is it surprising that microorganisms can fix nitrogen at ambient temperatures whereas the industrial process occurs between 400 and 600° C? Calculate the temperature at which k_1 equals the value of k_{2a} at 27° C.

7. By planting legumes between corn rows in late August and plowing this "green manure" under in early spring, 133 pounds of nitrogen per acre can be added to the soil. The total energy cost for legume seeds and fuel requirements is 90,000 kcal/acre. Calculate the saving in energy relative to the amount of inorganic nitrogen fertilizer applied if the Haber process requires 8,000 kcal/pound of fixed nitrogen. The total amount of energy needed to grow an acre of corn, excluding the 133-pound nitrogen requirement, is 2×10^6 kcal. What percentage of the total energy budget can be conserved by using legumes rather than inorganic nitrogen?

8. a) Consider a *para*-substituted phenyldiethylphosphate insecticide of the following form:

$$ X-\langle\underline{\ \ }\rangle-O-\overset{\overset{O}{\|}}{P}(OC_2H_5)_2 $$

Why does the toxicity of the insecticide increase as the electron-withdrawing capacity of X increases?

b) The electronegativity value of P is 2.1, that of S is 2.5, and for O it is 3.5. Using these facts, explain why phosphorothionate insecticides (containing phosphorus-sulfur double bonds rather than phosphorus-oxygen double bonds) are unreactive with cholinesterase but are activated in the insect's body by oxidizing enzymes. What advantage is there to using sulfur-containing insecticides?

9. Suppose a fruit fly is being killed with an insecticide. However, one out of a million fruit flies possesses an enzyme that breaks down the insecticide into nontoxic metabolic products. Assume that as the normal fruit flies quickly die off, the population of the resistant flies increases geometrically (i.e., 1, 2, 4, 8, ...). If a new generation occurs every 23.5 days, in how many days will the fruit fly population be restored?

10. a) A DNA template segment has the sequence of base pairs, TAG TAG TAG TAG. Into what complementary base pairs will mRNA transcribe this segment? Using Table 4.12 determine the amino acid sequence that results from the DNA code.

b) Describe the new amino acid sequence formed during the following frame-shift mutations in the DNA: (1) a C is added after the first G; (2) the second A is deleted.

11. Nitrous acid (HNO_2) can convert cytosine to uracil. Since uracil pairs with adenine, show how nitrous acid can cause a cytosine-guanine pair to be transformed into a thymine-adenine pair during DNA replication.

12. Ample evidence indicates that cancer is largely an environmental disease. However, the body is not a passive partner in the induction of the disease. Using benzanthracene and dimethylnitrosamine as examples (Figures 4.50 and 4.51), explain how the body actively participates in its own destruction. Correlate your reasoning with the fact that the Ames bacterial test for known carcinogens gives negative results unless a mammalian liver extract is added to the test medium.

13. Relate how mercury accumulation in the food chain led to the Minimata disaster. Why is the conversion to methyl mercury the key step in mercury toxicity?

14. In the human body, the half-life of organic mercury is 70 days, and for inorganic mercury it is 6 days. Why is there such a marked difference? What is the maximum body accumulation of each type of mercury at a constant ingestion rate of 2 mg/day? (The solution is similar to that of problem 4.)

15. Summarize the biochemical mechanism whereby chlorinated dioxins and PCBs can upset hormone function in animals. Why are the geometric dimensions of the molecule so important?

16. a) Assume the concentration of K^+ ions in a nerve cell is 0.1 M, and the concentration of Na^+ ions is 0.005 M. In the extracellular fluid, the concentration of K^+ is 0.005 M and the concentration of Na^+ is 0.1 M. Calculate the free energy required to exclude Na^+ from the cell and to replace it by K^+. The free energy expression is:

$$\Delta G = 2.3 \ RT \ \log \frac{C_2}{C_1}$$

C_2 and C_1 are the concentrations inside and outside of the cell, respectively, $R = 1.98$ calories/°K/mol, and T of the body = 310 °K.

b) K^+ ions are blocked from diffusing out of the cell by an electric potential across the cell membrane that is equal and opposite to the diffusional potential. Calculate this potential (in millivolts). Utilize the relation:

$$2.3 \ RT \ \log \frac{C_2}{C_1} = ZF \Delta V$$

where Z is the charge of the ion; F is the Faraday, or 23.062 kcal/v/mol; and ΔV is the potential across the membrane (in millivolts).

c) Describe how an insecticide may upset the regulation of the active transport of K^+ and Na^+ ions across the neural membrane.

17. Why are chemicals that are known to produce mutations in bacteria and insects generally known to induce cancer in humans?

18. Unlike a heat engine, which does work at constant pressure only when heat can be passed from a higher temperature to a lower temperature, the body utilizes chemical free energy stored in ATP at constant temperature and pressure. Given that the free energy obtained from burning a mole of glucose in air is 686 kcal, what is the thermodynamic efficiency of ATP free energy storage in the body given the following reaction:

glucose + 36 ADP + 36 P_i + 36H^+ + 6O_2 → 6CO_2 + 36 ATP + 42H_2O

and the fact that ΔG^0 for the hydrolysis of one mole of ATP is -7.3 kcal?

19. a) An aromatic amine undergoes the following reactions in the body:

Why is step (2) with the subsequent products necessary for the induction of cancer?
b) What general property do all ultimate carcinogens possess for binding with DNA?

20. The chemistry of cadmium is quite homologous to that of zinc, and it replaces zinc with great facility in enzymes. However, the activity of cadmium-substituted enzymes differs greatly from that of the normal zinc-containing ones. To illustrate this, data are presented below for cadmium substitution in the zinc-containing enzyme, carboxypeptidase. This digestive enzyme catalyzes two different hydrolysis reactions as shown:

peptide bond hydrolysis

ester bond hydrolysis

Plot the data for the two reactions given in the following table. Graph both plots on the same axes. Label the y-axis "% Cd substituted." Use the x-axis twice, once to plot peptidase activity and once to plot esterase activity. Draw the best straight line through the points.

% Cd Substituted	Relative Peptidase Activity	% Cd Substituted	Relative Esterase Activity
0	7.5	0	1.1
50	3.2	50	1.4
75	1.9	75	1.6
90	0.8	100	·1.7
97	0.2		

Data taken from J. E. Coleman and B. L. Vallee, *J. Biol. Chem.* 236 (1961): 2244.

Notes

1. For further reading on the Calvin cycle, see L. Stryer, *Biochemistry* (San Francisco: W. H. Freeman and Co. Publishers, 1975), pp. 469–73.
2. P. Mitchell, *Biol. Rev.* 41 (1965):445.
3. J. Chatt, A. J. Pearman, and R. L. Richards, *Nature* 253 (1975):39.
4. J. Chatt, A. J. Pearman, and R. L. Richards, *J. Organometal. Chem.* 101C (1975):45–47.

5. L. Pauling, *Vitamin C and the Common Cold* (San Francisco: W. H. Freeman and Co. Publishers, 1970).

6. F. Matsumura and K. C. Patil, *Science* 166 (1969):121.

7. F. Matsumura and T. Narahashi, *Biochem. Pharmacol.* 20 (1971):825.

8. C. Pert and S. Snyder, *Science* 179 (1973):1011.

9. A. P. Feinberg, I. Creese, and S. Snyder, *Proc. Natl. Acad. Sci. USA* 73 (1976):4215.

10. J. Hughes, *Brain Res.* 88 (1975):296.

11. G. W. Pasternak, R. Goodman, and S. H. Snyder, *Life Sci.* 16 (1975):1765.

12. J. Hughes, T. Smith, H. W. Kosterlitz, L. A. Fothergill, B. A. Morgan, and H. R. Morris, *Nature* 258 (1975):577.

13. L. Lykken, *Environmental Toxicology of Pesticides*, edited by F. Matsumura, G. M. Boush, and T. Misato (New York: Academic Press, 1972), pp. 449–69.

14. M. Eto, *Organophosphorus Pesticides—Organic and Biological Chemistry* (Cleveland: CRC Press, 1974), p. 161.

15. W. C. Evans, *J. Gen. Microbiol.* 32 (1963):177.

16. T. F. Castro and T. Yoshida, *J. Agric. Food Chem.* 19 (1971):1168.

17. P. P. Williams, *Residue Rev.* 66 (1977):90.

18. B. N. Ames, W. E. Durston, E. Yamasaki, and F. D. Lee, *Proc. Natl. Acad. Sci. USA* 70 (1973):2281.

19. B. N. Ames, H. O. Kammen, and E. Yamasaki, *Proc. Natl. Acad. Sci. USA* 72 (1975):2423.

Suggestions for Further Reading

Nitrogen Cycle

Delwiche, C. C. "The Nitrogen Cycle." *Sci. Am.* 223 (September 1970):136.

Skinner, K. J. "Nitrogen Fixation." *Chem. Eng. News,* October 4, 1976, p. 22.

Brill, W. J. "Biological Nitrogen Fixation." *Sci. Am.* 236 (March 1977):68.

Brill, W. J. "Nitrogen Fixation: Basic to Applied."*Am. Sci.* 67 (July–August 1979):458.

Eady, R. R., and Postgate, J. R. "Nitrogenase." *Nature* 249 (1974):805.

Hardy, R., Burns, R., and Parshall, G. "Bioinorganic Chemistry of Dinitrogen Fixation." In *Inorganic Biochemistry,* vol. 2, edited by G. L. Eichhorn. New York: Elsevier Science, 1973.

Aleem, M. "Oxidation of Inorganic Nitrogen Compounds." *Annu. Rev. Plant Physiol.* 21 (1970):67.

Payne, W. J. "Reduction of Nitrogenous Oxides by Microorganisms." *Bacteriol. Rev.* 37 (1973):409.

Miyata, M., and Mori, T. "Studies on Denitrification." *J. Biochem.* 60 (1969):463.

Delwiche, C. C., and Bryan, B. A. "Denitrification." *Annu. Rev. Microbiol.* 30 (1976):241.

Nutrition and Food Production

Deathrage, F. E. *Food for Life.* New York: Plenum Press, 1975.

Sanders, H. J. "Nutrition and Health." *Chem. Eng. News,* March 26, 1979, p. 27.

Zelitch, I. "Photosynthesis and Plant Productivity." *Chem. Eng. News*, February 5, 1979, p. 28.

Miller, K. R. "The Photosynthetic Membrane." *Sci. Am.* 241 (October 1979):102.

Food and agriculture issue of *Scientific American* 235 (September 1976).

Food issue of *Science* 188 (May 9, 1975). Also published along with other articles in Abelson, P. H., ed. *Food: Politics, Economics, Nutrition and Research*, Science Compendium. Washington, D.C.: American Association for the Advancement of Science, 1975.

Steinhart, J., and Steinhart, C. "Energy Use in the U.S. Food System." *Science* 184 (1974):307.

Pimentel, D., et al. "Food Production and the Energy Crisis." *Science* 182 (1973):443.

Pimentel, D., Dritschilo, W., Krummel, J., and Kurtzman, J. "Energy and Land Constraints in Food Protein Production." *Science* 190 (1975):754.

Johnson, W. A., Stolzfus, V., and Craumer, P. "Energy Conservation in Amish Agriculture." *Science* 198 (1977):373.

Wortman, S. "Agriculture in China." *Sci. Am.* 232 (June 1975):13.

Revelle, R. "Energy Use in Rural India." *Science* 192 (1976):969.

Brink, R. A., Densmore, J., and Hill, G. A. "Soil Deterioration and the Growing World Demand for Food." *Science* 197 (1977):625.

Eckholm, E. P. *Losing Ground; Environmental Stress and World Food Prospects.* New York: W. W. Norton Co., Inc., 1976.

Lerza, C., and Jacobsen, M., eds. *Food for People, Not for Profit.* New York: Ballantine Books, Inc., 1975.

Lappé, F. M., and Collins, J. *Food First.* New York: Ballantine Books, Inc., 1978.

Insecticides and Neurochemistry

White-Stevens, R., ed. *Pesticides in the Environment*, vol. 1, parts I and II. New York: Marcel Dekker, Inc., 1971.

Eto, M. *Organophosphorus Pesticides: Organic and Biological Chemistry.* Cleveland: CRC Press, 1974.

Casida, J. "Insecticide Biochemistry." *Annu. Rev. Biochem.* 42 (1973):259.

Matsumura, F., Boush, G., and Misato, T. *Environmental Toxicology of Pesticides.* New York: Academic Press, 1972.

Kupfer, D. "Effects of Pesticides and Related Compounds on Steroid Metabolism and Function," *CRC Crit. Rev. Toxicol.* 4, no. 1 (1975):83.

Street, J. C. "Organochlorine Insecticides and the Stimulation of Liver Microsome Enzymes." *Ann. NY Acad. Sci.* 160 (1969):274.

Peakall, D. B. "Pesticides and the Reproduction of Birds." *Sci. Am.* 222 (April 1970):72.

Kaiser, K. "Pesticide Report: The Rise and Fall of Mirex." *Environ. Sci. Technol.* 12 (May 1978):520.

Weber, J. "The Pesticide Scorecard." *Environ. Sci. Technol.* 11 (August 1977):756.

Edwards, C. A. *Persistent Pesticides in the Environment*, 2nd ed. Cleveland: CRC Press, 1973.

Crosby, D. G. "The Fate of Pesticides in the Environment." *Annu. Rev. Plant Physiol.* 24 (1973):467.

Williams, P. P. "Metabolism of Synthetic Organic Pesticides by Anaerobic Microorganisms," *Residue Rev.* 66 (1977):63.

Stevens, C. F. "The Neuron," *Sci. Am.* 241 (September 1979):54.

Keynes, R. D. "Ion Channels in the Nerve-Cell Membrane," *Sci. Am.* 240 (March 1979):126.

Lester, H. A. "The Response to Acetylcholine," *Sci. Am.* 236 (February 1977):106.

Snyder, S. H. "Opiate Receptors and Internal Opiates," *Sci. Am.* 236 (March 1977):44.

Snyder, S. H. "The Brain's Own Opiates," *Chem. Eng. Bews,* November 28, 1977, p. 26.

Organic and Inorganic Toxic Chemicals

Kimbrough, R. D. "The Toxicity of Polychlorinated Compounds and Related Chemicals," *CRC Crit. Rev. Toxicol.* 2, no. 4 (1974):445.

Nisbet, I. C. T. "Criteria Document for PCB's," Environmental Protection Agency, 440/76-021, 1976.

"Subcommittee on the Health Effects of PCB's and PBB's, Final Report," Washington, D.C.: Department of Health, Education and Welfare, 1976.

Rawls, R. "Italy Seeks Answers Following Toxic Release," *Chem. Eng. News,* August 23, 1976, p. 27.

Walsh, J. "Seveso: The Questions Persist Where Dioxin Created a Wasteland," *Science* 197 (1977):1064.

Thomasson, W. A. "Deadly Legacy: Dioxin and the Vietnam Veteran," *Bull. Atom. Sci.* 35 (May 1979):15.

Vallee, B. L., and Ulmer, D. D. "Biochemical Effects of Mercury, Cadmium, and Lead," *Annu. Rev. Biochem.* 41 (1972):91.

Clarkson, T. W. "Recent Advances in the Toxicology of Mercury with Emphasis on the Alkylmercurials." *CRC Crit. Rev. Toxicol.* 1 (1972):203.

Chisholm, J. J. "Lead Poisoning." *Sci. Am.* 224 (February 1971):15.

Wessel, M., and Dominski, A. "Our Children's Daily Lead." *Am. Sci.* 65 (May–June 1977):294.

Fox, J. L. "Research Solving Body's Detoxifying System." *Chem. Eng. News,* June 4, 1979, p. 24.

Gillette, J. R., Davis, D. C., and Sasame, H. A. "Cytochrome P450 and Its Role in Drug Metabolism." *Annu. Rev. Pharmacol.* 12 (1972):57.

Ridley, W. P., Dizikes, L. J., and Wood, J. M. "Biomethylation of Toxic Elements in the Environment." *Science* 197 (1977):329.

Wood, J. M. "Biological Cycles for Toxic Elements in the Environment." *Science* 183 (1974):1049.

Poland, A., and Kende, A. "2,3,7,8-Tetrachlorodibenzo-*p*-dioxin: Environmental Contaminant and Molecular Probe." *Fed. Proc.* 35 (1976):2404.

Suess, M. J. "The Environmental Load and Cycle of Polycyclic Aromatic Hydrocarbons." *The Science of the Total Environment* 6 (1976):239.

Carter, L. "Chemical Plants Leave Unexpected Legacy to Two Virginia Rivers." *Science* 198 (1977):1015.

Hartung, R., and Dinman, B., eds. *Environmental Mercury Contamination.* Ann Arbor, Mich.: Ann Arbor Science Publications, 1972.

Friberg, L., Piscator, M., and Nordberg, G. *Cadmium in the Environment.* Cleveland: CRC Press, 1971.

Goldwater, L. J. "Mercury in the Environment." *Sci. Am.* 224 (May 1971):15.

"Airborne Lead in Perspective." Washington, D.C.: National Academy of Sciences, 1972.

Murray, C. "EPA Criticized for Chemical Wastes Handling." *Chem. Eng. News,* November 13, 1978, p. 18.

Pojasek, R. B. "Disposing of Hazardous Chemical Wastes." *Environ. Sci. Technol.* 13 (July 1979):810.

Murray, C. "Chemical Waste Disposal, A Costly Problem." *Chem. Eng. News,* March 12, 1979, p. 12.

Maugh, T. "Toxic Waste Disposal, A Growing Problem." *Science* 204 (1979):819.

Maugh, T. "Hazardous Wastes Technology Is Available." *Science* 204 (1979):930.

Maugh, T. "Incineration, Deep Wells Gain New Importance." *Science* 204 (1979):1188.

Maugh, T. "Burial Is Last Resort for Hazardous Wastes." *Science* 204 (1979):1295.

Cancer

Cairns, J. "The Cancer Problem." *Sci. Am.* 233 (November 1975):64.

Miller, E. C., and Miller, J. A. *Molecular Biology of Cancer,* edited by H. Busch. New York: Academic Press, 1974.

Croce, C., and Koprowski, H. "The Genetics of Human Cancer." *Sci. Am.* 238 (February 1978):117.

Setlow, R. B. "Repair Deficient Human Disorders and Cancer." *Nature* 271 (February 23, 1978):713.

Nicolson, G. L. "Cancer Metastasis." *Sci. Am.* 240 (March 1979):66.

Heidelberger, C. "Chemical Carcinogenesis." *Annu. Rev. Biochem.* 44 (1975):81.

Epstein, S. "Cancer and the Environment." *Bull. Atom. Sci.* 33 (March 1977):22.

Weisburger, E. K. "Natural Carcinogenic Products." *Environ. Sci. Technol.* 13 (March 179):278.

Maugh, T. "Chemical Carcinogens: How Dangerous Are Low Doses?" *Science* 202 (1978):137.

Maugh, T., "Chemical Carcinogens: The Scientific Basis for Regulation." *Science* 201 (1978):1200.

"Public Policy: Chemicals and Cancer." *Chem. Eng. News,* January 16, 1978, p. 34.

"News Forum: Should the Delaney Clause Be Changed?" *Chem. Eng. News,* June 27, 1977, p. 24.

Devoret, R. "Bacterial Tests for Potential Carcinogens." *Sci. Am.* 241 (August 1979):40.

McCann, J., and Ames, B. N. "A Simple Method for Detecting Environmental Carcinogens as Mutagens." *Ann. NY Acad. Sci.* 271 (1976):5.

Fox, J. L. "Ames Test Success Paves Way for Short-Term Cancer Testing." *Chem. Eng. News,* December 12, 1977, p. 34.

Ames, B. N. "Identifying Environmental Chemicals Causing Mutations and Cancer." *Science* 204 (1979):587.

APPENDIX

Units of Energy and Radiation

1. Forms and units of energy.
    a) Heat and work are interconvertible forms of energy.
        (1) *Heat* is energy that flows from one body to another because of a difference in their temperatures. Common units of heat energy are:
            (i) One calorie* is the heat needed to raise the temperature of 1 g of water 1° C (specifically, from 14.5 to 15.5° C, since the heat capacity of water varies somewhat with temperature).
            (ii) One British thermal unit (Btu) is the heat needed to raise the temperature of 1 lb of water 1° F (from 63 to 64° F).
        (2) *Work* is energy that is transmitted when a force acts against a resistance to produce motion. Work = force × distance, and force = mass × acceleration. Common units of work energy are:
            (i) One erg is the work done by a force that accelerates a 1-g mass at 1.0 cm/sec² for a distance of 1 cm.
            (ii) One joule is the work done by a force that accelerates a 1-kg mass at 1.0 m/sec² for a distance of 1 m.
            (iii) One foot-pound (ft-lb) is the work done by a force of 1 lb (a 453.59-g mass accelerated at 32.1740 ft/sec²) over a distance of 1 ft.
    b) Kinetic and potential energy; Power.
        (1) Kinetic energy (K) is the work that a body can do by virtue of its motion:

$$K = \frac{1}{2} \, (\text{mass}) \times (\text{velocity})^2$$

        (2) Potential energy is the work that a system of bodies is capable of doing by virtue of the relative position of its parts, that is, by virtue of its configuration (e.g., water falling from a height or chemicals reacting in a battery).

*Nutritionists use the Calorie (capital C), which equals 1,000 calories, or 1 kilocalorie (kcal).

359

(3) *Power* is the rate at which work is done. Power = work/time. Common units of power are:

   (i) 1 watt (w) = 1 joule/second

   (ii) 1 horsepower = 33,000 ft-lb/minute

(*Note:* power × time = work; hence, watts × seconds = joules; watts × hours = 3,600 joules; and 1 kilowatt-hour (kwh) = 3.6 × 10⁶ joules.)

c) Radiant energy. Energy is also caused by light waves. The photons of electromagnetic radiation have no rest mass and travel with a constant velocity, depending only on the medium (air, water, glass, etc.). In a vacuum (empty space), the velocity of light is $c = 3 \times 10^{10}$ cm/second. The oscillations of the light wave are measured by the wavelength, λ (in meters or subunits of meters), or by the frequency, $\nu = c/\lambda$ (in cycles per second, cps or hertz). The energy of a light wave is directly proportional to its frequency, $E = h\nu$, where h is Planck's constant, 6.626×10^{-27} erg·second. Often the frequency is expressed in wave numbers, $\bar{\nu} = 1/\lambda$, leaving out the velocity of light.

    The electromagnetic spectrum covers a wide range of wavelengths, from radiowaves (λ in meters) through microwaves (centimeters), infrared waves (micrometers), ultraviolet waves (tenths of micrometers), x-rays (angstroms, i.e., atomic dimensions), and γ rays (thousandths of angstroms, i.e., nuclear dimensions). The visible region of the spectrum, to which the human eye responds, is quite narrow, from about 0.4 μ (blue light) to about 0.7 μ (red light). This is also the region of maximum sunlight intensity.

d) Some useful units and conversion factors:

   (1) Length: meters (m)

     1 meter = 10^{-3} kilometer (km) = 10^2 centimeter (cm) = 10^3 millimeter (mm) = 10^6 micrometer (μm or μ) = 10^9 nanometer (nm) = 10^{10} angstrom (Å)

   (2) Mass: grams (g)

     1 gram = 10^{-3} kilogram (kg) = 10^3 milligram (mg) = 10^6 microgram (μg) = 10^9 nanogram (ng) = 10^{12} picogram (pg)

   (3) Temperature: Degrees Kelvin or absolute (°K) = degrees centigrade (°C) + 273. Degrees Farenheit (°F) = (9/5)°C + 32

   (4) Energy: As we have seen, there are many units of energy, relating to the different forms that energy can take:

     calorie: This is the basic unit of heat energy. Chemists are accustomed to using calories or kilocalories (kcal). Nutritionists use Calories, which are actually kilocalories.

British thermal unit (Btu): This unit of heat energy is used in engineering practice.

$$1 \text{ Btu} = 252 \text{ calories}$$

joule: This is the basic unit of work and has been adopted as the fundamental unit of energy of the International System of Units.

$$1 \text{ calorie} = 4.184 \text{ joules}$$

kilowatt-hour (kwh): This unit is used in measuring electrical energy production or consumption.

$$1 \text{ kwh} = 3.6 \times 10^6 \text{ joule} = 860.4 \text{ kcal}$$

cm^{-1}: The energy of light waves is proportional to their frequency, which is usually expressed as the wave number ($\bar{\nu} = 1/\lambda$) in cm^{-1}. For example, green light with 500-nm wavelength has a wave number, or "energy," of $(500 \times 10^{-7} \text{ cm})^{-1} = 20,000 \text{ cm}^{-1}$. It is possible to relate the wave number to the equivalent quantity of heat, or chemical energy per mole of photons; thus

$$1 \text{ kcal/mol} = 349.8 \text{ cm}^{-1}$$

electron volts (ev): This unit is commonly used by physicists in describing radiation and elementary particles. It is the amount of energy acquired by any charged particle that carries unit electronic charge when it falls through a potential difference of 1 v. It can be related to the equivalent wave number of electromagnetic radiation:

$$1 \text{ ev} = 8,064.9 \text{ cm}^{-1}$$

A multiple of this unit that is commonly used is the megaelectron volt = Mev = 10^6 ev.

2. Units of radiation. Radiation is measured in different ways, depending on the purpose of the measurement. The *curie* is a unit of radiation *rate:* One curie corresponds to 3.7×10^{10} radioactive disintegrations per second.

The *roentgen* is a unit of radiation exposure that specifies what radiation *would do:* One roentgen is the intensity of radiation that, on passing through 1 cm^3 of dry air (at 0° C and 1 atm pressure), would create 1 electrostatic unit (esu)* of positively charged ions and 1 esu of negatively charged ions.

The *rad* is a unit of absorbed dose. It describes what radiation *has done:* One rad is the amount of radiation that deposits 100 ergs of energy per gram of tissue. (It happens that 1 roentgen of radiation deposits about 100 ergs of

*1 esu = 2.08×10^9 times the charge of a single electron.

energy in 1 g of biological tissue, so exposure to 1 roentgen is equivalent to a 1-rad dose.)

The *rem* (roentgen-equivalent-man) is a unit of biological dose, based on the rad, multiplied by a modifying factor to allow for the biological effectiveness of different kinds of radiation:

$$1 \text{ rem } = 1 \text{ rad } \times M$$

M is taken to be unity for β and γ rays, but is assigned a value of 10–20 for α rays, depending on their energy, to allow for the higher density of damage.

Index

Absorption of solar radiation, 63; by ozone, 118, 120, 121

Acetylcholine, 293-97, 303-5

Acid mine drainage, 199

Acid rain: composition of, 196-97; effect of on fish, 197-99; increased mineral leaching from, 199; from tall smokestacks, 171-72

Acids: in buffer solutions, 202-3; definition of, 195; polyprotic acids, 204; strong acids, 200-201; weak acids, 201

Actinides, 50

Action spectrum, 121

Activated carbon: in industrial wastewater treatment, 243; in tertiary sewage treatment, 240; in treatment of drinking water, 247

Activated charcoal. See Activated carbon

Activated sludge. See Sewage sludge

Activation barrier: for carbon oxidation, 139; for NO oxidation, 141

Aflatoxin, 329, 346, 349

Agriculture: in poor countries, 261-65; water pollution from, 247-49

Air, composition of, 107

Airplanes, energy efficiency of, 81-82

Albedo, 1-2; effect of human activities on, 99-100

Aldrin, 292

Algae: blooms of, 231; in lake productivity, 223

Alpha rays: damage to biological tissue from 43-44, 49; definition of, 29; natural emission of, 33-34

Alum (aluminum sulfate): in drinking water treatment, 246; in phosphate removal, 230

Aluminosilicate clays: as builder, 208; as ion exchanger, 213; in neutralization of rain, 196; in oil spills, 235; in regulating pH of ocean, 217, 218, 220; types of, 214-16

Aluminum, recycling of, 84

Americium-243, 50

Ames test, 349

Amino acids: essential amino acids, 280; frequency of, 280-82; in protein systhesis, 335-38

Ammonia: annual atmospheric emissions of, 161-62; from catalytic converter, 168; from nitrogenase enzyme, 257-58, 275-76

Ammonia stripping, 237-39; energy requirements for, 240

Ammonium nitrate. See Fertilizer

Amphiphilic solutes, 220

Anaerobic bacteria: decomposition of toxic organic chemicals by, 315-16; in origin of fossil fuels, 4; in water pollution, 232

Animal, wastes of. See Cattle feedlots

Anion exchangers, 212-13; synthetic, 243

Anthracite coal, 23

Aquifer: depletion of by coal industry, 25; pollution of by fertilizer, 249; U.S. reserves of, 185, 186

Aromatic amines as carcinogens, 346

Aromatic hydrocarbons: as carcinogens, 341; environmental decomposition of, 315; as lead substitute in gasoline, 168; from oil refining, 16

Asbestos, health effects of, 176

Atmosphere: density profile of, 118; lapse rates in, 118; temperature profile of, 118. See also Troposphere; Stratosphere

Atmospheric window, 108-9; and CFM spectra, 113

ATP (adenosine triphosphate), 146, 266-68

Automobile emissions: air to fuel ratio in, 165, 166; chemical composition of, 165, 166; control of, 166-71; from diesel engines, 176; relation of carbon monoxide to, 152-53; relation of to smog, 165

Avogadro's number, 194

Band gap in semiconductors, 66

Base: definition of, 195; strong base, 201; weak base, 202. See also pH

Benzanthracene, as carcinogen, 330, 332-33

Benzo(a)pyrene: as carcinogen, 346, 349; as constituent of soot, 176

Beta rays; damage to biological tissue from, 44-45, 49; definition of, 29